Generative AI and Large Language Models

Generative AI and Large Language Models

Guest Editors

Fabrizio Marozzo
Riccardo Cantini

MDPI

Basel • Beijing • Wuhan • Barcelona • Belgrade • Novi Sad • Cluj • Manchester

Guest Editors
Fabrizio Marozzo
Department of Informatics, Modeling, Electronics and Systems Engineering (DIMES)
University of Calabria
Rende
Italy

Riccardo Cantini
Department of Informatics, Modeling, Electronics and Systems Engineering (DIMES)
University of Calabria
Rende
Italy

Editorial Office
MDPI AG
Grosspeteranlage 5
4052 Basel, Switzerland

This is a reprint of the Special Issue, published open access by the journal *Big Data and Cognitive Computing* (ISSN 2504-2289), freely accessible at: https://www.mdpi.com/journal/BDCC/special_issues/1XP11D36SD.

For citation purposes, cite each article independently as indicated on the article page online and as indicated below:

Lastname, A.A.; Lastname, B.B. Article Title. *Journal Name* **Year**, *Volume Number*, Page Range.

ISBN 978-3-7258-7703-4 (Hbk)
ISBN 978-3-7258-7704-1 (PDF)
https://doi.org/10.3390/books978-3-7258-7704-1

Contents

About the Editors

Fabrizio Marozzo

Fabrizio Marozzo is an Associate Professor of Computer Engineering with the Department of Informatics, Modeling, Electronics and Systems Engineering at the University of Calabria, Italy. His research activity concerns big data analytics, machine learning, generative artificial intelligence, large language models, and distributed cloud-edge computing systems. He has also worked extensively on social media analysis, scalable data-intensive applications, and explainable AI.

Riccardo Cantini

Riccardo Cantini is an Assistant Professor of Computer Engineering with the Department of Informatics, Modeling, Electronics and Systems Engineering at the University of Calabria, Italy. His research interests include big data analytics, social media analysis, deep learning, machine learning, natural language processing, large language models, sustainable AI, and edge AI. His recent research focuses on generative AI methods and intelligent data analysis in complex application domains.

Preface

The following Reprint was developed to provide a coherent snapshot of recent advances in generative artificial intelligence and large language models. The collected contributions reflect the breadth of a rapidly evolving research area, spanning model-centered questions such as retrieval, reasoning, faithfulness, and explainability, in addition to application-driven studies in domains where reliability and responsible adoption are essential. One of the main motivations behind this Reprint is the need to move beyond a narrow focus on model performance and to consider how LLM-based systems can be grounded, evaluated, and integrated into real-world workflows. The volume is intended for researchers, practitioners, and advanced-level students interested in the design, assessment, and application of generative AI systems. Taken together, the included articles demonstrate both the maturity the field has already reached and the many open directions that deserve further investigation.

Fabrizio Marozzo and Riccardo Cantini
Guest Editors

big data and cognitive computing

MDPI

Editorial

Generative AI and Large Language Models

Fabrizio Marozzo * and Riccardo Cantini

Department of Informatics, Modeling, Electronics and Systems Engineering (DIMES), University of Calabria, 87036 Rende, Italy; rcantini@dimes.unical.it
* Correspondence: fabrizio.marozzo@unical.it

1. Introduction

In recent years, generative artificial intelligence and, in particular, large language models (LLMs) have rapidly transformed the landscape of data analysis, knowledge extraction, content generation, and intelligent decision support. The emergence of increasingly capable foundation models has accelerated progress in natural language processing and has also expanded the reach of AI into a wide variety of domains, including, among others, healthcare, education, cybersecurity, public administration, finance, accessibility, and social media analysis [1–3]. Beyond their strong performance in text-generation and question-answering, these models are now being employed as general-purpose tools for summarization, reasoning, annotation, explanation, and interaction, often serving as the core computational component of more complex intelligent systems.

This fast-moving evolution has produced major opportunities, but it has also made visible a number of important gaps in current research and practice. Although the capabilities of LLMs continue to improve, several issues remain insufficiently addressed, including factual reliability, hallucination mitigation, ambiguity handling, explainability, reproducibility, bias control, and the robust integration of external knowledge sources [4–6]. At the same time, there is a growing need for more systematic evidence on how these models behave in domain-specific and high-stakes settings, where performance alone is not enough and must be complemented by trustworthiness, transparency, safety, and meaningful human oversight. Recent studies have also shown the value of LLMs in supporting advanced interpretability and analytical tasks; for example, in the analysis of online opinions, reviews, and social media content [7,8]. These developments suggest that the field is entering a new phase, in which the focus is shifting from raw model capability to the effective, responsible, and context-aware deployment of generative AI.

This Special Issue, entitled "Generative AI and Large Language Models", was conceived precisely in response to these challenges. Its objective was to collect contributions capable of advancing the field along multiple complementary directions: novel methods for retrieval and reasoning, rigorous approaches to evaluation and trustworthiness, analytical studies able to structure the state-of-the-art, and application-oriented investigations in socially relevant domains. The ten papers published in this Special Issue reflect the diversity and vitality of the field. Together, they offer a useful picture of how current research is addressing open questions related to grounded generation, agentic systems, domain adaptation, security, explainability, accessibility, and real-world adoption.

2. Overview of the Published Papers

The ten papers included in this Special Issue cover a broad set of research directions and application areas, highlighting both the methodological richness of the field and its growing practical relevance. The first cluster of contributions focuses on retrieval-augmented generation (RAG), contextual reasoning, and the evaluation of grounded responses. Ye et al. propose TRACE, a topical reasoning framework with adaptive contextual experts for long-text summarization, showing how document structure and semantic relationships can be exploited to improve structure-aware retrieval and multi-expert reasoning [9]. Mansurova et al. investigate QA-RAG and study the extent to which LLMs effectively rely on external knowledge, emphasizing both the potential of retrieval-based pipelines and the challenges that still remain in integrating external truth in a reliable way [10]. In their paper, Papageorgiou et al. examine faithfulness in agentic RAG systems for e-governance and introduce a modular framework based on LLM judges to analyze hallucination and redundancy across alternative retrieval pipelines [11]. Collectively, these studies show that retrieval is not merely an auxiliary component of LLM-based systems, but a central design dimension whose quality must be considered together with rigorous evaluation of grounding, faithfulness, and attribution.

The second group of papers addresses the use of LLMs in human-centered and socially relevant contexts. Andruccioli et al. explore the role of LLMs in sustainable and inclusive web accessibility, showing how these models can support the identification of accessibility issues in dynamically generated web content that may be overlooked by conventional validation tools, while also discussing the risks associated with redundant or hallucinated warnings [12]. Alostad investigates the use of LLMs as annotators for stance detection in the Kuwaiti dialect, demonstrating that carefully prompted open models can produce promising results even in a low-resource linguistic setting [13]. In the educational domain, Mitroulias and Sioutas present a systematic review and bibliometric analysis of automated multiple-choice question generation, offering a structured perspective on the development of this research area and its intersection with recent LLM-based methods [14]. These contributions illustrate the increasing ability of generative AI to support inclusion, education, and language technologies beyond high-resource scenarios, while also reinforcing the importance of prompt design, careful benchmarking, and domain-sensitive evaluation.

Healthcare is another area prominently represented in the Special Issue, reflecting both the promise and the sensitivity of LLM adoption in critical environments. In their contribution, Hamid and Brohi provide a review of LLMs in healthcare, discussing major application categories together with threats, vulnerabilities, and security frameworks needed to support safer deployment in real-world medical contexts [15]. Karami et al. analyze ChatGPT (GPT-3) prompts shared through social media discourse to identify health-related uses of AI chatbots, thus offering an interesting empirical perspective on how users perceive and employ these systems in everyday practice [16]. Taken together, these papers suggest that healthcare is one of the most promising domains for generative AI, but also one in which concerns about privacy, reliability, accountability, and security must remain central.

The Special Issue also includes studies focused on cybersecurity and risk-sensitive analytical scenarios. Daniel et al. compare machine learning models and LLMs for labeling network intrusion detection system rules with MITRE ATT&CK techniques, showing that LLMs provide interesting opportunities in terms of automation and explainability, while conventional machine learning approaches still maintain advantages in predictive accuracy [17]. Roumeliotis et al. investigate LLMs and other NLP models for cryptocurrency sentiment analysis, comparing advanced language models for classifying the sentiment of crypto-related news and discussing their relevance for investment intelligence and risk management [18]. These contributions demonstrate how generative AI is increasingly

 https://doi.org/10.3390/bdcc10040127

entering operational and high-impact settings, where effectiveness must be balanced with interpretability, robustness, and informed decision support.

3. Discussion

Although the ten papers address different problems, methods, and domains, several common themes emerge clearly from this collection. First, the Special Issue confirms that one of the most pressing gaps in current LLM research concerns the relationship between generative capability and grounded knowledge. The contributions on RAG, agentic reasoning, and evaluation frameworks show that future progress will depend not only on larger or more capable base models, but also on better integration with external information sources and on stronger methods for assessing factual consistency, transparency, and attribution [9–11]. In this respect the Special Issue contributes to an important ongoing shift in the field: from viewing LLMs as standalone text generators to treating them as components of broader knowledge-intensive systems.

Second, the papers collected here help address another key gap, namely the limited understanding of how LLMs behave in domain-specific, socially relevant, and high-stakes contexts. The studies on healthcare, accessibility, education, cybersecurity, finance, and low-resource language processing show that the value of generative AI cannot be measured exclusively in terms of benchmark performance [12–18]. Instead, the practical usefulness of these systems depends on broader qualities such as trustworthiness, safety, interpretability, fairness, privacy protection, cost efficiency, and the degree to which human actors can remain meaningfully involved in the loop. By presenting evidence from multiple domains, this Special Issue helps broaden the discussion beyond purely technical performance and toward the conditions required for responsible real-world adoption.

Third, the Special Issue highlights the importance of analytical, comparative, and review-oriented studies in a field that is evolving extremely quickly. Some of the published papers do not simply propose new systems, but instead offer taxonomies, surveys, bibliometric analyses, and benchmarking frameworks that help organize current knowledge and clarify the state-of-the-art [11,14,15]. This is especially valuable in generative AI research, where rapid innovation can easily outpace conceptual clarity. In this sense, the Special Issue addresses not only technical gaps, but also the need for more structured understanding of where the field currently stands and where it should move next.

4. Future Research Directions

The papers in this Special Issue make clear that future research on generative AI and LLMs should move decisively toward more trustworthy, grounded, and context-aware systems. One major direction concerns the improvement of retrieval and reasoning mechanisms, especially in environments where generated content must remain closely aligned with external evidence. More work is needed on hybrid architectures that combine LLMs with retrieval modules, knowledge graphs, domain repositories, and agentic workflows, as well as on evaluation protocols capable of measuring faithfulness, attribution, and robustness in a reproducible way.

A second priority concerns domain adaptation and responsible deployment in high-impact sectors. The growing use of LLMs in healthcare, education, accessibility, governance, finance, and cybersecurity shows that these systems are increasingly expected to support consequential decisions and sensitive interactions. Future studies should therefore pay greater attention to safety guarantees, privacy-preserving mechanisms, bias mitigation, human oversight strategies, and the design of interfaces that help users understand model limitations and uncertainties. In many cases, progress will likely depend not only on

 https://doi.org/10.3390/bdcc10040127

stronger models, but also on interdisciplinary collaboration capable of integrating technical, legal, organizational, and ethical perspectives.

A third important direction is the development of more transparent and interpretable forms of generative AI. As LLMs become more deeply embedded in research and professional workflows, it will be increasingly important to understand features such as how they produce outputs, how they respond to ambiguity, how they fail, and how their behavior can be made more controllable. Comparative studies, benchmark creation, and explanatory frameworks will continue to play a fundamental role in this process. More generally, future research should aim to ensure that generative AI systems are not only more powerful, but also more reliable, explainable, inclusive, and socially responsible.

5. Conclusions

The papers collected in this Special Issue provide a broad and timely perspective on current research in generative AI and large language models. Together, they show a field that is progressing rapidly, but also becoming more mature in the questions it asks and in the criteria by which success should be judged. Beyond raw performance, the studies published here underscore the importance of grounding, explainability, safety, transparency, and domain-aware evaluation.

Overall, this Special Issue contributes to addressing important gaps in the current literature by bringing together methodological advances, application-driven investigations, and analytical studies across a diverse set of contexts. At the same time, it makes evident that many open challenges remain. We believe that future research should focus increasingly on the trustworthy integration of LLMs into real-world systems, on rigorous and reproducible evaluation methodologies, and on approaches that combine technical innovation with human-centered and socially responsible design. We hope that this collection will stimulate further work in these directions and support the development of generative AI systems that are not only more capable, but also more dependable and beneficial.

Author Contributions: F.M. and R.C. writing—original draft preparation. All authors have read and agreed to the published version of the manuscript.

Conflicts of Interest: The authors declare no conflict of interest.

References

1. Brown, T.B.; Mann, B.; Ryder, N.; Subbiah, M.; Kaplan, J.; Dhariwal, P.; Neelakantan, A.; Shyam, P.; Sastry, G.; Askell, A.; et al. Language Models are Few-Shot Learners. *Adv. Neural Inf. Process. Syst.* **2020**, *33*, 1877–1901.
2. Ouyang, L.; Wu, J.; Jiang, X.; Almeida, D.; Wainwright, C.; Mishkin, P.; Zhang, C.; Agarwal, S.; Slama, K.; Ray, A.; et al. Training Language Models to Follow Instructions with Human Feedback. *Adv. Neural Inf. Process. Syst.* **2022**, *35*, 27730–27744.
3. Touvron, H.; Lavril, T.; Izacard, G.; Martinet, X.; Lachaux, M.A.; Lacroix, T.; Rozière, B.; Goyal, N.; Hambro, E.; Azhar, F.; et al. LLaMA: Open and Efficient Foundation Language Models. *arXiv* **2023**, arXiv:2302.13971. [CrossRef]
4. Bommasani, R.; Hudson, D.A.; Adeli, E.; Altman, R.; Arora, S.; von Arx, S.; Bernstein, M.S.; Bohg, J.; Bosselut, A.; Brunskill, E.; et al. On the Opportunities and Risks of Foundation Models. *arXiv* **2021**, arXiv:2108.07258. [CrossRef]
5. Wei, J.; Wang, X.; Schuurmans, D.; Bosma, M.; Ichter, B.; Xia, F.; Chi, E.; Le, Q.; Zhou, D. Chain-of-Thought Prompting Elicits Reasoning in Large Language Models. *Adv. Neural Inf. Process. Syst.* **2022**, *35*, 24824–24837.
6. Marozzo, F. Iterative resolution of prompt ambiguities using a progressive cutting-search approach. In *Proceedings of the IFIP International Conference on Artificial Intelligence Applications and Innovations*; Springer: Berlin/Heidelberg, Germany, 2025; pp. 210–224.
7. Cosentino, C.; Gündüz-Cüre, M.; Marozzo, F.; Öztürk-Birim, Ş. Exploiting large language models for enhanced review classification explanations through interpretable and multidimensional analysis. In *Proceedings of the International Conference on Discovery Science*; Springer: Berlin/Heidelberg, Germany, 2024; pp. 3–18.
8. Belcastro, L.; Cantini, R.; Marozzo, F.; Talia, D.; Trunfio, P. Detecting mental disorder on social media: A ChatGPT-augmented explainable approach. *Online Soc. Netw. Media* **2025**, *48*, 100321. [CrossRef]

https://doi.org/10.3390/bdcc10040127

9. Ye, J.; Xin, Q.; Zhang, C.; Qi, H. TRACE: Topical Reasoning with Adaptive Contextual Experts. *Big Data Cogn. Comput.* **2026**, *10*, 31. [CrossRef]
10. Mansurova, A.; Mansurova, A.; Nugumanova, A. QA-RAG: Exploring LLM Reliance on External Knowledge. *Big Data Cogn. Comput.* **2024**, *8*, 115. [CrossRef]
11. Papageorgiou, G.; Sarlis, V.; Maragoudakis, M.; Magnisalis, I.; Tjortjis, C. Evaluating Faithfulness in Agentic RAG Systems for e-Governance Applications Using LLM-Based Judging Frameworks. *Big Data Cogn. Comput.* **2025**, *9*, 309. [CrossRef]
12. Andruccioli, M.; Bassi, B.; Delnevo, G.; Salomoni, P. Leveraging Large Language Models for Sustainable and Inclusive Web Accessibility. *Big Data Cogn. Comput.* **2025**, *9*, 247. [CrossRef]
13. Alostad, H. Large Language Models as Kuwaiti Annotators. *Big Data Cogn. Comput.* **2025**, *9*, 33. [CrossRef]
14. Mitroulias, D.; Sioutas, S. A Systematic Review and Bibliometric Analysis of Automated Multiple-Choice Question Generation. *Big Data Cogn. Comput.* **2026**, *10*, 35. [CrossRef]
15. Hamid, R.; Brohi, S. A Review of Large Language Models in Healthcare: Taxonomy, Threats, Vulnerabilities, and Framework. *Big Data Cogn. Comput.* **2024**, *8*, 161. [CrossRef]
16. Karami, A.; Qiao, Z.; Zhang, X.; Kharrazi, H.; Bozorgi, P.; Bozorgi, A. Health Use Cases of AI Chatbots: Identification and Analysis of ChatGPT Prompts in Social Media Discourses. *Big Data Cogn. Comput.* **2024**, *8*, 130. [CrossRef]
17. Daniel, N.; Kaiser, F.K.; Giladi, S.; Sharabi, S.; Moyal, R.; Shpolyansky, S.; Murillo, A.; Elyashar, A.; Puzis, R. Labeling Network Intrusion Detection System (NIDS) Rules with MITRE ATT&CK Techniques: Machine Learning vs. Large Language Models. *Big Data Cogn. Comput.* **2025**, *9*, 23. [CrossRef]
18. Roumeliotis, K.I.; Tselikas, N.D.; Nasiopoulos, D.K. LLMs and NLP Models in Cryptocurrency Sentiment Analysis: A Comparative Classification Study. *Big Data Cogn. Comput.* **2024**, *8*, 63. [CrossRef]

https://doi.org/10.3390/bdcc10040127

big data and cognitive computing

MDPI

Systematic Review

A Systematic Review and Bibliometric Analysis of Automated Multiple-Choice Question Generation

Dimitris Mitroulias * and Spyros Sioutas

Department of Engineering & Informatics, University of Patras, 26504 Rio, Greece; sioutas@ceid.upatras.gr
* Correspondence: mitroulias@ceid.upatras.gr

Abstract

The aim of this study is to systematically capture, synthesize, and evaluate current research trends related to Automated Multiple-Choice Question Generation as they emerge within the broader landscape of natural language processing (NLP) and large language model (LLM)-based educational and assessment research. A systematic search and selection process was conducted following PRISMA (Preferred Reporting Items for Systematic Reviews and Meta-Analyses) guidelines, using predefined inclusion and exclusion criteria. A total of 240 eligible publications indexed in the Scopus database were identified and analyzed. To provide a comprehensive overview of this evolving research landscape, a bibliometric analysis was performed utilizing performance analysis and scientific mapping methods, supported by the Bibliometrix (version 4.2.2) R package and VOSviewer (version 1.6.19) software. The findings of the performance analysis indicate a steady upward trend in publications and citations, with significant contributions from leading academic institutions—primarily from the United States—and a strong presence in high quality academic journals. Scientific mapping through co-authorship analysis reveals that, despite the increasing research activity, there remains a need for enhanced collaborative efforts. Bibliographic coupling organizes the analyzed literature into seven thematic clusters, highlighting the main research axes and their diachronic evolution. Furthermore, co-word analysis identifies emerging research trends and underexplored directions, indicating substantial opportunities for future investigation. To the best of our knowledge, this study represents the first systematic bibliometric analysis that examines Automated Multiple-Choice Question Generation research within the context of the broader LLM-driven educational assessment literature. By mapping the relevant scientific production and identifying research gaps and future directions, this work contributes to a more coherent understanding of the field and supports the ongoing development of research at the intersection of generative AI and educational assessment.

Keywords: natural language processing; education; bibliometric analysis; systematic review; Scopus; VOSviewer; Bibliometrix R

1. Introduction

In recent years, the rapid development of natural language processing (NLP) technologies and large language models (LLMs) has radically transformed the field of educational technology, introducing new capabilities for the automatic creation, assessment, and personalization of learning materials. Within this broader landscape of LLM-driven educational and assessment research, the automatic generation of multiple-choice questions (MCQs) from educational texts has emerged as a particularly relevant application, supporting formative assessments and the enhancement of active learning [1,2]. Within this context, automatic question generation is increasingly recognized as a core component of automated assessment systems, addressing the limitations of time-consuming and labor-intensive manual question design. Prior survey-based research highlights that the integration of automatic question generation and answer assessment mechanisms plays a crucial role in identifying learners' knowledge gaps and supporting scalable, technology-enhanced learning environments [3].

This study focuses on Automated Multiple-Choice Question Generation, as this form of assessment plays a central role in modern educational environments, especially in the context of formative assessments and the support of active learning. Unlike other forms of assessment, such as open-ended questions or development tasks, multiple-choice questions offer the possibility of immediate feedback, automated grading, and easy integration into large-scale digital learning platforms. Furthermore, the automation of multiple-choice question generation addresses a critical practical issue in the educational process, namely the increased workload of teachers related to the design of quality assessment tools. At the same time, the widespread use of MCQs in formal and distance education, combined with their structured nature, makes them particularly suitable for applications of artificial intelligence and machine learning. Therefore, the choice of this specific category of tools is not intended to exclude other forms of automatic assessment, but reflects the importance, widespread application, and high practical utility of multiple-choice questions in modern educational systems.

The existing literature on automated question generation and generative AI in education addresses a wide range of topics, including key-concept extraction, question and distractor generation, as well as broader issues related to assessment design and evaluation, often employing machine learning and neural network methodologies [4–8]. Despite the growing volume of publications, this body of research remains fragmented, with a substantial heterogeneity in datasets, modeling approaches, and evaluation metrics [7]. In recent years, several systematic and bibliometric reviews have examined specific aspects of the broader research landscape related to generative AI-driven educational assessment, within which Automated Multiple-Choice Question Generation is typically addressed as part of wider analytical frameworks rather than as an isolated research focus. For example, Al Faraby et al. [9] provide an extensive systematic review of neural question generation for educational purposes, while Awalurahman and Budi [10] focus on the automatic generation of distractors, identifying prevailing models and their limitations. Other studies, such as Artsi et al. [8], investigate the use of large language models (LLMs), including GPT and BERT, for examination question generation in professional domains such as medicine, highlighting both their potential and associated ethical challenges. Similarly, the bibliometric review by Ahadi et al. [11] analyzes the contribution of text mining techniques to education more broadly, documenting the rapid growth of NLP-related research without explicitly focusing on multiple-choice question generation as a distinct analytical focus.

Although the above studies offer important insights into individual aspects of automated question generation and generative AI in education, there is no comprehensive bibliometric mapping that systematically examines how Automated Multiple-Choice Question Generation research is positioned and evolves within the broader landscape of NLP- and LLM-based educational assessment. Unlike the existing systematic and narrative reviews, which primarily synthesize algorithmic approaches, model architectures, or application cases of automatic question generation [2,3,9,10], the present study adopts a large-scale bibliometric perspective to systematically map the scientific structure and evolution of Automated Multiple-Choice Question Generation research. To the best of our knowledge, no prior study has conducted a comprehensive quantitative bibliometric anal-

 https://doi.org/10.3390/bdcc10010035

ysis that situates MCQ generation explicitly within the rapidly expanding landscape of LLM-driven educational assessment. By combining performance analysis with science mapping techniques (co-authorship, bibliographic coupling, and co-word analysis), this review goes beyond descriptive synthesis to reveal publication dynamics, collaboration patterns, dominant thematic clusters, and emerging research directions. In doing so, it offers a macro-level, evidence-based perspective that complements the existing technical reviews and provides a clearer understanding of how this research field has developed, diversified, and positioned itself within the broader ecosystem of artificial intelligence in education. This research gap necessitates a systematic mapping of publication trends, thematic areas, research collaborations, and emerging directions that shape this evolving research landscape. This study adopts the methodology of bibliometric analysis (BA). Through BA, it becomes possible to map the evolution of the knowledge field, identify the most important research components, and reveal thematic correlations and research trends. The study utilizes performance analysis and science mapping techniques, which allow for the visualization and quantitative analysis of publications, citations, authorship collaborations, and thematic foci [12,13]. Specifically, the analysis aims to answer the following research questions (RQ) within the context of LLM-driven educational and assessment research: (RQ1) What are the publication and citation trends in the field under consideration? (RQ2) What are the most important countries (a), scientific sources (b), researchers (c), institutions (d), and articles (e) contributing to the development of the field? (RQ3) What is the level of collaboration among authors in the relevant literature? (RQ4) What are the dominant thematic areas and how have they evolved over time? (RQ5) What are the future directions of research and what research gaps are emerging?

Therefore, following established practices [14,15], we collected data from the Elsevier Scopus database and selected for evaluation relevant studies published in quality journals. We then collected and analyzed bibliometric data, offering a comprehensive mapping of scientific production in the field.

In contrast to the existing systematic and narrative reviews that examine automatic question generation mainly at the level of algorithmic approaches, implementation techniques, and pedagogical applications, the present study adopts a bibliometric approach with the aim of mapping the overall scientific structure of the field. Specifically, through the analysis of publication trends, citation patterns, collaboration networks, and bibliographic coupling, the research captures the evolution, dynamics, and dominant research trends at a macro level.

The contribution of this research is multidimensional. First, to the authors' knowledge, no other study has attempted a bibliometric analysis by offering a systematic mapping of the research landscape in this field and highlighting its historical and thematic developments. Second, it provides a comprehensive overview of the knowledge structure of the field, identifying the leading research elements, the most productive countries, and thematic convergences. Third, it identifies unexplored areas and suggests future research directions, facilitating the further academic development and practical application of automatic question generation using NLP.

Finally, the paper is organized as follows: Section 2 provides an in-depth literature review discussing prior research on the topic; Section 3 describes in detail the methodology of the BA; Section 4 presents the results of the performance and science mapping analyses; and Section 5 summarizes the main conclusions and discusses the limitations of the study.

 https://doi.org/10.3390/bdcc10010035

2. Literature Review

Research on Automatic Multiple-Choice Question Generation (MCQG) has experienced remarkable development in the last decade, with an emphasis on the utilization of natural language processing (NLP) techniques and, more recently, large language models (LLMs). The first reviews [16–18] focused mainly on early methods of extracting questions from texts, offering a general picture of the landscape up to 2014. Later, Ch and Saha [19], as well as Papasalouros and Chatzigiannakou [20], expanded on semi-automatic question generation, with an emphasis on the use of semantic patterns and concept extraction techniques, without, however, quantitatively examining the evolution of the field or the thematic associations of the publications. Kurdi et al. [2] collected 93 studies published between 2015 and 2019, documenting the progress in automatic question generation techniques and their educational application forms. Although their contribution is substantial, this study is limited in time and subject matter, as it does not include the latest developments related to the use of transformers and LLMs, nor does it provide a bibliometric analysis for mapping the intellectual structure of the field.

In recent years (2019–2025), the literature shows a remarkable increase in both research interest and the sophistication of techniques. Contemporary studies, such as those by Bitew et al. [21], Ghanem and Fyshe [22], and Feng et al. [23], have utilized deep neural networks and transformers to optimize distractor generation, while others, such as those by Yu et al. [24] and Cavusoglu et al. [25], have explored the use of pre-training models with knowledge graph integration and retrieval-augmented generation.

In addition to the above, additional reviews and surveys have appeared that focus on individual aspects—for example, Pan et al. [26] and Guo, Liao et al. [27] present a summary of neural approaches to question generation (NQG), while Mulla and Gharpure [28] offer a review with a methodological emphasis (datasets, metrics, applications). Another important development is the emergence of systematic reviews for the sub-field of distractor generation (e.g., [10,29]), which highlight the centrality of the issue of the quality of misleading options.

In parallel, Awalurahman and Budi [10] conducted a systematic literature review exclusively on distractor generation, highlighting the need for unified evaluative criteria and comparative studies. In addition, Lin et al. [30] and Bitew et al. [21] applied fine-tuning and predictive prompting approaches, respectively, to achieve more realistic and pedagogically reliable questions. The recent study by Mucciaccia et al. [31] is one of the first applications of LLMs for the automatic generation of university questions, focusing on the assessment of the quality and validity of the produced results.

Examples of bibliometric/systematic studies in the broader field of NLP application in education that support this observation include work on text mining NLP in education [11], a bibliometric study on automated assessments in programming [32], and a broader review of NLP AI in education [1]. These works show that there are valuable bibliometric approaches in branches of educational technology, but they do not specifically focus on a comprehensive bibliometric mapping of automated MCQ generation as a single field.

Of notable interest is also the research in the article by Dong et al. [33], which proposes an advanced multi-level system for generating diverse and pedagogically useful answer choices. Overall, these new approaches demonstrate the transition of the field from traditional NLP techniques to deeply modeled architectures, which offer greater accuracy and generalizability.

Furthermore, several bibliometric and systematic reviews [34–38] demonstrate that research on automatic question generation (AQG) has grown significantly in recent years, particularly with the incorporation of large language models (LLMs) and technical transformers. However, most studies focus on technical or algorithmic aspects, without com-

https://doi.org/10.3390/bdcc10010035

prehensively examining the cognitive, pedagogical, and methodological dimensions of the phenomenon [39–41]. Although Ng and Ho [42] and Guo et al. [43] attempt to map the contribution of artificial intelligence to educational evaluation, none of the existing bibliometric analyses focuses exclusively on the NLP–MCQ generation–education interface, as this study seeks to do.

However, despite the rapid increase in publications and the variety of methodologies, a comprehensive bibliometric approach that captures the structure, dynamics, and evolution of research in the field of automatic MCQ generation is lacking. In contrast to previous systematic reviews that methodically document techniques, datasets, and evaluations [2,44], or to specialized reviews on distractors [10], our work offers the first systematic bibliometric mapping that combines quantitative performance analyses (TP, TC, h-index, etc.) with mappings of science (co-authorship, co-citation, co-word analysis). Furthermore, the study updates and extends the time window (2018–2025) and applies strict quality criteria (AJG) to deliver a reproducible, interdisciplinary mapping of trends, collaboration networks, and emerging thematic axes in the field of automatic MCQ generation with NLP techniques. In this way, the study contributes both to theoretical understanding and to the practical routing of future research directions (e.g., evaluation of LLM-generated items, bias and fairness, applications in education).

3. Methodology and Data

This study presents a systematic review and bibliometric analysis conducted in accordance with the PRISMA 2020 guidelines (Preferred Reporting Items for Systematic Reviews and Meta-Analyses) [45]. The review was not prospectively registered in a protocol registry (e.g., PROSPERO). BA was employed as the primary methodological approach, given its significant advancement in recent years as a robust quantitative tool for organizing, analyzing, and mapping extensive bodies of scientific literature [46,47].

Its utility lies in the ability to process extensive, often unstructured data in a systematic and methodologically rigorous manner, offering a high level of objectivity and reproducibility in research findings [48]. BA is particularly useful in rapidly evolving fields where the systematic exploration of emerging thematic directions and the revelation of the intellectual structure of the scientific field are required [49,50].

In this context, BA leverages two main pillars: performance analysis and science mapping. These techniques are well-established approaches in the international literature [12] and have been widely used in recent studies to understand the evolution of scientific fields, such as artificial intelligence, computational linguistics, and educational technology [51–53].

Performance analysis is the foundation of BA and examines the contribution of key research components—such as authors, institutions, countries, scientific journals, and subject areas—using criteria such as the number of publications (TP), total citations (TC), and the Hirsch index (h-index) [54,55]. These measures are used to capture productivity and scientific impact, providing an overall picture of the evolution of the research field [56].

In addition, science mapping explores the intellectual and thematic structure of the field. In the context of this study, three main techniques were used: (i) Bibliographic coupling, which is based on the logic that two articles that share common references show thematic and intellectual affinity [57]. This technique aims to identify thematic groups and evolutionary patterns [58]. (ii) Co-authorship analysis, which visualizes the networks of collaboration between authors and organizations [59] and highlights the degree of international collaboration [60]. (iii) Co-word analysis, which examines the associations between terms that appear simultaneously and reveals the conceptual structure and future directions of the field [48].

https://doi.org/10.3390/bdcc10010035

The three techniques were applied to answer the corresponding research questions: co-authorship analysis for the third question, bibliographic coupling for the fourth, and co-word analysis for the fifth. To perform these analyses, the software Bibliometrix [12] and VOSviewer [13] were used, which are leading platforms for bibliometric analyses and have been adopted in a multitude of recent studies [61–63]. The data collection process followed a rigorous, reproducible, and transparent methodological approach, aligned with the PRISMA guidelines [45] and previous relevant studies [64–66].

Several established scholarly databases were evaluated for data collection purposes, namely Scopus, Web of Science (WoS), and Google Scholar. Scopus was selected based on its stringent quality control standards [67], its broad interdisciplinary scope, and its extensive use in bibliometric and science mapping studies [68,69]. In comparison with WoS, Scopus demonstrates a wider disciplinary coverage, particularly in the fields of computer science, engineering, and social sciences, which are comparatively less represented in WoS, thereby supporting a more inclusive and multidisciplinary BA [70]. Moreover, Scopus indexes approximately 60% more journals than WoS, further strengthening the depth and completeness of the dataset [71]. Google Scholar was not considered suitable due to limitations related to indexing transparency, the inclusion of discontinued journals, and the high proportion of non-English publications, all of which may affect data reliability and reproducibility in bibliometric research [72]. Overall, Scopus constitutes a robust and comprehensive source for bibliometric inquiry, offering access to over 40,000 peer-reviewed publications across diverse subject areas, along with structured and reliable metadata that support advanced BA and visualization techniques [73,74].

The search was performed using combinations of keywords for the title, abstract, and keywords (TITLE-ABS-KEY), aiming to retrieve as many relevant publications in the field as possible. The final query that was defined and employed was as follows: ("large language model" OR "LLM" OR "GPT" OR "transformer-based model" OR "retrieval-augmented generation" OR RAG OR "fusion-in-decoder") AND ("chatbot" OR "AI agent" OR "conversational agent" OR "intelligent assistant" OR "virtual assistant" OR "autonomous agent") AND ("education" OR "educational technology" OR "school administration" OR "teacher support" OR "academic management" OR "payroll" OR "HR system" OR "administrative process" OR "institutional management" OR "database assistant" OR "SQL agent" OR "human evaluation" OR "grounded"). The selection of keywords and data collection time frame was based on the need to capture the most recent and substantial developments in the field of large language models (LLMs), AI agents, and their applications in educational technology. The period 2022–2025 was purposefully chosen, as it represents the phase of explosive development and scientific maturity of LLM technologies and related tools such as GPT and RAG (retrieval-augmented generation). During this period, an exponential increase in publications, research projects, and practical applications of these models in educational settings was observed [75,76].

The selection of specific search terms (e.g., LLM, GPT, transformer-based model, RAG, chatbot, AI agent, intelligent assistant, virtual assistant) was based on two main criteria: (i) scientific accuracy and representativeness, as these terms are the prevailing research labels in the field of AI and education [77]; and (ii) ensuring thematic coverage, so as to include both technological approaches (such as transformer models and NLP techniques), as well as applied pedagogical and administrative uses of AI agents in school and university environments. In addition, the terms "education", "educational technology", "school management", and "administrative processes" were incorporated into the search query to ensure that the results focus on studies that explore the interconnection of LLMs with the educational and organizational sector [78]. This strategy is in line with modern approaches to BA, where keywords are determined based on thematic relevance and the tendency to

https://doi.org/10.3390/bdcc10010035

appear in top journals [79,80]. The period 2022–2025 is considered ideal for this study, as it represents the post-ChatGPT era, where LLMs began to be actively integrated into education platforms, learning support systems, and autonomous administrative systems [81]. Therefore, the choice of this temporal focus allows for the capture of the most modern scientific and technological developments, offering an updated and realistic framework for mapping the cognitive field.

4. Results

4.1. PRISMA Flow Diagram and Study Selection

Figure 1 illustrates the stepwise process of identification, screening, eligibility assessment, and inclusion of publications, in accordance with PRISMA guidelines. The initial search covering the period 2022–2025 (November) yielded 1090 records. Sequential filtering steps were applied to ensure the validity, thematic relevance, and methodological quality of the dataset. Health-related studies were not excluded a priori during the screening process. However, publications focusing exclusively on medical or clinical education, without a direct emphasis on Automated Multiple-Choice Question Generation or related assessment methodologies, were excluded in order to preserve thematic coherence and methodological consistency with the objectives of this bibliometric analysis. Specifically, 40 publications without a defined author were removed, resulting in 1026 papers. The sample was then limited to publications in the fields of computer science, engineering, and social sciences, reducing the number to 725 articles. Subsequently, only journal articles were retained, excluding conference proceedings, book chapters, and other document types, leaving 245 publications. Finally, five non-English publications were excluded, resulting in a final sample of 240 articles for BA. Although concepts such as learning effectiveness, item analysis, and adaptive testing are highly relevant to multiple-choice question design, they appear only sporadically in the retrieved literature. Their limited and fragmented presence in studies focusing on automated MCQ generation indicates an important research gap, particularly with regard to the pedagogical evaluation and learning impact of automatically generated assessment items.

To enhance validity and reduce bias, the relevance assessment was independently performed by three researchers, with a fourth acting as a moderator. Disagreements were resolved through discussion until consensus was reached, following best practices in scientific methodology [82,83]. This rigorous process ensures that the selected dataset is representative of the current research landscape and suitable for systematic bibliometric analysis.

After completing the filtering process, it was observed that the time period of the selected papers finally extended from 2023 to November 2025. This reduction compared to the initial period (2022–2025) is due to the fact that a large part of the 2022 publications did not meet the thematic relevance or quality classification criteria according to the Academic Journal Guide (AJG, 2021), as they focused on traditional or rule-based NLP approaches. Moreover, the shift in the analysis period reflects the rapid evolution of the field after 2023, a period during which there was an explosive increase in interest and research output around the use of LLMs, such as GPT-4 and Claude, in educational technology and automated question generation applications [9,27,29]. In addition, the tightening of selection filters, aimed at ensuring qualitatively reliable and thematically relevant works, contributed to the natural shrinkage of the time range, without, however, affecting the validity or representativeness of the sample [47,48].

https://doi.org/10.3390/bdcc10010035

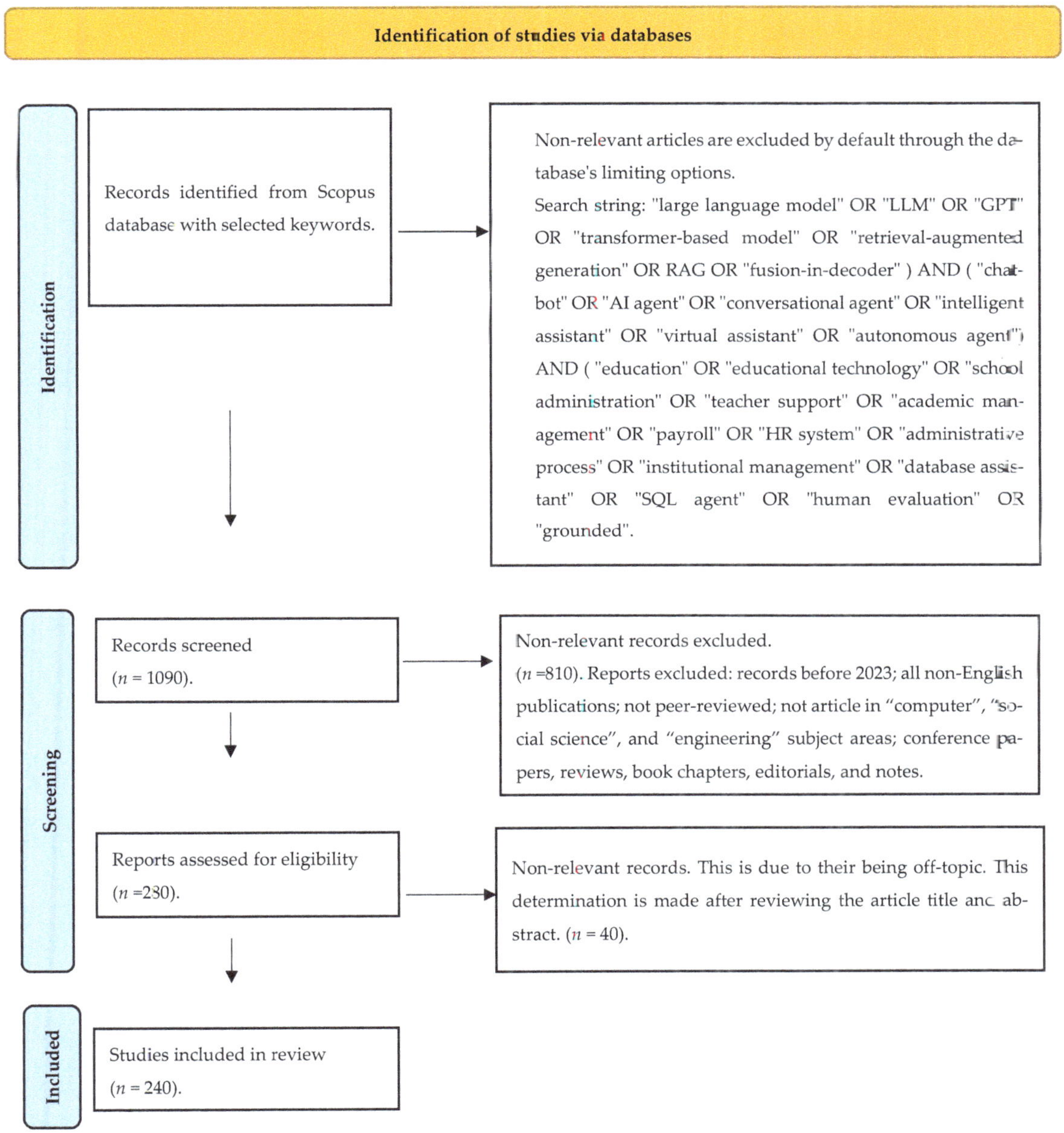

Notes: This diagram illustrates the stages of BA.
Source(s): Prepared by authors.

Figure 1. PRISMA flowchart diagram.

The choice to focus on the most recent publications enhances the timeliness and relevance of the analysis, as it reflects the latest technological and scientific developments in the field of automatic question generation and NLP systems in education. A similar methodological approach has been adopted in modern bibliometric studies, which emphasize emerging research trends and thematic clusters [58,84]. Consequently, the selection of

https://doi.org/10.3390/bdcc10010035

the final sample enhances thematic homogeneity, ensures the reproducibility of the results, and provides a realistic depiction of the current research reality in the field.

4.2. Descriptive Analysis Results

The basic information about the research is deployed in this sub-section (Table 1). The bibliometric analysis carried out for the period 2023–2025 includes 240 publications from 149 scientific journals, which demonstrates intense research activity in the field of automatic MCQ generation and, more generally, in the applications of artificial intelligence in education. The impressive annual growth rate of publications, reaching 97.71%, confirms that the field is in a phase of rapid development, mainly due to the rapid progress in LLMs and in neural approaches to natural language processing [27].

Table 1. Main information about data.

Description	Results	Description	Results
Timespan	2023:2025	AUTHORS	
Sources (Journals)	149	Authors	239
Documents	240	Authors of Single-Authored Docs	0
Annual Growth Rate %	97.71	AUTHORS COLLABORATION	
Document Average Age	0.6	Single-Authored Docs	0
Average Citations Per Doc	42.5	Co-Authors Per Doc	11.7
References	1993	International Co-Authorships %	25
DOCUMENT CONTENTS		DOCUMENT TYPES	
Keywords Plus (ID)	923	Article	240
Author's Keywords (DE)	880		

Note(s): This was produced using Biblioshiny. Source(s): Table by authors.

The articles of this period have a very short average age (0.6 years) and a high average number of citations (42.5 per article), which reflects both the modern and scientifically active nature of the field. The increased impact of these studies reflects the broadening interest of the research community in the use of artificial intelligence for automatic question generation, the support for educational assessment, and the development of intelligent learning systems [2].

Regarding authorship, the 1405 authors participating in the writing of the 240 articles demonstrate the highly collaborative nature of the research. No single-author works were identified, while the average number of co-authors per publication (11.7) reveals a high level of interdisciplinary collaboration, with international contributions in 25% of the works. This trend is characteristic of new, rapidly developing research fields, where knowledge is developed through synergies and exchanges between different scientific areas [48].

Regarding thematic content, the 923 plus keywords and 880 author keywords highlight the wide variety of topics covered by the publications. The most frequent terms are associated with concepts such as neural networks, deep learning, automatic content generation, adaptive learning, and NLP-based question generation. This thematic diversity indicates the gradual transition of research from traditional normative questioning methods to advanced approaches that utilize machine learning techniques and transformers.

The reduction in the time frame of the analysis (2023–2025 versus 2022–2025 initially) is explained by the rapid concentration of publications in the last two years, where technological progress in models such as GPT and T5 [85] led to increased interest and the production of new knowledge. This trend is consistent with recent bibliometric studies in related fields of educational technology, where a shift in research interest towards applications of LLMs is observed [86,87].

 https://doi.org/10.3390/bdcc10010035

Overall, the results highlight a dynamic, rapidly evolving, and highly collaborative research ecosystem, which is consolidating its position in the international scientific scene. The present study, by mapping this new phase of development (2023–2025), provides a holistic picture of the course of the field and contributes substantially to the understanding of contemporary research trends, thematic correlations, and future prospects in the field of automatic question generation through NLP and artificial intelligence technologies in education.

4.3. Performance Analysis Results

This subsection focuses on the performance analysis, which examines the overall scientific productivity and influence of the field through key bibliometric indicators. This analysis aims to capture both the quantitative and qualitative dimensions of research activity, highlighting the way in which the relevant research has evolved over time. To this end, five main evaluation criteria were applied: (RQ1a) The temporal evolution of publications, which captures the dynamic development and level of maturity of the research field. (RQ2b) The geographical distribution of research production, in order to identify the regions or countries with the greatest contribution to the bibliography. (RQ3c) The most active and influential authors, as well as their international or institutional collaborations, which reveal the networks of scientific partnership. (RQ4d) The most productive publication sources, i.e., the scientific journals and conferences that shape the research field. (RQ5e) The most cited articles, which constitute the theoretical and methodological pillars of the specific field of knowledge.

In general, the above criteria allow for the formation of a holistic picture of research activity, providing essential information on the structure, key factors, and trends in the diffusion of knowledge in the field of study.

4.3.1. Number of Publications per Year (RQ1)

From Table 2, it is observed that there is a significant variation in the influence of publications by year, based on citations. In 2023, the 33 publications show a high average number of citations per article (257.36) and average number of citations per year (85.79), suggesting that these articles are particularly influential and likely include fundamental or early works that serve as a reference for subsequent research.

Table 2. Annual scientific production and citation.

Year	Articles	Mean TC Per Article	Mean TC Per Year
2023	33	257.36	85.79
2024	78	18.78	9.39
2025	129	1.87	1.87

Source(s): Table by authors. Note(s): TC = total citations.

For 2024, although the number of articles increases (78), the average number of citations per article decreases significantly (18.78), suggesting that these are mainly newer publications with a limited time to accumulate citations. Accordingly, the average number of citations per year is much lower (9.39). The year 2025 presents the highest number of articles (129), but the average number of citations per article is very low (1.87), reflecting the newness of these publications and the limited time period to accumulate citations.

In conclusion, the trends show that early publications in the field have greater influence and constitute the foundation for newer research, while more recent publications, despite their increased volume (Figure 2), have not yet acquired a significant number of citations, something expected in bibliometric analyses [47,88].

 https://doi.org/10.3390/bdcc10010035

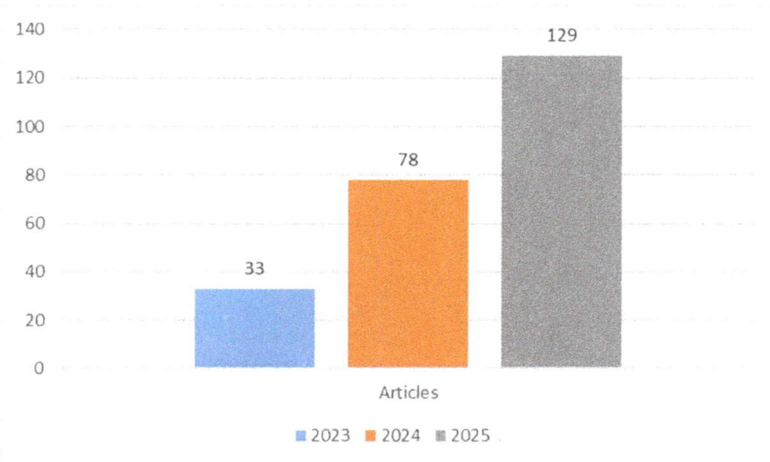

Figure 2. Publication trends. Source: By authors.

4.3.2. Country-Wise Analysis (RQ2a)

The analysis of the data (Table 3) shows that there is a strong variation between countries in terms of the volume and quality of scientific production. The United States stands out for the largest number of publications, as it accumulates 61 articles and 5836 citations in total. This is followed by China, with 27 articles, Germany, with 19, and the United Kingdom, with 16. These countries are the main producers of scientific work in the field, although the average impact per article (C/A) is not always particularly high. For example, China has a low impact index (9.56), which indicates that, despite the increased production, its publications do not have the same research impact as other countries.

Table 3. Top 20 contributing countries.

Country	Articles	Citations	C/A	Country	Articles	Citations	C/A
USA	61	5836	95.67	Japan	9	204	22.67
China	27	258	9.56	Canada	8	155	19.38
Germany	19	3040	160.00	Taiwan	7	2846	406.57
UK	16	2965	185.31	Norway	6	2854	475.67
Australia	14	3576	255.43	Italy	6	2739	456.50
Singapore	12	4578	381.50	Saudi Arabia	6	2733	455.50
India	12	3110	259.17	Switzerland	5	2765	553.00
Spain	12	2880	240.00	Turkey	5	83	16.60
South Korea	12	673	56.08	Portugal	5	38	7.60
Hong Kong	11	3042	276.55	New Zealand	4	2815	703.75

Notes: The table reports the results for productivity and influence of each country. Abbreviations: C/A = citations per article. Source: Prepared by authors based on Biblioshiny.

In contrast, some countries with a smaller number of articles have an extremely high average impact. For example, New Zealand, with just four articles, records the highest C/A index (703.75), which indicates that its publications have a very high impact on the scientific community. Correspondingly, Switzerland (C/A 553), Norway (475.67), Italy (456.50), Saudi Arabia (455.50), and Taiwan (406.57) have particularly high impact values, which indicates focused but high-quality research.

In an intermediate category are countries such as Singapore (381.50), Australia (255.43), India (259.17), Spain (240), and Hong Kong (276.55), which combine a satisfactory number

 https://doi.org/10.3390/bdcc10010035

of publications with a relatively high impact. These cases show a balance between the quantity and quality of scientific production. In contrast, countries such as Turkey (16.60), Canada (19.38), and Portugal (7.60) show low impact indices, which can be attributed either to the low international visibility of their publications or to their lower participation in international collaboration networks.

Overall, it appears that the volume of publications does not necessarily imply a high scientific influence. Large countries, such as the United States and China, dominate in terms of quantity, while smaller countries, such as New Zealand and Switzerland, are distinguished by the quality and visibility of their research. This picture reveals a field with a strong imbalance, where a few countries produce the largest volume of research, but the highest quality is found in more specialized and research-mature environments.

4.3.3. Most Contributing Journals (RQ2b)

The analysis of publication sources shows that the research field of automated MCQ generation is attracting the interest of a variety of scientific journals active at the intersection of educational technology, artificial intelligence, and medical education (Table 4). At the top of the list is the journal *JMIR Medical Education* with 24 publications, which indicates the intense research activity around the application of automated assessment methods in medical and clinical education. The high number of publications is also accompanied by a significant number of references (1742 citations), an element that confirms the influence of the journal in this scientific field.

Table 4. Contributing journals.

Source	Articles	Source	Citations
JMIR Medical Education	24	*International Journal of Information Management*	2712
Education and Information Technologies	8	*JMIR Medical Education*	1742
Computers and Education: Artificial Intelligence	7	*Journal of Applied Learning and Teaching*	1696
British Journal of Educational Technology	6	*Education and Information Technologies*	488
Frontiers in Education	5	*Journal of University Teaching and Learning Practice*	421
IEEE Access	5	*Benchcouncil Transactions on Benchmarks, Standards and Evaluations*	349
Electronics (Switzerland)	4	*International journal of educational Technology in Higher Education*	246
Frontiers in Artificial Intelligence	4	*European Journal of Engineering Education*	219
Journal of Applied Learning and Teaching	3	*Information* (Switzerland)	170
Information (Switzerland)	3	*Computers and Education: Artificial Intelligence*	163

Source(s): By authors.

Next are *Education and Information Technologies* (eight articles) and *Computers and Education: Artificial Intelligence* (seven articles), which function as the pre-eminent international forum for research combining natural language processing (NLP), machine learning, and pedagogical assessment techniques. Also, the presence of journals such as the *British Journal of Educational Technology* and *Frontiers in Education* demonstrates the interdisciplinary nature of the field, as they cover topics ranging from learning technology to psychopedagogical assessment.

IEEE Access deserves a special mention, with five publications and a strong technological focus, indicating an involvement of the engineering research community in

https://doi.org/10.3390/bdcc10010035

the development of algorithmic approaches for the automatic production of educational content. The presence of the journals *Electronics* (Switzerland) and *Frontiers in Artificial Intelligence* further strengthens the connection of the field with technological and computational sciences.

In terms of the impact of publications, the journal with the most citations is the *International Journal of Information Management* with 2712 citations, which shows that the relevant works touch on issues of information management, data, and artificial intelligence in organizational or educational contexts. *JMIR Medical Education* itself, although leading in the number of articles, also ranks very high in citations, which highlights its double influence: both in terms of production volume and scientific awareness. The position of the *Journal of Applied Learning and Teaching* (1696 citations) is also noteworthy, which shows that the topic of automatic question generation is closely linked to the practical dimension of teaching and educational design. At the same time, the presence of journals such as *Education and Information Technologies*, *Journal of University Teaching and Learning Practice*, and *European Journal of Engineering Education* proves that the research impact of the field is not limited only to technical approaches, but also extends to pedagogical and institutional dimensions.

In summary, the multidimensional nature of the field is reflected in the combination of journals from the fields of education, technology, engineering, and medicine. *JMIR Medical Education* and the *International Journal of Information Management* emerge as key journals in both production and citations, acting as research hubs. The strong presence of journals such as *Computers and Education: Artificial Intelligence* and *IEEE Access* indicates a shift in research interest towards more automated, technology-oriented solutions. The increasing number of articles in educational technology journals indicates that artificial intelligence in educational assessment is evolving into an emerging scientific field with a broad interdisciplinary reach.

4.3.4. Author-Wise Analysis (RQ2c)

Table 5 captures the ten most productive and influential researchers in the emerging scientific field of artificial intelligence and, in particular, large language models (LLMs), with applications in education, assessment, and cognition. The data demonstrate not only the geographical diversity of the researchers, but also the interdisciplinary nature of the field, where specialties from education, social sciences, computer science, and machine learning converge.

Table 5. Contributing authors.

Author	Articles	Citations	h	Affiliation
Crawford, J	3	515	24	Tasmanian School of Business and Economics, Australia
Cwiertny, D	3	226	43	University of Iowa, US
Demir, I	3	226	37	Tulane University, US
Manrique, R	3	2	8	FLAGlab, Colombia
Mondal, H	3	2	13	All India Institute of Medical Sciences Deoghar, India
Rudolph, J	3	1696	15	Kaplan Higher Education Academy, Singapore
Sermet, Y	3	226	18	Tulane University, US
Tan, S	3	1696	7	Institute for Adult Learning, Singapore
Allen, K.A.	2	483	37	Monash University, Australia
Caccavale, F	2	21	5	Technical University of Denmark, Denmark

Source(s): By authors.

At the top of the ranking based on the influence index (citations and h-index) is Rudolph J. from the Kaplan Higher Education Academy (Singapore), with 1696 citations

https://doi.org/10.3390/bdcc10010035

and an h-index of 15, which underlines his systematic contribution to the study of the impacts of genetic artificial intelligence in higher education. Rudolph is one of the most recognized figures in the discussion around the transformation of assessment and learning in the light of AI, as he is the author of some of the most cited articles in the field (e.g., "ChatGPT: Bullshit spewer or the end of traditional assessments in higher education?").

Tan S., also from Singapore (Institute for Adult Learning), holds a significant position, with 1696 citations, confirming that the Southeast Asian region has emerged as a key research center for investigating the relationship between AI and lifelong learning. The high concentration of citations for researchers from Singapore reflects the country's strong investment in innovation and educational technology.

Crawford J. (Tasmanian School of Business and Economics, Australia) follows with 515 citations and an h-index of 24, demonstrating his interdisciplinary contribution to the ethical dimension of artificial intelligence and the management of education through digital transformations. Similarly, Allen K.A. (Monash University, Australia), with 483 citations and an h-index of 37, emerges as a key representative of the psychopedagogical approach to artificial intelligence, examining the emotional well-being and adaptability of students in the new era of learning.

In the United States, Demir I. and Sermet Y. (Tulane University), as well as Cwiertny D. (University of Iowa), all with 226 citations, stand out, focusing on the use of LLMs for STEM education and skill assessments. Their presence indicates the increasing research activity of American universities, especially in projects that combine machine learning and pedagogical technology. On the other hand, Manrique R. (FLAGlab, Colombia) and Mondal H. (All India Institute of Medical Sciences, India) contribute with lower impact metrics (h-index 8 and 13); however, their presence demonstrates the expansion of research interest beyond the Western context towards emerging regions, with an increasing activity in educational technology. Finally, Caccavale F. (Technical University of Denmark), with a smaller research output (2 articles, 21 citations), reveals the integration of the field in technological institutions in Europe, which demonstrates the European interest in the interdisciplinary study of AI in education.

From the above, it is found that there is a high level of international collaboration, with researchers from Asia, Oceania, Europe, and the Americas. In addition, a concentration of influence is observed in a few leading authors, mainly from Singapore and Australia. Also, a shift in scientific interest is observed from the technical applications of artificial intelligence (e.g., machine learning) to its pedagogical, ethical, and social dimensions. This distribution reflects a new phase of maturation of the field, where the emphasis is shifting from technological development to the human dimension of education in artificial intelligence.

4.3.5. Contributing Institutions (RQ2d)

The analysis of the leading institutions active in research in the field of Automated Multiple-Choice Question Generation reveals interesting findings both in terms of geographical distribution and level of research impact (Table 6). It is observed that the primacy belongs to institutions in the United States, with the University of Iowa accumulating three publications, confirming its constant presence in issues linking artificial intelligence, education, and automated assessment. Correspondingly, the College of Engineering and the College of Liberal Arts and Sciences (also from the USA) show the same number of publications (three), which indicates a balanced research activity between technological and humanities scientific fields. Their presence confirms that research in the field of automated question generation requires an interdisciplinary approach—combining algorithmic techniques with pedagogical theories and linguistic analysis.

https://doi.org/10.3390/bdcc10010035

Table 6. Top ten contributing institutions.

Institutions	Articles	h	Institutions	Citations
University of Iowa, US	3	6	Indiana University Bloomington, US	595
College of Engineering, US	3	5	Director of Research, Singapore	510
College of Liberal Arts and Sciences, US	3	5	University of Tasmania, Australia	440
Department of Physiology, Ministry of Health and Family Welfare, India	3	4	Monash University, Australia	411
Hannam University, South Korea	2	4	Cquniversity, Australia	408

Source(s): By authors.

At the international level, the participation of Asian institutions is also notable. The Department of Physiology, Ministry of Health and Family Welfare, India (India), records three publications and h-index = 4, which can be interpreted as a result of the increasing application of natural language processing (NLP) and computational assessment technologies in medical education and training. Similarly, Hannam University, South Korea (with two publications and h-index = 4), shows that the East Asian region is starting to gain research momentum in the subject, especially in the context of English language teaching through intelligent assessment systems.

In terms of citations, we observe that the institutions with the highest impact are Indiana University Bloomington (595 citations), the Director of Research, Singapore (510), and the University of Tasmania (440). This high visibility indicates not only productivity but also a significant influence in the research communities dealing with assessment automation, natural language processing, and educational technology. Also, of interest is the presence of Australian universities (Monash University and CQU University), which seem to be shaping an emerging research stream in the area of computational education.

On the whole, the data suggest that this field is interdisciplinary and globalized, with contributions from universities on different continents. The United States continues to maintain a strong leadership position in the production and dissemination of knowledge. Asia (India, Korea, Singapore) is emerging as a rapidly growing research power, mainly through the application of artificial intelligence technologies in teaching and assessment. Australian university structures occupy significant positions in the citations, reflecting mature networks of international collaboration and research impact.

4.3.6. The Most Cited Global Publications (RQ2e)

Table 7 presents the ten most influential articles in the field of artificial intelligence research, and, in particular, large language models (LLMs), such as ChatGPT, with applications in education, assessment, and society. The data clearly highlight the rapid rise and intense research activity that occurred in 2023 and 2024, years that marked the explosion of scientific engagement with genetic models.

The high citation impact of the articles listed in Table 7 can be attributed to their foundational role in shaping the early discourse on large language models in education and assessment. Most of these studies were published in 2023, a pivotal year that marked the rapid diffusion of generative AI tools such as ChatGPT into educational practice. Their multidisciplinary scope, addressing assessment integrity, ethical implications, professional education, and policy considerations, positioned them as reference points for subsequent empirical and conceptual research. As a result, these publications function not only as highly cited works, but also as intellectual anchors that structure the development of the field.

 https://doi.org/10.3390/bdcc10010035

Table 7. Top cited articles.

Author(s)/Year	Title	TC	TCY
[89]	"So what if ChatGPT wrote it? Multidisciplinary perspectives on opportunities, challenges and implications of generative conversational AI for research, practice and policy"	2712	904.00
[90]	"How Does ChatGPT Perform on the United States Medical Licensing Examination? The Implications of Large Language Models for Medical Education and Knowledge Assessment"	1357	452.33
[91]	"ChatGPT: Bullshit spewer or the end of traditional assessments in higher education?"	1154	384.67
[92]	"War of the chatbots: Bard, Bing Chat, ChatGPT, Ernie and beyond. The new AI gold rush and its impact on higher education"	510	170.00
[93]	"Large language models in education: A focus on the complementary relationship between human teachers and ChatGPT"	441	147.00
[94]	"Leadership is needed for ethical ChatGPT: Character, assessment, and learning using artificial intelligence (AI)"	408	136.00
[95]	"ChatGPT for healthcare services: An emerging stage for an innovative perspective"	349	116.33
[96]	"ChatGPT versus engineering education assessment: a multidisciplinary and multi-institutional benchmarking and analysis of this generative artificial intelligence tool to investigate assessment integrity"	219	73.00
[97]	"Not quite eye to A.I.: student and teacher perspectives on the use of generative artificial intelligence in the writing process"	185	61.67
[98]	"Artificial Intelligence-Enabled Intelligent Assistant for Personalized and Adaptive Learning in Higher Education"	163	81.50

Notes: This table is sorted based on TC to find 10 influential topics in the literature. Abbreviations: TC = total citations; TCY = total citations per year. Source(s): Prepared by authors based on Biblioshiny.

The article by Dwivedi, Kshetri et al. [89], with 2712 total citations and 904 per year, occupies the first place by far, demonstrating its multidisciplinary nature and its importance in setting the research and policy agenda for generative AI systems. This work serves as a reference foundation for the study of the social, ethical, and political implications of generative AI. Next is the study by Gilson et al. [90] with 1357 citations, which examines the relationship of ChatGPT to medical education and its ability to answer professional certification exams (USMLE). This article is a landmark, as it introduced the dialog on the use of LLMs as cognitive learning and assessment tools.

The two studies by Rudolph et al. [91,92], with 1154 and 510 citations, respectively, analyze the impact of LLMs on higher education, focusing on the integrity of assessment and the change in traditional teaching formats. The repeated presence of the same author highlights the consistency and impact of his research contribution. The study by Jeon and Lee [93] (441 citations) examines the complementary relationship between humans and machines in teaching, laying the foundation for pedagogical hybrid learning models, while Crawford et al. [94] highlight the importance of ethical leadership and the responsible use of artificial intelligence in education, showing the shift in interest to ethical issues.

In the health sector, Javaid et al. [95] analyze the potential of ChatGPT in health services, opening new perspectives in diagnostic support and in the education of health professionals. At the same time, Nikolic et al. [96] focus on assessing the validity of AI tools in engineering education, proposing control frameworks to ensure academic integrity. Barrett & Pack [97] examine student and teacher perceptions of the use of generative AI in writing, highlighting issues of critical thinking, authenticity, and creativity. Finally,

 https://doi.org/10.3390/bdcc10010035

Sajja et al. [98] is one of the most recent, introducing AI-enabled personalized and adaptive learning, a framework for personalized education that integrates LLMs into adaptive learning systems.

All in all, the analysis shows that the most influential papers focus on three main thematic areas: ethical, social, and pedagogical dimensions of LLMs [89,91,94], applications in education and assessment [90,93,96], and innovative uses in professional fields, such as health [95] and personalized learning [98].

The high concentration of citations in articles from 2023 indicates that this year was a milestone for the foundation of the scientific discussion around LLMs, while the gradual decrease in citations in later papers (2024) reflects the phenomenon of a delayed diffusion of new publications in the literature [12,48].

It should be noted that the identified thematic clusters are not mutually exclusive. Several influential studies span multiple dimensions simultaneously, combining ethical considerations, pedagogical implications, and domain-specific applications. For example, research addressing assessment integrity often intersects both ethical and pedagogical perspectives, while studies conducted in professional domains such as medicine also contribute to broader discussions on educational assessment. This thematic overlap reflects the inherently interdisciplinary and evolving nature of AI-driven research in education.

4.4. Science Mapping

4.4.1. Co-Authorship Analysis of Authors (RQ3)

Co-author analysis provides a comprehensive picture of the collaborative landscape that has emerged in the field of Automated Multiple-Choice Question Generation. The network visualization (Figure 3) captures the dynamic relationships between researchers, highlighting the axes of collaboration and research clusters that have developed in recent years.

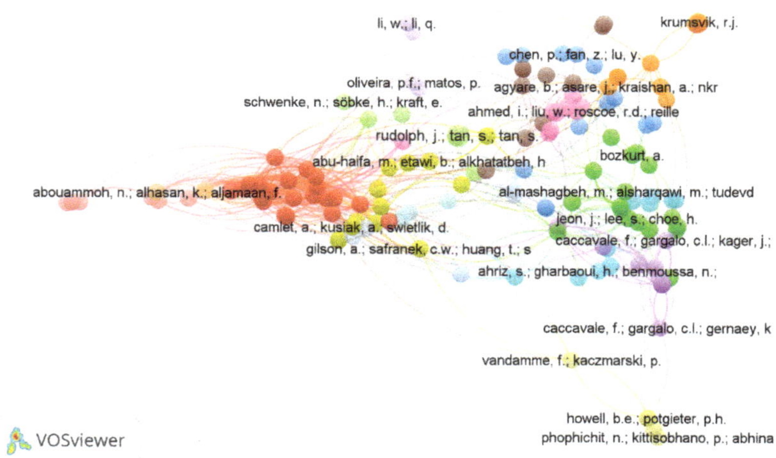

Figure 3. Co-authorship network and cluster density of the author. Labels were adjusted to improve readability. Note(s): Each node represents an author, with node size proportional to the author's total link strength (TLS), indicating the extent of collaboration. Links between nodes represent co-authorship relations, with thicker links denoting stronger collaborative ties. Colors indicate distinct collaboration clusters identified by VOSviewer. The visualization highlights the collaborative structure and research groupings within the field. Source(s): Figure by authors.

 https://doi.org/10.3390/bdcc10010035

To enhance interpretability, node size and link thickness were adjusted to reflect collaboration intensity, following established visualization practices in bibliometric mapping. Specifically, each node corresponds to an author, with the size of the node or name reflecting its academic productivity or influence, while the color separation indicates the formation of distinct research groups. To capture and analyze this collaborative structure, the VOSviewer tool was used, which is an established choice for mapping bibliometric networks [13]. The analysis revealed a network of 239 authors, who are connected through 660 collaborative ties, with a total connection strength (TLS = 726). The total number of authors was divided into 16 groups, indicating a fragmented but active and interacting research ecosystem. The thickness of the lines connecting the nodes illustrates the degree of collaboration: the thicker the line, the closer and more frequent the intellectual interactions between the researchers involved. The existence of many active links in different subsets of the network highlights the multidimensional and interdisciplinary nature of the field, where artificial intelligence, educational technology, computational linguistics, and data science meet and feed off each other.

Overall, the analysis demonstrates that the level of collaboration in this research field is satisfactory and is steadily growing. The structure of the network indicates not only the existence of central, highly productive authors, but also the presence of many smaller groups that contribute to the continuous evolution and expansion of the literature.

4.4.2. Bibliographic Coupling of Publications (RQ4)

To capture the research structure and thematic directions of a scientific field, the bibliographic coupling method is a particularly suitable tool. This approach is based on the idea that two publications are conceptually related when they draw references from a common bibliographic base, thus forming a "conjugation pair" [47,57]. Through this logic, publications are grouped into clusters that reflect underlying intellectual and thematic affinities.

In the context of the present study, the application of bibliographic coupling to the 240 articles in the sample revealed that 153 of them presented strong connections in terms of their common references. The bibliographic coupling analysis revealed seven distinct thematic areas that capture the structure and research trends in the field of automated MCQs and the use of LLMs in assessment. These themes emerged from the grouping of related publications that share common bibliographic foundations and compose a coherent picture of the field. Table 8 depicts the main focus of each group, accompanied by the most representative publications.

Acknowledging that the labeling of clusters always involves an element of interpretative judgment, each group was examined in depth through a close reading of its constituent studies and their citation patterns. The thematic descriptors assigned to each cluster therefore do not merely serve as categorical labels; they encapsulate recurring conceptual motifs, dominant research priorities, and intellectual commonalities that emerged across the included works. The keywords and titles associated with each cluster support the visualization of broader themes in the field and underscore the contributions of the grouped publications to the cumulative knowledge base.

Cluster 1: "AI-Assisted Assessment and Automated MCQ Generation". The first and largest cluster focuses directly on Automated Multiple-Choice Question Generation. The focus is on comparative studies on the reliability of MCQ generation from GPT-3.5, GPT-4, LLaMA, as well as applications in specialized fields, such as medical education. Works such as those by K. Hwang et al. [99], Ling and Afzaal [100], and Workum et al. [101] highlight issues of quality, alignment with Bloom's cognitive levels, and the need for human editing. In parallel, some studies [102,103] focus on the comparison between human and

https://doi.org/10.3390/bdcc10010035

automated MCQ generation, demonstrating that LLMs can achieve a comparable quality on well-structured topics. Roumeliotis et al.'s [104] research argues that cryptocurrencies are becoming increasingly popular, but investment sentiment is strongly influenced by news, creating opportunities but also significant risks. The study examines how advanced language models, such as GPT-4, BERT, and FinBERT, can analyze news sentiment about cryptocurrencies, enhancing market understanding and investment decisions. Hamid and Brohi's [105] work shows that, although LLMs can automate critical processes in the healthcare sector, the existence of vulnerabilities makes it necessary to address serious risks such as data interception and corruption. The research proposes an application taxonomy, a threat model, and a framework for the secure implementation of LLMs in healthcare, filling gaps that have not been addressed in the literature so far.

Table 8. Bibliographic coupling.

Cluster	Central Focus	Description	Indicative Sources
1	AI-Assisted Assessment and Automated MCQ Generation	Automatic MCQ generation; quality assessment; GPT/human comparison	[99–105]
2	AI in Education Systems and Teacher Support	LLMs as educational tools, analytics, teacher support	[85,106–109]
3	Ethical and Responsible AI in Education	Transparency, bias, ethics, philosophy of using AI	[110–113]
4	AI Governance and Institutional Policy	Policy, adoption, legislation, usage concerns	[114–116]
5	AI Literacy and Public Perception	Digital literacy, perceptions, adoption	[117–121]
6	NLP, NLG, and Technical Modeling	Semantic control, dialog models, LLM techniques	[122,123]
7	Scientometric and Meta-Analysis of AI in Education	Bibliometrics, epistemological trends	[124–129]

Note(s): This table presents the results of science mapping analysis. It was produced by VOSviewer Source(s): Table by authors.

Cluster 2: "AI in Education Systems, Learning Analytics, and Teacher Support". The second cluster focuses on the use of LLMs in educational ecosystems, including learning systems, data analytics, and teacher support. The research here shows that LLMs function as digital assistants, capable of analyzing student behavior, generating personalized recommendations, and supporting the development of learning materials, such as mathematical proofs or assessment questions [106]. The discussion of "Education 4.0" [107] is often reoccurring, with researchers arguing that LLMs can extend personalized learning and support teachers in particularly demanding tasks, reducing cognitive load. Moreover, this cluster includes studies that explore how AI fits into the broader education ecosystem: as a digital assistant, as a teacher support system, or as a tool for diagnosing learning patterns. Works such as [85,108,109] highlight cases where LLMs support the creation of learning activities, feedback, and even the analysis of student behavior.

Cluster 3: "Ethical, Responsible, and Philosophical Perspectives of AI in Education". The third cluster focuses on issues of accountability, transparency, and ethical implications of the use of AI. Publications such as those by [110–113] analyze the inequalities that may arise from algorithmic processes, the illusion of "personalization" created by LLMs, and the philosophical implications of knowledge production.

Cluster 4: The fourth cluster concerns governance policies and the institutional adoption of artificial intelligence systems. As the introduction of LLMs in universities rapidly progresses, research projects examine how organizations adapt regulations, management

 https://doi.org/10.3390/bdcc10010035

practices, and assessment processes to safely and responsibly integrate these systems [114]. The literature highlights the need for clear usage frameworks, quality assurance, data protection, and ongoing staff training, as the adoption of LLMs creates challenges as well as new opportunities. This cluster covers governance and educational policy related to AI systems. Studies such as [115,116] examine academic perceptions of LLMs, the challenges of integrating AI practices into institutional settings, and the emerging regulatory needs.

Cluster 5: "AI Literacy, Technology Adoption, and Public Perception". In the fifth cluster, issues of technological literacy, technology adoption, and social acceptance of artificial intelligence emerge. Articles in this cluster examine how students and the wider public perceive artificial intelligence tools, what factors influence their intention to use them, and how sociocultural conditions influence the diffusion of these technologies [117]. Research such as that of authors [118,119] shows that the social legitimacy of LLMs in education is closely linked to the level of trust, perceived usefulness, and familiarity with the technology. This cluster brings together studies that examine user attitudes, the diffusion of AI tools, and factors influencing acceptance. For example, Semeler et al. [120] and Kajiwara and Kawabata [121] explore social indicators, digital literacy, subjective utility, and concerns surrounding the use of generative AI.

Cluster 6: "NLP, Natural Language Generation, and Technical Modeling".

This cluster concerns technical approaches to natural language modeling, dialog generation, and methodologies that enable accurate, coherent, and controlled text production. Works such as [122,123] focus on coherent dialog generation, semantic control, and foundation models for large-scale tasks—which form the technical foundation of automatic MCQ generation.

Cluster 7: "Scientometric and Meta-Analytical Studies of AI in Education". Finally, the seventh cluster includes scientometric and meta-analytic studies that map the totality of research activity around artificial intelligence in education [124–129]. These studies use bibliometric tools to identify research trends, gaps, and shifts in interest in the field. This section is particularly important, as it offers an overall picture of the evolution of the field and contributes to the formulation of strategic directions for future research.

Despite the inherent limitations of bibliographic coupling, such as its dependence on available data and the inability to capture the temporal evolution of knowledge, the results of this analysis have substantial practical value for practitioners and researchers in the field. Specifically, bibliographic coupling allows the identification of thematic clusters and research streams that are actively developing, facilitating an understanding of the structure and dynamics of the research ecosystem. In this way, practitioners can leverage the findings to identify mature and emerging areas of research, monitor key research directions, and support evidence-based decisions at the level of educational design, policy, or technological implementation.

Overall, the bibliographic coupling analysis reveals a rapidly evolving field, where automated MCQ generation is no longer seen as a stand-alone technical capability but as a central element of a broader dialog on reflective learning, artificial intelligence, organizational policies, and social processes. The interdisciplinary nature of the field suggests that future research will need to consider not only technological innovations but also the pedagogical, ethical, and social dimensions associated with the widespread application of LLMs in the educational process.

Beyond the descriptive mapping of publication trends and thematic clusters, the bibliometric patterns identified in this study reflect deeper theoretical and technological transformations in the field of artificial intelligence in education (AIED). The sharp increase in research output after 2023 coincides with the widespread adoption of transformer-based architectures and large language models, which have fundamentally altered approaches

 https://doi.org/10.3390/bdcc10010035

to automated content generation and assessment. The dominance of clusters related to AI-assisted assessment and educational support systems indicates a paradigm shift from rule-based NLP methods towards generative, data-driven models capable of supporting formative assessment, adaptive learning, and scalable feedback mechanisms.

Furthermore, the emergence of clusters focusing on ethics, governance, and AI literacy aligns with contemporary theoretical debates in AIED regarding responsible AI, assessment validity, and human–AI collaboration. The relatively limited presence of automated MCQ generation as a standalone theme suggests that this area remains theoretically under-conceptualized, offering opportunities to integrate insights from assessment theory, cognitive taxonomies (e.g., Bloom's taxonomy), and learning analytics. Overall, the bibliometric findings highlight how technological innovation in AI is increasingly intertwined with pedagogical and theoretical considerations, reinforcing the need for interdisciplinary research that bridges computational advances with educational theory.

4.4.3. Keywords Analysis (RQ5)

The mapping captures the historical evolution of research around Automated Multiple-Choice Question Generation and related technologies. Shades of blue correspond to early publications, while green–yellow highlight more recent studies. The size of the nodes indicates the relative importance of each topic area; for example, AI in education appears as one of the most influential nodes, in contrast to smaller topics such as educational performance.

Strong connecting lines indicate a high level of co-authorship or close thematic correlation. A significant increase in activity is observed in the period 2023–2024, during which terms such as AI, chatbot, ChatGPT, and LLM dominate, reflecting the rapid spread of large language models in educational research. In contrast, smaller nodes—such as Automated Multiple-Choice Question Generation, AI agents, and conversational AI—indicate scientific fields that remain underexplored. The relatively limited literature specifically on automated MCQ generation for educational purposes was one of the main motivations for this study, reinforcing our interest in examining the field in depth and developing a corresponding system.

Figure 4 presents a co-word analysis of the most frequently occurring topics, as they are identified in publications in this scientific field. All keywords that met the frequency criteria were selected, resulting in a fairly extensive network with 7072 links and 8858 TLS. The keywords with the highest frequency and TLS are AI (occ.: 135, TLS: 345), LLM (occ.: 115, TLS: 312), ChatGPT (occ.: 102, TLS: 303), and NLP (occ.: 95, TLS: 295). In addition, related topics such as chatbots, Gemini, machine learning, automated MCQ generation, and educational technology appear. To illustrate the temporal evolution of keywords, an overlay visualization was applied, in which each term is colored based on the average year of its appearance. According to this method, older topics appear in blue shades, while more recent ones appear in green and yellow. Some notable trends emerge from the coexistence network. Early research focused mainly on more general issues, such as artificial intelligence, AI in education, and meaningful learning, supported by LLM-based educational systems that facilitate conceptual understanding, feedback, and adaptive assessment. Over time, new topics began to gain momentum. NLP, machine learning, and automated code generation have been prominent since 2024 and continue to increase in frequency to this day, signaling the broadening and specialization of research interest.

The overall picture of the network highlights that, despite the rapid growth of research around artificial intelligence and large language models, Automated Multiple-Choice Question Generation in education remains a relatively limited and less mature field. This gap creates significant opportunities for new studies, experimentation, and applications,

https://doi.org/10.3390/bdcc10010035

such as the development of question generation systems that can effectively support teachers and students. The ever-expanding research landscape leaves room for deeper analysis, and this study seems to be positioned precisely at this dynamic point.

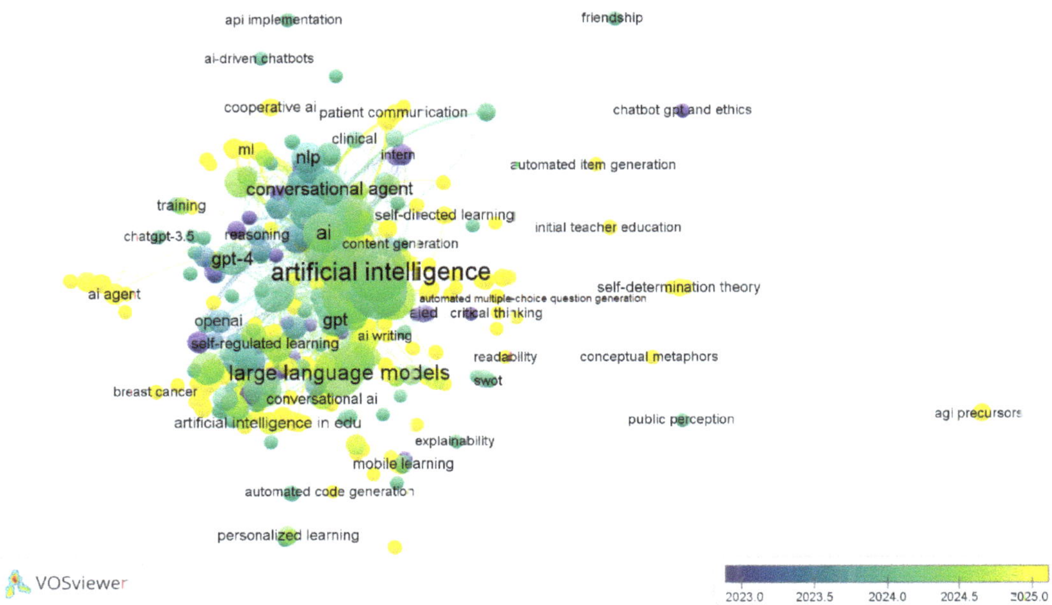

Figure 4. Co-word analysis (overlay visualization). Labels were adjusted to improve readability. Notes: This figure presents the analysis co-words to illustrate the temporal allocation of authors' keywords in each thematic group. The colors in the spectrum differ, with blue reflecting the early years and green and yellow the newer ones. Source(s): Figure by authors.

5. Conclusions

From a theoretical and practical standpoint, the bibliometric findings of this study extend beyond descriptive mapping by explicitly linking observed research patterns to current theoretical and technological developments in artificial intelligence in education. Overall, utilizing bibliometric techniques and approaches from information systems and educational sciences, this study carries out a comprehensive and retrospective assessment of research on automated MCQ generation. Its contribution is structured around three main axes, which substantially strengthen the relevant literature. First, it presents an updated and systematic mapping of the main thematic trends, highlighting their evolution and their place in the broader scientific ecosystem of artificial intelligence in education. Second, it offers an overall assessment of the productivity and scientific impact of the field, highlighting the dynamics that characterize automated MCQ generation. Third, it suggests new, evidence-based directions for future research, with substantial implications for academics, practitioners, and policymakers. The study's contribution is of particular value to researchers and doctoral candidates, as it offers a coherent and in-depth view of the available body of knowledge, facilitating the identification of emerging thematic areas and new research avenues. At the same time, it helps practitioners understand the challenges and technological developments that may affect the implementation of automated question generation systems in the future. Finally, it provides useful indications to policymakers, contributing to strategic planning and the formulation of regulatory frameworks that can support the adoption and safe utilization of such technologies.

https://doi.org/10.3390/bdcc10010035

This study constitutes an in-depth retrospective overview of the field, utilizing a combination of various bibliometric methods. Through these techniques, important information was revealed regarding productivity, the structure of scientific knowledge, and the conceptual foundations that support research in Automated Multiple-Choice Question Generation. To achieve our objectives, we answered five research questions.

The first question explored publication and citation trends, revealing a steady upward trend, as well as an increasing diffusion of the topic in high-prestige scientific journals, which demonstrates an increased interest and scientific maturity. The second question focused on identifying the most important research institutions. The findings show that the research core is located mainly in the USA, while the United Kingdom and Australia also play an important role. Then, scientific mapping techniques were utilized to answer the following questions. A literature review was conducted to explore the main thematic axes and their evolution. This analysis revealed that, in recent years, interest has been strongly focused on topics such as artificial intelligence in education, LLMs, NLP techniques, chatbots, ChatGPT, and new models such as Gemini, indicating the close connection of the field with modern developments in computational linguistics. The third question examined the collaborative patterns of authors through a co-authorship analysis. The results indicate that research activity is characterized by a significant degree of collaboration, which reflects the increased interdisciplinarity and dynamic nature of the field. Finally, the fifth question focused on identifying future directions. Through co-word analysis, emerging trends were identified, most notably Automated Multiple-Choice Question Generation itself, which are expected to gain even greater importance, especially when combined with applications in education and the creation of intelligent learning systems.

From a broader theoretical and technological perspective, the findings of this bibliometric analysis indicate that Automated Multiple-Choice Question Generation is increasingly embedded within the evolving ecosystem of AIED. The dominance of themes related to large language models, AI-assisted assessment, and educational support systems reflects a shift in the field towards generative and adaptive paradigms, where assessment is no longer treated as a static evaluative process but as a dynamic component of learning design. At the same time, the relatively limited consolidation of automated MCQ generation as an autonomous research stream suggests that this area remains under-theorized in comparison to other AI-driven educational applications. This gap highlights the need for a stronger integration between technological advances in natural language generation and established educational theories, such as formative assessments, cognitive taxonomies, and learning analytics. Future research is therefore encouraged to move beyond technical performance and address issues of pedagogical validity, cognitive alignment, and the responsible deployment of generative AI in assessment contexts. In this sense, automated MCQ generation can be seen not merely as a technical capability, but as a critical interface between artificial intelligence, educational theory, and instructional practice.

From a practical perspective, the findings of this study offer several implications for key stakeholders in education. For educators, automated MCQ generation systems supported by LLMs can be used to reduce the time and cognitive effort required for assessment design, while enabling more frequent formative assessments and immediate feedback. The bibliometric evidence indicates a growing interest in aligning AI-generated questions with cognitive taxonomies and learning objectives, suggesting that educators may increasingly employ such tools to support adaptive learning, diagnostic assessment, and personalized feedback in both face-to-face and online environments. For system developers, the identified thematic clusters and emerging research trends provide guidance for the design of assessment platforms that integrate natural language generation with learning analytics and instructional design principles. Developers may leverage insights from the literature

https://doi.org/10.3390/bdcc10010035

to enhance question quality, ensure pedagogical validity, and incorporate features such as difficulty control, distractor plausibility, and the transparency of AI-generated outputs. The observed fragmentation of research in automated MCQ generation also highlights opportunities for developing modular, interoperable systems that can be embedded within existing learning management systems. For policy makers and educational administrators, the rapid growth of AI-driven assessment technologies underscores the need for evidence-informed governance frameworks. The results of this study can support policy decisions related to quality assurance, the ethical use of generative AI, data protection, and academic integrity. In particular, bibliometric trends emphasizing ethics, governance, and AI literacy suggest that institutional policies should promote responsible adoption, teacher training, and the continuous evaluation of AI-based assessment tools to ensure fairness, transparency, and pedagogical effectiveness.

Despite its systematic and comprehensive design, this study is subject to several methodological limitations that should be considered when interpreting the results. First, the exclusive use of the Scopus database, while ensuring high-quality and well-structured metadata, may have led to the omission of relevant studies indexed in other sources such as Web of Science or specialized conference proceedings. This choice may partially affect the observed distribution of publications, citations, and geographical contributions. Second, the construction of the search query and the selection of keywords inevitably shaped the scope of the retrieved literature. Although the query was designed to capture recent and impactful developments in automated assessments and large language models in education, certain studies focusing on Automated Multiple-Choice Question Generation using alternative terminology or earlier NLP approaches may not have been fully represented. As a result, some thematic areas may appear less consolidated than they are in practice. Third, the selected time window reflects the rapid evolution of the field in the post-2023 period; however, it also limits the ability to capture long-term citation dynamics and historical continuities. Consequently, highly recent publications may appear underrepresented in terms of citation impact, while earlier influential works may exert a disproportionate influence on bibliometric indicators. Finally, bibliometric techniques inherently emphasize structural and quantitative patterns rather than the qualitative depth of individual contributions. Methods such as bibliographic coupling and co-word analysis depend on citation practices and keyword selection, which may not always fully reflect the conceptual richness of the underlying studies. Future research could address these limitations by integrating bibliometric approaches with qualitative content analysis, expert-driven systematic reviews, and empirical investigations of educational effectiveness. Recognizing these limitations is essential for the appropriate interpretation of the findings and for guiding future research. These implications demonstrate how bibliometric evidence can inform instructional practice, system design, and policy decisions in AI-driven educational assessment.

Author Contributions: Conceptualization, D.M. and S.S.; methodology, D.M.; software, D.M.; validation, D.M. and S.S.; formal analysis, D.M. and S.S.; investigation, D.M.; resources, D.M.; data curation, D.M.; writing—original draft preparation, D.M.; writing—review and editing, D.M. and S.S.; visualization, D.M.; supervision, S.S. All authors have read and agreed to the published version of the manuscript.

Funding: This research received no external funding.

Data Availability Statement: The data we use for our calculations are derived from the Scopus Database.

Conflicts of Interest: The authors declare no conflicts of interest.

 https://doi.org/10.3390/bdcc10010035

References

1. Lan, Y.; Li, X.; Du, H.; Lu, X.; Gao, M.; Qian, W.; Zhou, A. Survey of natural language processing for education: Taxonomy, systematic review, and future trends. *IEEE Trans. Knowl. Data Eng.* **2025**, *38*, 659–678. [CrossRef]
2. Kurdi, G.; Leo, J.; Parsia, B.; Sattler, U.; Al-Emari, S. A Systematic Review of Automatic Question Generation for Educational Purposes. *Int. J. Artif. Intell. Educ.* **2020**, *30*, 121–204. [CrossRef]
3. Das, B.; Majumder, M.; Phadikar, S.; Sekh, A.A. Automatic question generation and answer assessment: A survey. *Res. Pract. Technol. Enhanc. Learn.* **2021**, *16*, 5. [CrossRef]
4. Memarzadeh, H.; Ghadiri, N.; Samwald, M.; Lotfi Shahreza, M. Applying unsupervised keyphrase methods on concepts extracted from discharge sheets. *Pattern Anal. Appl.* **2023**, *26*, 1715–1727. [CrossRef]
5. Martínez-Comesaña, M.; Rigueira-Díaz, X.; Larrañaga-Janeiro, A.; Martínez-Torres, J.; Ocarranza-Prado, I.; Kreibel, D. Impact of artificial intelligence on assessment methods in primary and secondary education: Systematic literature review. *Rev. Psicodidáctica* **2023**, *28*, 93–103. [CrossRef]
6. Kotsiantis, S.B. Use of machine learning techniques for educational proposes: A decision support system for forecasting students' grades. *Artif. Intell. Rev.* **2012**, *37*, 331–344. [CrossRef]
7. Goyal, R.; Kumar, P.; Singh, V.P. A Systematic survey on automated text generation tools and techniques: Application, evaluation, and challenges. *Multimed. Tools Appl.* **2023**, *82*, 43089–43144. [CrossRef]
8. Artsi, Y.; Sorin, V.; Konen, E.; Glicksberg, B.S.; Nadkarni, G.; Klang, E. Large language models for generating medical examinations: Systematic review. *BMC Med. Educ.* **2024**, *24*, 354. [CrossRef] [PubMed]
9. Al Faraby, S.; Adiwijaya, A.; Romadhony, A. Review on neural question generation for education purposes. *Int. J. Artif. Intell. Educ.* **2024**, *34*, 1008–1045. [CrossRef]
10. Awalurahman, H.W.; Budi, I. Automatic distractor generation in multiple-choice questions: A systematic literature review. *PeerJ Comput. Sci.* **2024**, *10*, e2441. [CrossRef]
11. Ahadi, A.; Singh, A.; Bower, M.; Garrett, M. Text mining in education—A bibliometrics-based systematic review. *Educ. Sci.* **2022**, *12*, 210. [CrossRef]
12. Aria, M.; Cuccurullo, C. Bibliometrix: An R-tool for comprehensive science mapping analysis. *J. Informetr.* **2017**, *11*, 959–975. [CrossRef]
13. van Eck, N.J.; Waltman, L. Software survey: VOSviewer, a computer program for bibliometric mapping. *Scientometrics* **2009**, *84*, 523–538. [CrossRef]
14. Dwivedi, Y.K.; Sharma, A.; Rana, N.P.; Giannakis, M.; Goel, P.; Dutot, V. Evolution of artificial intelligence research in Technological Forecasting and Social Change: Research topics, trends, and future directions. *Technol. Forecast. Soc. Change* **2023**, *192*, 122579. [CrossRef]
15. Jain, K.; Tripathi, P.S. Mapping the environmental, social and governance literature: A bibliometric and content analysis. *J. Strateg. Manag.* **2023**, *16*, 397–428. [CrossRef]
16. Kaur, J.; Bathla, A.K. A review on automatic question generation system from a given Hindi text. *International. J. Res. Comput. Appl. Robot. (IJRCAR)* **2025**, *3*, 87–92.
17. Rakangor, S.; Ghodasara, Y.R. Literature review of automatic question generation systems. *Int. J. Sci. Res. Publ.* **2025**, *5*, 1–5.
18. Le, N.-T.; Kojiri, T.; Pinkwart, N. Automatic question generation for educational applications–the state of art. In *Advances in Intelligent Systems and Computing, Proceedings of the Advanced Computational Methods for Knowledge Engineering, Budapest, Hungary, 8–9 May 2014*; van Do, T., Thi, H., Nguyen, N., Eds.; Springer: Berlin/Heidelberg, Germany, 2014; pp. 325–338. [CrossRef]
19. Ch, D.R.; Saha, S.K. Automatic multiple choice question generation from text: A survey. *IEEE Trans. Learn. Technol.* **2018**, *13*, 14–25. [CrossRef]
20. Papasalouros, A.; Chatzigiannakou, M. Semantic Web and Question Generation: An Overview of the State of the Art. In Proceedings of the International Conference E-Learning, ERIC, Cape Town, South Africa, 5–6 July 2018. Available online: https://scispace.com/pdf/semantic-web-and-question-generation-an-overview-of-the-3v81u9f0h8.pdf (accessed on 11 October 2025).
21. Bitew, S.K.; Deleu, J.; Develder, C.; Demeester, T. Distractor generation for multiple-choice questions with predictive prompting and large language models. In *Communications in Computer and Information Science, Proceedings of the International Workshops of ECML PKDD 2023, Turin, Italy, 18–22 September 2023*; Springer: Berlin/Heidelberg, Germany, 2023; pp. 48–63. [CrossRef]
22. Ghanem, B.; Fyshe, A. Disto: Evaluating textual distractors for multi-choice questions using negative sampling based approach. *arXiv* **2023**, arXiv:2304.04881. [CrossRef]
23. Feng, W.; Lee, J.; McNichols, H.; Scarlatos, A.; Smith, D.; Woodhead, S.; Ornelas, N.O.; Lan, A. Exploring automated distractor generation for math multiple-choice questions via large language models. In *Findings of the Association for Computational Linguistics: NAACL*; Association for Computational Linguistics: Mexico City, Mexico, 2024; pp. 3067–3082. [CrossRef]

 https://doi.org/10.3390/bdcc10010035

24. Yu, H.-C.; Shih, Y.-A.; Law, K.-M.; Hsieh, K.-Y.; Cheng, Y.-C.; Ho, H.-C.; Lin, Z.-A.; Hsu, W.-C.; Fan, Y.-C. Enhancing distractor generation for multiple-choice questions with retrieval augmented pretraining and knowledge graph integration. In Proceedings of the Annual Meeting of the Association for Computational Linguistics, Bangkok, Thailand, 11–16 August 2024; pp. 11019–11029. [CrossRef]
25. Cavusoglu, D.; Sen, S.; Sert, U. DisGeM: Distractor Generation for Multiple Choice Questions with Span Masking. In Proceedings of the EMNLP 2024—2024 Conference on Empirical Methods in Natural Language Processing, Findings of EMNLP 2024, Association for Computational Linguistics (ACL), Miami, FL, USA, 12–16 November 2024; pp. 9714–9732. [CrossRef]
26. Pan, L.; Lei, W.; Chua, T.-S.; Kan, M.-Y. Recent advances in neural question generation. *arXiv* **2019**, arXiv:1905.08949. [CrossRef]
27. Guo, S.; Liao, L.; Li, C.; Chua, T.-S. A survey on neural question generation: Methods, applications, and prospects. In Proceedings of the 33rd International Joint Conference on Artificial Intelligence (IJCAI-24), Jeju, Republic of Korea, 3–9 August 2024; pp. 8038–8047. [CrossRef]
28. Mulla, N.; Gharpure, P. Automatic question generation: A review of methodologies, datasets, evaluation metrics, and applications. *Prog. Artif. Intell.* **2023**, *12*, 1–32. [CrossRef]
29. Alhazmi, E.; Sheng, Q.Z.; Zhang, W.E.; Zaib, M.; Alhazmi, A. Distractor generation in multiple-choice tasks: A survey of methods, datasets, and evaluation. In Proceedings of the EMNLP 2024—2024 Conference on Empirical Methods in Natural Language Processing, Miami, FL, USA, 12–16 November 2024; pp. 14437–14458. [CrossRef]
30. Lin, R.; Xu, D.; Wang, H.; Chen, Z.; Wang, Y.; Liu, S. DGRC: An Effective Fine-tuning Framework for Distractor Generation in Chinese Multi-choice Reading Comprehension. In Proceedings of the 2024 IEEE International Conference on Systems, Man, and Cybernetics (SMC), Kuching, Malaysia, 6–10 October 2024; IEEE: New York, NY, USA, 2024; pp. 815–820. [CrossRef]
31. Mucciaccia, S.S.; Paixão, T.M.; Mutz, F.; De Souza, A.F.; Badue, C.S.; Oliveira-santos, T. Automatic Multiple-Choice Question Generation and Evaluation Systems Based on LLM: A Study Case With University Resolutions. In Proceedings of the 31st International Conference on Computational Linguistics, Abu Dhabi, United Arab Emirates, 19–24 January 2025; pp. 2246–2260. Available online: https://aclanthology.org/2025.coling-main.154/ (accessed on 12 October 2025).
32. Paiva, J.C.; Figueira, Á.; Leal, J.P. Bibliometric Analysis of Automated Assessment in Programming Education: A Deeper Insight into Feedback. *Electronics* **2023**, *12*, 2254. [CrossRef]
33. Dong, X.; Li, Z.; Su, H.; Xue, J.; Dang, X. Transformer-enhanced hierarchical encoding with multi-decoder for diversified MCQ distractor generation. *Artif. Intell. Rev.* **2025**, *58*, 229. [CrossRef]
34. Ait, O.A.; Mohib, Z.; Adrdour, M. Natural Language Processing in Higher Education Institutions: A Bibliometric Analysis Using Scopus Database. In Proceedings of the International Conference on Artificial Intelligence in Education Technology, Barcelona, Spain, 29–31 July 2024; pp. 99–120. [CrossRef]
35. Shaik, T.; Tao, X.; Li, Y.; Dann, C.; McDonald, J.; Redmond, P.; Galligan, L. A review of the trends and challenges in adopting natural language processing methods for education feedback analysis. *IEEE Access* **2022**, *10*, 56720–56739. [CrossRef]
36. Awalurahman, H.W.; Aji, R.F.; Budi, I. Transformer and Large Language Models for Automatic Multiple-Choice Question Generation: A Systematic Literature Review. *IEEE Access* **2025**, *13*, 127100–127112. [CrossRef]
37. Gavira Durón, N.; Jiménez-Preciado, A.L. Exploring the role of AI in higher education: A natural language processing analysis of emerging trends and discourses. *TQM J.* 2025, *ahead-of-print*. [CrossRef]
38. Al Shuraiqi, S.; Aal Abdulsalam, A.; Masters, K.; Zidoum, H.; AlZaabi, A. Automatic generation of medical case-based multiple-choice questions (MCQs): A review of methodologies, applications, evaluation, and future directions. *Big Data Cogn. Comput.* **2024**, *8*, 139. [CrossRef]
39. Xue, H.; Liu, W. Bibliometric Analysis of Natural Language Processing Technology in Education: Hot Topics, Frontier Evolution, and Future Prospects. *SAGE Open* **2025**, *15*, 21582440251319891. [CrossRef]
40. Paladines, J.; Ramirez, J. A systematic literature review of intelligent tutoring systems with dialogue in natural language. *IEEE Access* **2020**, *8*, 164246–164267. [CrossRef]
41. Mousavinasab, E.; Zarifsanaiey, N.; Kalhori, S.R.N.; Rakhshan, M.; Keikha, L.; Saeedi, M.G. Intelligent tutoring systems: A systematic review of characteristics, applications, and evaluation methods. *Interact. Learn. Environ.* **2021**, *29*, 142–163. [CrossRef]
42. Ng, S.-L.; Ho, C.-C. Generative AI in Education: Mapping the Research Landscape Through Bibliometric Analysis. *Information* **2025**, *16*, 657. [CrossRef]
43. Guo, S.; Zheng, Y.; Zhai, X. Artificial intelligence in education research during 2013– 2023: A review based on bibliometric analysis. *Educ. Inf. Technol.* **2024**, *29*, 16387–16409. [CrossRef]
44. Ch, D.R.; Saha, S.K. Generation of multiple-choice questions from textbook contents of school-level subjects. *IEEE Trans. Learn. Technol.* **2022**, *16*, 40–52. [CrossRef]
45. Page, M.J.; McKenzie, J.E.; Bossuyt, P.M.; Boutron, I.; Hoffmann, T.C.; Mulrow, C.D.; Shamseer, L.; Tetzlaff, J.M. Akl, E.A.; Brennan, S.E. The PRISMA 2020 statement: An updated guideline for reporting systematic reviews. *BMJ* **2021**, *372*, 71. [CrossRef]
46. Marles, E.; Gomez-Luna, E.; Guerrero, J.; Vasquez, J. Innovative Bibliometric Methodology: A New Big Data-Based Framework for Scientific Research. *Energies* **2025**, *18*, 2437. [CrossRef]

47. Mukherjee, D.; Lim, W.M.; Kumar, S.; Donthu, N. Guidelines for advancing theory and practice through bibliometric research. *J. Bus. Res.* **2022**, *148*, 101–115. [CrossRef]
48. Donthu, N.; Kumar, S.; Mukherjee, D.; Pandey, N.; Lim, W.M. How to conduct a bibliometric analysis: An overview and guidelines. *J. Bus. Res.* **2021**, *133*, 285–296. [CrossRef]
49. Tian, K.; Zhu, Z.; Mbachu, J.; Ghanbaripour, A.; Moorhead, M. Artificial intelligence in risk management within the realm of construction projects: A bibliometric analysis and systematic literature review. *J. Innov. Knowl.* **2025**, *10*, 100711. [CrossRef]
50. Klarin, A. How to conduct a bibliometric content analysis: Guidelines and contributions of content co-occurrence or co-word literature reviews. *Int. J. Consum. Stud.* **2024**, *48*, e13031. [CrossRef]
51. Mitroulia, M.; Armakolas, S.; Krotký, J. A bibliometric analysis on research trends of distance education using scopus database. *J. Educ. Technol. Comput. Sci.* **2023**, *34*, 153–164. [CrossRef]
52. Lachheb, A.; Leung, J.; Abramenka-Lachheb, V.; Sankaranarayanan, R. AI in higher education: A bibliometric analysis, synthesis, and a critique of research. *Internet High. Educ.* **2025**, *67*, 101021. [CrossRef]
53. Alduais, A.; Yassin, A.A.; Allegretta, S. Computational linguistics: A scientometric review. In *Quality and Quantity*; Springer: Dordrecht, The Netherlands, 2025; Volume 59. [CrossRef]
54. Hirsch, J. An Index to Quantify An Individual's Scientific Research Output. *Proc. Natl. Acad. Sci. USA* **2005**, *102*, 16569–16572. [CrossRef]
55. Cobo, M.J.; López-Herrera, A.G.; Herrera-Viedma, E.; Herrera, F. An approach for detecting, quantifying, and visualizing the evolution of a research field: A practical application to the Fuzzy Sets Theory field. *J. Informetr.* **2011**, *5*, 146–166. [CrossRef]
56. Mingers, J.; Leydesdorff, L. A Review of Theory and Practice in Scientometrics. *Eur. J. Oper. Res.* **2015**, *246*, 1–19. [CrossRef]
57. Kessler, M.M. Bibliographic coupling between scientific papers. *Am. Doc.* **1963**, *14*, 10–25. [CrossRef]
58. Zupic, I.; Čater, T. Bibliometric Methods in Management and Organization. *Organ. Res. Methods* **2014**, *18*, 429–472. [CrossRef]
59. Crane, D. Social Structure in a Group of Scientists: A Test of the "Invisible College" Hypothesis. *Am. Sociol. Rev.* **1969**, *34*, 335–352. [CrossRef]
60. Sigala, M.; Kumar, S.; Donthu, N.; Sureka, R.; Joshi, Y. A bibliometric overview of the Journal of Hospitality and Tourism Management: Research contributions and influence. *J. Hosp. Tour. Manag.* **2021**, *47*, 273–288. [CrossRef]
61. Chytis, E.; Eriotis, N.; Mitroulia, M. ESG in Business Research: A Bibliometric Analysis. *J. Risk Financ. Manag.* **2024**, *17*, 460. [CrossRef]
62. Samara, H.H.; Qudah, H.A.; Mohsin, H.J.; Abualhijad, S.; Hani, L.Y.B.; Al Rahamneh, S.; AlQudah, M.Z. Artificial intelligence and machine learning in corporate governance: A bibliometric analysis. *Hum. Syst. Manag.* **2025**, *44*, 349–375. [CrossRef]
63. Kavitha, K.; Joshith, V.P.; Rajeev, N.P.; Asha, S. Artificial Intelligence in Higher Education: A Bibliometric Approach. *Başlık* **2024**, *13*, 1121–1137. [CrossRef]
64. Lampropoulos, G. Intelligent Virtual Reality and Augmented Reality Technologies: An Overview. *Futur. Internet* **2025**, *17*, 58. [CrossRef]
65. Mitroulia, M.; Chytis, E.; Kitsantas, T.; Skordoulis, M.; Kalantonis, P. ESG Strategy and Tax Avoidance: Insights from a Meta-Regression Analysis. *J. Risk Financ. Manag.* **2025**, *18*, 503. [CrossRef]
66. Mitroulia, M.; Chytis, E.; Kitsantas, T.; Mitroulias, D. ESG Reported Activities and Corporate Tax Planning: A Meta-Analysis. In Proceedings of the 14th International Conference of the Financial Engineering and Banking Society (FEBS), Montpellier, France, 11–13 May 2025; Available online: https://febs2025.eventsadmin.com/Home/Welcome (accessed on 7 October 2025).
67. Durán-Sánchez, A.; Río-Rama, M.d.l.C.D.; Álvarez-García, J.; García-Vélez, D.F. Mapping of scientific coverage on education for Entrepreneurship in Higher Education. *J. Enterprising Communities People Places Glob. Econ.* **2019**, *13*, 84–104. [CrossRef]
68. Ragazou, K.; Passas, I.; Garefalakis, A.; Galariotis, E.; Zopounidis, C. Big Data Analytics Applications in Information Management Driving Operational Efficiencies and Decision-Making: Mapping the Field of Knowledge with Bibliometric Analysis Using R. *Big Data Cogn. Comput.* **2023**, *7*, 13. [CrossRef]
69. Soliman, M.; Fatnassi, T.; Elgammal, I.; Figueiredo, R. Exploring the Major Trends and Emerging Themes of Artificial Intelligence in the Scientific Leading Journals amidst the COVID-19 Era. *Big Data Cogn. Comput.* **2023**, *7*, 12. [CrossRef]
70. Gusenbauer, M. Search where you will find most: Comparing the disciplinary coverage of 56 bibliographic databases. *Scientometrics* **2022**, *127*, 2683–2745. [CrossRef]
71. Comerio, N.; Strozzi, F. Tourism and its economic impact: A literature review using bibliometric tools. *Tour. Econ.* **2019**, *25*, 109–131. [CrossRef]
72. Clermont, M.; Dyckhoff, H. Coverage of business administration literature in Google Scholar: Analysis and comparison with Econbiz, Scopus and Web of Science. *Bibliometr. Forsch.* **2012**, *1*, 54. [CrossRef]
73. Joshi, A. Comparison between Scopus & ISI Web of Science. *J. Glob. Values ISSN* **2016**, *7*, 976–9447.
74. Nobanee, H.; Dilshad, M.N.; Al Dhanhani, M.; Al Neyadi, M.; Al Qubaisi, S.; Al Shamsi, S. Big data applications the banking sector: A bibliometric analysis approach. *Sage Open* **2021**, *11*, 21582440211067230. [CrossRef]

75. Fan, L.; Li, L.; Ma, Z.; Lee, S.; Yu, H.; Hemphill, L. A Bibliometric Review of Large Language Models Research from 2017 to 2023. *ACM Trans. Intell. Syst. Technol.* **2024**, *15*, 91. [CrossRef]
76. Hadi, M.U.; Al-Tashi, Q.; Shah, A.; Qureshi, R.; Muneer, A.; Irfan, M.; Zafar, A.; Shaikh, M.; Akhtar, N.; Wu, J.; et al. Large Language Models: A Comprehensive Survey of its Applications, Challenges, Limitations, and Future Prospects. *Authorea Prepr.* **2023**, *1*, 1–26. [CrossRef]
77. Nguyen, T.N.; Truong, H.T. Trends and emerging themes in the effects of generative artificial intelligence in education: A systematic review. *Eurasia J. Math. Sci. Technol. Educ.* **2025**, *21*, em2613. [CrossRef]
78. Fu, Y.; Weng, Z.; Wang, J. Examining AI Use in Educational Contexts: A Scoping Meta-Review and Bibliometric Analysis. *Int. J. Artif. Intell. Educ.* **2024**, *35*, 1388–1444. [CrossRef]
79. Pessin, V.Z.; Yamane, L.H.; Siman, R.R. Smart bibliometrics: An integrated method of science mapping and bibliometric analysis. *Scientometrics* **2022**, *127*, 3695–3718. [CrossRef]
80. Sureka, R.; Donthu, N.; Kumar, S. Three Decades of the Journal of Teaching in International Business: A Bibliometric Overview. *J. Teach. Int. Bus.* **2020**, *31*, 259–285. [CrossRef]
81. Kasneci, E.; Seßler, K.; Küchemann, S.; Bannert, M.; Dementieva, D.; Fischer, F.; Gasser, U.; Groh, G.; Günnemann, S.; Hüllermeier, E. ChatGPT for good? On opportunities and challenges of large language models for education. *Learn. Individ. Differ.* **2023**, *103*, 102274. [CrossRef]
82. Frandsen, T. Evolution of modularity literature: A 25-year bibliometric analysis. *Int. J. Oper. Prod. Manag.* **2017**, *37*, 703–747. [CrossRef]
83. Seyedghorban, Z.; Matanda, M.J.; LaPlaca, P. Advancing theory and knowledge in the business-to-business branding literature. *J. Bus. Res.* **2016**, *69*, 2664–2677. [CrossRef]
84. Ferreira, B.; Diz, A.; Silva, P.; Sousa, L.; Pinho, L.; Fonseca, C.; Lopes, M. Bibliometric Analysis of the Informal Caregiver's Scientific Production. *J. Pers. Med.* **2022**, *12*, 61. [CrossRef]
85. Meyer, J.G.; Urbanowicz, R.J.; Martin, P.C.N.; O'Connor, K.; Li, R.; Peng, P.-C.; Bright, T.J.; Tatonetti, N.; Won, K.J.; Gonzalez-Hernandez, G.; et al. ChatGPT and large language models in academia: Opportunities and challenges. *BioData Min.* **2023**, *16*, 20. [CrossRef]
86. Guizani, S.; Mazhar, T.; Shahzad, T.; Ahmad, W.; Bibi, A.; Hamam, H. A systematic literature review to implement large language model in higher education: Issues and solutions. *Discov. Educ.* **2025**, *4*, 35. [CrossRef]
87. Hassan, A.; Eid, M. A Systematic Review of Automatic Neural Question Generation. *J. ACS Adv. Comput. Sci.* **2025**, *16*. [CrossRef]
88. Bornmann, L.; Daniel, H. What do citation counts measure? A review of studies on citing behavior. *J. Doc.* **2008**, *64*, 45–80. [CrossRef]
89. Dwivedi, Y.K.; Kshetri, N.; Hughes, L.; Slade, E.L.; Jeyaraj, A.; Kar, A.K.; Baabdullah, A.M.; Koohang, A.; Raghavan, V.; Ahuja, M.; et al. Opinion Paper: "So what if ChatGPT wrote it?" Multidisciplinary perspectives on opportunities, challenges and implications of generative conversational AI for research, practice and policy. *Int. J. Inf. Manage.* **2023**, *71*, 102642. [CrossRef]
90. Gilson, A.; Safraneck, C.; Huang, T.; Socrates, V.; Chi, L.; Taylor, R.; Chartash, D. How Does ChatGPT Perform on the United States Medical Licensing Examination? The Implications of Large Language Models for Medical Education and Knowledge Assessment. *JMIR Med. Educ.* **2023**, *9*, e45312. [CrossRef] [PubMed]
91. Rudolph, J.; Tan, S.S.S.; Tan, S.S.S. ChatGPT: Bullshit spewer or the end of traditional assessments in higher education? *J. Appl. Learn. Teach.* **2023**, *6*, 342–363. [CrossRef]
92. Rudolph, J.; Tan, S.; Tan, S. War of the chatbots: Bard, Bing Chat, ChatGPT, Ernie and beyond. The new AI gold rush and its impact on higher education. *J. Appl. Learn. Teach.* **2023**, *6*, 364–389. [CrossRef]
93. Jeon, J.; Lee, S. Large language models in education: A focus on the complementary relationship between human teachers and ChatGPT. *Educ. Inf. Technol.* **2023**, *28*, 15873–15892. [CrossRef]
94. Crawford, J.; Cowling, M.; Allen, K.-A. Leadership is needed for ethical ChatGPT: Character, assessment, and learning using artificial intelligence (AI). *J. Univ. Teach. Learn. Pract.* **2023**, *20*, 1–19. [CrossRef]
95. Javaid, M.; Haleema, A.; Singh, R.P. ChatGPT for healthcare services: An emerging stage for an innovative perspective. *BenchCouncil Trans. Benchmarks, Stand. Eval.* **2023**, *3*, 100105. [CrossRef]
96. Nikolic, S.; Daniel, S.; Haque, R.; Belkina, M.; Hassan, G.M.; Grundy, S.; Lyden, S.; Neal, P.; Sandison, C. ChatGPT versus engineering education assessment: A multidisciplinary and multi-institutional benchmarking and analysis of this generative artificial intelligence tool to investigate assessment integrity. *Eur. J. Eng. Educ.* **2023**, *48*, 559–614. [CrossRef]
97. Barrett, A.; Pack, A. Not quite eye to AI: Student and teacher perspectives on the use of generative artificial intelligence in the writing process. *Int. J. Educ. Technol. High. Educ.* **2023**, *20*, 59. [CrossRef]
98. Sajja, R.; Sermet, Y.; Cikmaz, M.; Cwiertny, D.; Demir, I. Artificial intelligence-enabled intelligent assistant for personalized and adaptive learning in higher education. *Information* **2024**, *15*, 596. [CrossRef]

99. Hwang, K.; Challagundla, S.; Alomair, M.; Chen, L.K.; Choa, F.-S. Towards AI-assisted multiple choice question generation and quality evaluation at scale: Aligning with Bloom's Taxonomy. In Proceedings of the Artificial Intelligence in Education, Recife, Brazil, 8–12 July 2024. [CrossRef]
100. Ling, J.; Afzaal, M. Automatic question-answer pairs generation using pre-trained large language models in higher education. *Comput. Educ. Artif. Intell.* **2024**, *6*, 100252. [CrossRef]
101. Workum, J.; Volkers, B.; Van de Sande, D.; Arora, S.; Goeijenbier, M.; Gommers, D.; van Genderen, M. Comparative evaluation and performance of large language models on expert level critical care questions: A benchmark study. *Crit. Care* **2025**, *29*, 72. [CrossRef]
102. Azzi, A.; Erdős, F.; Németh, R.; Varadarajan, V.; Afrifa, S. Comparative analysis of NLP-driven MCQ generators from text sources. *Comput. Educ. Artif. Intell.* **2025**, *9*, 100440. [CrossRef]
103. Wu, H.; Zerner, T.; Lee, D.; Court-Kowalski, S.; Devitt, P.; Palmer, E. GPT-4 versus human authors in clinically complex MCQ creation: A blinded analysis of item quality. *Med. Teach.* **2025**, *47*, 1–14. [CrossRef]
104. Roumeliotis, K.I.; Tselikas, N.D.; Nasiopoulos, D.K. LLMs and NLP Models in Cryptocurrency Sentiment Analysis: A Comparative Classification Study. *Big Data Cogn. Comput.* **2024**, *8*, 63. [CrossRef]
105. Hamid, R.; Brohi, S. A Review of Large Language Models in Healthcare: Taxonomy, Threats, Vulnerabilities, and Framework. *Big Data Cogn. Comput.* **2024**, *8*, 161. [CrossRef]
106. Zhan, X.; Xu, Y.; Abdi, N.; Collenette, J.; Abu-Salma, R.; Sarkadi, S. Banal Deception Human-AI Ecosystems: A Study of People's Perceptions of LLM-generated Deceptive Behaviour. *arXiv* **2024**, arXiv:2406.08386. [CrossRef]
107. Caccavale, F.; Gargalo, C.L.; Gernaey, K.V.; Krühne, U. Towards Education 4.0: The role of Large Language Models as virtual tutors in chemical engineering. *Educ. Chem. Eng.* **2024**, *49*, 1–11. [CrossRef]
108. Mutanga, M.B.; Msane, J.; Mndaweni, T.N.; Hlongwane, B.B.; Ngcobo, N.Z. Exploring the Impact of LLM Prompting on Students' Learning. *Trends High. Educ.* **2025**, *4*, 31. [CrossRef]
109. Venter, J.; Coetzee, S.A.; Schmulian, A. Exploring the use of artificial intelligence (AI) in the delivery of effective feedback. *Assess. Eval. High. Educ.* **2025**, *50*, 516–536. [CrossRef]
110. Calderon, R.; Herrera, F. And Plato met ChatGPT: An ethical reflection on the use of chatbots in scientific research writing, with a particular focus on the social sciences. *Humanit. Soc. Sci. Commun.* **2025**, *12*, 713. [CrossRef]
111. Grundmann, S.; Al Owayyed, M.; Bruijnes, M.; Vroonhof, E.; Brinkman, W.-P. Lilobot: A Cognitive Conversational Agent to Train Counsellors at Children's Helplines. *J. Med. Syst.* **2025**, *49*, 5. [CrossRef]
112. Isiaku, L.; Kwala, A.; Sambo, K.; Isiaku, H. Academic Evolution in the Age of ChatGPT: An In-depth Qualitative Exploration of its Influence on Research, Learning, and Ethics in Higher Education. *J. Univ. Teach. Learn. Pract.* **2024**, *21*, 67–91. [CrossRef]
113. Medina-Romero, M.Á.; Jinchuña Huallpa, J.; Flores-Arocutipa, J.; Panduro, W.; Huete, L.; Flores Limo, F.; Herrera, E.; Callacna, R.; Ariza Flores, V.; Quispe, I.; et al. Exploring the ethical considerations of using Chat GPT in university education. *Period. Eng. Nat. Sci.* **2023**, *11*, 105–115. [CrossRef]
114. Peykani, P.; Ramezanlou, F.; Tanasescu, C.; Ghanidel, S. Large Language Models: A Structured Taxonomy and Review of Challenges, Limitations, Solutions, and Future Directions. *Appl. Sci.* **2025**, *15*, 8103. [CrossRef]
115. Fuligni, C.; Figaredo, D.D.; Stoyanovich, J. "Would You Want an AI Tutor?" Understanding Stakeholder Perceptions of LLM-based Chatbots in the Classroom. *arXiv* **2025**, arXiv:2503.02885.
116. Wang, J.; Huang, C.; Yan, S.; Xie, W.; He, D. When young scholars cooperate with LLMs in academic tasks: The influence of individual differences and task complexities. *Int. J. Hum.–Comput. Interact.* **2025**, *41*, 4624–4639. [CrossRef]
117. Sáez-Velasco, S.; Alaguero-Rodríguez, M.; Rodríguez-Cano, S.; Delgado-Benito, V. Students' Attitudes Towards AI and How They Perceive the Effectiveness of AI in Designing Video Games. *Sustainability* **2025**, *17*, 3096. [CrossRef]
118. Idris, M.D.; Feng, X.; Dyo, V. Revolutionizing higher education: Unleashing the potential of large language models for strategic transformation. *IEEE Access* **2024**, *12*, 67738–67757. [CrossRef]
119. Liu, L. AI and the Crisis of Legitimacy in Higher Education. *Am. J. STEM Educ.* **2025**, *4*, 16–26.
120. Semeler, A.; Pinto, A.; Koltay, T.; Dias, T.; Oliveira, A.; González, J.; Rozados, H.B.F. Algorithmic literacy: Generative artificial intelligence technologies for data librarians. *EAI Endorsed Trans. Res. Artic. Scalable Inf. Syst.* **2024**, *11*. [CrossRef]
121. Kajiwara, Y.; Kawabata, K. AI literacy for ethical use of chatbot: Will students accept AI ethics? *Comput. Educ. Artif. Intell.* **2024**, *6*, 100251. [CrossRef]
122. Nguyen, T.A.; Kharitonov, E.; Copet, J.; Adi, Y.; Hsu, W.-N.; Elkahky, A.; Tomasello, P.; Algayres, R.; Sagot, B.; Mohamed, A.; et al. Generative Spoken Dialogue Language Modeling. *Trans. Assoc. Comput. Linguist.* **2023**, *11*, 250–266. [CrossRef]
123. Hwang, Y.; Kang, D.; Bak, J. Dialogue response coherency evaluation with feature sensitive negative sample using multi list-wise ranking loss. *Eng. Appl. Artif. Intell.* **2025**, *150*, 110609. [CrossRef]
124. Demirkol, M.; Malkoç, N. Assessing the Intellectual Structure of the Evolving Knowledge Base on ChatGPT in the Field of Education and Health. *Educ. Process Int. J.* **2023**, *12*, 36–64. [CrossRef]

 https://doi.org/10.3390/bdcc10010035

125. Bozkurt, A. Unleashing the Potential of Generative AI, Conversational Agents and Chatbots in Educational Praxis: A Systematic Review and Bibliometric Analysis of GenAI in Education. *Open Prax.* **2023**, *15*, 261–270. [CrossRef]
126. Ismail, F.; Tan, E.; Rudolph, J.; Crawford, J.; Tan, S. Artificial intelligence in higher education. A protocol paper for a systematic literature review. *J. Appl. Learn. Teach.* **2023**, *6*, 56–63. [CrossRef]
127. Zhai, X.; Chu, X.; Chai, C.S.; Jong, M.S.Y.; Istenic, A.; Spector, M.; Liu, J.-B.; Yuan, J.; Li, Y. A Review of Artificial Intelligence (AI) in Education from 2010 to 2020. *Complexity* **2021**, *2021*, 8812542. [CrossRef]
128. Tahiru, F. AI in education: A systematic literature review. *J. Cases Inf. Technol.* **2021**, *23*, 1–20. [CrossRef]
129. Zhang, K.; Aslan, A.B. AI technologies for education: Recent research & future directions. *Comput. Educ. Artif. Intell.* **2021**, *2*, 100025. [CrossRef]

 https://doi.org/10.3390/bdcc10010035

big data and cognitive computing

MDPI

Article

TRACE: Topical Reasoning with Adaptive Contextual Experts

Jiabin Ye, Qiuyi Xin, Chu Zhang and Hengnian Qi *

School of Information Engineering, Huzhou University, Huzhou 313000, China; 2023388014@stu.zjhu.edu.cn (J.Y.); 2023388123@stu.zjhu.edu.cn (Q.X.); chuzh@zjhu.edu.cn (C.Z.)

* Correspondence: qhn@zjhu.edu.cn

Abstract

Retrieval-Augmented Generation (RAG) is widely used for long-text summarization due to its efficiency and scalability. However, standard RAG methods flatten documents into independent chunks, disrupting sequential flow and thematic structure, resulting in significant loss of contextual information. This paper presents MOEGAT, a novel graph-enhanced retrieval framework that addresses this limitation by explicitly modeling document structure. MOEGAT constructs an Orthogonal Context Graph to capture sequential discourse and global semantic relationships—long-range dependencies between non-adjacent text spans that reflect topical similarity and logical associations beyond local context. It then employs a query-aware Mixture-of-Experts Graph Attention Network to dynamically activate specialized reasoning pathways. Experiments conducted on three public long-text summarization datasets demonstrate that MOEGAT achieves state-of-the-art performance. Notably, on the WCEP dataset, it outperforms the previous state-of-the-art Graph of Records (GOR) baseline by 14.9%, 18.1%, and 18.4% on ROUGE-L, ROUGE-1, and ROUGE-2, respectively. These substantial gains, especially the 14.9% improvement in ROUGE-L, reflect significantly better capture of long-range coherence and thematic integrity in summaries. Ablation studies confirm the effectiveness of the orthogonal graph and Mixture-of-Experts components. Overall, this work introduces a novel structure-aware approach to RAG that explicitly models and leverages document structure through an orthogonal graph representation and query-aware Mixture-of-Experts reasoning.

Keywords: graph-based retrieval-augmented generation; MOEGAT; long-text summarization; document structure

1. Introduction

The rapid advancements of Large Language Models have recently led to remarkable performance across a wide array of language modeling tasks [1]. Within this landscape, the ability to accurately and efficiently comprehend and summarize long-form documents has emerged as a key frontier challenge [2,3]. To address this, the research community has largely pursued two principal technical approaches: one focusing on long-context architectures that expand the model's native context window, and the other on the Retrieval-Augmented Generation paradigm [4,5]. Unlike long-context strategies that attempt to process the entire document in one pass, RAG offers a more flexible and computationally efficient solution. It functions by precisely locating and extracting a small set of critical information snippets to guide the LLM's generation process. This fundamental "retrieve-then-generate" principle has demonstrated its efficacy in a multitude of knowledge-intensive tasks [6,7]. Notably, our approach operates in a zero-shot manner without dataset-specific fine-tuning, prioritizing strong generalization while maintaining competitive generation quality.

However, despite these advantages, conventional RAG methods face a critical limitation: they often fail to capture the holistic meaning and global context necessary for understanding complex documents [6–8]. This deficiency arises primarily from the widely used "chunk flattening" strategy. Unlike human reading, which follows a continuous narrative flow, this approach mechanically partitions documents into fixed-size segments based on token counts rather than semantic boundaries [9,10]. Such arbitrary fragmentation fundamentally undermines sequential coherence by severing long-range dependencies—often cutting through cause-and-effect chains and leaving premises detached from their conclusions [11]. By treating segments as independent units, the retriever becomes blind to the cross-referential links and recurrent motifs that bind scattered information into a unified whole, leading to phenomena such as the "lost in the middle" effect where central contextual information is overlooked [11,12]. Consequently, the intrinsic connections between semantic units are lost, making the reconstruction of global context exceptionally difficult. This issue is particularly pronounced in domains that rely heavily on deep contextual understanding, such as clinical documents [13] and legal texts [14]. To overcome these structural deficiencies, Graph-Augmented Retrieval Generation has gradually emerged. Its core idea is to convert a document into a graph structure, thereby explicitly modeling entities, concepts, and the complex relationships among them. This paradigm has undergone a notable research evolution: early work primarily focused on enhancing language models with pre-constructed external knowledge graphs [15,16], but this approach was constrained by high construction costs and limited flexibility. Consequently, recent research has shifted towards text-native Graph RAG, which dynamically constructs graph structures directly from the source text, treating "graph construction for content" as a core task [17]. This approach has already demonstrated potential in general-purpose frameworks [18] and for tasks such as summarization [19,20].

Despite this progress, Graph RAG still faces several significant challenges in the application of long-document summarization. At the representation level, existing graph construction methods typically compress the rich semantic hierarchy of a document into a single-layer graph structure. Such methods, including those that rely on entity-relation extraction to identify named entities and their connections or those that link co-occurring [21] or similar terms through keyword association, fail to preserve the multi-level logical hierarchy from high-level themes and mid-level arguments down to low-level details [22]. Although some studies have begun to explore hierarchical or multi-granularity graph construction, including hierarchical Graph Neural Networks [23,24] and hierarchical Transformers [25,26], the challenge of systematically representing the complete logical hierarchy of a document remains unsolved. At the reasoning level, mainstream homogeneous graph models, such as standard Graph Neural Networks or Graph Language Models [27], apply the same aggregation mechanism to all nodes in the graph. This approach fails to differentiate between the distinct reasoning patterns required for processing abstract concepts and concrete facts. Although the Mixture-of-Experts architecture, which routes different inputs to specialized sub-networks, has proven effective in multi-task scenarios [28,29], its potential when combined with graph attention networks to handle heterogeneous nodes has yet to be thoroughly explored. At the training level, the lack of fine-grained, node-level annotations [14] for long-document summarization tasks means that existing Graph RAG methods often focus on optimizing intermediate stages, such as graph construction and retrieval [17,30]. This practice creates a significant gap between their training objectives and the final summarization task. Lacking the direct supervisory signals needed to iden-

https://doi.org/10.3390/bdcc10010031

tify critical nodes, the model struggles to learn precise information selection strategies, rendering the training process fraught with uncertainty [31,32].

Motivated by challenges in representation, reasoning, and training in standard RAG systems, we propose MOEGAT, a graph-augmented retrieval framework (Figure 1). MOEGAT takes a document represented as an Orthogonal Context Graph and a user query as inputs. The query is encoded into an embedding that serves two roles: (1) driving a Router module to dynamically select the top-K most relevant Graph Attention Network experts, and (2) guiding final node scoring. The selected experts process graph nodes independently along two orthogonal subspaces—sequential discourse structure and long-range semantic dependencies—followed by non-linear integration of their outputs. The fused node representations are then scored against the query embedding in a Scoring Head. The top-K highest-scoring nodes (e.g., top 6 in Figure 1) are retrieved and passed to a Large Language Model for generation.

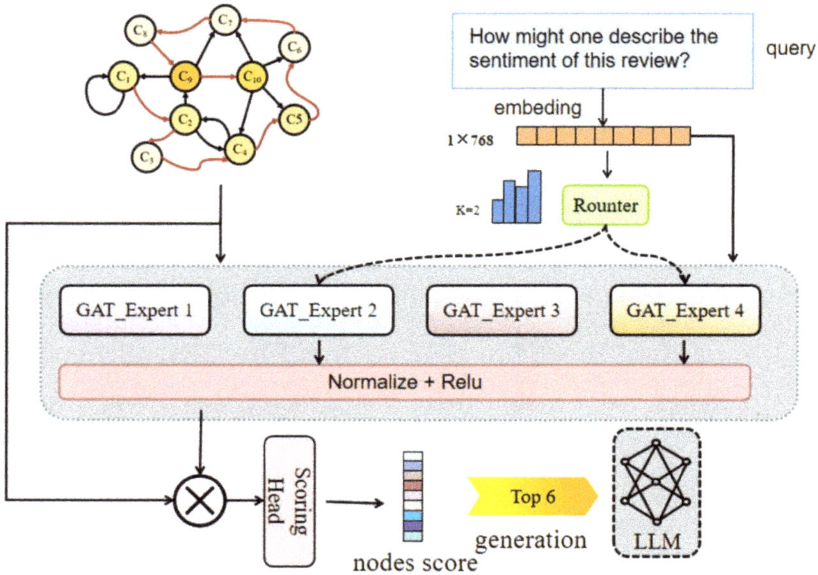

Figure 1. Overview of the MOEGAT architecture, illustrating the Orthogonal Context Graph construction, query-aware Mixture-of-Experts routing, node scoring, and top-K retrieval process. The red line indicates local sequential coherence. The black line indicates global semantic associations.

MOEGAT consists of three synergistic modules that work together to enable structure-aware retrieval and reasoning. The first module constructs an Orthogonal Context Graph. This graph explicitly encodes the document's intrinsic structure through two types of orthogonal edges: sequential adjacency edges that preserve the linear narrative flow and textual order, and semantic proximity edges that capture global thematic relationships across distant segments. This dual representation provides a comprehensive structural prior that mitigates the context loss in traditional chunk-based approaches. The second module is a query-aware Mixture-of-Experts Graph Attention Network. Given the query embedding, a router dynamically selects a sparse set of specialized experts. Each chosen expert operates along a distinct reasoning pathway—corresponding to a specific semantic subspace such as sequential discourse or long-range semantics—by performing query-modulated attention and neighborhood aggregation within that pathway. This enables adaptive, task-specific context propagation across the graph. The third module introduces self-supervised training objectives to address the supervision gap. We generate

https://doi.org/10.3390/bdcc10010031

differentiable soft labels by computing BERT-Score-based [33] semantic similarity between each node and the reference summary. Training is then formulated as a pairwise ranking task, supplemented by auxiliary objectives that promote balanced expert utilization and stable optimization.

Experiments on multiple public long-document summarization datasets show that MOEGAT achieves competitive performance. Our main contributions are summarized as follows:

(1) Orthogonal Context Graph Modeling: A dual-edge graph that jointly captures sequential discourse and global semantic relationships, providing a richer structural prior for retrieval.
(2) Hierarchical Graph Reasoning with Dynamic Expert Routing: A sparse Mixture-of-Experts GAT with query-guided expert selection and subspace-specific attention, enabling efficient and adaptive context aggregation.
(3) Self-supervised Multi-objective Training: A ranking-based paradigm with soft semantic labels and balance regularization, facilitating effective training without fine-grained annotations.

2. Related Work

While prior Graph-RAG approaches mainly improve local retrieval for question-answering tasks using pre-constructed graphs [34–36], they treat documents as flat chunks. This fails to preserve sequential flow and global thematic structure needed for holistic long-document summarization. In contrast, MOEGAT introduces an Orthogonal Context Graph to disentangle local sequential and long-range semantic dependencies within the document. It pairs this with a query-aware Mixture-of-Experts Graph Attention Network for dynamic reasoning. Thus, it enables effective holistic long-document summarization.

Building on these Graph-RAG efforts, Retrieval-Augmented Generation has emerged as a mainstream paradigm to address the inherent knowledge limitations of Large Language Models and to mitigate their generation of hallucinations. Conventional RAG methods primarily rely on vector-based retrieval over unstructured text corpora, which essentially treats knowledge as isolated information fragments, thereby struggling to effectively capture and utilize the complex structural relationships embedded within the text [37]. To overcome this limitation, researchers have recently begun to explore the integration of graph structures into the RAG framework, leading to the development of Graph-Augmented RAG methods. Graph structures can explicitly model the semantic associations between entities and have been demonstrated to enhance model performance in various question-answering and reasoning tasks. Specifically, current research is advancing along two primary fronts: one focused on structured retrieval enhancement based on graph indexing, and the other dedicated to leveraging Graph Neural Networks for representation learning and reasoning enhancement.

Structured Retrieval Enhancement Based on Graph Indexing. The core idea of this direction is to index knowledge by constructing text into a graph structure, which enables the retrieval of semantically coherent knowledge subgraphs to mitigate semantic drift and provide LLMs with precise context. For instance, some studies construct domain-specific knowledge graphs to support complex fault diagnosis [38], while others utilize graph structures to address the challenges of cross-document information extraction and fusion, thereby improving the accuracy and detail of information retrieval [39]. Other work models question-answering as an optimization problem on the graph, seeking an optimal subgraph to balance retrieval relevance with generation efficiency [34].

GNN-Driven Representation Learning and Reasoning Enhancement. In contrast to static graph indexing, this line of research aims to integrate the dynamic learning capabili-

https://doi.org/10.3390/bdcc10010031

ties of Graph Neural Networks (GNNs) to mine the deep, implicit semantic information within the graph. Through its characteristic message-passing mechanism, a GNN aggregates features from neighboring nodes, allowing the vector representation of a node to encapsulate not only its own information but also the semantics of its contextual environment. This creates a deep complementarity with the text comprehension abilities of LLMs. This capability serves multiple roles within the RAG pipeline: during the retrieval phase, GNNs can enhance recall quality by modeling semantic relations between passages [35]; in the post-retrieval stage, they can function as re-rankers, optimizing the organizational logic of candidate documents based on graph-based structural associations [40]; furthermore, end-to-end GNN-RAG frameworks have been developed to tackle question-answering scenarios that require complex graph reasoning [36].

Although existing Graph-RAG research, while varied in its technical approaches, is typically based on pre-constructed graph structures, its application paradigms have primarily centered on question-answering tasks. The objective is to enhance the quality of retrieval and generation for locally relevant information [34,35]; even when applied to long-document summarization, these methods are often confined to query-focused summarization [9]. However, for summarization tasks that require a holistic comprehension of long documents, such QA-centric paradigms face significant challenges due to their inability to effectively integrate global information. Therefore, this paper explores the application of graph structures to enhance global summarization capabilities for long documents, with a focus on identifying and integrating the core themes and logical threads that span the entire text to produce a summary that reflects the document's overall content.

3. Methods

We designed a graph-augmented retrieval framework for the task of long-document summarization, the overall architecture of which is illustrated in Figure 1. The framework first constructs a long document into an Orthogonal Context Graph (Ortho-Graph). Subsequently, we employ a query-aware Mixture-of-Experts Graph Attention Network (MoeGAT) to rank nodes on the Orthogonal Context Graph and retrieve query-relevant information. The Mixture-of-Experts module uses a gating network to route the input query to a subset of specialized experts, each comprising a lightweight Graph Attention layer focused on one graph subspace (sequential or semantic). The activated experts collectively form a query-tailored reasoning pathway—a dynamic sub-network that aggregates information along sequential or semantic edges based on the query's topical demands. The method for graph construction and the specific architecture of our model is detailed in the following sections.

3.1. Construction of the Orthogonal Context Graph (Ortho-Graph)

Conventional RAG approaches often process long documents by flattening them into independent, sequential chunks. This process inherently discards the rich structural information vital for deep comprehension. To address this limitation, we propose the Orthogonal Context Graph (Ortho-Graph). The Ortho-Graph is designed to explicitly represent two fundamental dimensions of text understanding: local sequential coherence and global semantic associations. We treat these dimensions as conceptually orthogonal. This orthogonality is formally realized by separating the information flow into two mutually exclusive axes: a sequential axis, which preserves the linear narrative flow, and a semantic axis, which captures long-range logical dependencies independent of linear proximity.

The Ortho-Graph is constructed by first splitting the document D into an ordered sequence of text chunks $C = \{c_1, c_2, \ldots, c_n\}$ (chunk-size w, overlap s). Each chunk c_i

https://doi.org/10.3390/bdcc10010031

corresponds to a node v_i, and a pre-trained embedding model Φ maps each node to a representation vector $x_i = \Phi(v_i)$, forming the node feature matrix $x_i = \Phi(v_i)$.

Graph connectivity is defined via an adjacency matrix A, which is decomposed into two structurally distinct components:

$$A = A^{sec} + A^{sem} \tag{1}$$

An edge exists between nodes v_i and v_j if $A_{ij} = 1$.

The sequential adjacency matrix A^{seq} captures local narrative flow by linking only consecutive chunks:

$$A_{ij}^{seq} = \delta(|i - j|, 1) \tag{2}$$

where δ is the Kronecker delta (see Supplementary Section S1 for details).

The semantic adjacency matrix A^{sem} connects nodes based on content similarity while deliberately excluding local sequential neighbors to maintain orthogonality. This is enforced by a neighborhood exclusion mask, ensuring disjoint supports ($A^{seq} \odot A^{sem} = 0$) and restricting semantic edges to long-range associations. Full details of the masking and top-k selection process are provided in Supplementary Section S2.

By integrating sequential coherence with global semantic relations, the Ortho-Graph provides a rich structural prior that enhances retrieval and supports more coherent summarization.

3.2. Node-Adaptive Dynamic Routing

Nodes in the Ortho-Graph have different functional roles. Standard Graph Neural Networks use uniform message passing. This ignores node heterogeneity. To solve this, we introduce a node-adaptive dynamic routing mechanism. It builds a customized reasoning pathway for each node. The pathway consists of a sparse subset of expert modules.

The process works as follows. Given node features $X \in \mathbb{R}^{N \times Dim}$, we first compute expert affinities:

$$L = XW_{router} \tag{3}$$

where $W_{router} \in \mathbb{R}^{Dim \times E}$ is learnable. Each L_{ij} measures how well node i matches expert j. For efficiency and specialization, we apply sparse activation. For each node i, we select the top-k experts with highest affinity (See Supplementary Section S3 for selection details):

$$\mathcal{T}_i = \arg\max_{S \in 1,\ldots,E, |S| = K} \sum_{j \in S} L_{ij} \tag{4}$$

We then normalize weights locally over the selected experts:

$$g_{ij} = \begin{cases} \frac{exp(L_{ij})}{\sum_{k \in \mathcal{T}_i} exp(L_{ik})}, & j \in \mathcal{T}_i \\ 0, & otherwise \end{cases} \tag{5}$$

This ensures $\sum_{j \in \mathcal{T}_i} g_{ij} = 1$ for each node. After experts process the graph in parallel, the final node representation is a weighted combination:

$$h_i^* = \sum_{j \in \mathcal{T}_i} g_{ij} \cdot E_j(q, X, A)[j] \tag{6}$$

Here, $E_j(q, X, A)[j]$ is the output of expert j for node i. This design promotes expert specialization. It also keeps computation efficient through sparsity.

https://doi.org/10.3390/bdcc10010031

3.3. Query-Modulated Graph Attention Expert

Each activated expert is a Query-Modulated Graph Attention Expert (QM-GAE). Its goal is query-aware relational reasoning on the Ortho-Graph. Figure 2 illustrates the overall process. The process has three steps. First, the input query is encoded as a dense vector q. Second, each node feature x_i is made query-aware. We concatenate x_i and q, then pass them through an MLP:

$$F_{latent} = MLP([x_i \,||\, q]) \tag{7}$$

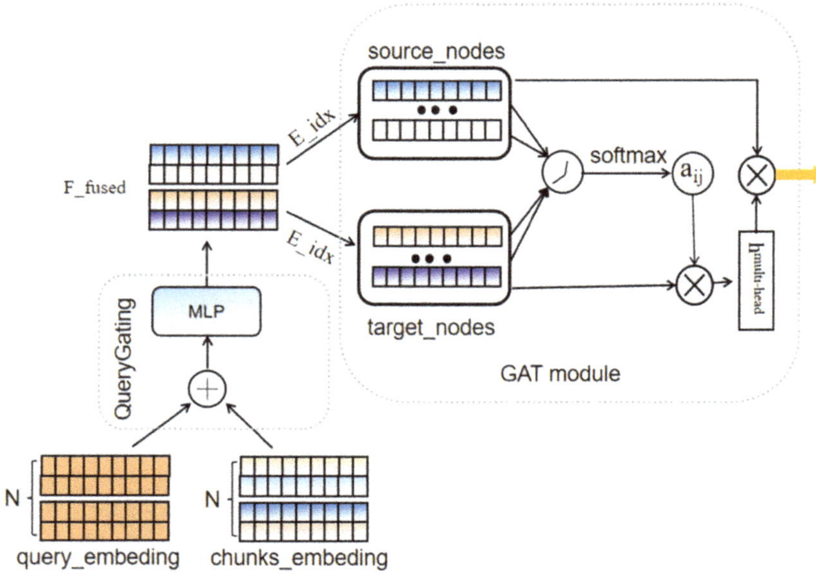

Figure 2. Model Structure of Query-Modulated Graph Attention Expert.

Third, multi-head graph attention aggregates information from neighbors. For head h, the attention coefficient is:

$$\alpha_{ij}^{(h)h} = \frac{exp\left(LeakyReLU\left(a^T\left[W^h f_i \,\middle|\middle|\, W^h f_j\right]\right)\right)}{\sum_{k\in N_i} exp(LeakyReLU(a^T[W^h f_i \,||\, W^h f_k]))} \tag{8}$$

where N_i includes node i and its direct neighbors. a^T is a shared weight vector and W^h is the weight matrix for the h-th attention head. The final node representation is the concatenation of all heads:

$$h_i' = ||_{h=i}^{H} \sigma\left(\sum_{j\in N_i} \alpha_{ij}^{(h)} W^h f_j\right) \tag{9}$$

By injecting query semantics into both feature projection and attention (as shown in Figure 2), QM-GAE produces task-relevant node representations. See Supplementary Section S4 for full notation and implementation details.

3.4. Node Ranking and Summary Generation

Upon completion of the query-aware graph reasoning by the expert modules, a final representation h_i', is generated for each node. This representation is rich in contextual information and aligned with the query's intent. The ultimate task of this stage is to convert these complex node representations into a coherent, natural language summary that synthesizes the core information. This process is initiated by a Scoring Head. The

https://doi.org/10.3390/bdcc10010031

objective of this module is to quantify the relevance of each node by projecting its final representation h_i', back into the semantic space of the query q. This is achieved by computing the inner product of h_i' and q, which generates a scalar relevance score s_i, for each node v_i. These scores provide the quantitative basis for information selection. Based on these scores, the top-N nodes with the highest values are selected. The set of indices for these nodes represents the most salient content fragments within the document. Finally, this context is injected into an instruction template and is synthesized into the final summary S, by a Large Language Model.

3.5. Self-Supervised Semantic Alignment and Expert Load Balancing

To train the model effectively, we employ a composite loss function that pursues two main objectives: learning a meaningful node importance ranking and ensuring balanced utilization of experts. The total loss combines a ranking term and a load-balancing term:

$$\mathcal{L}_{total} = \lambda_{ranking}\mathcal{L}_{ranking} + \lambda_{balance}\mathcal{L}_{balance} \quad (10)$$

The ranking loss is self-supervised. It uses semantic relevance scores derived from BERTScore, computed with DeBERTa-xlarge-mnli embeddings between each node and the reference summary [20]. Nodes whose relevance exceeds the mean form the positive set $\mathcal{P}^+$; the remainder form the negative set $\mathcal{P}^-$. A pairwise margin ranking loss is then applied over all positive-negative pairs:

$$\mathcal{L}_{ranking} = \frac{1}{|\mathcal{P}|}\sum_{(p,n)\subseteq\mathcal{P}} \max(0, m - (f_p - f_n)) \quad (11)$$

where $\mathcal{P}$ represents the set of all positive-negative sample pairs in the graph, m is a margin hyperparameter that controls the degree of separation between positive and negative samples, and f_p and f_n are the model's predicted scores for the positive and negative sample nodes, respectively. This encourages the model to assign higher scores to more relevant nodes without requiring manual annotations.

To prevent routing collapse and promote expert specialization, we introduce an auxiliary load-balancing loss. This term combines a utilization component, which encourages uniform assignment of nodes across experts, and a confidence component, which favors decisive routing decisions. The detailed formulation, including both components averaged over layers, is provided in Supplementary Section S5. Together, these objectives enable stable training and high-quality summarization performance.

4. Results

The preceding sections have introduced our core contributions: an Orthogonal Context Graph that explicitly separates local discourse from global semantic associations, and a node-adaptive Mixture-of-Experts routing mechanism that forms query-tailored reasoning pathways under self-supervised objectives. We now turn to comprehensive experimental evaluation on three public long-text summarization datasets to demonstrate these designs' effectiveness.

Experimental Setup

Datasets: Experiments were conducted on three public long-text summarization datasets to ensure the robustness and generalizability of our evaluation. These datasets cover diverse domains and introduce distinct structural challenges. QMSum [41] consists of meeting transcripts from various domains; in this study, we focused on its "general query" portion, which allows validation of the model's ability to integrate global information in informal, multi-speaker conversational scenarios. BookSum [42] provides long narrative

 https://doi.org/10.3390/bdcc10010031

texts from literary works, thereby testing the model's effectiveness in capturing long-range dependencies within extremely long contexts and complex narrative structures. Finally, WCEP [43] addresses multi-document summarization of news events, enabling assessment of cross-document information deduplication, fusion, and organization. Performance was quantified using the standard ROUGE metrics [44], namely ROUGE-1, ROUGE-2, and ROUGE-L, which measure content coverage and accuracy through lexical overlap between generated and reference summaries.

Implementation Details: In our experiments, long documents were segmented into text chunks of 256 tokens with an overlap of 64 tokens. Initial embeddings were generated using the Contriever model. Based on these text chunks as nodes, we constructed a base graph by connecting adjacent chunks to preserve the local narrative flow and by connecting each chunk to its 5 semantically closest non-adjacent chunks to establish global relationships. This graph was then input into a 3-layer Moe-GAT model, where the node and hidden layer dimensions were both set to 768. Each layer contained 4 experts, and a Top-2 routing strategy was used to dynamically select experts for each node. The model was trained using the AdamW optimizer with an initial learning rate of 1×10^{-4}. The composite loss function consisted of two components: a self-supervised ranking loss (with weight $\mathcal{L}_{ranking}$) and an expert load-balancing loss (with weight $\mathcal{L}_{balance}$), to ensure that the model learned node importance while maintaining a balanced utilization of experts. During the final summary generation stage, our trained Moe-GAT model functioned as the retriever. The query and the complete Orthogonal Context Graph were fed into the model, which then computed relevance scores for all nodes in the graph relative to the query. The top 6 most relevant nodes were selected based on these scores, and their content was input into the LLaMA-2-7b-chat model to generate the final summary via a greedy decoding strategy.

Baselines: To ensure a comprehensive evaluation, we compare our proposed Moe-GAT model with multiple representative baselines, including: (1) Sparse Retrievers (i.e., BM25 [41] and TF-IDF [42]), (2) Dense Retrievers (i.e., Contriever [43], DPR [44], SBERT [45], and Dragon [46]), (3) Full-context Modeling (i.e., directly processing entire documents without retrieval), and (4) Structured Retrieval Methods (i.e., Node2Vec [47], GOR [16], and Thought-R [48]). This systematic comparison enables thorough validation of our model's effectiveness across different technical approaches.

4.1. Main Results

We conducted comprehensive experiments on the QMSum, WCEP, and BookSum datasets, comparing our proposed method against several baselines to evaluate its long-context global summarization capabilities. The results are presented in Table 1. Our proposed Moe-GAT consistently outperforms all baseline methods across nearly all evaluation metrics and datasets. Thanks to the mixture-of-experts architecture combined with graph attention mechanisms, our model can effectively capture and integrate complex semantic relationships across different text chunks, thereby enhancing the retrieval and representation of key information for summarization. Moreover, the structured modeling of document content enables more precise identification of salient content, which is crucial for generating high-quality summaries.

Moe-GAT shows clear superiority over traditional retrieval methods. While structured retrieval methods like GOR demonstrate competitive performance, our approach further advances the state-of-the-art by leveraging more sophisticated graph-based representations. Compared to full-context modeling, Moe-GAT achieves better performance with significantly shorter input lengths (approximately 1.5K tokens), demonstrating its efficiency in handling long documents without information loss from truncation.

https://doi.org/10.3390/bdcc10010031

Additional Findings. (1) Sparse retrievers (BM25 and TF-IDF) produce suboptimal results as they rely solely on lexical matching without capturing semantic meanings. (2) Dense retrievers show varying performance, with Contriever achieving relatively better results, though still inferior to our method due to limitations in modeling global document structure. (3) Node2Vec produces unsatisfactory results since its random walk-based embeddings cannot be effectively optimized for the summarization task. (4) Although Thought-R demonstrates competitive results, it is still inferior to Moe-GAT due to insufficient exploration of the hierarchical relationships between document segments. (5) The "Full Context" approach suffers from information loss when processing extremely long documents, resulting in suboptimal performance despite accessing the complete document content.

Overall, Moe-GAT achieves the best results compared with various baselines across all three datasets, demonstrating the effectiveness of our proposed method in addressing the challenges of long-context global summarization.

Table 1. Experimental results for the long-context global summarization task on the WCEP, QMSum, and BookSum datasets, reporting ROUGE-L (R-L), ROUGE-1 (R-1), and ROUGE-2 (R-2). Note that the average LLM input token length is 6 × 256 (≈1.5K). The highest scores are shown in bold.

Model	WCEP			QMSUM			BookSum		
	R-L	R-1	R-2	R-L	R-1	R-2	R-L	R-1	R-2
BM25 [45]	15.5	22.6	7.3	18.4	32.1	6.1	13.7	26.7	4.9
TF-IDF [46]	15.3	22.3	7.3	18.3	31.2	6.3	13.6	26.6	4.9
SBERT [47]	13.7	20.5	5.5	19.0	33.0	7.4	14.4	28.9	5.4
Dragon [48]	14.6	21.8	6.8	19.2	33.5	7.7	13.7	27.2	4.8
Contriever [49]	15.7	23.5	7.7	19.1	32.7	7.7	14.4	29.8	5.5
DPR [50]	15.6	22.5	7.5	18.6	32.1	6.7	13.8	27.1	4.8
Full Context	14.4	21.0	7.1	19.4	33.1	6.8	14.4	28.9	5.9
Node2Vec [51]	13.9	20.1	6.3	18.5	31.8	6.3	13.6	27.4	4.6
Thought-R [52]	15.2	22.4	7.4	19.0	33.9	7.6	14.2	29.5	5.7
GOR [20]	18.1	25.4	9.2	19.8	34.5	7.8	14.9	**31.5**	6.6
ours	**20.7**	**30.0**	**10.8**	**22.1**	**39.6**	**9.6**	**15.2**	30.2	**7.3**

4.2. Generalization Capability of the Framework Across Different Large Language Models

To rigorously evaluate the generalization capability and model-agnostic nature of the proposed framework, a comprehensive experimental analysis was conducted on three representative text summarization datasets: QMSum, Booksum, and WCEP. The experiments utilized several different backbone language models with the aim of verifying that the performance improvements stem from the intrinsic advantages of the Moe-GAT architecture itself, rather than from a coincidental synergy with any specific large model. We selected a series of high-performing and representative open-source large language models as backbones and evaluated them under two settings: "LLM-Only" and "Ours + LLM". By comparing the performance of each backbone model, both standalone and in conjunction with the Moe-GAT framework, on the ROUGE-L, ROUGE-1, and ROUGE-2 metrics (with results presented in Tables 2–4), we have derived the following key findings.

The experimental results demonstrate that the Moe-GAT framework induces universal and robust performance gains across various summarization tasks. On the QMSum dataset, which is characterized by multi-turn dialogs with complex interlocutor dependencies, all tested backbone models achieved consistent improvements in their ROUGE-L and ROUGE-1 scores after the integration of Moe-GAT. This improvement stems primarily

https://doi.org/10.3390/bdcc10010031

from the Orthogonal Context Graph, which effectively preserves sequential discourse flows across turns. Such flows are frequently disrupted during direct full-text summarization by standalone LLMs.

Table 2. Performance comparison of the proposed Moe-GAT framework before and after integration with different Large Language Models (LLMs) on the QMSum dataset. The highest scores are shown in bold.

LLM Model	LLM-Only (Baseline)			Ours + LLM		
	R-L	R-1	R-2	R-L	R-1	R-2
gpt5-nano	14.9	29.93	4.3	**16.8**	**32.7**	**5.7**
gemini-2.5	12.8	22.0	5.7	**18.1**	**33.7**	**6.6**
QwenLong-L1-32B	15.5	29.5	4.7	**17.0**	**32.0**	**5.6**
glm-4-9b	20.3	37.3	7.3	**21.2**	**38.5**	**8.8**
Hunyuan-MT-7B	21.2	37.2	8.2	**21.7**	**39.2**	**8.7**
Qwen2.5-7B-Instruct	20.1	36.3	**9.7**	**20.7**	**38.7**	8.9
internlm2-5-7b-chat	20.7	35.7	**9.6**	**21.4**	**38.1**	9.1

Table 3. Performance comparison of the proposed Moe-GAT framework before and after integration with different Large Language Models (LLMs) on the Booksum dataset. The highest scores are shown in bold.

LLM Model	LLM-Only (Baseline)			Ours + LLM		
	R-L	R-1	R-2	R-L	R-1	R-2
gpt5-nano	14.9	32.3	6.5	**15.1**	**32.9**	**6.7**
gemini-2.5	16.1	34.8	**8.2**	**16.4**	**41.6**	8.1
QwenLong-L1-32B	12.8	25.9	4.3	**13.0**	**26.8**	**5.1**
glm-4-9b	14.8	32.5	5.5	**16.3**	**37.7**	**8.2**
Hunyuan-MT-7B	9.2	14.6	2.7	**21.7**	**39.2**	**8.7**
Qwen2.5-7B-Instruct	15.1	33.9	6.8	**15.8**	**35.6**	**7.8**
internlm2-5-7b-chat	13.3	25.6	5.8	**15.1**	**33.1**	**7.2**

Table 4. Performance comparison of the proposed Moe-GAT framework before and after integration with different Large Language Models (LLMs) on the WCEP dataset. The highest scores are shown in bold.

LLM Model	LLM-Only (Baseline)			Ours + LLM		
	R-L	R-1	R-2	R-L	R-1	R-2
gpt5-nano	14.8	22.4	7.7	**15.5**	**24.2**	**8.1**
gemini-2.5	14.5	22.3	7.6	**16.7**	**25.6**	**9.4**
QwenLong-L1-32B	15.3	22.8	**8.1**	**15.4**	**24.6**	7.7
glm-4-9b	18.9	26.2	9.6	**20.4**	**29.5**	**10.9**
Hunyuan-MT-7B	18.4	26.5	9.8	**19.4**	**28.8**	**10.4**
Qwen2.5-7B-Instruct	14.8	21.7	8.4	**16.9**	**24.6**	**9.2**
internlm2-5-7b-chat	13.9	19.8	7.7	**16.3**	**24.6**	**8.8**

This positive trend was further validated on the Booksum and WCEP datasets. On the Booksum dataset, which features lengthy narrative texts with strong sequential coherence, all seven models exhibited clear performance improvements when combined with our framework. The gains for Hunyuan-MT-7B were especially significant, achieving substantial leaps of over 12 points in ROUGE-L and 24 points in ROUGE-1. These pronounced gains highlight the framework's strength in modeling long-range sequential dependencies via its dedicated sequential axis. This specifically benefits models that struggle with processing extended contexts in full-text mode.

https://doi.org/10.3390/bdcc10010031

Similarly, a comprehensive and consistent performance enhancement was observed across all models on the WCEP dataset, a multi-document news clustering task rich in thematic overlaps. In this case, the semantic axis of the Orthogonal Context Graph plays a pivotal role by capturing cross-document thematic links. This enables more accurate consensus identification than direct full-text processing by standalone LLMs. Such systematic improvement across different domains and task difficulties provides strong evidence for the universal effectiveness of the Moe-GAT framework in enhancing summary generation quality.

Furthermore, the Moe-GAT framework possesses excellent versatility and broad enhancement capabilities. Evaluation across text summarization tasks confirms that the framework is effective for a diverse range of large language models with heterogeneous architectures, including those from the GPT, Gemini, and Qwen families. Regardless of the backbone model, the introduction of Moe-GAT consistently improved summary quality. This confirms that its success relies on universal design principles rather than the internal mechanisms of any specific model.

Further quantitative analysis reveals an important pattern: the magnitude of the performance gain is inversely correlated with the baseline capability of the backbone model. Stronger models, such as InternLM2.5-7B-Chat or GLM-4-9B, already possess relatively effective internal context modeling for full-text summarization, leaving less room for external structural augmentation. In contrast, weaker baselines suffer more severely from context limitations in direct full-text processing. Examples include Hunyuan-MT-7B on Booksum or various Gemini variants. For these models, the query-aware Moe-GAT and Orthogonal Context Graph provide substantial complementary structural signals, resulting in larger absolute gains. Specifically, the framework provides robust yet modest improvements for highly optimized models. Conversely, it yields more substantial performance leaps for models with weaker baseline capabilities. This phenomenon indicates that Moe-GAT can adaptively provide a commensurate level of optimization based on the potential of different models, thereby universally elevating summarization performance across a wide range of architectures.

The experimental results demonstrate that: (1) The Moe-GAT framework induces universal and robust performance gains across different types of summarization tasks. On the QMSum dataset (characterized by multi-turn dialogs with complex interlocutor dependencies), all tested backbone models achieved consistent improvements in their ROUGE-L and ROUGE-1 scores after the integration of Moe-GAT. This is primarily because the Orthogonal Context Graph effectively preserves sequential discourse flows across turns, which are frequently disrupted in direct full-text summarization by standalone LLMs. This positive trend was further validated on the Booksum and WCEP datasets. Particularly on the Booksum dataset (featuring lengthy narrative texts with strong sequential coherence), all seven models exhibited clear performance improvements when combined with our framework, with the improvement for Hunyuan-MT-7B being especially significant, achieving substantial leaps of over 12 points in ROUGE-L and 24 points in ROUGE-1. These pronounced gains on Booksum highlight the framework's strength in modeling long-range sequential dependencies via its dedicated sequential axis, particularly benefiting models that struggle with processing extended contexts in full-text mode. On the WCEP dataset (a multi-document news clustering task rich in thematic overlaps), a comprehensive and consistent performance enhancement was also observed across all models. Here, the semantic axis of the Orthogonal Context Graph plays a pivotal role by capturing cross-document thematic links, enabling more accurate consensus identification than direct full-text processing by standalone LLMs. This systematic improvement, spanning different domains and task difficulties, provides strong evidence for the universal effectiveness of the

 https://doi.org/10.3390/bdcc10010031

Moe-GAT framework in enhancing the quality of summary generation. (2) The Moe-GAT framework possesses excellent versatility and broad enhancement capabilities. In the evaluation of text summarization tasks, the framework was effectively validated on a diverse range of large language models with heterogeneous architectures, including those from the GPT, Gemini, and Qwen families. Regardless of the model used as the backbone, the introduction of Moe-GAT consistently improved the quality of the generated summaries, confirming the universal applicability of its design principles rather than a dependency on the internal mechanisms of any specific model. Further quantitative analysis reveals an important pattern: the magnitude of the performance gain is inversely correlated with the baseline capability of the backbone model. This pattern arises because stronger models (e.g., internlm2-5-7b-chat or glm-4-9b) already possess relatively effective internal context modeling for full-text summarization, leaving less room for external structural augmentation. In contrast, weaker baselines (e.g., Hunyuan-MT-7B on Booksum or gemini-2.5 variants) suffer more severely from context limitations in direct full-text processing; the query-aware MoE-GAT and Orthogonal Context Graph therefore provide substantial complementary structural signals, resulting in larger absolute gains. Specifically, for highly optimized models such as internlm2-5-7b-chat, the framework provides robust yet modest improvements. Conversely, for models with weaker baseline capabilities, it yields more substantial performance leaps. This phenomenon clearly indicates that Moe-GAT can adaptively provide a commensurate level of optimization based on the potential of different models, thereby universally elevating the summarization performance across a wide range of models.

4.3. Ablation Study

We performed a series of ablation experiments to deeply investigate the contribution of each core component in the proposed framework. The results appear in Table 5. Our analysis reveals the distinct and complementary roles of each component, allowing us to quantify their relative importance to the overall performance.

Table 5. Results of the ablation study on the QMSum, WCEP, and BookSum datasets. The highest scores are shown in bold.

Variant	QMSUM			WCEP			BookSum		
	R-L	R-1	R-2	R-L	R-1	R-2	R-L	R-1	R-2
w/o Moe	18.9	34.7	6.9	18.2	27.2	9.5	12.9	25.6	5.6
w/o Semantic	19.1	35.2	6.9	18.4	26.3	8.7	10.3	17.1	2.6
w/o Sequential	18.3	34.4	6.6	17.2	26.6	8.8	10.6	16.8	3.4
w/o $\mathcal{L}_{ranking}$	19.6	37.9	8.6	17.8	26.0	8.2	12.4	23.7	4.9
w/o $\mathcal{L}_{balance}$	20.2	37.7	9.3	20.0	28.8	9.6	11.4	21.2	4.3
Full Model (ours)	**22.1**	**39.6**	**9.6**	**20.7**	**30.0**	**10.8**	**15.2**	**30.2**	**7.3**

(1) The Moe architecture is fundamental for modeling long and heterogeneous documents. We implemented the "w/o Moe" variant by setting the expert number to 1, forcing all graph nodes to be processed by a single expert with identical parameters. The resulting performance degradation, consistent across all datasets, underscores that expert specialization is non-trivial. The impact is most pronounced on BookSum, which features the longest and most thematically diverse narratives, with a 15.1% relative drop in ROUGE-L. This indicates that the Moe framework contributes most significantly to handling the varied reasoning demands in lengthy texts.

(2) The orthogonal graph decomposition is crucial, with the semantic and sequential structures contributing differentially depending on the dataset characteristics. The "w/o Semantic" variant, which removes semantic adjacency, causes the most severe drops

 https://doi.org/10.3390/bdcc10010031

on datasets rich in thematic content; for instance, ROUGE-1 on BookSum plunges from 30.2 to 17.1 (a 43.3% relative drop), highlighting that the semantic graph is the primary driver for capturing long-range topical dependencies. Conversely, the "w/o Sequential" variant, which removes sequential links, more significantly harms coherence in structured dialogs or narratives, as seen in the notable ROUGE-L decrease on QMSum (from 22.1 to 18.3). Therefore, while both structures are essential, the semantic component contributes most to overall informativeness on content-rich datasets, whereas the sequential component is vital for maintaining local flow.

(3) The composite training objective ensures task alignment and training stability. The "w/o $\mathcal{L}_{ranking}$" variant removes the self-supervised ranking loss and causes clear performance reductions across datasets. This result highlights the loss's role in producing discriminative node representations optimized for relevance ranking in summarization. The "w/o $\mathcal{L}_{balance}$" variant removes the balancing loss and leads to moderate but consistent declines. For example, ROUGE-1 drops from 30.2 to 21.2 on BookSum. The drop is larger here because longer documents generate more nodes and amplify load imbalance issues. This outcome confirms that explicit load balancing prevents expert collapse and preserves the full representational power of the Moe architecture.

4.4. Computational Efficiency Analysis

We address concerns regarding the computational complexity of MOEGAT by distinguishing between graph construction (preprocessing) and inference stages. Measurements are conducted on the WCEP dataset using a consistent LLM backbone, excluding identical LLM generation time across methods.

Graph construction entails splitting the document into overlapping chunks, encoding them with a pre-trained embedding model to generate node representations, and constructing the sparse sequential and masked top-k semantic adjacency matrices. The dominant cost lies in the embedding step and varies significantly with the embedding model. Subsequent steps—building the sparse sequential adjacency matrix (O(N)) and the masked top-k semantic adjacency matrix—are considerably lighter, as they operate on precomputed embeddings with efficient sparse operations. Graph construction is performed once per document and can be fully offline, making it amortizable in practical deployments.

During inference, MOEGAT performs dynamic routing, query-aware Mixture-of-Experts Graph Attention propagation over the pre-constructed sparse Orthogonal Context Graph, and node ranking via composite losses. The highly sparse graph ensures efficient attention. As shown in Table 6, MOEGAT averages 1.2 s per query, versus 0.58 s for GoR—a modest 0.6-s increase mainly from dynamic routing and multi-expert layers. Given the substantial gains (+14.9% ROUGE-L, +18.1% ROUGE-1, +18.4% ROUGE-2 over GoR), this minor overhead is well-justified for practical applications.

Table 6. Inference efficiency analysis inference time per query on the WCEP dataset.

Baselines	Node2Vec	BM25	Contriever	SBERT	GOR	MOEGAT
Inference Time (s)	9.40	0.02	0.20	0.01	0.58	1.16

5. Discussion

5.1. Efficacy of the Scoring Mechanism

This mechanism is a critical component of the framework, with its core function being the accurate ranking of nodes. To this end, the model-predicted score for each node on the test set was calculated and compared against its corresponding ground-truth score to

 https://doi.org/10.3390/bdcc10010031

evaluate the consistency between the two. Specifically, a plot of the model's output scores versus the target scores was generated to visually investigate the correlation between them.

We conducted a quantitative analysis on the test set to evaluate the effectiveness of our scoring mechanism. Results are visualized in Figure 3. Figure 3a shows the linear regression fit between model-predicted relevance scores and ground-truth scores for each node. We observe a strong positive linear correlation, evidenced by a Pearson correlation coefficient of r = 0.759 ($p < 0.001$). Additionally, Spearman's rank correlation coefficient of ρ = 0.714 confirms high monotonic consistency in ranking. The coefficient of determination $R^2 = 0.576$ indicates that the model explains more than half of the variance in ground-truth scores. Compared to typical relevance prediction performance reported in complex natural language understanding tasks [53], these results demonstrate robust and reliable score prediction capabilities. This finding is further supported by the two-dimensional kernel density estimation in Figure 3b, where the joint distribution reveals that most data points concentrate tightly around the regression line. This pattern confirms consistent performance across the majority of samples and validates that our scoring head successfully assigns higher relevance to critical content segments.

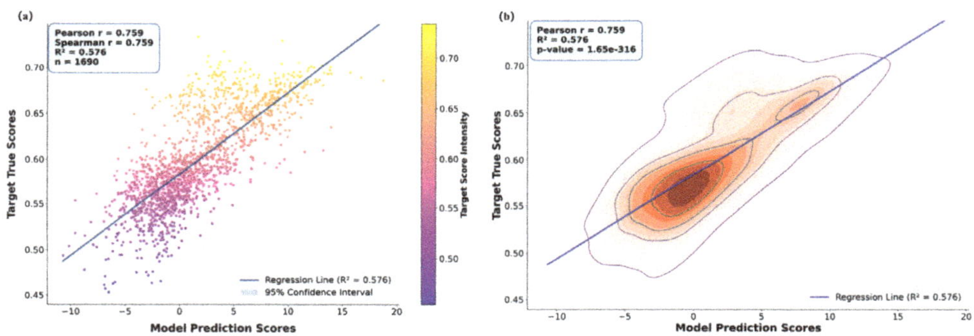

Figure 3. Efficacy evaluation of the scoring mechanism. (**a**) Regression fit between model-predicted and ground-truth node scores on the test set. (**b**) Two-dimensional kernel density estimation of the joint distribution of predicted and ground-truth scores.

5.2. Sensitivity Analysis of the Number of Semantic Neighbors

We conducted a systematic study to examine the influence of k, the number of semantic neighbors in the Orthogonal Context Graph, on ranking performance. Results for the WCEP and QMSum datasets are shown in Figure 4. As k increases from small values, performance on both datasets improves rapidly at first, reflecting the benefit of incorporating more long-range semantic connections. Performance then reaches a peak and subsequently declines or plateaus, indicating the onset of noise from overly distant or irrelevant neighbors. The optimal k and the model's sensitivity to this hyperparameter vary markedly between datasets. On the WCEP dataset, which features high content heterogeneity due to multi-document news clusters containing diverse topics, advertisements, and ancillary elements, the model achieves peak ranking performance at $k = 5$. Beyond this point, further increases in k lead to a steady decline, as additional semantic edges frequently connect core content to noisy or irrelevant segments. This noise dilutes the signal during graph propagation and reduces retrieval precision. In contrast, the QMSum dataset consists of meeting transcripts that are more semantically dense and thematically coherent within each document. Here, the model attains its highest performance at $k = 7$, with only minor degradation even as k continues to increase up to 10 or higher. This greater robustness suggests that extra semantic neighbors in QMSum are more likely to link genuinely related utterances across speakers or agenda items, providing useful supplementary context rather than noise.

 https://doi.org/10.3390/bdcc10010031

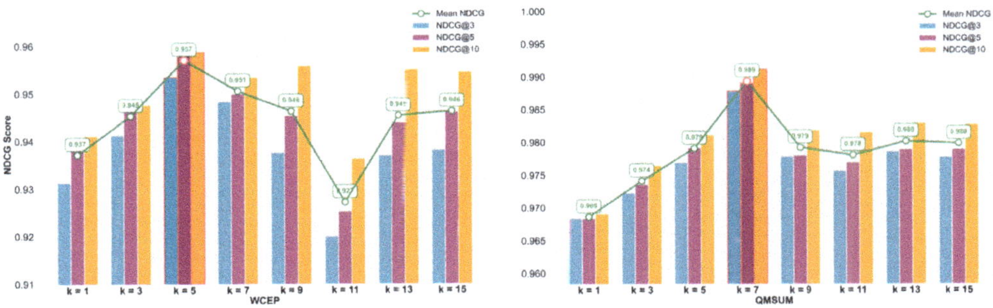

Figure 4. Influence of the number of semantic neighbor's k on ranking performance. Results are shown for the WCEP and QMSum datasets.

These dataset-specific patterns underscore the value of tuning k based on document characteristics: lower values suit heterogeneous or noisy sources to minimize spurious connections, while higher values are preferable for focused, cohesive texts. Overall, the results confirm that our Orthogonal Context Graph construction is not only effective but also exhibits appropriate sensitivity to this key hyperparameter, enabling strong adaptability across diverse long-document scenarios in practice.

5.3. Analysis of the Impact of the Load-Balancing Loss on Architectural Stability

We performed a quantitative comparison between the full model, which incorporates the load-balancing loss, and an ablated variant without this loss (w/o load-balancing). Results are presented in Figure 5 from two perspectives: the dynamic evolution of expert load during training (a) and the steady-state distribution after convergence (b). Without the load-balancing loss, the routing mechanism exhibits severe imbalance after convergence, as shown in Figure 5b. One expert (expert 5) processes 45.9% of the input tokens—nearly four times the ideal uniform share of 12.5% for 8 experts—while experts 2, 3, 4, and 7 receive almost no tokens. This "winner-take-all" phenomenon causes the multi-expert system to degenerate into a structure dominated by a single expert, substantially reducing overall model capacity. The load balance score drops dramatically from 0.912 in the full model to 0.341 in the ablated version, confirming routing collapse.

In contrast, the full model with the load-balancing loss maintains healthy utilization. Figure 5a illustrates that, despite initial fluctuations, the load on all eight experts rapidly converges and stabilizes around the ideal average. This demonstrates that the load-balancing loss serves as an effective regularizer, enforcing uniform input distribution and ensuring each expert receives sufficient training signal. By preserving expert diversity and capacity, this mechanism contributes directly to the superior ROUGE performance observed in the full model.

5.4. Analysis of the Role of the Self-Supervised Ranking Loss in the Separability of the Representation Space

We investigated the role of the self-supervised ranking loss in representation learning through a comparative visualization study. Final node representations from the full model and an ablated variant without the ranking loss are projected into two dimensions using UMAP. Results are shown in Figure 6, where red points represent golden nodes that are highly relevant to the reference summary and blue points represent ordinary nodes. In the ablated model (right panel), golden and ordinary nodes are heavily intermingled with no discernible separable structure. This indicates that the main task objective alone provides insufficient signal for the model to distinguish nodes of varying importance, resulting in

 https://doi.org/10.3390/bdcc10010031

poor representation separability. The full model (left panel) exhibits markedly different behavior. Golden nodes form a compact, well-defined cluster clearly separated from the region occupied by ordinary nodes. This pronounced boundary demonstrates that the self-supervised ranking loss supplies a task-aligned supervisory signal that effectively guides the encoder to enhance separability between critical and secondary content. By serving as a carefully designed proxy task, the ranking loss imposes structuredness on the representation space, enabling better differentiation of node importance and contributing directly to improved summary quality.

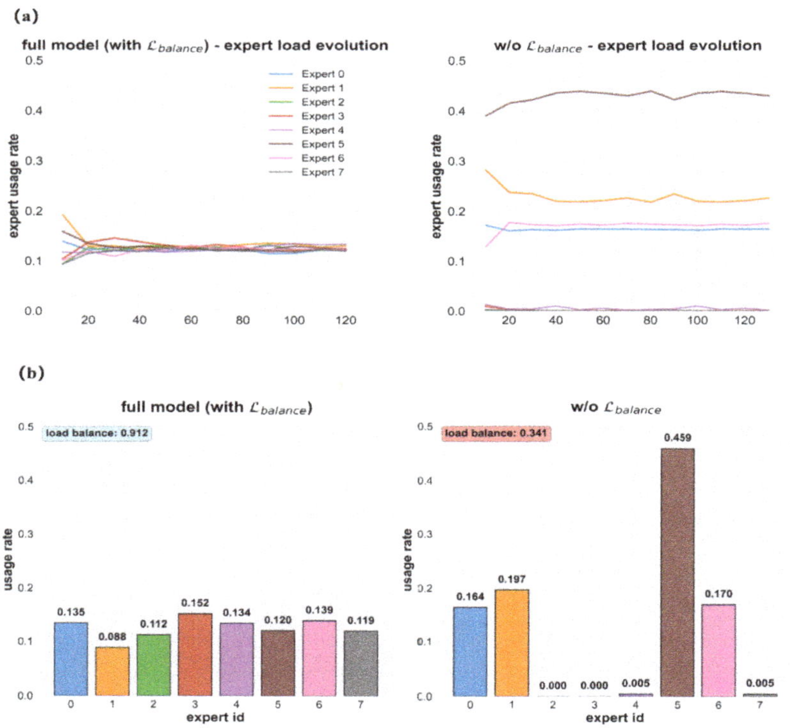

Figure 5. Impact of the load-balancing loss on expert utilization in the multi-expert architecture. (**a**) Dynamic evolution of expert load during training with the load-balancing loss. (**b**) Steady-state expert load distribution after convergence, comparing the full model and the model without the load-balancing loss.

5.5. Analysis of the Correlation Between Internal Decision Mechanisms and Summarization Performance

High-quality summarization depends critically on the model's ability to accurately assess sentence importance. To examine this internal decision-making process and its relation to generation performance, we conducted a qualitative visual analysis on 34 test samples from the QMSum dataset. Results are presented in Figure 7, with the top panel showing ROUGE-L scores for each sample and the bottom panel displaying a heatmap of model-assigned importance scores for sentences in the corresponding source document (darker colors indicate higher importance; selected summary sentences are bordered in dark gray). Based on this visual analysis, the following conclusions were drawn:

(1) Accurate Judgments and an Effective Scoring Mechanism: The heatmaps collectively indicate that the model can precisely identify salient sentences. In the vast majority of samples, the sentences ultimately selected for the summary (highlighted with dark

 https://doi.org/10.3390/bdcc10010031

gray borders) show a high degree of correspondence with the most intensely colored regions in the heatmap, which represent the highest importance scores. For example, in samples 17, 20, and 34, the model exhibits a pronounced "peak" effect, where a few sentences are assigned extremely high scores while the rest receive markedly lower ones. This demonstrates a strong alignment between the model's internal scoring and its summary generation behavior, confirming that the designed scoring architecture can effectively identify high-information-density content. (2) Overcoming Positional Bias with Global Information Awareness: The analysis reveals that the model successfully avoids the "lead bias" commonly found in traditional summarization methods. Observing the vertical axis of the heatmaps (normalized sentence position), high-scoring salient sentences are not concentrated at the beginning of the documents (in the 0.0–0.2 range) but are instead distributed widely throughout the text. For instance, the key information in sample 20 is concentrated in the initial part of the text, whereas the salient sentences in samples 5, 15, and 33 are located primarily in the middle and latter sections. This indicates that the model possesses a global information-aware capability, enabling it to assess sentence importance based on semantic value rather than positional cues, which is particularly crucial for processing long documents with diverse structures.

(3) Positive Correlation between Scoring Confidence and Summary Quality: A comparison of the ROUGE-L scores and the heatmap patterns reveals a clear association between the two. In samples with high ROUGE-L scores (e.g., samples 17 and 34), the heatmaps exhibit high contrast, with a few sentences receiving scores significantly higher than the rest. Conversely, in samples with lower scores (e.g., samples 5 and 29), the color distribution is relatively uniform. This suggests that the more "confident" the model is in its judgments—that is, when the scores of salient sentences are highly prominent—the higher the quality of the generated summary tends to be. In summary, the model demonstrates high accuracy and global awareness in assessing sentence importance, providing a solution for long-document summarization that is both effective and interpretable.

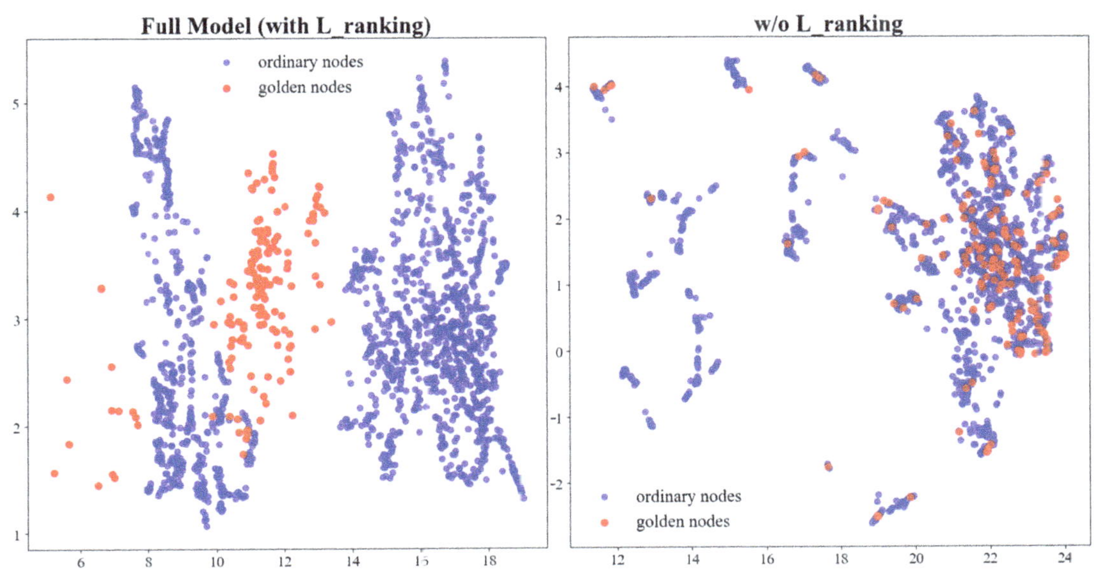

Figure 6. UMAP visualization of node representation spaces. Red points denote golden nodes (highly relevant to the reference summary); blue points denote ordinary nodes. **Left**: full model with self-supervised ranking loss. **Right**: ablated model without the ranking loss.

https://doi.org/10.3390/bdcc10010031

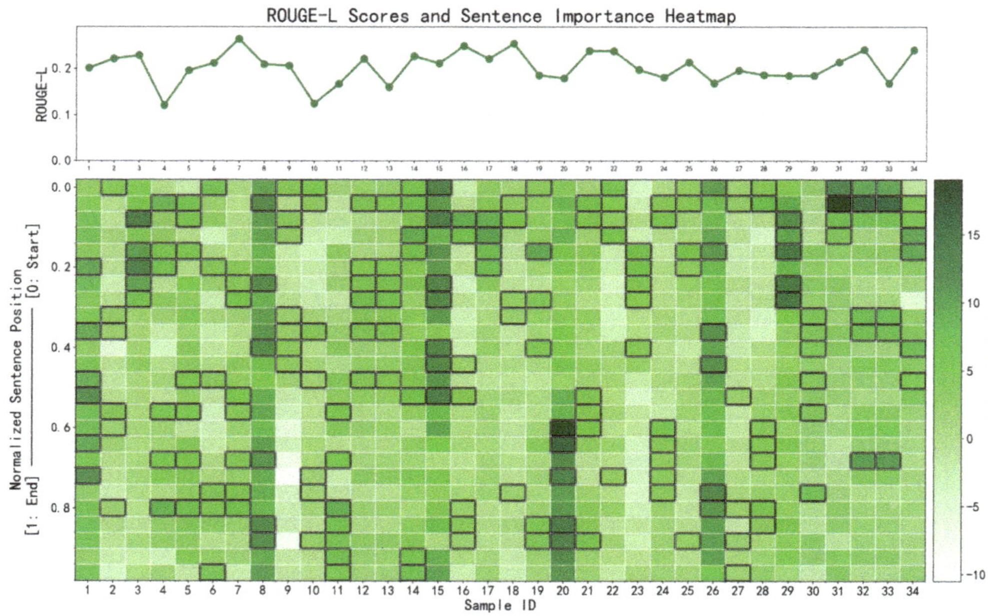

Figure 7. Qualitative analysis of the relationship between internal sentence importance scoring and summarization performance on 34 QMSum test samples. **Top**: line plot of ROUGE-L scores per sample. **Bottom**: heatmap of model-assigned importance scores for sentences in each corresponding source document (darker regions indicate higher importance; sentences selected for the summary are highlighted with dark gray borders).

5.6. Limitations

A primary limitation of the proposed method lies in its strong dependence on the quality of the graph construction. We front-load the complex semantic analysis task; while this reduces the computational burden on the model, it also shifts the performance bottleneck to the graph construction stage. This limitation is particularly pronounced on the BookSum dataset, where for extremely long and complex texts such as books, the current graph construction method struggles to fully capture the macroscopic narrative structure. This reveals a critical issue: even a model with a highly stable and load-balanced internal architecture (see Figure 5) will have its ultimate efficacy constrained by the quality of its input representation (i.e., the graph structure). Another limitation stems from the implicit division of labor among the experts, which restricts the model's controllability. While we successfully ensured that all experts are activated via the load-balancing loss, we did not explicitly guide their functional differentiation. This causes the model to function as an effective "generalist" rather than a collection of interpretable and steerable "specialists" Consequently, the model lacks the flexibility required for applications that involve generating summaries from a specific perspective.

6. Conclusions

In this paper, we proposed Orthogonal Graph Expert Network, an innovative framework designed to enhance the performance of long-document summarization. Our method uniquely combines a hierarchical graph structure with a Mixture-of-Experts architecture to effectively model the complex, long-range, and heterogeneous semantic relationships inherent in long texts. Intuitively, we construct a graph to capture both local and global dependencies within the document and apply a Graph Attention Network (GAT) on top of

 https://doi.org/10.3390/bdcc10010031

it. We then leverage the Moe architecture to dynamically route different types of textual information to specialized experts for processing, thereby achieving a more fine-grained and adaptive content comprehension. To optimize this framework, we designed a composite training objective centered on a self-supervised ranking loss function, which directly aligns the node representations with the downstream summarization task, and a load-balancing loss function, which ensures the stability and full utilization of the model's capacity. Extensive experiments conducted on multiple long-document summarization datasets demonstrate that Orthogonal Graph Expert Network significantly outperforms a variety of strong baseline models, including retrieval-based methods, long-context large language models, and other graph-based approaches. This validates the effectiveness and superiority of our proposed framework.

Supplementary Materials: The following supporting information can be downloaded at: https://www.mdpi.com/article/10.3390/bdcc10010031/s1. Section S1: Sequential Adjacency Matrix; Section S2: Semantic Adjacency Matrix and Orthogonality Constraint; Section S3: Node-Adaptive Dynamic Routing; Section S4: Query-Modulated Graph Attention Expert (QM-GAE); Section S5: Load-Balancing Loss.

Author Contributions: J.Y.: Investigation, Data curation, Software, Methodology, Formal analysis, Visualization, Writing—original draft, Writing—review and editing; Q.X.: Investigation, Writing—review and editing; C.Z.: Methodology, Validation, Supervision, Writing—review and editing; H.Q.: Conceptualization, Resources, Methodology, Funding acquisition, Project administration, Writing—review and editing. All authors have read and agreed to the published version of the manuscript.

Funding: This research was funded by Zhejiang Key R&D Plan; grant number: 2017C03047.

Institutional Review Board Statement: Not applicable.

Informed Consent Statement: Not applicable.

Data Availability Statement: The original data presented in the study are openly available in references [37–39].

Conflicts of Interest: The authors declare no conflicts of interest.

References

1. Chang, Y.; Wang, X.; Wang, J.; Wu, Y.; Yang, L.; Zhu, K.; Chen, H.; Yi, X.; Wang, C.; Wang, Y.; et al. A Survey on Evaluation of Large Language Models. *ACM Trans. Intell. Syst. Technol.* **2024**, *15*, 39. [CrossRef]
2. AbuRa'ed, A.; Saggion, H.; Shvets, A.; Bravo, À. Automatic related work section generation: Experiments in scientific document abstracting. *Scientometrics* **2020**, *125*, 3159–3185. [CrossRef]
3. Luo, Z.; Xie, Q.; Ananiadou, S. Factual Consistency Evaluation of Summarization in the Era of Large Language Models. *Expert Syst. Appl.* **2024**, *254*, 124456. [CrossRef]
4. Asai, A.; Wu, Z.; Wang, Y.; Sil, A.; Hajishirzi, H. Self-rag: Learning to retrieve, generate, and critique through self-reflection. In Proceedings of the International Conference on Learning Representations, Vienna, Austria, 7–11 May 2024.
5. Ratner, N.; Levine, Y.; Belinkov, Y.; Ram, O.; Magar, I.; Abend, O.; Karpas, E.; Shashua, A.; Leyton-Brown, K.; Shoham, Y. Parallel Context Windows for Large Language Models. In Proceedings of the 61st Annual Meeting of the Association for Computational Linguistics, Toronto, ON, Canada, 9–14 July 2023; pp. 6383–6402. [CrossRef]
6. Jiang, Z.; Xu, F.F.; Gao, L.; Sun, Z.; Liu, Q.; Dwivedi-Yu, J.; Yang, Y.; Callan, J.; Neubig, G. Active retrieval augmented generation. In Proceedings of the 2023 Conference on Empirical Methods in Natural Language Processing, Sentosa, Singapore, 6–10 December 2023; pp. 7969–7992.
7. Shi, W.; Min, S.; Yasunaga, M.; Seo, M.; James, R.; Lewis, M.; Zettlemoyer, L.; Yih, W.-t. Replug: Retrieval-augmented black-box language models. In Proceedings of the 2024 Conference of the North American Chapter of the Association for Computational Linguistics: Human Language Technologies (Volume 1: Long Papers), Washington, DC, USA, 16–21 June 2024; pp. 8371–8384.
8. Liu, N.F.; Lin, K.; Hewitt, J.; Paranjape, A.; Bevilacqua, M.; Petroni, F.; Liang, P. Lost in the Middle: How Language Models Use Long Contexts. *Trans. Assoc. Comput. Linguist.* **2024**, *12*, 157–173. [CrossRef]

https://doi.org/10.3390/bdcc10010031

9. Edge, D.; Trinh, H.; Cheng, N.; Bradley, J.; Chao, A.; Mody, A.; Truitt, S.; Metropolitansky, D.; Ness, R.O.; Larson, J. From local to global: A graph rag approach to query-focused summarization. *arXiv* **2024**, arXiv:2404.16130. [CrossRef]
10. Procko, T.T.; Ochoa, O. Graph Retrieval-Augmented Generation for Large Language Models: A Survey. In Proceedings of the Conference on AI, Science, Engineering, and Technology (AIxSET), Laguna Hills, CA, USA, 30 September–2 October 2024; pp. 166–169. [CrossRef]
11. Peng, B.; Zhu, Y.; Liu, Y.; Bo, X.; Shi, H.; Hong, C.; Zhang, Y.; Tang, S. Graph Retrieval-Augmented Generation: A Survey. *ACM Trans. Inf. Syst.* **2024**, *44*, 1–52. [CrossRef]
12. Kim, D.; Yoo, S.; Jeong, O. MedSumGraph: Enhancing GraphRAG for Medical QA with Summarization and Optimized Prompts. *Artif. Intell. Med.* **2025**, *172*, 103311. [CrossRef]
13. Zakka, C.; Shad, R.; Chaurasia, A.; Dalal, A.R.; Kim, J.L.; Moor, M.; Fong, R.; Phillips, C.; Alexander, K.; Ashley, E.; et al. Almanac—Retrieval-Augmented Language Models for Clinical Medicine. *NEJM AI* **2024**, *1*, AIoa2300068. [CrossRef] [PubMed]
14. Borchmann, L.; Wisniewski, D.; Gretkowski, A.; Kosmala, I.; Jurkiewicz, D.; Szalkiewicz, L.; Palka, G.; Kaczmarek, K.; Kaliska, A.; Gralinski, F. Contract Discovery: Dataset and a Few-Shot Semantic Retrieval Challenge with Competitive Baselines. In Proceedings of the Conference on Empirical Methods in Natural Language Processing, Online, 16–20 November 2020; pp. 4254–4268. [CrossRef]
15. Gubanov, M.; Pyayt, A.; Karolak, A. Cancerkg. org-a web-scale, interactive, verifiable knowledge graph-llm hybrid for assisting with optimal cancer treatment and care. In Proceedings of the 33rd ACM International Conference on Information and Knowledge Management, Boise, ID, USA, 21–25 October 2024; pp. 4497–4505.
16. Sarmah, B.; Mehta, D.; Hall, B.; Rao, R.; Patel, S.; Pasquali, S. Hybridrag: Integrating knowledge graphs and vector retrieval augmented generation for efficient information extraction. In Proceedings of the 5th ACM International Conference on AI in Finance, Brooklyn, NY, USA, 14–17 November 2024; pp. 608–616.
17. Hu, Y.; Lei, Z.; Zhang, Z.; Pan, B.; Ling, C.; Zhao, L. GRAG: Graph Retrieval-Augmented Generation. In *Human Language Technology—The Baltic Perspectiv*; IOS Press: Amsterdam, The Netherlands, 2025; pp. 4145–4157. [CrossRef]
18. Zhao, Y.; Zhu, J.; Guo, Y.; He, K.; Li, X. E^ 2GraphRAG: Streamlining Graph-based RAG for High Efficiency and Effectiveness. *arXiv* **2025**, arXiv:2505.24226.
19. Wu, W.; Li, W.; Xiao, X.; Liu, J.; Cao, Z.; Li, S.; Wu, H.; Wang, H. BASS: Boosting Abstractive Summarization with Unified Semantic Graph. In Proceedings of the 59th Annual Meeting of the Association for Computational Linguistics and the 11th International Joint Conference on Natural Language Processing, Online, 1–6 August 2021; pp. 6052–6067. [CrossRef]
20. Zhang, H.; Feng, T.; You, J. Graph of Records: Boosting Retrieval Augmented Generation for Long-context Summarization with Graphs. In Proceedings of the 63rd Annual Meeting of the Association for Computational Linguistics, Vienna, Austria, 27 July–1 August 2025; pp. 23780–23799. [CrossRef]
21. Zhang, Z.; Yu, B.; Shu, X.; Mengge, X.; Liu, T.; Guo, L. From what to why: Improving relation extraction with rationale graph. In Proceedings of the Findings of the Association for Computational Linguistics: ACL-IJCNLP 2021, Online, 1–6 August 2021; pp. 86–95.
22. Garg, M.; Kumar, M. KEST: A graph-based keyphrase extraction technique for tweets summarization using Markov decision process. *Expert Syst. Appl.* **2022**, *209*, 118110. [CrossRef]
23. Ying, Z.; You, J.; Morris, C.; Ren, X.; Hamilton, W.; Leskovec, J. Hierarchical Graph Representation Learning with Differentiable Pooling. *Adv. Neural Inf. Process. Syst.* **2018**, *31*, 4800–4810.
24. Zhao, C.; Zhou, X.; Xie, X.; Zhang, Y. Hierarchical Attention Graph for Scientific Document Summarization in Global and Local Level. In *Human Language Technology—The Baltic Perspectiv*; IOS Press: Amsterdam, The Netherlands, 2024. [CrossRef]
25. Liu, Y.; Lapata, M. Hierarchical Transformers for Multi-Document Summarization. In Proceedings of the Annual Meeting of the Association for Computational Linguistics, Florence, Italy, 28 July–2 August 2019; pp. 5070–5081. [CrossRef]
26. Zhang, X.; Wei, F.; Zhou, M. HIBERT: Document Level Pre-training of Hierarchical Bidirectional Transformers for Document Summarization. In Proceedings of the Annual Meeting of the Association for Computational Linguistics, Florence, Italy, 28 July 28–2 August 2019; pp. 5059–5069. [CrossRef]
27. Plenz, M.; Frank, A. Graph Language Models. In Proceedings of the Annual Meeting of the Association for Computational Linguistics, Bangkok, Thailand, 11–16 August 2024; pp. 4477–4494. [CrossRef]
28. Chen, T.; Chen, X.; Du, X.; Rashwan, A.; Yang, F.; Chen, H.; Wang, Z.; Li, Y. AdaMV-MoE: Adaptive Multi-Task Vision Mixture-of-Experts. In Proceedings of the IEEE International Conference on Computer Vision, Paris, France, 1–6 October 2023; pp. 17346–17357. [CrossRef]
29. Li, Y.; Jiang, S.; Hu, B.; Wang, L.; Zhong, W.; Luo, W.; Ma, L.; Zhang, M. Uni-MoE: Scaling Unified Multimodal LLMs with Mixture of Experts. *IEEE Trans. Pattern Anal. Mach. Intell.* **2025**, *47*, 3424–3439. [CrossRef]
30. Zhang, J.; Zhang, X.; Yu, J.; Tang, J.; Tang, J.; Li, C.; Chen, H. Subgraph Retrieval Enhanced Model for Multi-hop Knowledge Base Question Answering. In Proceedings of the Annual Meeting of the Association for Computational Linguistics, Dublin, Ireland, 22–27 May 2022; pp. 5773–5784. [CrossRef]

 https://doi.org/10.3390/bdcc10010031

31. Liang, X.; Niu, S.; Li, Z.; Zhang, S.; Song, S.; Wang, H.; Yang, J. Xiong, F.; Tang, B.; Xi, C. Empowering Large Language Models to Set Up a Knowledge Retrieval Indexer Via Self-Learning. *arXiv* **2024**, arXiv:2405.16933. [CrossRef]
32. Liu, S.; Cao, J.; Yang, R.; Wen, Z. Generating a Structured Summary of Numerous Academic Papers: Dataset and Method. *Comput. Res. Repos.* **2022**, 4280–4288. [CrossRef]
33. Gutierrez, B.J.; Shu, Y.; Gu, Y.; Yasunaga, M.; Su, Y. HippoRAG: Neurobiologically Inspired Long-Term Memory for Large Language Models. In Proceedings of the 38th Conference on Neural Information Processing Systems, Vancouver, BC, Canada, 10–15 December 2024; pp. 59532–59569. [CrossRef]
34. He, X.; Tian, Y.; Sun, Y.; Chawla, N.V.; Laurent, T.; LeCun, Y.; Bresson, X.; Hooi, B. G-Retriever: Retrieval-Augmented Generation for Textual Graph Understanding and Question Answering. In Proceedings of the 38th Conference on Neural Information Processing Systems, Vancouver, BC, Canada, 10–15 December 2024; pp. 132876–132907. [CrossRef]
35. Li, Z.; Guo, Q.; Shao, J.; Song, L.; Bian, J.; Zhang, J.; Wang, R. Graph Neural Network Enhanced Retrieval for Question Answering of Large Language Models. In Proceedings of the 2025 Conference of the Nations of the Americas Chapter of the Association for Computational Linguistics: Human Language Technologies, Albuquerque, NM, USA, 29 April–4 May 2025; pp. 6612–6633. [CrossRef]
36. Mavromatis, C.; Karypis, G. GNN-RAG: Graph Neural Retrieval for Efficient Large Language Model Reasoning on Knowledge Graphs. In Proceedings of the Findings of the Association for Computational Linguistics: ACL 2025, Vienna, Austria, 27 July–1 August 2025; pp. 16682–16699. [CrossRef]
37. Hu, Y.; Lu, Y. RAG and RAU: A Survey on Retrieval-Augmented Language Model in Natural Language Processing. *arXiv* **2024**, arXiv:2404.19543. [CrossRef]
38. Bahr, L.; Wehner, C.; Wewerka, J.; Bittencourt, J.; Schmid, U.; Daub, R. Knowledge Graph Enhanced Retrieval-Augmented Generation for Failure Mode and Effects Analysis. *J. Ind. Inf. Integr.* **2025**, 45, 100807. [CrossRef]
39. Suryawanshi, S.; Waghmode, S.; Sawant, R.; Gupta, M. A Knowledge Graph-based RAG for Cross-Document Information Extraction. In Proceedings of the 5th International Conference on Pervasive Computing Social Networking, Salem, India, 14–16 May 2025. [CrossRef]
40. Zhu, X.; Xie, Y.; Liu, Y.; Li, Y.; Hu, W. Knowledge Graph-Guided Retrieval Augmented Generation. In Proceedings of the 2025 Conference of the Nations of the Americas Chapter of the Association for Computational Linguistics: Human Language Technologies, Albuquerque, NM, USA, 29 April–4 May 2025; pp. 8912–8924. [CrossRef]
41. Zhong, M.; Yin, D.; Yu, T.; Zaidi, A.; Mutuma, M.; Jha, R.; Awadallah, A.H.; Celikyilmaz, A.; Liu, Y.; Qiu, X.; et al. QMSum: A New Benchmark for Query-based Multi-domain Meeting Summarization. In Proceedings of the North American Chapter of the Association for Computational Linguistics, Online, 6–11 June 2021; pp. 5905–5921. [CrossRef]
42. Kryściński, W.; Rajani, N.; Agarwal, D.; Xiong, C.; Radev, D. BookSum: A Collection of Datasets for Long-form Narrative Summarization. *arXiv* **2022**, arXiv:2105.08209. [CrossRef]
43. Ghalandari, D.G.; Hokamp, C.; Pham, N.T.; Glover, J.; Ifrim, G. A Large-Scale Multi-Document Summarization Dataset from the Wikipedia Current Events Portal. In Proceedings of the Annual Meeting of the Association for Computational Linguistics, Online, 5–10 July 2020; pp. 1302–1308. [CrossRef]
44. Lin, C.-Y. ROUGE: A Package for Automatic Evaluation of Summaries. In Proceedings of the Annual Meeting of the Association for Computational Linguistics, Barcelona, Spain, 25–26 July 2004; pp. 74–81.
45. Robertson, S.E.; Zaragoza, H. The Probabilistic Relevance Framework: BM25 and Beyond. *Found. Trends Inf. Retr.* **2009**, 3, 333–389. [CrossRef]
46. Tawfeeq, N.Z.; Abed, W.S.; Ghazal, O.G. A semantic model of morphological information retrieval: A comparative accumulative analysis. In Proceedings of the 2020 2nd Annual International Conference on Information and Sciences (AiCIS), Fallujah, Iraq, 24–25 November 2020. [CrossRef]
47. Reimers, N.; Gurevych, I. Sentence-BERT: Sentence Embeddings Using Siamese BERT-Networks. In Proceedings of the Conference on Empirical Methods in Natural Language Processing, Hong Kong, China, 3–7 November 2019; pp. 3982–3992. [CrossRef]
48. Lin, S.-C.; Asai, A.; Li, M.; Oguz, B.; Lin, J.; Mehdad, Y.; Yih, W.-t.; Chen, X. How to Train Your Dragon: Diverse Augmentation Towards Generalizable Dense Retrieval. In Proceedings of the Findings of the Association for Computational Linguistics: EMNLP 2023, Singapore, 6–10 December 2023; pp. 6385–6400.
49. Izacard, G.; Caron, M.; Hosseini, L.; Riedel, S.; Bojanowski, P.; Joulin, A.; Grave, E. Unsupervised Dense Information Retrieval with Contrastive Learning. *Trans. Mach. Learn. Res.* **2021**. *2022*, 2835–8856.
50. Karpukhin, V.; Oğuz, B.; Min, S.; Lewis, P.; Wu, L.; Edunov, S.; Chen, D.; Yih, W.-t. Dense passage retrieval for open-domain question answering. In Proceedings of the 2020 Conference on Empirical Methods in Natural Language Processing (EMNLP), Online, 16–20 November 2020; pp. 6769–6781.
51. Grover, A.; Leskovec, J. Node2vec: Scalable Feature Learning for Networks. In Proceedings of the 22nd ACM SIGKDD International Conference on Knowledge Discovery and Data Mining (KDD '16), New York, NY, USA, 13–17 August 2016; pp. 855–864. [CrossRef]

52. Feng, T.; Han, P.; Lin, G.; Liu, G.; You, J. Thought-Retriever: Don't Just Retrieve Raw Data, Retrieve Thoughts. International Conference on Learning Representations Workshop: How Far Are We from AGI. 2024. Available online: https://openreview.net/pdf/006ed5ed24038d996f1ced687940c3a1078d72d0.pdf (accessed on 12 November 2025).
53. Zhou, Y.; Camacho-Collados, J.; Bollegala, D. A Predictive Factor Analysis of Social Biases and Task-Performance in Pretrained Masked Language Models. In Proceedings of the 2023 Conference on Empirical Methods in Natural Language Processing, Singapore, 6–10 December 2023; pp. 11082–11100. [CrossRef]

https://doi.org/10.3390/bdcc10010031

big data and cognitive computing

MDPI

Article

Evaluating Faithfulness in Agentic RAG Systems for e-Governance Applications Using LLM-Based Judging Frameworks

George Papageorgiou [1], Vangelis Sarlis [1], Manolis Maragoudakis [2,*], Ioannis Magnisalis [1] and Christos Tjortjis [1]

[1] School of Science and Technology, International Hellenic University, 57001 Thessaloniki, Greece; gpapageorgiou2@ihu.edu.gr (G.P.); e.sarlis@ihu.edu.gr (V.S.); i.magnisalis@ihu.edu.gr (I.M.); c.tjortjis@ihu.edu.gr (C.T.)

[2] Department of Informatics, Ionian University, 49100 Corfu, Greece

* Correspondence: mmarag@ionio.gr

Abstract: As Large Language Models (LLMs) are core components in Retrieval-Augmented Generation (RAG) systems for knowledge-intensive tasks, concerns regarding hallucinations, redundancy, and unverifiable outputs have intensified, particularly in high-stakes domains, such as e-government. This study proposes a modular, multi-pipeline framework for statement-level faithfulness evaluation for characterizing hallucination and redundancy across both simple and agentic RAG pipelines. Using GPT-4.1, Claude Sonnet-4.0, and Gemini 2.5 Pro as LLM-based judges, this study examines how tool-specific attribution within agentic multi-tool architectures influences the interpretability and traceability of the generated content. By using a modular agentic RAG framework combining symbolic (GraphRAG), semantic (embedding), and real-time (web) retrieval, we benchmark hallucination and redundancy patterns, using state-of-the-art LLM judges. The study examines RAG and agent-based pipelines that attribute outputs to distinct tools, in contrast to traditional single-source RAG systems that rely on aggregated retrieval. Using e-government data sourced from the European Commission's Press Corner, our evaluation framework assesses not only the frequency, but also the source-aware detectability of hallucinated content. The findings provide actionable insights into how source granularity and retrieval orchestration impact faithfulness evaluation across different pipeline architectures, while also suggesting new directions for explainability-aware RAG design. The study contributes a reproducible, modular framework for automated faithfulness assessment, with implications for transparency, governance compliance, and trustworthy AI deployment.

Keywords: faithfulness evaluation; generative artificial intelligence (GAI); GraphRAG; large language models (LLMs); retrieval-augmented generation (RAG)

1. Introduction

Retrieval-Augmented Generation (RAG) architectures have significantly improved the factual grounding of Large Language Models (LLMs) by incorporating external evidence into response generation. However, the integration of retrieved content does not guarantee answer accuracy or faithfulness, as hallucinations and redundant statements still frequently emerge, especially in complex, multi-source environments. While manual evaluations of LLM outputs remain the standard for hallucination detection, they are time-consuming, non-scalable, and often lack granularity. Recent advancements in LLM-based evaluators now offer the potential for scalable, automated, and statement-level assessments of faithfulness, including hallucination, repetition, and source attribution errors.

At the same time, the evolution of agentic RAG architectures, which orchestrates multiple retrieval pipelines (e.g., embeddings, graph traversal, web search), introduces new layers of complexity, and opportunity, for monitoring the origins and quality of generated responses. In contrast to single RAG systems, agentic systems can attribute individual answer components to specific retrieval tools, making it possible to assess hallucination risk and redundancy per pipeline, aiming for further fine-tuning. However, the benefits of this tool-specific granularity for automated evaluation have not yet been rigorously studied.

This study develops and validates an LLM-based framework to address these challenges for automated hallucination at the statements level, with a particular focus on evaluating the role of attribution and architecture in enhancing interpretability, traceability, and system-level reliability.

In addition, we conduct a sophisticated performance evaluation of the most common RAG architectures, analyzing their effectiveness across Question Answering (QA), reasoning depths, and different retrieval modes to comprehensively assess their suitability for structured, policy-relevant AI deployment.

This study aims to address two key objectives:

RQ1: What is the effectiveness and accuracy of content generated by RAG architecture, based on state-of-the-art LLMs for evaluation of both standards and agentic RAG pipelines?

This question explores the effectiveness and accuracy of state-of-the-art LLM judges for identifying unfaithful or repetitive content, comparing their performance across standard RAG and multi-agent retrieval architectures.

RQ2: To what extent does tool-specific attribution within agentic pipelines support more interpretable and granular monitoring of answer faithfulness, compared to single-source RAG systems, under LLM-based evaluation?

This question investigates whether segmenting generated content by RAG tool (e.g., graph, embedding, web) enables better interpretability and quality of answer generation.

1.1. Aims and Objectives

The central aim of this study is to design, implement, and evaluate an automated framework for statement-level hallucination and redundancy detection in RAG systems, with particular emphasis on comparing agentic and non-agentic architectures. This involves exploring how LLM-based evaluators can provide an overview of unfaithful content, and whether tool-specific attribution in multi-agent systems supports deeper insights into retrieval quality and output trustworthiness.

To achieve this aim, the research first constructs a representative evaluation dataset, generating answers from both traditional single-source RAG systems and modular agentic pipelines. It uses e-governance sources to evaluate three common RAG architectures: knowledge graphs, embeddings, and real-time web content.

With e-governance related dataset, the study then overviews the performance of LLM evaluators in detecting hallucinated claims, redundant statements, and unsupported assertions across both architectures. A key objective is to assess whether segmenting responses by their originating retrieval tools, available in agentic pipelines, improves the interpretability, and diagnostic clarity of evaluation outputs.

The study also aims to analyze patterns in hallucination frequency and location across pipelines, enabling insights into retrieval-specific vulnerabilities. Finally, the research seeks to define actionable design recommendations for building faithfulness-aware RAG architectures that are not only robust and informative, but also easier to monitor, explain, and regulate, laying the groundwork for more trustworthy and ethically deployable LLM systems in the public sector and beyond. In addition, we present a sophisticated performance evaluation of graph creation, demonstrating use cases that support e-government services, public communication, and policy intelligence grounded in survey data.

1.2. Study Significance

As RAG systems continue to evolve into modular, agent-driven frameworks, the need for granular, automated faithfulness evaluation becomes increasingly urgent, particularly in governance, legal, and regulatory contexts. This study addresses a pressing gap in current research, by systematically evaluating whether LLM-based hallucination detection methods can meaningfully characterize output quality across diverse retrieval sources. By comparing standard RAG systems to agentic architectures with tool attribution, the study contributes to an understanding of how architectural transparency influences evaluation performance.

Furthermore, our research offers practical tools and reproducible methods for faithfulness auditing contributing to the development of more trustworthy, traceable, and verifiable LLM systems, capable of supporting real-world decision-making in complex and high-stakes domains, such as e-government

The remainder of this paper is organized as follows: Section 2 reviews related work on RAG architectures and faithfulness evaluation in LLM-based systems. Section 3 presents the proposed modular framework, dataset, and experimental design. Section 4 reports the main results and comparative analyses across RAG pipelines, while Section 5 discusses key findings, limitations, and practical implications. Finally, Section 6 concludes the study and outlines future research directions.

2. Background

As LLMs continue to redefine the boundaries of natural language processing, their integration with RAG frameworks has significantly improved factual grounding in open-domain and task-specific question answering. Despite these advances, LLMs remain prone to hallucination, the generation of fluent but incorrect content, and redundancy, particularly in multi-hop or information-dense contexts. Traditional RAG systems, which rely on flat document retrieval, often fail to capture semantic relationships between entities and provide limited support for attribution.

GraphRAG addresses these limitations by incorporating structured representations, such as knowledge graphs and layout-aware textual graphs. This enables relational reasoning, subgraph extraction, and provenance tracking, making GraphRAG particularly well-suited to knowledge-intensive tasks. However, hallucinations persist even in graph-based systems due to noise propagation and ambiguous entity resolution. At the same time, emerging agentic RAG pipelines, which orchestrate multiple retrieval tools (e.g., symbolic graphs, semantic embeddings, and web search), offer modularity and transparency, but their evaluation frameworks remain underdeveloped.

While early work such as [1] introduced the RAG paradigm by combining parametric and non-parametric memories, subsequent research has increasingly focused on the trustworthiness and faithfulness of RAG outputs. For instance, ref. [2] demonstrates that citation correctness does not guarantee faithfulness, and [3] proposes fine-grained monitoring of unfaithful segments in RAG systems. Recent surveys [4,5] have also begun to explore graph-based RAG architectures and domain-specific applications, highlighting gaps in retrieval quality, source attribution, and evaluation benchmarks. More recently, ref. [6] proposes self-supervised faithfulness optimization, signaling the evolving sophistication of this area. By integrating these contributions with our statement-level evaluation framework, our study extends the literature by comparing simple, graph-based, and agentic

RAG pipelines in an e-governance domain, using multi-LLM evaluators and a detailed analysis of hallucination and attribution errors.

This study investigates the intersection of these architectures by focusing on statement-level hallucination detection and tool-specific attribution within both simple and agentic systems. By leveraging LLM-based evaluation frameworks, we aim to improve transparency, faithfulness, and trustworthiness of complex QA pipelines across structured domains.

2.1. Symbolic and Graph-Based RAG Architectures

LLMs have transformed natural language understanding and generation, but remain constrained by their static pretraining, often producing hallucinations, confidently generated yet ungrounded or incorrect information. RAG frameworks were introduced to address this limitation by conditioning generation on retrieved external knowledge. However, traditional RAG systems typically rely on unstructured or flat document retrieval, limiting their interpretability, multi-hop reasoning, and transparency in knowledge attribution. GraphRAG has emerged as a promising evolution of RAG, incorporating structured knowledge representations, such as knowledge graphs (KGs) or textual graphs. By enabling explicit reasoning over entity relationships, subgraph traversal, and chain-of-thought generation, it improves both answer fidelity and interpretability. Studies, such as G-Retriever and Graphusion, have demonstrated the potential of graphs in knowledge-intensive tasks, showing their ability to retrieve semantically coherent subgraphs and generate structured responses grounded in high-quality KGs [7,8].

GraphRAG encodes knowledge in graph-based structures that capture entity relationships, document layouts, and multi-modal associations, enabling nuanced, semantically grounded, and explainable retrievals [9]. Unlike flat, vector-based similarity retrieval, GraphRAG supports multi-hop reasoning, semantic disambiguation, and context-aware retrieval [4]. Recent designs further modularize GraphRAG architectures with dual-level retrieval strategies, combining symbolic graph traversal and embedding-based soft matching to enhance adaptability, domain transferability, and noise reduction [10].

Frameworks, such as HuixiangDou2, implement dual-level retrieval (keyword-level and logic-form) with fuzzy matching and multi-stage verification, achieving substantial gains in accuracy from 60% to 74.5% with the Qwen2.5-7B-Instruct model on domain-specific datasets, highlighting GraphRAG's applicability to structured reasoning and hallucination mitigation [11]. SubgraphRAG employs adaptive triple scoring and Directional Distance Encoding (DDE) to retrieve semantically rich subgraphs without fine-tuning, relying on in-context learning to produce answers and reasoning chains. It further encourages abstention, when evidence is insufficient, reducing hallucinations and improving robustness across LLM sizes [12].

The GraphRAG pipeline can be formalized into three stages: (1) Graph-Based Indexing (G-Indexing), (2) Graph-Guided Retrieval (G-Retrieval), and (3) Graph-Enhanced Generation (G-Generation). By integrating textual and relational structures, this architecture enhances interpretability and faithfulness, with successful applications in domains such as scientific publishing [13], government transparency [14], and chronic disease management [15].

Traditional RAG approaches, which focus on semantic similarity-based retrieval from flat corpora, often suffer from fragmented retrieval, contextual drift, and loss of semantic relationships, thereby exacerbating hallucination risks. GraphRAG addresses these shortcomings by employing entity-centric subgraph generation and multi-hop reasoning [13,16]. Nevertheless, vulnerabilities remain; for instance, GraphRAG under Fire illustrates that while graph-based indexing improves robustness against naïve poisoning attacks, shared entity relations can propagate misinformation across multiple queries [17].

Hallucination, defined as the generation of factually incorrect content, remains a critical issue for both standard and graph-based RAG systems. While RAG aims to improve factual accuracy by conditioning on retrieved evidence, models still hallucinate when context is insufficient or misaligned with the query. Traditional evaluation metrics (e.g., BLEU, ROUGE) fail to capture factual consistency, prompting the adoption of LLM-based evaluators that assess hallucination and faithfulness at the statement level by cross-validating claims with retrieved evidence [10].

Structured retrieval variants, such as PathRAG and PolyG reduce noise via path pruning and adaptive traversal [18,19], while HyperGraphRAG extends coverage to n-ary relational facts for richer domain-specific representations [20]. Recent advances, such as SuperRAG, introduce layout-aware graph modeling (LAGM) to preserve structural hierarchies like section headers, tables, and diagrams, enabling more accurate retrievals in multimodal contexts [21]. PathRAG and PolyG similarly manage graph complexity and retrieval overhead, while maintaining relevance [9,22]. Frameworks, including GraphRAG-FI, DynaGRAG, and CG-RAG, combine symbolic reasoning, dynamic evidence weighting, and hierarchical citation networks to improve retrieval accuracy, semantic richness, and attribution [23,24].

Agentic RAG pipelines extend this paradigm by orchestrating multiple retrieval modalities, symbolic graph traversal, dense semantic search, and real-time web retrieval through a unified orchestration layer. This enables fine-grained, tool-specific attribution, tracing which pipeline component contributed to each segment of a generated response, and thereby improving transparency and faithfulness evaluation. Graphusion advances this concept with fusion-based graph operations, such as entity merging and conflict resolution between expert-annotated and LLM-generated subgraphs, proving particularly effective for scientific knowledge curation from ACL papers and enhancing relation consistency across models like GPT-4 and LLaMA3 [8].

2.2. Embedding, Web Search and Hybrid Retrieval

Parallel efforts in LLM-based evaluation frameworks, such as MLLM-as-a-Judge and GraphEva, investigate how large models can serve as reliable evaluators for generated content, enabling automated hallucination and faithfulness scoring at the statement level. Despite their promise, current evaluation methods often lack fine-grained tool attribution, making it difficult to trace specific factual claims in generated answers back to their retrieval sources, whether symbolic graphs, semantic embeddings, or live web search [25,26]. RAG has become a pivotal strategy to mitigate hallucinations and strengthen the factual grounding of LLMs by enriching prompts with contextually relevant knowledge. Nevertheless, traditional RAG systems typically operate on flat, unstructured corpora and lack visibility into how retrieved information contributes to generated outputs. This opacity poses challenges for diagnosing hallucinations and redundancies, especially in high-fidelity domains, such as medicine, law, and scientific research [27].

A complementary research direction examines the limitations of current LLM-based evaluation methods. State-of-the-art models like GPT-4 and GPT-4o are increasingly employed, not only for content generation, but also as evaluators of factuality, redundancy, and consistency. LLM-as-a-Judge (LLM-J) frameworks assess faithfulness at the statement level, providing interpretability aligned with human judgment. However, these evaluations are typically holistic, lacking the granularity to identify which retrieval tool, embedding-based search, web search, or graph traversal produced each specific output segment [28].

Addressing this gap, recent works incorporate tool-specific attribution into agentic RAG pipelines, where modularized agents specialize in different retrieval modes and annotate generated responses with provenance tags. This segmentation enables statement-level hallucination diagnosis, detection of redundant agent contributions, and dynamic routing of sub-queries to the most suitable tool depending on semantic or structural requirements [27,28].

Several retrieval architectures complement these evaluation-focused innovations. SubgraphRAG implements scalable, lightweight retrieval by scoring graph triples and extracting semantically compact subgraphs. This adaptability allows it to accommodate LLM context length constraints and to tailor retrieval strategies for both small and large models, while reducing hallucinations by grounding reasoning in structured subgraphs.

SuperRAG advances multimodal reasoning by transforming text, tables, and diagrams into layout-aware graphs, a capability critical for domains like e-government, where document structure and multi-modal context heavily influence extraction quality. It integrates layout analysis, graph construction, and multi-retriever pipelines (e.g., vector search, graph traversal) to enhance both retrieval relevance and downstream QA performance.

Comparative studies, such as RAG vs. GraphRAG, reveal that GraphRAG surpasses vanilla RAG on multi-hop QA and complex summarization tasks, whereas RAG excels in retrieving fine-grained factoid information. These findings highlight the value of combining both paradigms, particularly in hybrid or agent-based systems designed to minimize hallucinations through fine-grained content tracing and tool-specific attribution [25].

Traditional RAG architectures are typically monolithic, treating retrieval as a single unified process. In contrast, agentic RAG frameworks decompose retrieval into modular, source-specific agents, such as graph retrievers, dense embedding retrievers, and web search modules, enabling more granular attribution of evidence to system components. This modular design enhances scalability, interpretability, and the potential for tool-specific hallucination detection and redundancy mitigation [29].

Similarly, approaches like GRAG and FastRAG adopt hybrid, task-adaptive retrieval pipelines, combining structural, semantic, and symbolic methods to achieve superior factual grounding and reduced hallucinations, particularly in domains involving semi-structured data, healthcare, and scientific reasoning [30,31]. Recent comparative analyses across tasks such as single-hop QA, multi-hop QA, and query-focused summarization confirm that, while RAG remains strong in factoid retrieval and short-form QA, GraphRAG outperforms in multi-hop reasoning, complex summarization, and managing incomplete or distributed knowledge. In scenarios requiring traversal of entity chains or synthesis of contrasting viewpoints (e.g., multi-year, multi-country survey analysis), GraphRAG consistently provides a performance edge.

Moreover, hybrid approaches, either dynamically selecting between RAG and GraphRAG based on query type or integrating their outputs, achieve statistically significant improvements over method alone [25,32]. These results support the rationale for hybrid architectures that combines symbolic (graph) and dense (vector + web) retrieval within policy intelligence systems.

2.3. Terminology and Conceptual Definitions

To ensure terminological clarity, the following definitions are adopted throughout this study:

- Faithfulness refers to the degree to which a model's generated content accurately reflects and aligns with the retrieved or provided source evidence. It serves as the overarching criterion for factual reliability in RAG systems.
- Factual grounding denotes the process of conditioning a model's responses on explicit, verifiable information from external sources, such as databases, graphs, or web content. It represents the mechanism through which faithfulness is achieved.

- Hallucination describes any generated statement that lacks support in the retrieved sources or contradicts the underlying evidence.

While these concepts are closely related, they serve distinct roles in our evaluation framework: factual grounding is a design property of the RAG pipeline, faithfulness is the measurable outcome of that property, and hallucination represents its primary failure mode. This consistent terminology is applied across all sections of the paper to avoid ambiguity.

2.4. Hallucination and Redundancy Evaluation Frameworks

By systematically evaluating hallucination and redundancy at the statement level and incorporating attribution-aware evaluation, this study advances the goal of trustworthy generation in structured retrieval contexts. The proposed approach evaluates RAG pipelines not only on output quality but also on the transparency, granularity, and reliability of their internal processes. Leveraging LLM-based evaluators that operate at the statement level and embedding tool-specific provenance enables a deeper understanding of how different components symbolic, semantic, or real-time, contribute to final answers, improving both performance and trustworthiness.

Hallucinations remain a critical limitation of LLMs, particularly when the content generated is unsupported by either pre-trained knowledge or retrieved evidence. While RAG architectures mitigate this risk by grounding responses in retrieved text or structured data, they are not immune to introducing hallucinations. Systems without fine-grained evaluation mechanisms often inject irrelevant or misleading information, due to poor retrieval precision or overreliance on extraneous data. In parallel, redundancy repeated inclusion of similar or overlapping content reduces efficiency and interpretability [33].

To address these issues, new evaluation frameworks use LLMs not only as generators but also as judges, assessing hallucination, redundancy, and factual alignment at the statement level. Benchmarks, such as DeepEval, MLLM-as-a-Judge, and SELF-RAG, exemplify this trend, employing attention scores, logits, and context-aware scoring to quantify and explain hallucination sources [33,34].

Structured retrieval approaches further reduce hallucinations by constraining generation to validated domain-grounded facts. For example, GraphRAG for Finance and G-Retriever leverage knowledge graphs to focus reasoning on verified triples, while HybridRAG and FactRAG apply pre-generation filtering to construct and validate subgraphs before passing them to the LLM. Notably, G-Retriever formalizes retrieval as a Prize-Collecting Steiner Tree optimization problem, ensuring subgraph construction balances relevance, connectivity, and semantic coverage enhancing both explainability and accuracy [7,10].

Recent advancements shift from monolithic RAG architectures toward multi-agent (agentic) systems, where specialized retrieval modules graph-based, dense embedding, and web-search agents operate in parallel or sequence. These agentic frameworks enable tool-specific attribution, allowing evaluators and users to trace each segment of an answer back to its originating source. Such provenance tracking is vital for fine-grained error diagnosis, as demonstrated by CypherBench for structured query evaluation [35] and GraphEval for viewpoint-based content scoring [36]. Moreover, modular architectures can reduce hallucinations through internal redundancy checks and cross-agent verification, particularly when paired with statement-level evaluators. Tools like MLLM-as-a-Judge, SELF-RAG, and GraphEval-GNN exemplify this next generation of automated faithfulness scoring, offering rigorous and scalable validation pipelines [15,36].

The move toward statement-level diagnostics allows LLM evaluators to verify individual claims within generated outputs, improving detection of nuanced hallucinations that may be contextually subtle or structurally embedded in complex answers. Approaches such as IdepRAG and Hypergraph-based GraphRAG increase robustness by encoding multivariate relationships and prioritizing evidence based on statement-specific usefulness scores, reducing the likelihood of superficial or semantically misaligned responses [37]. This capability is especially important in domains requiring structured, interconnected knowledge, such as legislative corpora, citation networks, or scientific datasets, where single-source RAG may overlook critical relational dependencies.

Such approaches are particularly relevant in applications involving structured, interconnected information (e.g., legislative texts, citation graphs, and scientific datasets), where single-source RAG may miss critical relational dependencies. Statement-level evaluation frameworks, when combined with tool-specific attribution, allow researchers to dissect whether hallucinations arise from model bias, retrieval error, or faulty integration.

LLM-based evaluators now present a viable alternative to human-in-the-loop validation, offering the ability to assess hallucinations, redundancy, and factual consistency at the sentence or claim level—capabilities far beyond traditional BLEU-style metrics. For example, GraphEval applies viewpoint decomposition and graph-based label propagation to score originality and correctness, revealing prompt sensitivity and latent biases in LLMs [36]. Systematic comparisons further show that RAG performs well for short, factoid-style QA, while GraphRAG excels in tasks requiring reasoning, aggregation, or document-wide synthesis. Hybrid strategies, whether via query-based routing (selection) or output integration consistently outperform single-method approaches, reinforcing the value of combining symbolic (graph) and dense (vector + web) retrieval in architectures designed to maximize faithfulness and minimize hallucination.

2.5. Trustworthiness, Verification & Advanced RAG Control

Recent advances in RAG aim to address core limitations of LLMs, such as hallucinations, knowledge cutoffs, and lack of attribution, by dynamically integrating external knowledge sources into the generation process [38]. Beyond conventional pipelines, emerging approaches leverage hybrid retrieval techniques, domain-specific knowledge graphs, and adaptive query strategies to improve factual grounding and reasoning capabilities.

Adaptive and graph-based RAG architectures, such as WeKnow-RAG, combine multi-stage web retrieval with structured knowledge representations to enhance accuracy and trustworthiness in real-world scenarios [39]. In long-form and complex question answering, reinforcement learning frameworks like RioRAG optimize informativeness and factual completeness via nugget-level reward modeling, reducing unsupported content, while preserving coherence [40]. These developments align with a broader shift toward faithfulness-aware evaluation and optimization, a focus central to this study's aim of assessing and improving the reliability of agentic RAG systems in knowledge-intensive applications.

Persistent challenges in RAG pipelines stem from both retrieval and generation stages, including incomplete or inaccurate evidence and inconsistencies between generated outputs and supporting references. The Chain-of-Verification RAG (CoV-RAG) framework addresses these issues through a verification module that scores, judges, and revises retrieved documents and generated responses, enabling iterative refinement via query reformulation and factuality checks [41]. Complementary to such technical advances, recent surveys have stressed the need for trustworthiness in RAG encompassing reliability, privacy, safety, fairness, explainability, and accountability especially in high-stakes domains, where factual grounding and bias mitigation are critical [42].

Several architectures explicitly focus on improving factual grounding. FaithfulRAG introduces fact-level conflict modeling to detect and mitigate discrepancies between retrieved content and generated text. SFR-RAG integrates semantic filtering and reranking to improve contextual fidelity, while other work distinguishes correctness from faithfulness, noting that accurate answers may still lack evidence support. Domain-specific systems, such as context-aware travel assistants, demonstrate the benefits of hybrid retrieval approaches (e.g., HyDE, GraphRAG) and persona-based augmentation for improving retrieval precision and generative relevance. Collectively, these advances emphasize a dual focus on retrieval optimization and generative verification, aligning closely with this study's objective of strengthening faithfulness in agentic RAG [43,44].

While many evaluations assess only answer or citation correctness, correctness alone does not ensure grounding in retrieved evidence. The concept of citation faithfulness addresses this by requiring a causal link between cited documents and generated statements, avoiding post-rationalization and misplaced trust [2]. Synchronous Faithfulness Monitoring (SYNCHECK) offers a lightweight, real-time detection mechanism that combines sequence likelihood, uncertainty estimation, context influence, and semantic alignment to identify unfaithful sentences during decoding [45]. These synchronous interventions, combined with faithfulness-oriented decoding, improve the grounding of generated outputs, while balancing informativeness and reliability.

For domain personalization, context-aware assistants integrate strategies like HyDE and GraphRAG with persona-driven prompt adaptation to enhance contextual relevance and reduce hallucinations [46]. On the structured knowledge side, FiDeLiS combines deductive-verification beam search with Path-RAG reasoning to anchor inference in verifiable KG steps, lowering hallucination rates, while maintaining computational efficiency [47]. Together, these approaches demonstrate the value of coupling retrieval optimization with reasoning verification to achieve faithful, interpretable, and contextually grounded outputs.

Traditional RAG pipelines, which follow a static retrieve-then-generate pattern, often suffer from shallow reasoning, limited adaptability, and retrieval inadequacy in complex tasks. This has led to Synergized RAG–Reasoning systems, where reasoning guides retrieval and evidence iteratively informs reasoning, enabling deeper inference and improved factuality [48]. Trustworthiness efforts in these settings include metrics like TRUST-SCORE, which measures groundedness via refusal accuracy, answer correctness, and citation validity, and alignment methods like TRUST-ALIGN, which train models to refuse when evidence is insufficient and produce verifiable citations [49]. These methods signal a shift toward adaptive, evidence-grounded agentic RAG frameworks.

Retrieval-Free Generation (RFG) offers speed advantages, but is more prone to hallucinations, due to reduced explicit grounding. Methods such as RA2FD distill the faithfulness capacity of RAG "teacher" models into efficient RFG "students" using sequence-level distillation and contrastive learning, narrowing the trade-off between accuracy and efficiency [50]. Evaluation frameworks like FRANQ complement these efforts by differentiating faithfulness (alignment with retrieved evidence) from factuality (objective correctness), enabling targeted uncertainty quantification for improved hallucination detection [51]. These works highlight the importance of integrating knowledge infusion, faithfulness-aware evaluation, and efficiency-driven design for developing trustworthy LLM pipelines in both simple and agentic RAG scenarios.

Although large-context models can process entire documents, studies show that well-designed RAG pipelines can match or exceed their performance, while reducing computational cost and latency [52]. Research in this area emphasizes the role of retrieval strategies, ranking mechanisms, and prompt engineering in ensuring generated output remains grounded in retrieved evidence, rather than relying on parametric memory [53]. Additional work demonstrates that combining retrieval quality metrics with output verification improves both correctness and contextual grounding, underscoring the need for systematic evaluation frameworks in high-trust settings.

In multimodal contexts, RAG introduces further risks of selection hallucination and context-generation hallucination when retrieved visual or textual elements are irrelevant or incorrectly processed. The RAG-Check framework addresses this with relevance scores (RS) and correctness scores (CS) to quantify retrieval quality and response faithfulness in multimodal RAG [54]. Recent advances also shift toward agentic search, where models autonomously plan, iteratively query, and integrate information from multiple sources. Conventional evaluation frameworks often fail to capture such complexity, focusing narrowly on final answers or overlooking intermediate reasoning and tool usage. RAVine addresses these gaps with fine-grained, attributable nugget-based assessments combined with process-oriented and efficient metrics, enabling more comprehensive analysis of task completeness, faithfulness, and tool effectiveness [55]. Complementary efforts, including RAG-Check and large-context comprehension benchmarks, reinforce the need for robust, interpretable, and cost-efficient evaluation methods that reflect real-world, multi-agent, and multimodal information seeking scenarios [56].

2.6. Necessity and Feasibility of the Proposed Study

Recent advances in LLMs have significantly improved text generation quality; however, the faithfulness and factual reliability of RAG systems remain underexplored particularly in high-stakes, evidence-dependent domains, such as e-Governance. Existing research primarily focuses on domain-general question answering or open-domain retrieval, with limited emphasis on statement-level evaluation and agentic multi-tool reasoning. This gap highlights the necessity for a framework capable of systematically quantifying hallucination, redundancy, and attribution across diverse RAG architectures.

The feasibility of the proposed approach is ensured by the maturity of current LLM APIs (e.g., GPT-4.1, Claude Sonnet-4.0, Gemini 2.5 Pro), which enable consistent, scalable, and reproducible evaluation at the statement level, as well as by the structured nature of publicly available European Commission (EC) press releases, which provide a reliable and policy-relevant testbed. Together, these factors establish both the need and practical viability of the study's experimental design.

2.7. Main Innovation Points of This Study

Building on the identified research gaps, this study introduces several key innovations that advance the evaluation of RAG systems:

1. Statement-Level Faithfulness Evaluation: We utilize a fine-grained, LLM-driven framework that evaluates factual alignment at the statement level, capturing nuanced forms of redundancy and conflict often overlooked in prior work.
2. Cross-Evaluator Consistency Analysis: The framework leverages three distinct LLM families (GPT-4.1, Claude Sonnet-4.0, Gemini 2.5 Pro) to assess inter-model reliability and mitigate evaluator bias.
3. Application to E-Governance Contexts: We apply the framework to official EC press releases, offering the first large-scale assessment of faithfulness in high-stakes, policy-relevant AI systems.
4. Open and Reproducible Design: All prompt templates, low-code source code, and evaluation scripts are documented and released for replication and extension.

These innovations contribute to a practical, transparent, and domain-grounded methodology for advancing trustworthy LLM applications in public-sector decision support.

3. Technical Architecture and Solution

The technical architecture presented in this research is designed to be modular and rigorously evaluate and improve the factual reliability of RAG systems for e-governance applications, from single-pipeline configurations to complex agent-based orchestration. Using publicly available e-governance data from the EC's official online platform for media and public communications, Press Corner integrates four complementary components.

Firstly, a modular RAG orchestration framework, as presented in Figure 1, built on embedding-based, graph-based, and web-based retrieval pipelines. Secondly, a triples evaluation configuration for verifying the accuracy and completeness of knowledge graph construction. Thirdly, a faithfulness assessment configuration for measuring the factual grounding of standard RAG pipelines. Lastly, an agentic RAG faithfulness assessment, enabling fine-grained evaluation of multi-source reasoning, attribution, and conflict handling. Each component is designed to be reproducible, model-agnostic, and traceable, with standardized prompts, deterministic evaluation settings, and structured outputs that facilitate large-scale benchmarking. For the experiments, Goggle Colab was used (Intel Xeon CPU at 2.20 GHz, 12.67 GiB RAM, NVIDIA Tesla T4 with 14.74 GiB memory, CUDA 12.4 support, Operating Environment: 64-bit x86_64 architecture with little-endian byte order, Python 3.11.13. The low-code source is openly available at https://github.com/gpapageorgiouedu/Evaluating-Faithfulness-in-Agentic-RAG-Systems-for-e-Governance-applications-LLM-Based (accessed on 9 September 2025).

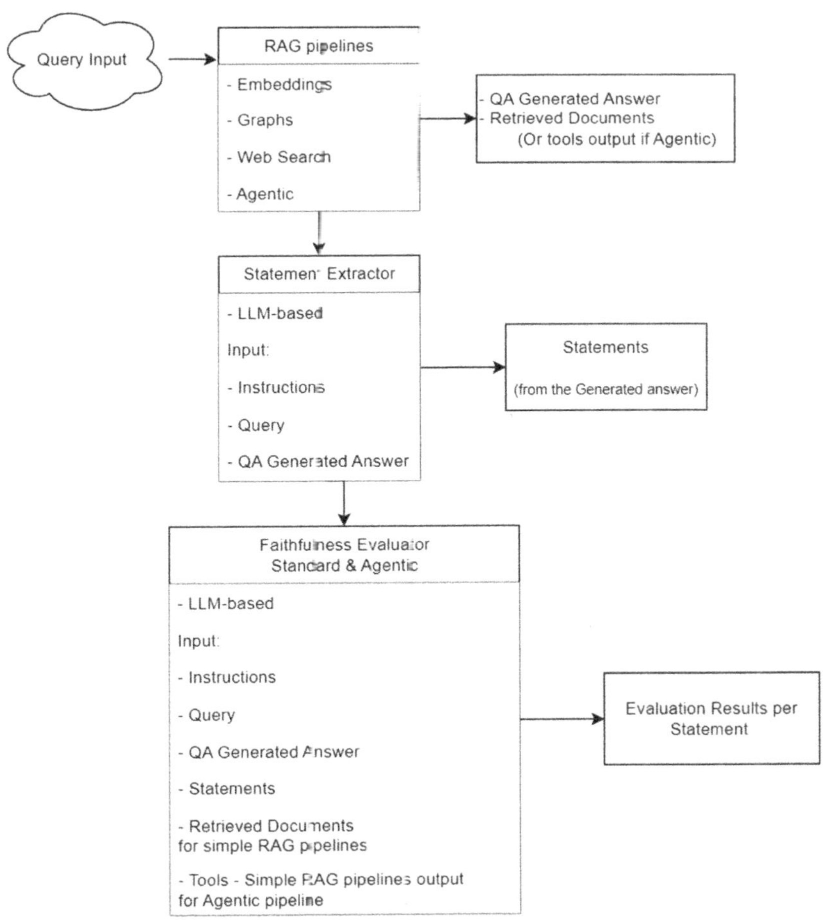

Figure 1. Faithfulness evaluation architectural overview diagram.

The faithfulness evaluation process of the proposed framework, as presented in Figure 1, begins with an input query that is passed through three baseline RAG pipelines and an agentic multi-tool pipeline. Each pipeline generates an answer, along with its supporting retrieved documents. The generated answer, together with the original query, is then processed by an LLM-based statement extractor, which identifies and isolates individual factual statements. These statements are subsequently evaluated by LLM-based judges against the retrieved documents and the generated answer to determine factual consistency and potential redundancy; in the agentic case, this judgment is instead grounded in the outputs of the baseline RAG pipelines, which function as its evaluated evidence layer. This modular workflow enables a systematic, pipeline-agnostic comparison of hallucination and redundancy patterns across both traditional and agentic RAG architectures.

Together, these elements provide a transparent and extensible solution for assessing and improving RAG performance in domains that demand high accuracy, explainability, and evidence-backed reasoning.

3.1. Data Sources

For our chosen use case, centered on the public sector and e-governance, we sourced data from the Press Corner, the EC's official online platform for media and public communications. To focus on specific topics and find related data, we conducted a search for four key subjects: the Clean Industrial Deal, Invest EU, US tariffs and REPowerEU. For those topics, aiming to conduct a broader experiment covering different subjects, we selected the 36 most recent press releases and statements; ten for each, with four documents to overlap between subjects, resulting in total 36 documents. In addition to the main content, we captured titles and publication dates as supplementary metadata.

We also integrated SerpAPI [57] via Haystack's [58] live content retrieval components, using it to perform a Google search and extract the five most relevant results. To support modular data orchestration within Haystack, our setup allows for easy inclusion of additional sources in various formats (e.g., PDF, CSV, TXT), including the corresponding converters, enabling users to upload and process their own selected content with minimal adjustments.

3.2. RAG Orchestration

The assessed RAG orchestration is based on three standard RAG pipelines, one based on embeddings, one based on graphs and a last one based on Web Search. The complete information regarding architecture can be found in [59]. This work is based on previous research as referenced, using the same architecture, with a slight modification to the RAG backend prompt, which was optimized for conducting a complete LLM-based faithfulness evaluation. Each of those pipelines has a distinctive indexing process, based on the data handling, using embedding-ada-002 model from OpenAI [60] for embeddings calculation, along with GPT-4.1-mini [61] (gpt-4_1-mini-2025-04-14) for text generation, with a temperature of 0 (fully deterministic generation) and top_p of 0 (restricting output to the highest-probability tokens only).

The GraphRAG pipeline is built on two core processes, the indexing and the retrieval/generation, while both were designed to be modular and with adjustable configuration. In the indexing phase, we used GPT-4.1-mini to extract structured factual triples from unstructured documents, which were then stored in a Neo4j graph database. Each triple (subject, relation, object) was linked to its source, ensuring semantic richness and traceability. For the initial X documents, this process yielded X triples, X unique relationship types, and X unique entity types, all captured reliably and without ingestion errors.

For retrieval and answer generation, the system leverages the knowledge graph to respond to user queries. Search terms are extracted and used to generate dynamic Cypher queries to find relevant entities and relationships. Retrieved results are re-ranked for relevance using the cross-encoder model intfloat/simlm-msmarco-reranker, which predicts how well each document matches the query. The top documents are then used to build a prompt for GPT-4.1-mini, which generates a markdown-formatted answer strictly grounded in the graph-based knowledge, with inline citations to original sources. This approach enables accurate, transparent, and explainable responses, well-suited for domains that demand high reliability.

The embedding pipeline adopted a modular two-stage process, comprising embedding-based indexing and querying, designed for adaptability across diverse applications. During indexing, JSON documents containing text, titles, and source URLs were cleansed and then embedded using OpenAI's embedding-ada-002 model to generate semantic vectors, which were stored in Neo4j with cosine similarity enabled for efficient retrieval. The system supported different embedding models as needed, and all document processing was managed to ensure clean, high-quality input for embedding.

For querying, the pipeline used a RAG approach: user queries are embedded and matched against stored document vectors to emerge the most relevant content. Results were then reranked for relevance with intfloat/simlm-msmarco-reranker, before being passed to a prompt builder for answer generation, using GPT-4.1-mini. The prompt enforced strict grounding in the retrieved documents and includes inline HTML links to the original sources for transparency. This setup maintained high flexibility, allowing integration of various open-source and commercial models, ensuring reliable, context-aware responses grounded in cited evidence.

The web-based RAG pipeline was built for real-time content retrieval and generation, leveraging GPT-4.1-mini for answer synthesis. In this approach, live web searches were performed using SerpAPI, and content was extracted from URLs with LinkContentFetcher, allowing the pipeline to collect up-to-date information in direct response to user queries dynamically. Retrieved web pages were processed to extract clean text, titles, and source URLs, ensuring all content was structured consistently for downstream processing.

To ensure relevance and diversity, the pipeline used intfloat/simlm-msmarco-reranker to refine the top five document snippets before generating a response. The prompt builder then enforced strict grounding in the retrieved content, structuring answers in Markdown and citing sources with inline HTML links for transparency. If no sufficient evidence was found, the system returns an "inconclusive" statement, maintaining clarity and reliability. By combining live web search, RAG methods, and modular components, this pipeline delivered timely, well-sourced, and transparent answers grounded in the latest available information.

The agentic configuration combined the embedding pipeline, the GraphRAG pipeline, and web search as modular tools, allowing each to leverage its unique retrieval method for comprehensive and adaptable responses. Queries were processed through all three specialized pipelines, embedding-based internal document search, graph-based retrieval internal document search, and real-time web search, with outputs standardized for seamless multi-tool integration. Each pipeline-maintained modularity and processed its respective data sources independently, ensuring scalability and consistency within the agentic framework.

When a query was received, an agent-based RAG approach coordinated the three retrieval tools in parallel, synthesizing structured reasoning using insights from embeddings, the knowledge graph, and live web results. A customizable system prompt guided the agent and used GPT-4.1 [61] as the final answer generator, enforcing step-by-step logic and clear separation between internal and web-derived information. Responses were formatted into defined sections "thought process", internal search findings, web insights, and any conflicts identified between sources, with inline HTML links for source attribution. This design supports transparent, robust, and nuanced answers, making it ideal for complex domains such as policy research and e-government.

3.3. Triples Evaluation Configuration

The triples evaluation configuration is designed to provide a rigorous, transparent assessment of the accuracy and completeness of extracted knowledge triples. For each document, using GPT-4.1, the original text and its corresponding set of extracted triples are submitted to an evaluation workflow powered by a large language model with the prompt configuration in Table A2 in Appendix A. This process systematically reviewed each generated triple, determining if it was "Correct" (fully supported by the underlying text) or "Hallucinated" (not directly substantiated by the passage). Additionally, the LLM-based evaluator supplied concise, context-sensitive explanations for each classification, offering clear insights into why a triple is considered accurate or inaccurate.

In addition to validating existing triples, the configuration is attentive to recall by instructing the evaluator to identify any factual triples present in the text that were not captured by the extraction process, reporting these as "missed triples." This dual focus ensured that both over-generation (hallucinations) and under-generation (misses) were captured, providing a more holistic view of extraction performance.

The evaluation methodology emphasizes structure and consistency, requiring the LLM to return all results in a standardized, machine-readable format suitable for further analysis and benchmarking, with the prompt configuration presented in Table A1 in Appendix A. Moreover, detailed metadata, such as processing latency and input token counts, were logged for each evaluation, supporting robust comparisons of extraction faithfulness across large document sets.

By leveraging LLM-driven evaluation with transparent output requirements and comprehensive coverage of both precision and recall, the built LLM-based triples evaluation component configuration delivers a highly explainable and reproducible framework for diagnosing strengths and weaknesses in information graph creation. The approach is designed with the aim of being well-suited for complex domains where accuracy, completeness, and traceability are critical.

3.4. Simple RAG Faithfulness Assessment Configuration

To assess the factual reliability of the RAG pipelines, a dedicated faithfulness evaluation component was built and employed. This component is designed as a modular architecture that can interface with different language model providers. It supports multiple evaluation backends, allowing the use of state-of-the-art models from OpenAI (GPT-4.1) [61], Anthropic (Claude Sonnet-4.0) [62], and Google (Gemini-2.5-Pro) [63] to independently assess the grounding of each generated answer. First, for every generated answer, using GPT-4.1, the model was instructed as presented in Table A1 in the Appendix A, to extract factual statements from the generated answer.

For every question, the associated context passages and the list of extracted factual statements are passed to the evaluator. The evaluator then prompts the chosen model with standardized scoring instructions, with the prompt configuration, as presented in Table A4 (Appendix A), ensuring a consistent assessment regardless of the provider. Each statement is assigned a score based on whether it is explicitly supported by the retrieved evidence, unsupported, or marked as inconclusive. Special handling is applied for inconclusive cases, distinguishing between justified uncertainty, where the context truly lacks sufficient information, and unjustified uncertainty, where a definitive answer was in fact available.

Multiple evaluator models are employed intentionally, with each model independently assessing the faithfulness of a single pipeline. This approach leverages the complementary strengths of different providers, reducing the risk of evaluator bias and increasing the robustness of the evaluation. By incorporating diverse evaluation perspectives, it ensures a more reliable and model-agnostic comparison of pipeline performance.

The evaluation results include per-statement scores and justifications, along with an aggregated score representing the overall alignment between the answer and its supporting evidence. This architecture enables the interchangeable use of multiple evaluator models while preserving a unified output format, ensuring comparability across the embedding-based, graph-based, and web-based retrieval pipelines.

3.5. Agentic RAG Faithfulness Assessment Configuration

Moreover, we assessed the Agentic pipeline by building and using a custom LLM-based evaluator as a haystack component. The agent faithfulness evaluation configuration was designed to strictly assess the grounding, attribution, and conflict handling of answers produced by the agent-based RAG orchestration. This evaluation, similar to the standard RAG pipelines evaluator, was conducted using three independent evaluator backends, OpenAI's GPT-4.1 (gpt-4_1-2025-04-14), Anthropic's Claude Sonnet-4.0 (claude-sonnet-4-20250514), and Google's Gemini-2.5-Pro (gemini-2 5-pro), all configured with temperature 0 (and top_p of 0 for GPT) to ensure deterministic and reproducible results aimed at producing stable scoring outputs across repeated runs, enabling reliable benchmarking of agent performance.

Each evaluation instance was provided with the following inputs: the original query, the predicted answer generated by the agent, the embedding search context, the graph search context, the web search context, and a pre-extracted list of factual statements from the answer. The evaluator was explicitly instructed, as presented in Table A5 (Appendix A), not to extract statements on their own, but to analyze and score only the provided list, ensuring controlled and auditable scoring.

For each statement, the evaluator applied a standardized (configurable) scoring rubric (discrete, not continuous) tailored to multi-source RAG assessment. This rubric covered a broad set of conditions, as follows:

- Whether a statement was supported exclusively by the embedding search context, the graph search context, or by both (scored 1, 2, or 3, respectively).
- Whether a statement represented a conflict between internal knowledge and web search findings, and if so, whether this conflict was correctly identified and explicitly marked (score 4 for correct conflict identification, score 5 for incorrectly marked conflicts, and score 6–7 for unmarked conflicts).
- Whether a statement was unsupported by any context (score 0).
- Whether a statement originated from the web context and was properly attributed (score 9 for correct attribution, or −9 if the web attribution was missing).
- Whether the answer explicitly indicated the absence of conflict, where none existed (score 8).

Each score was accompanied by a concise justification, referencing the specific context(s) that either supported the statement or demonstrated its conflict. This ensured traceability and a clear link between each evaluation decision and the underlying evidence.

The evaluation prompt was carefully designed to enforce strict JSON output formatting, with one object per statement, maintaining the exact wording of each statement. This structure enabled automated aggregation of evaluation results and further analysis of agent behavior. By combining a deterministic evaluation setup, a detailed conflict-aware scoring rubric, and multi-model redundancy across three evaluator backends, the faithfulness evaluation provided a transparent and reproducible method to measure how well the agent grounded its answers in retrieved evidence and properly attributed its sources.

This configuration ensured that evaluation results not only highlighted factual correctness but also exposed weaknesses in conflict handling and source attribution, providing a fine-grained diagnostic framework for improving multi-source RAG agent reliability.

4. Results

The following section presents the results of a comprehensive evaluation of the simple RAG and Agentic pipelines, focusing on factual grounding, retrieval accuracy, and source attribution. Results start with the triple extraction component, which underpins the graph-based retrieval pipeline and was assessed for accuracy and completeness using a precision-recall framework. This is followed by a detailed comparison of the embedding-based, graph-based, and web-based RAG pipelines, evaluated independently by three leading large language models: GPT-4.1, Claude Sonnet-4.0, and Gemini 2.5 Pro. Each model assessed the factual alignment of generated responses with the retrieved context across pipelines. Finally, the section concludes with the evaluation of the agent-based RAG orchestration, which integrates all retrieval modes. This part examines how effectively the agent reasons over multi-source inputs, flags and resolves conflicts, and attributes evidence. The tables and narrative that follow detail the performance of each component, providing a grounded view of reliability and areas for improvement across the system.

4.1. *Triples Extraction Evaluation*

The triple extraction component was evaluated on a set of 36 documents, resulting in the assessment of 1591 extracted factual triples, while 1589 were classified as correct, and only 2 were identified as hallucinated, reflecting an extremely high precision of 0.999 as presented in Table 1. This indicates that the system almost never generates unsupported triples. Moreover, the evaluation identified 63 missed triples; factual information present in the text that was not captured during extraction, resulting in a recall score of 0.962. While slightly lower than precision, this still represents a strong ability to extract relevant facts comprehensively. Precision ensures reliability by minimizing hallucinations, ensuring that the factual information is captured, while high recall is critical when the goal is comprehensive coverage of official documents. Lastly, the combined F1 score of 0.980 demonstrates a high overall performance, balancing accuracy with completeness.

Table 1. Triple Extraction Evaluation Results.

Metric	Value
Documents Evaluated	36
Total Triples Evaluated	1591
Correct Triples	1589
Hallucinated Triples	2
Missed Triples	63
Precision	0.999
Recall	0.962
F1 Score	0.98

These results confirm that the triple extraction pipeline is highly reliable and exhibits minimal hallucination, making it a solid foundation for graph-based retrieval systems in domains like e-governance that demand traceable factual accuracy.

4.2. Simple RAG Pipelines Faithfulness Evaluation

The following subsection presents a comparative assessment of the three RAG pipelines, embedding-based, graph-based, and web-based, based on evaluations conducted by GPT-4.1, Claude Sonnet-4.0, and Gemini 2.5 Pro. Each model independently judged the factual grounding of responses, highlighting the relative reliability of each retrieval approach and revealing subtle differences in how each model interprets support, conflict, and uncertainty. The results below provide a breakdown of performance per model across all three retrieval pipelines.

Regarding GPT-4.1-based faithfulness evaluation (Table 2), all three simple RAG pipelines exhibited strong factual alignment, with consistently high support rates and minimal uncertainty. Specifically, the embedding-based pipeline performed reliably, with 97.7% of statements marked as supported and only 2.2% as unsupported. Moreover, the graph-based pipeline achieved slightly higher accuracy, with 98.4% of statements supported and only 1.5% unsupported, reflecting strong consistency in structured retrieval. Additionally, the web-based pipeline reached 99.9% support and only two unsupported cases, making it the most faithful pipeline in this evaluation. Across all modes, GPT-4.1 detected just four inconclusive cases, all correctly identified, highlighting strong confidence in the quality of evidence used across the pipelines.

Table 2. GPT-4.1 Evaluation Results Across Embedding, Graph, and Web Pipelines.

Statement Category	Embeddings	Graphs	Web	Statement Category
Supported	1995 (97.7%)	1638 (98.4%)	2508 (99.9%)	Supported
Unsupported	44 (2.2%)	25 (1.5%)	2 (0.1%)	Unsupported
Inconclusive correct	2 (0.1%)	2 (0.1%)	0 (0.0%)	Inconclusive correct
Inconclusive incorrect	0 (0.0%)	0 (0.0%)	0 (0.0%)	Inconclusive incorrect

Claude Sonnet-4.0 (Table 3) provided a consistent and moderately more conservative evaluation of the RAG pipelines. The embedding pipeline scored 97.0% supported and 2.9% unsupported statements, reflecting strong, but slightly reduced alignment compared to GPT-4.1. Additionally, in the graph pipeline, performance dipped slightly further, with 96.2% supported and 3.7% unsupported. In comparison, the web-based pipeline remained a strong performer under Claude's assessment, with 99.4% support and just 0.6% unsupported statements. Like GPT-4.1, Claude identified two correct inconclusive cases per pipeline and no incorrect ones. Overall, Claude's evaluation reinforces the relative strength of the web-based pipeline, while identifying slightly more gaps in internally retrieved content.

Table 3. Claude Sonnet-4.0 Evaluation Results Across Embedding, Graph, and Web Pipelines.

Statement Category	Embeddings	Graphs	Web	Statement Category
Supported	1980 (97.0%)	1602 (96.2%)	2495 (99.4%)	Supported
Unsupported	59 (2.9%)	61 (3.7%)	15 (0.6%)	Unsupported
Inconclusive correct	2 (0.1%)	2 (0.1%)	0 (0.0%)	Inconclusive correct
Inconclusive incorrect	0 (0.0%)	0 (0.0%)	0 (0.0%)	Inconclusive incorrect

Gemini 2.5 Pro (Table 4) exhibited more selective evaluation patterns across the simple RAG pipelines, with lower support rates and higher identification of unsupported statements. Based on the results, the embedding-based pipeline reached 95.9% support, with 4.0% of statements marked as unsupported, while the graph-based pipeline showed a similar trend, with 95.8% support and 4.1% unsupported. Moreover, the web-based

pipeline still performed well, achieving 98.4% supporting statements and 1.6% unsupported. Gemini identified two correct inconclusive cases in the internal pipelines and none in the web mode, with no incorrect inconclusive reported. This suggests that while all pipelines maintained high faithfulness, Gemini applied stricter standards, especially to non-web-based retrievals.

Table 4. Gemini 2.5 Pro Evaluation Results Across Embedding, Graph, and Web Pipelines.

Statement Category	Embeddings	Graphs	Web	Statement Category
Supported	1958 (95.9%)	1595 (95.8%)	2469 (98.4%)	Supported
Unsupported	81 (4.0%)	68 (4.1%)	41 (1.6%)	Unsupported
Inconclusive correct	2 (0.1%)	2 (0.1%)	0 (0.0%)	Inconclusive correct
Inconclusive incorrect	0 (0.0%)	0 (0.0%)	0 (0.0%)	Inconclusive incorrect

4.3. *Agentic RAG Faithfulness Evaluation*

The agent-based RAG orchestration was evaluated across multiple evidence types and conflict-handling scenarios by three top-tier language models. Across all evaluators, the results reveal strong grounding fidelity based on individual pipelines' outputs, robust multi-source integration, and effective conflict handling, with slight variation in sensitivity between models.

Internal Evidence Use was prominent: the majority of statements were supported by internal sources, either embeddings, graphs, or both. GPT-4.1 rated the highest proportion as supported by both internal sources (36.5%), followed by Claude Sonnet-4.0 (32.8%) and Gemini 2.5 Pro (28.5%). Embedding-only and graph-only supports remained relatively low across all three, confirming balanced multi-source utilization (Table 5).

Table 5. Agentic Evaluation—Statement Classification by Evaluator.

Statement Category	GPT-4.1	Claude Sonnet-4.0	Gemini 2.5 Pro
Embedding Only	146 (7.9%)	133 (7.2%)	115 (6.2%)
Graph Only	79 (4.3%)	83 (4.5%)	125 (6.8%)
Both Internal Sources	672 (36.5%)	604 (32.8%)	524 (28.5%)
Conflict (Flagged & Correct)	23 (1.2%)	32 (1.7%)	47 (2.6%)
Conflict (Flagged but Incorrect)	0 (0.0%)	1 (0.1%)	2 (0.1%)
Conflict (Web/Internal, Not Flagged)	1 (0.1%)	0 (0.0%)	3 (0.2%)
Conflict Not Acknowledged	0 (0.0%)	0 (0.0%)	1 (0.1%)
Consensus (No Conflict)	215 (11.7%)	210 (11.4%)	191 (10.4%)
Web Supported (Marked)	704 (38.2%)	711 (38.6%)	658 (35.7%)
Web Supported (Unmarked)	0 (0.0%)	60 (3.3%)	135 (7.3%)
Unsupported	1 (0.1%)	7 (0.4%)	40 (2.2%)
Missing	0 (0.0%)	0 (0.0%)	0 (0.0%)

Web-based support was also frequently recognized. All evaluators flagged around 35–39% of statements as supported by web evidence. GPT-4.1 showed perfect attribution with no unmarked web-supported statements, while Gemini marked a notable 7.3% as web-supported but unmarked, suggesting a potential attribution issue in that context. Claude reported 3.3% unmarked.

Conflict handling was largely accurate, but with some divergence. Claude and Gemini identified more correctly flagged conflicts (1.7% and 2.6%, respectively) than GPT (1.2%), but Gemini also surfaced a small number of unflagged or unacknowledged conflicts, indicating stricter scrutiny. Only Gemini found a case of unacknowledged conflict.

Unsupported statements were rare. GPT flagged only one (0.1%), Claude seven (0.4%), and Gemini forty (2.2%), again suggesting that Gemini applies more rigorous standards in evaluating factual alignment.

5. Discussion

To assess the factual reliability of each RAG pipeline for e-governance use cases, we analyzed the performance of embedding-based, graph-based, web-based, and agentic retrieval strategies using evaluations conducted by three top-tier language models: GPT-4.1, Claude Sonnet-4.0, and Gemini 2.5 Pro. The evaluation focused on question-level fidelity, particularly emphasizing the rate of fully supported answers evidence. This was the most meaningful metric in contexts demanding high accountability such as e-government service delivery and policy decision support.

As presented in Table 6, the embedding-based pipeline produced fully supported answers in 85.0% of the 120 evaluated cases, whereas the graph-based pipeline achieved 90.0%. The difference becomes particularly relevant when considering that graph-based indexing is designed for structured, traceable fact storage, and is thus well-suited to governance-related tasks such as benefits eligibility, policy audits, or regulation retrieval, where factual completeness and low hallucination rates are paramount. The same table shows that hallucinations appeared in 13.3% of embedding queries versus only 8.3% in the graph pipeline, supporting the observation that embeddings, while flexible, are more prone to surface semantically relevant yet unsupported material.

Table 6. GPT-4.1 Evaluation Question Type Coverage.

Metric	Embedding	Graph	Web	Agentic
Total Questions Evaluated	120	120	120	120
With ≥1 Supported Statement	118 (98.3%)	116 (96.7%)	120 (100.0%)	119 (99.2%)
With ≥1 Unsupported Statement	16 (13.3%)	10 (8.3%)	2 (1.7%)	1 (0.8%)
With ≥1 Inconclusive (Correct) Statement	2 (1.7%)	2 (1.7%)	0 (0.0%)	0 (0.0%)
With ≥1 Inconclusive (Incorrect) Statement	0 (0.0%)	0 (0.0%)	0 (0.0%)	0 (0.0%)
Fully Supported Answers (All statements = 1)	102 (85.0%)	108 (90.0%)	118 (98.3%)	119 (99.2%)
With Any Hallucination	16 (13.3%)	10 (8.3%)	2 (1.7%)	1 (0.8%)

The same pattern is confirmed in Table 7, where the graph pipeline slightly outperforms embeddings again, producing 80.8% fully supported answers compared to 80.0%. Claude's more conservative judgment also raises the hallucination rates for both pipelines, but the relative gap remains.

Table 7. Claude Sonnet-4.0 Evaluation Question Type Coverage.

Metric	Embedding	Graph	Web	Agentic
Total Questions Evaluated	120	120	120	120
With ≥1 Supported Statement	118 (98.3%)	116 (96.7%)	120 (100.0%)	120 (100.0%)
With ≥1 Unsupported Statement	22 (18.3%)	21 (17.5%)	4 (3.3%)	5 (4.2%)
With ≥1 Inconclusive (Correct) Statement	2 (1.7%)	2 (1.7%)	0 (0.0%)	0 (0.0%)
With ≥1 Inconclusive (Incorrect) Statement	0 (0.0%)	0 (0.0%)	0 (0.0%)	0 (0.0%)
Fully Supported Answers (All statements = 1)	96 (80.0%)	97 (80.8%)	116 (96.7%)	115 (95.8%)
With Any Hallucination	22 (18.3%)	21 (17.5%)	4 (3.3%)	5 (4.2%)

Similarly, Table 8 further supports this finding, showing 79.2% fully supported answers for graph-based queries compared to 75.8% for embeddings. Across all models, then, the graph pipeline demonstrates more consistent grounding, which is especially relevant for applications requiring strict traceability of public-sector knowledge graphs, such as legislation mapping or procurement tracking.

Table 8. Gemini 2.5 Pro Evaluation Question Type Coverage.

Metric	Embedding	Graph	Web	Agentic
Total Questions Evaluated	120	120	120	120
With ≥1 Supported Statement	118 (98.3%)	115 (95.8%)	120 (100.0%)	120 (100.0%)
With ≥1 Unsupported Statement	27 (22.5%)	23 (19.2%)	17 (14.2%)	19 (15.8%)
With ≥1 Inconclusive (Correct) Statement	2 (1.7%)	2 (1.7%)	0 (0.0%)	0 (0.0%)
With ≥1 Inconclusive (Incorrect) Statement	0 (0.0%)	0 (0.0%)	0 (0.0%)	0 (0.0%)
Fully Supported Answers (All statements = 1)	91 (75.8%)	95 (79.2%)	103 (85.8%)	101 (84.2%)
With Any Hallucination	27 (22.5%)	23 (19.2%)	17 (14.2%)	19 (15.8%)

Web-based RAG emerged as the most faithful among standalone pipelines, achieving the highest rate of fully supported answers across all evaluators, 98.3% under GPT-4.1, 96.7% under Claude, and 85.8% under Gemini. These results reflect the benefits of real-time retrieval and effective synthesis for answering queries tied to dynamic public information, such as election updates or policy changes.

However, despite low hallucination rates, the credibility of retrieved web sources remains a critical factor, while, in contrast to internal documents, which are inherently trustworthy, web content may introduce inaccuracies if not properly sourced. Therefore, even when factual alignment appears strong, the overall accuracy of the answer still depends on the reliability of the underlying sources.

Moreover, it is critical that attribution issues, such as missing web citations or unmarked content conflicts, are carefully examined. While this study did not evaluate the credibility of web domains, it is worth noting that information from non-accredited or unverified publishers can potentially introduce inaccuracies. In comparison, when using internal documents, identifying and addressing potential conflicts within the context retrieved can help mitigate these risks and enhance trust in the final output.

The agentic RAG pipeline, which integrates all three retrieval modes (embedding, graph, and web), demonstrated the highest faithfulness scores in evaluation. However, this result is not directly comparable to the standalone pipelines, because the agent was not grounded in raw documents; instead, it operated on the already-generated outputs of the embedding, graph, and web systems. In practice, this means the agent's faithfulness reflects a second-layer verification task, assessing how effectively it synthesizes, reconciles, and preserves factual content distilled by the base pipelines, rather than performing first-order retrieval grounding itself.

According to GPT-4.1's coverage results, 119 out of 120 answers (99.2%) were fully supported, with only one hallucinated case. Claude's results also show strong reliability, with 95.8% of agentic answers fully supported. Even Gemini's stricter evaluation confirmed the robustness of the agentic strategy, with 84.2% fully supported answers, marginally above the web-only pipeline and ahead of embedding and graph-based retrievals. These outcomes are detailed in the agentic column of each model's table's results, reinforcing the benefit of multi-source evidence fusion in complex reasoning tasks.

What distinguishes the agentic pipeline is its architectural design, which explicitly separates evidence sources and applies step-by-step logic for synthesis, allowing it to identify and manage conflicts, attribute sources correctly, and maximize contextual alignment. This is especially critical in governance applications involving multi-agency data, evolving legislation, or public transparency initiatives, where conflicting or incomplete information must be overseen responsibly.

Across pipelines, the evaluators operated over markedly different token volumes, which shape how comparative results should be interpreted, as presented in Table 9. The embedding, graph, and web-based pipelines each supplied full retrieved evidence to the LLM judges, averaging 7063, 11,029, and 8628 input tokens per evaluation, respectively.

Table 9. Average Input Tokens per Evaluation Prompt Across Pipelines (GPT-4.1 tokenizer).

Pipeline/Evaluation Type	Avg Prompt Tokens
Embeddings	7063.38
Graph	11,029.46
Web	8627.98
Agentic	4891.21

The agentic evaluation was considerably more compact at 4891 tokens, not due to reduced context depth, but because the agent's evaluation prompt did not include raw documents; instead, it passed the generated answers produced by the individual pipelines, meaning the evaluator assessed an abstraction layer above the source retrieval. This positions the agentic scoring process as second-order faithfulness verification, where the model is judged on how well it maintains factual integrity when summarizing, merging, and reconciling evidence already distilled by embedding, graph, and web retrieval streams.

Importantly, all three evaluators, GPT-4.1, Claude Sonnet-4.0, and Gemini 2.5 Pro, were presented with the same input prompt per question, ensuring that differences in scoring reflect evaluative behavior, rather than variation in instructions or evidence exposure. Additionally, token estimates for all augmented prompts were computed using the GPT-4.1 tokenizer, meaning absolute values reflect that encoding standard and should be interpreted with this baseline in mind, particularly given that the agentic configuration is assessed at a more distilled knowledge layer rather than directly against full document context.

Lastly, the evaluation results captured across all evaluators confirm that the graph-based pipeline offers a measurable advantage over embeddings in internal document retrieval tasks, particularly in terms of producing fully supported answers and minimizing hallucination. The web-based pipeline is accurate for up-to-date factual coverage and real-world responsiveness, especially by accredited domains retrieval, while the agentic configuration delivers a combination of those pipelines, making it a promising candidate for large-scale, high-stakes e-governance deployments, where different architects and sources are combined. These findings underscore the importance of selecting pipeline architectures aligned with the fidelity, traceability, and recency demands of specific public-sector use cases.

Limitations and Threats to Validity

While this study controls three independent LLMs (GPT-4.1, Claude Sonnet-4.0, and Gemini 2.5 Pro) as automated evaluators, it does not yet incorporate a human-annotated gold standard for calibration. Establishing such a baseline would enable quantitative comparison of LLM judgments with human agreement levels and help validate their reliability in detecting hallucinations and redundancy. Although large-scale manual annotation was beyond the practical scope of the current work, we performed spot-checks on a random sample of evaluation outputs to ensure that model-judged labels aligned with human expectations. Nevertheless, future extensions of this framework will include a systematic human validation study using dual independent annotators and agreement measurement, in order to strengthen external validity and provide a reference standard for automated faithfulness evaluation.

The experiments presented in this study are intended primarily to demonstrate the proposed framework rather than to establish a benchmark dataset or comprehensive empirical evaluation. The set of 120 questions used for illustration was selected to cover representative topics within the e-government domain and serves as an example of how the framework can be applied in practice. The main contribution lies in the modular design and open availability of the framework itself; therefore, users can readily reproduce the workflow using their own question sets or domain data.

This study primarily aims to propose and demonstrate a modular framework for faithfulness evaluation in RAG systems, rather than to perform formal statistical hypothesis testing. The reported precision, recall, and fully supported answer rates serve as illustrative metrics to showcase how the framework can operate comparative analysis across different RAG architectures. Given the exploratory and methodological focus, the present version does not include formal significance testing or bootstrapped confidence intervals. The dataset size (36 press releases) was chosen to provide representative coverage of the e-government domain sufficient for framework validation. To mitigate evaluator variance, we report aggregated averages across three independent LLM judges, offering a stability check for the framework's evaluation layer. Future work will extend this framework to larger datasets and include statistical testing (e.g., bootstrapped confidence intervals and paired significance tests) to support more generalizable inferences.

A potential limitation of this study arises from evaluator circularity, as LLMs were used both as content generators and as evaluators of faithfulness. For example, different models could apply slightly different interpretive heuristics when judging "support" or "redundancy." Future work will include human-in-the-loop calibration to empirically assess evaluator bias by comparing human judgments with each LLM family's scoring trends, thereby quantifying the extent of circularity, and improving interpretive robustness.

6. Conclusions and Future Work

The comparative evaluation of the three standalone RAG pipelines on e-governance data, embedding-based, graph-based, and web-based pipelines, demonstrates distinct strengths. Across all evaluators, the graph-based pipeline consistently outperformed embeddings in internal document retrieval, delivering higher rates of fully supported answers and fewer hallucinations. This superiority is particularly evident under GPT-4.1 (90.0% vs. 85.0% fully supported), Claude (80.8% vs. 80.0%), and Gemini (79.2% vs. 75.8%), as shown in Tables 6–8. Starting with the graph pipeline, its advantage is derived from its ability to store and retrieve structured, traceable knowledge, making it well-suited for applications where factual completeness and verifiable provenance are essential, such as policy audits, legislative mapping, and regulatory compliance checks.

Continuing with the embedding-based pipeline, while showing slightly lower factual grounding than the graph approach, it offers significant advantages in speed, scalability, and operational cost. Embedding-based indexing and retrieval are computationally lighter, allowing for near-instantaneous query responses and efficient processing of large, diverse document collections. This makes it highly suitable for governance scenarios requiring rapid turnaround times and broad semantic coverage, such as citizen inquiry handling, public information portals, or early-stage policy research where comprehensiveness and timeliness outweigh the need for absolute traceability.

The web-based pipeline emerged as a strong performer retrieving content from the web in real-time, excelling in scenarios that demand live access to changing information. It achieved the highest rates of fully supported answers among the three pipelines, 98.3% under GPT-4.1, 96.7% under Claude, and 85.8% under Gemini, but its reliability strongly relies on the credibility of the retrieved sources. Unlike internal documents, web content can introduce inaccuracies if not drawn from accredited domains or trusted publishers. Even with low hallucination rates, attribution must be transparent, and issues such as missing web citations or unmarked content conflicts should be proactively addressed to sustain trust in outputs.

Moreover, by integrating the structured precision of graph retrieval, the flexibility and speed of embeddings, and the timeliness of web search, the agentic pipeline maintained strong factual support across evaluators, being 99.2% fully supported under GPT-4.1, 95.8% under Claude, and 84.2% under Gemini, with minimal hallucinations. Its architectural separation of evidence sources, explicit conflict handling, and step-by-step reasoning make it especially resilient for governance applications involving multi-agency datasets, evolving regulations, or situations where conflicting information must be responsibly reconciled. However, we should highlight the importance of the valid output of the tools (simple RAGs), the synthesized answer relies on them.

Moreover, it should be highlighted that the results reflect the specific pipeline configurations, indexing strategies, and prompting parameters used in this study. Performance may vary under different implementations, datasets, or evaluation settings, meaning that while the relative patterns are instructive, the absolute scores are tied to the evaluated setup.

Taken together, these results underscore that no single retrieval strategy is universally optimal; instead, pipeline selection should be driven by the faithfulness, traceability, and recency requirements of the target application. Graph-based retrieval offers the most dependable grounding for authoritative internal records. Embedding-based retrieval provides a good, faster, and more cost-efficient option, ideal for high-volume, low-latency use cases, but with a trade-off in precision and traceability. Web-based retrieval delivers unmatched responsiveness for dynamic information needs but demands strict source accreditation and attribution controls.

Agentic orchestration achieved high overall accuracy, reflecting its capacity to integrate and reason over the outputs of multiple specialized RAG pipelines. In this setup, however, its performance cannot be interpreted or compared independently of those pipelines as presented in Tables 6–8, since the agent's grounding is based on their generated answers rather than on the original documents.

Based on the presented results, agentic reliability reflects a second-order assessment, faithfulness to already-processed knowledge, rather than a direct evaluation against source material. This underscores the critical role of well-calibrated and domain-aligned base pipelines in ensuring factual integrity and interpretability within the orchestration process. Therefore, future work should extend evaluation to compare agent outputs against raw source material, rather than only pipeline-generated summaries.

Beyond its accuracy, the Agentic RAG framework offers enhanced source attribution by explicitly linking final responses to their originating pipelines, thereby improving traceability and transparency. Moreover, by operating on condensed, pipeline-level outputs rather than the entire raw retrieval context, it effectively reduces the context window required for reasoning, an advantage for efficiency and scalability in large-scale deployments.

Nevertheless, deploying Agentic systems in real-world e-governance scenarios presents notable challenges. Their multi-tool orchestration and iterative reasoning structures demand greater computational resources and longer inference times, while reliance on external APIs introduces potential latency, rate-limit, and data-privacy concerns. Consequently, their adoption must align with infrastructure readiness, governance standards, and ethical safeguards. Future research should focus on optimizing these architectures through techniques such as caching, model distillation, and hybrid offline–online retrieval setups to enhance their efficiency, reliability, and suitability for trustworthy large-scale deployment.

Future Work

Future research will focus on expanding the proposed evaluation framework to additional retrieval modalities and domains beyond the current structured settings. While this study primarily benchmarks hallucination and redundancy detection in simple and agentic GraphRAG systems, future work should explore multi-modal agentic pipelines that integrate textual, tabular, and visual knowledge sources, where attribution and faithfulness assessment become even more challenging. Incorporating temporal and streaming data could also enable dynamic provenance tracking in real-time decision-making scenarios, such as policy monitoring or crisis management, where context evolves continuously.

The present study utilizes 36 official press releases from the EC's Press Corner, distributed across four key policy domains. The current results should therefore be interpreted as a focused case study aimed at demonstrating the feasibility and diagnostic value of the proposed faithfulness evaluation framework. To further enhance robustness and generalizability, future work will expand the dataset to include a larger corpus of multilingual and multimodal policy documents, accompanied by per-topic performance analysis and sample complexity evaluation. This will allow more detailed insight into domain-specific behavior and potential scaling effects of Agentic RAG architectures.

Another direction involves refining tool-specific attribution mechanisms to support more granular provenance at the claim level. This would allow evaluators not only to detect hallucinations and redundancies but also to determine the exact retrieval path and source tool responsible for each statement, enabling targeted improvements in retrieval strategies. Enhancing the interoperability of the evaluation framework with existing LLM-as-a-Judge systems, such as GraphEval or SELF-RAG, could also facilitate broader adoption and standardization across research communities.

Future research will extend the present framework in several focused directions. First, we aim to expand the dataset to include multilingual and multimodal e-Governance documents for broader generalization. Second, future research will focus on extending the proposed framework to include a detailed and systematic qualitative analysis of hallucination types and their underlying causes. This will involve categorizing statement-level errors, examining linguistic and retrieval-related factors contributing to hallucinations, and validating evaluator judgments through human annotation. Third, optimization strategies, such as model distillation, caching, and tool selection heuristics will be explored to reduce computational cost and latency in agentic RAG pipelines. These directions represent practical and achievable next steps to enhance scalability, trustworthiness, and real-world applicability of the proposed framework.

Author Contributions: Conceptualization: G.P., M.M. and V.S.; methodology: G.P. and M.M.; software: G.P.; validation: M.M., C.T., G.P., I.M. and V.S.; formal analysis: V.S. and G.P.; investigation: G.P. and V.S.; resources: M.M., C.T., G.P., I.M. and V.S.; data curation: M.M., G.P. and V.S.; writing—original draft preparation: G.P. and V.S.; writing—review and editing: M.M., C.T., G.P., I.M. and V.S.; visualization: G.P. and V.S.; supervision: C.T. and M.M.; project administration: M.M., C.T., V.S. and G.P. All authors have read and agreed to the published version of the manuscript.

Funding: This research received no external funding.

Institutional Review Board Statement: Not applicable.

Informed Consent Statement: Not applicable.

Data Availability Statement: The original data presented in the study are openly available on GitHub at https://github.com/gpapageorgiouedu/Evaluating-Faithfulness-in-Agentic-RAG-Systems-for-e-Governance-applications-LLM-Based (accessed on 9 September 2025).

Conflicts of Interest: The authors declare no conflicts of interest.

Appendix A

The appendix includes prompts and system configurations used for indexing and querying procedures in the framework's construction.

Table A1. Knowledge Graph Triples Extractor.

Subcomponent	Configuration
System Prompt	You are an information extraction assistant. You are an expert in European Union's news, policies, laws, and actions. Extract all factual knowledge triples from the text in a structured format. Return the results as a JSON list where each item is an object with the keys: 'head', 'head_type', 'relation', 'tail', 'tail_type'. Guidelines: Resolve vague pronouns (like 'I', 'we', 'they', 'he/she') to actual entities based on context. Use the standard full format, even when abbreviations are used in the text. For example, when 'EU' is used, write it as 'European Union'. Use the standard full format for names, even if the full name is not used entirely in a specific sentence. If provide information please include the full context on triples. Maintain consistency: refer to entities by their full and most complete identifiers. Use concise relation phrases written in UPPER_SNAKE_CASE. Avoid vague, incomplete, or uninformative triples. Use full context to provide informative and comprehensive triples. Return only the JSON list of objects. Do not include any explanations, additional knowledge, or markdown. If an entity type is unclear, make a reasonable guess or use a general type like 'Entity'.

Table A2. Knowledge Graph Triples Evaluator.

Subcomponent	Configuration
System Prompt	You are a rigorous information extraction evaluator. You receive a passage of text and a set of knowledge triples. For each triple, determine if it is 'Correct' (supported by the text) or 'Hallucinated' (not fully supported by the text). Give a brief explanation for each. If there are factual triples in the text that are missing from the set, list them as 'missed_triples'. Return your evaluation as JSON in this format: {'results': [{'triple': {...}, 'evaluation': 'Correct' or 'Hallucinated', 'explanation': '...'}], 'missed_triples': [{...}, ...]}"

Table A3. Statements Extractor.

Subcomponent	Configuration

System Prompt	You will receive a question and a LLM-based generated answer.
	Your task is to break the generated answer into a list of factual statements by splitting it into sentences, leaving each sentence unchanged and exactly as it appears in the generated answer, only replace double with single quotes if double quotes are present.
	Do not rewrite, paraphrase, or alter the sentences in any way.
	Do not include the Disclaimer: This is AI generated content in the statements.
	Do not include sentences like For more detailed information, since there are no factual statements.
	Only use information from the answer itself (do NOT use any external knowledge or assumptions).
	
	All JSON keys and string values must use double quotes (").
	If it is required to quote something inside a statement, use ONLY single quotes (').
	Output only a valid JSON object with the key 'statements', which is a list of strings. Do not add any text before or after the JSON.
	
	Example:
	{
	"statements": [
	"The Clean Industrial Deal is designed to reduce industrial emissions.",
	"Affordable energy is the foundation of competitiveness."
	]
	}
	
	If the answer contains no factual statements, output an empty list.

Table A4. Simple RAG Faithfulness Evaluator.

Subcomponent	Configuration

System Prompt	You are evaluating the faithfulness of a list of factual statements with respect to a provided context.
	
	You will receive:
	-a question
	-a context: a set of retrieved documents or passages used to generate the answer
	-a list of factual statements (already extracted from a predicted answer)
	
	TASK:
	For each statement in the list, output an object with:
	-"statement": the statement, **repeated exactly as given, with no modifications**
	-"score": (see below)
	-"justification": a short explanation
	
	Scoring:
	a. If the statement is clearly supported by the context → score = 1
	b. If the statement is not supported or the context is silent → score = 0
	c. If the statement includes or is equivalent to 'Final Answer: inconclusive' AND this is justified by the lack of support in context → score = −1
	d. If the statement includes or is equivalent to 'Final Answer: inconclusive' BUT the context does contain sufficient information to answer the question → score = −2
	
	Formatting instructions:
	-Output a single valid JSON block, and **do not add any text before or after**.
	-Format the output as follows:
	{
	"evaluations": [
	{"statement": "...", "score": 1, "justification": "..."},
	{"statement": "...", "score": 1, "justification": "..."}
	]
	}
	-There MUST be one object for each statement, in the same order as given, and each 'statement' field must match the input exactly.
	-If you cannot score a statement, set "score": null and "justification": "MISSING".
	
	JSON Output Format instructions:
	-**All JSON keys and string values must use double quotes (").**
	-**If you must quote text inside any JSON string value (in either statement or justification), you MUST use single quotes ('), NEVER double quotes ("). Double quotes are reserved for JSON formatting only.**
	-**This also applies for nested quoting; even if you are quoting a phrase inside another quoted phrase. Use single quotes for all levels of quoting/referencing in the justifications.**
	-Do NOT add any commentary, markdown, or preamble; output only **VALID** JSON as shown above.
	
	Assess and score **every** statement.
	
	You should ALWAYS output the same number of statements given, along with their assessment.
	Be sure that you did not miss any given statement.

Table A5. Agentic RAG Evaluator.

Subcomponent	Configuration
System Prompt	You are evaluating the faithfulness and attribution of a list of factual statements, given specific tool contexts and a predicted answer from an agent. You will receive: -a question -embedding_search_context: information from internal knowledge from the embedding_search tool -graph_search_context: information from internal knowledge from the graph_search tool -web_search_context: information retrieved from the web_search tool -a predicted answer from an agent -a list of factual statements (already extracted from the answer; do NOT extract statements yourself) The predicted answer you receive SHOULD include: -an Internal Search Answer section, produced with embedding_search and graph_search tool results -a Web Search Insights section, produced with web_search tool results Your task is: For each provided statement, output an object with: -"statement": the statement, **repeated exactly as given, with no modifications** -"score": (see detailed rubric below) -"justification": a short explanation citing which context(s) support the statement and why that score applies Scoring rubric: a. If the statement is supported ONLY by embedding_search_context: → score = 1 justification: reference the specific content from embedding_search_context that supports the statement b. If the statement is supported ONLY by graph_search_context: → score = 2 justification: reference the specific content from graph_search_context that supports the statement c. If the statement is supported by BOTH embedding_search_context and graph_search_context: → score = 3 justification: show support from both contexts and explain how they jointly confirm the statement d. If the statement is a conflict statement AND is correctly identified because of conflict information from embedding_search_context or graph_search_context compared with web_search_context AND is clearly indicated/marked as conflict: → score = 4 justification: describe the conflict and how the answer clearly signals it as such e. If the statement is a conflict statement BUT is incorrectly identified (because there is no actual conflict in the contexts) AND is clearly indicated/marked as conflict: → score = 5 justification: note the false marking of conflict and explain how the sources do not disagree f. If the statement is supported by embedding_search_context or graph_search_context, but there is a conflict with web_search_context AND it is NOT clearly indicated/marked as conflict: → score = 6 justification: explain the internal vs. web disagreement and the lack of conflict signaling in the answer g. If there is a conflict between internal (embedding or graph) and web context BUT it is NOT clearly indicated/marked as conflict: → score = 7 justification: highlight the missed conflict and explain how it should have been addressed

Table A5. *Cont.*

Subcomponent	Configuration

System Prompt	h. If the statement reflects an explicit indication that no conflicts were found:
	→ score = 8
	justification: explain how the answer claims consensus and the contexts indeed show agreement
	
	i. If the statement is not supported by any context:
	→ score = 0
	justification: explain the absence of supporting evidence in all contexts
	
	j. If the statement is supported by web_search_context AND is clearly indicated/marked as coming from web search in the answer:
	→ score = 9
	justification: show the web-based support and cite how it was properly marked as web-sourced
	
	k. If the statement is supported by web_search_context BUT is NOT clearly indicated/marked as from the web:
	→ score = −9
	justification: provide evidence from the web_search_context and explain how the answer failed to mark it as web-sourced
	
	Formatting instructions:
	-Output a single valid JSON block, and **do not add any text before or after**.
	-Format the output as follows:
	{
	"evaluations": [
	{"statement": "...", "score": 1, "justification": "..."},
	{"statement": "...", "score": 2, "justification": "..."}
	]
	}
	-There MUST be one object for each statement, in the same order as given, and each 'statement' field must match the input exactly.
	-If you cannot score a statement, set "score": null and "justification": "MISSING".
	-**All JSON keys and string values must use double quotes (").**
	-**If you need to quote text inside a string value, use only single quotes (').**
	-Assess and score **every** statement.
	-Do NOT add any commentary, markdown, or preamble; output only valid JSON as shown above.

References

1. Lewis, P.; Perez, E.; Piktus, A.; Petroni, F.; Karpukhin, V.; Goyal, N.; Küttler, H.; Lewis, M.; Yih, W.-T.; Rocktäschel, T.; et al. Retrieval-Augmented Generation for Knowledge-Intensive NLP Tasks. In Proceedings of the 34th Conference on Neural Information Processing Systems, Online Conference, 6–12 December 2020.
2. Wallat, J.; Heuss, M.; de Rijke, M.; Anand, A. Correctness Is Not Faithfulness in RAG Attributions. *arXiv* **2024**, arXiv:2412.18004. [CrossRef]
3. Malin, B.; Kalganova, T.; Boulgouris, N. A Review of Faithfulness Metrics for Hallucination Assessment in Large Language Models. *IEEE J. Sel. Top. Signal Process.* 2025; *Early Access*. [CrossRef]
4. Abo El-Enen, M.; Saad, S.; Nazmy, T. A Survey on Retrieval-Augmentation Generation (RAG) Models for Healthcare Applications. *Neural Comput. Appl.* **2025**, *37*, 28191–28267. [CrossRef]
5. Arslan, M.B.; Ahmad, M.; Datta, R.; Majumdar, A.; Rao, A.R. Retrieval-Augmented Generation for Large Language Models: A Survey of Applications and Methods. *Procedia Comput. Sci.* **2024**, *232*, 899–906. [CrossRef]
6. Tang, X.; Wang, Y.; Hu, K.; Xu, R.; Li, C.; Sun, W.; Li, J.; Xie, S. SSFO: Self-Supervised Faithfulness Optimization for Retrieval-Augmented Generation. *arXiv* **2025**, arXiv:2508.17225.
7. He, X.; Tian, Y.; Sun, Y.; Chawla, N.V.; Laurent, T.; Lecun, Y.; Bresson, X.; Hooi, B. G-Retriever: Retrieval-Augmented Generation for Textual Graph Understanding and Question Answering. *Adv. Neural Inf. Process. Syst.* **2025**, *37*, 132876–132907.
8. Yang, R.; Yang, B.; Feng, A.; Ouyang, S.; Blum, M.; She, T.; Jiang, Y.; Lecue, F.; Lu, J.; Li, I. Graphusion: A RAG Framework for Knowledge Graph Construction with a Global Perspective. *arXiv* **2024**, arXiv:2410.17600. [CrossRef]

9. Procko, T.T.; Ochoa, O. Graph Retrieval-Augmented Generation for Large Language Models: A Survey. In Proceedings of the 2024 Conference on AI, Science, Engineering, and Technology, Laguna Hills, CA, USA, 30 September–2 October 2024; pp. 166–169. [CrossRef]
10. Barry, M.; Caillaut, G.; Halftermeyer, P.; Qader, R.; Mouayad, M.; Cariolaro, D.; Le Deit, F.; Gesnouin, J. GraphRAG: Leveraging Graph-Based Efficiency to Minimize Hallucinations in LLM-Driven RAG for Finance Data. In Proceedings of the Workshop on Generative AI and Knowledge Graphs (GenAIK), 31st International Conference on Computational Linguistics (COLING 2025), Abu Dhabi, United Arab Emirates, 19 January 2025; pp. 54–65. Available online: https://aclanthology.org/2025.genaik-1.6 (accessed on 2 September 2025).
11. Kong, H.; Wang, Z.; Wang, C.; Ma, Z.; Dong, N. HuixiangDou2: A Robustly Optimized GraphRAG Approach. *arXiv* **2025**, arXiv:2503.06474.
12. Li, M.; Miao, S.; Li, P. Simple Is Effective: The Roles of Graphs and Large Language Models in Knowledge-Graph-Based Retrieval-Augmented Generation. *arXiv* **2024**, arXiv:2410.20724.
13. Zhang, Q.; Chen, S.; Bei, Y.; Yuan, Z.; Zhou, H.; Hong, Z.; Dong, J.; Chen, H.; Chang, Y.; Huang, X. A Survey of Graph Retrieval-Augmented Generation for Customized Large Language Models. *arXiv* **2025**, arXiv:2501.13958.
14. Papageorgiou, G.; Sarlis, V.; Maragoudakis, M.; Tjortjis, C. A Multimodal Framework Embedding Retrieval-Augmented Generation with MLLMs for Eurobarometer Data. *AI* **2025**, *6*, 50. [CrossRef]
15. Evangelista, E.; Ruba, F.; Bukhari, S.M.S.; Nazir, A.; Sharma, R.S. Developing a GraphRAG-Enabled Local-LLM for Gestational Diabetes Mellitus. *medRxiv* **2025**. [CrossRef]
16. Mosolygo, B.; Fatemi, B.; Rabbi, F.; Opdahl, A.L. Evaluating GraphRAG's Role in Improving Contextual Understanding of News in Newsrooms. *medRxiv* **2025**. [CrossRef]
17. Liang, J.; Wang, Y.; Li, C.; Zhu, R.; Jiang, T.; Gong, N.; Wang, T. GraphRAG under Fire. *arXiv* **2025**, arXiv:2501.14050. [CrossRef]
18. Chen, B.; Guo, Z.; Yang, Z.; Chen, Y.; Chen, J.; Liu, Z.; Shi, C.; Yang, C. PathRAG: Pruning Graph-Based Retrieval Augmented Generation with Relational Paths. *arXiv* **2025**, arXiv:2502.14902.
19. Liu, R.; Jiang, H.; Yan, X.; Tang, B.; Li, J. PolyG: Effective and Efficient GraphRAG with Adaptive Graph Traversal. *arXiv* **2025**, arXiv:2504.02112.
20. Luo, H.; E, H.; Chen, G.; Zheng, Y.; Wu, X.; Guo, Y.; Lin, Q.; Feng, Y.; Kuang, Z.; Song, M.; et al. HyperGraphRAG: Retrieval-Augmented Generation with Hypergraph-Structured Knowledge Representation. *arXiv* **2025**, arXiv:2503.21322.
21. Yang, J.; Vu, D.-K.; Nguyen, M.-T.; Nguyen, X.-Q.; Nguyen, L.; Le, H. SuperRAG: Beyond RAG with Layout-Aware Graph Modeling. In Proceedings of the 2025 Conference of the North American Chapter of the Association for Computational Linguistics—Industry Track (NAACL 2025), Albuquerque, NM, USA, 30 April–2 May 2025; pp. 544–557. Available online: https://aclanthology.org/2025.naacl-industry.45/ (accessed on 2 September 2025). [CrossRef]
22. Ngangmeni, J.; Rawat, D.B. Swamped with Too Many Articles? GraphRAG Makes Getting Started Easy. *AI* **2025**, *6*, 47. [CrossRef]
23. Hu, Y.; Lei, Z.; Dai, Z.; Zhang, A.; Angirekula, A.; Zhang, Z.; Zhao, L. CG-RAG: Research Question Answering by Citation Graph Retrieval-Augmented LLMs. In Proceedings of the 48th International ACM SIGIR Conference on Research and Development in Information Retrieval (SIGIR '25), Bari, Italy, 13–18 July 2025; ACM: New York, NY, USA, 2025. [CrossRef]
24. Thakrar, K. DynaGRAG | Exploring the Topology of Information for Advancing Language Understanding and Generation in Graph Retrieval-Augmented Generation. *arXiv* **2024**, arXiv:2412.18644.
25. Han, H.; Shomer, H.; Wang, Y.; Lei, Y.; Guo, K.; Hua, Z.; Long, B.; Liu, H.; Tang, J. RAG vs. GraphRAG: A Systematic Evaluation and Key Insights. *arXiv* **2025**, arXiv:2502.11371. [CrossRef]
26. He, J.; Guo, Y.; Lam, L.K.; Leung, W.; He, L.; Jiang, Y.; Wang, C.C.; Xing, G.; Chen, H. OpenTCM: A GraphRAG-Empowered LLM-Based System for Traditional Chinese Medicine Knowledge Retrieval and Diagnosis. *arXiv* **2025**, arXiv:2504.20118.
27. Han, H.; Wang, Y.; Shomer, H.; Guo, K.; Ding, J.; Lei, Y.; Halappanavar, M.; Rossi, R.A.; Mukherjee, S.; Tang, X.; et al. Retrieval-Augmented Generation with Graphs (GraphRAG). *arXiv* **2024**, arXiv:2501.00309. [CrossRef]
28. Wei, J.; Wu, S.; Liu, R.; Ying, X.; Shang, J.; Tao, F. Tuning LLMs by RAG Principles: Towards LLM-Native Memory. *arXiv* **2025**, arXiv:2503.16071. [CrossRef]
29. Papageorgiou, G.; Sarlis, V.; Maragoudakis, M.; Tjortjis, C. Enhancing E-Government Services through State-of-the-Art, Modular, and Reproducible Architecture over Large Language Models. *Appl. Sci.* **2024**, *14*, 8259. [CrossRef]
30. Abane, A.; Bekri, A.; Battou, A. FastRAG: Retrieval Augmented Generation for Semi-Structured Data. *arXiv* **2024**, arXiv:2411.13773.
31. Hu, Y.; Lei, Z.; Zhang, Z.; Pan, B.; Ling, C.; Zhao, L. GRAG: Graph Retrieval-Augmented Generation. *arXiv* **2024**, arXiv:2405.16506. [CrossRef]
32. Chen, D.; Chen, R.; Zhang, S.; Liu, Y.; Wang, Y.; Zhou, H.; Zhang, Q.; Wan, Y.; Zhou, P.; Sun, L. MLLM-as-a-Judge: Assessing Multimodal LLM-as-a-Judge with Vision-Language Benchmark. In Proceedings of the 41st International Conference on Machine Learning (ICML), PMLR, Vienna, Austria, 21–27 July 2024; Volume 235, pp. 6562–6595. [CrossRef]

33. Guo, K.; Shomer, H.; Zeng, S.; Han, H.; Wang, Y.; Tang, J. Empowering GraphRAG with Knowledge Filtering and Integration. *arXiv* **2025**, arXiv:2503.13804. [CrossRef]
34. Li, J.; Wu, R.; Zhu, Y.; Zhang, H.; Chen, L.; Zheng, Z. Are Large Language Models In-Context Graph Learners? *arXiv* **2025**, arXiv:2502.13562. [CrossRef]
35. Feng, Y.; Papicchio, S.; Rahman, S. CypherBench: Towards Precise Retrieval over Full-Scale Modern Knowledge Graphs in the LLM Era. *arXiv* **2024**, arXiv:2412.18702.
36. Feng, T.; Sun, Y.; You, J. GraphEval: A Lightweight Graph-Based LLM Framework for Idea Evaluation. *arXiv* **2025**, arXiv:2503.12600.
37. Dou, C.; Zhang, Y.; Jin, Z.; Jiao, W.; Zhao, H.; Zhao, Y.; Tao, Z. Enhancing LLM Generation with Knowledge Hypergraph for Evidence-Based Medicine. *arXiv* **2025**, arXiv:2503.16530.
38. Ganatra, S.; Bhattacharyya, P. *Retrieval Augmented Generation: A Comprehensive Survey on Bridging Language Models and External Knowledge*; Center for Indian Language Technology (CFILT); Indian Institute of Technology Bombay: Mumbai, India, 2025; Available online: https://www.cfilt.iitb.ac.in/resources/surveys/2025/Shrey_Survey%20(1).pdf (accessed on 2 May 2025).
39. Xie, W.; Liang, X.; Liu, Y.; Ni, K.; Cheng, H.; Hu, Z. WeKnow-RAG: An Adaptive Approach for Retrieval-Augmented Generation Integrating Web Search and Knowledge Graphs. *arXiv* **2024**, arXiv:2408.07611.
40. Wang, Y.; Ren, R.; Wang, Y.; Zhao, W.X.; Liu, J.; Wu, H.; Wang, H. Reinforced Informativeness Optimization for Long-Form Retrieval-Augmented Generation. *arXiv* **2025**, arXiv:2505.20825.
41. He, B.; Chen, N.; He, X.; Yan, L.; Wei, Z.; Luo, J.; Ling, Z.-H. Retrieving, Rethinking and Revising: The Chain-of-Verification Can Improve Retrieval Augmented Generation. *arXiv* **2024**, arXiv:2410.05801.
42. Ni, B.; Liu, Z.; Wang, L.; Lei, Y.; Zhao, Y.; Cheng, X.; Zeng, Q.; Dong, L.; Xia, Y.; Kenthapadi, K.; et al. Towards Trustworthy Retrieval Augmented Generation for Large Language Models: A Survey. *arXiv* **2025**, arXiv:2502.06872. [CrossRef]
43. Zhang, Q.; Xiang, Z.; Xiao, Y.; Wang, L.; Li, J.; Wang, X.; Su, J. FaithfulRAG: Fact-Level Conflict Modeling for Context-Faithful Retrieval-Augmented Generation. *arXiv* **2025**, arXiv:2506.08938.
44. Nguyen, X.-P.; Pandit, S.; Purushwalkam, S.; Xu, A.; Chen, H.; Ming, Y.; Ke, Z.; Savarese, S.; Xong, C.; Joty, S. SFR-RAG: Towards Contextually Faithful LLMs. *arXiv* **2024**, arXiv:2409.09916. [CrossRef]
45. Wu, D.; Gu, J.-C.; Yin, F.; Peng, N.; Chang, K.-W. Synchronous Faithfulness Monitoring for Trustworthy Retrieval-Augmented Generation. *arXiv* **2024**, arXiv:2406.13692. [CrossRef]
46. Malamatinos, M.C. Enhancing Personalized Travel Assistance with Retrieval-Augmented Generation: A Context-Aware Approach. Master's Thesis, Aristotle University of Thessaloniki, Thessaloniki, Greece, 2025. Available online: https://ikee.lib.auth.gr/record/363388/files/GRI-2025-48885.pdf (accessed on 2 September 2025).
47. Sui, Y.; He, Y.; Liu, N.; He, X.; Wang, K.; Hooi, B. FiDeLiS: Faithful Reasoning in Large Language Model for Knowledge Graph Question Answering. *arXiv* **2025**, arXiv:2405.13873.
48. Li, Y.; Zhang, W.; Yang, Y.; Huang, W.-C.; Wu, Y.; Luo, J.; Bei, Y.; Zou, H.P.; Luo, X.; Zhao, Y.; et al. Towards Agentic RAG with Deep Reasoning: A Survey of RAG-Reasoning Systems in LLMs. *arXiv* **2025**, arXiv:2507.09477. [CrossRef]
49. Song, M.; Sim, S.H.; Bhardwaj, R.; Chieu, H.L.; Majumder, N.; Poria, S. Measuring and Enhancing Trustworthiness of LLMs in RAG through Grounded Attributions and Learning to Refuse. *arXiv* **2025**, arXiv:2409.11242.
50. Zhu, Z.; Liao, Y.; Xu, C.; Guan, Y.; Wang, Y.; Wang, Y. RA2FD: Distilling Faithfulness into Efficient Dialogue Systems. In Proceedings of the 2024 Conference on Empirical Methods in Natural Language Processing, Stroudsburg, PA, USA, 12–16 November 2024; pp. 12304–12317.
51. Fadeeva, E.; Rubashevskii, A.; Vashurin, R.; Dhuliawala, S.; Shelmanov, A.; Baldwin, T.; Nakov, P.; Sachan, M.; Panov, M. Faithfulness-Aware Uncertainty Quantification for Fact-Checking the Output of Retrieval Augmented Generation. *arXiv* **2025**, arXiv:2505.21072.
52. Sticha, A.; Braunschweiler, N.; Doddipatla, R.S.; Knill, K.M. Advancing Faithfulness of Large Language Models in Goal-Oriented Dialogue Question Answering. In Proceedings of the 6th Conference on ACM Conversational User Interfaces, Cambridge, UK, 8 July 2024.
53. Hindi, M.; Mohammed, L.; Maaz, O.; Alwarafy, A. Enhancing the Precision and Interpretability of Retrieval-Augmented Generation (RAG) in Legal Technology: A Survey. *IEEE Access* **2025**, *13*, 46171–46189. [CrossRef]
54. Mortaheb, M.; Khojastepour, M.A.A.; Chakradhar, S.T.; Ulukus, S. RAG-Check: Evaluating Multimodal Retrieval Augmented Generation Performance. *arXiv* **2025**, arXiv:2501.03995. [CrossRef]
55. Xu, Y.; Long, X.; Zheng, Z.; Gao, J. RAVine: Reality-Aligned Evaluation for Agentic Search. *arXiv* **2025**, arXiv:2507.16725. [CrossRef]
56. Lu, A. Evaluating LLMs on Large Contexts: A RAG Approach on Text Comprehension. Master's Thesis, University of Liège, Liège, Belgium, 2024. Available online: https://matheo.uliege.be/handle/2268.2/21150 (accessed on 2 September 2025).
57. Serper. Serper—Google Search API Documentation. 2024. Available online: https://serper.dev/ (accessed on 2 May 2025).

58. Pietsch, M.; Möller, T.; Kostic, B.; Risch, J.; Pippi, M.; Jobanputra, M.; Zanzottera, S.; Cerza, S.; Blagojevic, V.; Stadelmann, T. et al. Haystack: The End-to-End NLP Framework for Pragmatic Builders 2019. Available online: https://github.com/deepset-ai/haystack (accessed on 5 September 2025).
59. Papageorgiou, G.; Sarlis, V.; Maragoudakis, M.; Tjortjis, C. Hybrid Multi-Agent GraphRAG for E-Government: Towards a Trustworthy AI Assistant. *Appl. Sci.* **2025**, *15*, 6315. [CrossRef]
60. OpenAI Text-Embedding-Ada-002. 2023. Available online: https://platform.openai.com/docs/guides/embeddings (accessed on 1 September 2025).
61. OpenAI. Introducing GPT-4.1 in the API, 2025. Available online: https://openai.com/research/gpt-4-1 (accessed on 5 May 2025).
62. Anthropic. Introducing Claude 4. 2025. Available online: https://www.anthropic.com/news/claude-4 (accessed on 1 May 2025).
63. Google. Google Gemini 2.5: Our Most Intelligent AI Model. 2025. Available online: https://blog.google/technology/ai/google-gemini-2-5-our-most-intelligent-ai-model/ (accessed on 5 September 2025).

big data and cognitive computing

MDPI

Article

Leveraging Large Language Models for Sustainable and Inclusive Web Accessibility

Manuel Andruccioli, Barry Bassi, Giovanni Delnevo * and Paola Salomoni

Department of Computer Science and Engineering, University of Bologna, 47522 Cesena, Italy; manuel.andruccioli@unibo.it (M.A.); barry.bassi@unibo.it (B.B.); paola.salomoni@unibo.it (P.S.)
* Correspondence: giovanni.delnevo@unibo.it

Abstract: The increasing complexity of modern web applications, which are composed of dynamic and asynchronous components, poses a significant challenge for digital inclusion. Traditional automated tools typically analyze only the static HTML markup generated by frontend and backend frameworks. Recent advances in Large Language Models (LLMs) offer a novel approach to enhance the validation process by directly analyzing the source code. In this paper, we investigate the capacity of LLMs to interpret and reason dynamically generated content, providing real-time feedback on web accessibility. Our findings show that LLMs can correctly anticipate the presence of accessibility violations in the generated HTML code, going beyond the capabilities of traditional validators, also evaluating possible issues due to the asynchronous execution of the web application. However, together with legitimate issues, LLMs also produced a relevant number of hallucinated or redundant violations. This study contributes to the broader effort of employing AI with the aim of improving the inclusivity and equity of the web.

Keywords: web accessibility; large language models; human–AI interaction; digital sustainability

1. Introduction

The Web has moved from an information-sharing system for scientists and has become an essential tool that influences people's daily lives, professions, education, and social connections [1]. Considering its ever-increasing central role in society, it is important that its technological evolution is guided by principles of inclusivity and fairness [2]. In fact, while the Web can help in addressing sustainability challenges, it needs to follow sustainability principles [3]. On the one hand, it can have a central role in pursuing United Nations Sustainable Development Goals (SDGs), that take account of the economic, social, and ecological dimensions of sustainable development. On the other hand, the development and deployment of Web technologies must adhere to sustainable and ethical practices [4]. Guaranteeing accessibility, reducing both the digital divide and the environmental impact are all objectives mainly related to the SDG 10, which seeks to reduce inequalities within and among countries [5]. For these reasons, the Web must go beyond being a mere tool for sustainability, but incorporate it in its design, implementation, and usage. It is of fundamental importance that future Web systems empower everyone, particularly those from vulnerable and marginalized communities [6].

Web accessibility, which ensures that people with disabilities can perceive, understand, navigate, and interact with the Web, lies at the heart of this vision [7]. However, despite decades of standards and advocacy, accessibility remains an ongoing challenge—particularly in dynamic, component-based, and media-rich web environments [8].

Existing efforts have primarily focused on static content and compliance-driven evaluations, which often fall short in capturing the interactive and adaptive nature of modern applications [9]. This mismatch between established accessibility practices and the realities of contemporary web development highlights a significant research gap [10]. This gap calls for new approaches that can scale with the complexity of modern web development and bridge the divide between technical implementation and inclusive design [11].

Recent advances in Large Language Model (LLM) and Multimodal AI offer a promising path forward [12]. These models, exemplified by systems such as OpenAI's ChatGPT and Google's Gemini, have shown remarkable potential in a variety of domains, including code generation [13], natural language understanding [14], and image interpretation [15]. Their growing integration into software development workflows opens new possibilities for building more accessible, human-centered web systems [16]. Yet, these technologies also raise important questions about bias, sustainability, and the limits of automation in ethically sensitive contexts [17].

LLMs hold promise in streamlining the validation process for HTML code's adherence to accessibility standards. Their adeptness at interpreting code enables them to scrutinize web content, identifying potential accessibility shortcomings such as absent alternative text, inadequate semantic structuring, or other deviations from accessibility guidelines. This potential application stands to improve the accessibility auditing process while concurrently elevating the overall quality of web content. Ultimately, this ensures the content caters inclusively to the diverse needs of all users.

This paper investigates how LLMs can support web developers in designing accessible web applications, focusing on their ability to validate and improve accessibility at both the code and content level. Through a series of controlled experiments, we assess their performance in scenarios involving dynamically generated content and asynchronous data handling. We analyze the extent to which these tools can understand and reason about accessibility constraints, and we reflect on their potential—and limitations—as responsible AI agents in web development. In doing so, this work contributes to the broader conversation on how emerging web technologies can be leveraged for social good. Our findings aim to inform researchers and practitioners seeking to integrate LLMs into accessibility workflows in a safe, equitable, and sustainable manner—supporting the Web's evolution into a truly inclusive platform for all.

The remainder of the paper goes as follows. Section 2 establishes the background of web accessibility and the role of LLMs in such a context. Section 3 then details the proposed approach. The results of the experiments are presented in Section 4. Following this, Section 5 interprets these results in the context of existing literature and explores the implications for web development practices and accessibility tooling. Finally, Section 6 summarizes the main contributions of our work and suggests avenues for future research in the pursuit of more accessible web environments.

2. Background and Related Work

Several works investigated the application of LLMs for web accessibility. Othman et al. [18] study explored the potential of LLMs, specifically ChatGPT, to automatically remediate web accessibility issues and improve compliance with Web Content Accessibility Guidelines (WCAG) 2.1 guidelines. The research involved using the WAVE tool to identify accessibility errors on two non-compliant websites, subsequently employing ChatGPT for automated remediation. The effectiveness of this LLM-driven approach was evaluated by comparing its results against manual accessibility testing, offering insights for stakeholders aiming to enhance web accessibility for individuals with disabilities. In parallel to this, the study by Duarte et al. [12] explores the potential of LLMs to automate the detection of heading-related accessibility barriers on webpages, addressing limitations in existing automated tools. The authors evaluate three models—Llama 3.1, GPT-4o, and GPT-4o mini—using a controlled set of modified webpages derived from a WCAG-compliant baseline. They identify seven common heading-related barriers (e.g., missing headings, incorrect hierarchy) and design prompts to query the LLMs. Results reveal model-specific strengths: Llama 3.1 excels in detecting structural and semantic barriers (e.g., heading hierarchy), while GPT-4o mini performs better at identifying nuanced problems like accessible names. However, all models struggle with detecting missing headings, underscoring the need for complementary approaches. Then, in the study of Delnevo et al. [19], authors investigate the potential of LLMs, particularly ChatGPT 3.5, to enhance web accessibility by automating the evaluation and correction of HTML code. Research focuses on critical HTML elements such as forms, tables, and images, assessing their compliance with WCAG accessibility standards. Using a standardized prompt, they evaluate both accessible and non-accessible code snippets, highlighting cases where LLMs successfully identify and rectify issues—such as missing labels in forms or improper semantic structure in tables—while also noting limitations, such as inconsistent suggestions for equivalent accessibility attributes (e.g., scope vs. headers in tables). Moreover, López-Gil and Pereira [16] explore the potential of LLMs to automate the evaluation of WCAG success criteria that traditionally require manual inspection. Focusing on three specific criteria—1.1.1 (Non-text Content), 2.4.4 (Link Purpose), and 3.1.2 (Language of Parts)—the authors develop LLM-based scripts to assess accessibility compliance. Their approach leverages models like ChatGPT, Claude, and Bard to analyze HTML content, compare textual descriptions, and validate language tags. The results demonstrate that LLMs achieve an 87.18% accuracy in detecting issues missed by conventional automated tools, highlighting their potential to augment accessibility testing. Finally, Huynh et al. [20] instead tackled the problem of image accessibility. They presented SmartCaption AI, a tool that leverages LLMs for generating context-aware descriptions of images on web pages. Unlike traditional methods that rely solely on image-to-text algorithms, SmartCaption AI enhances accuracy by first summarizing the surrounding webpage content, providing the LLM with necessary contextual cues. This ensures that generated captions are not only precise but also relevant to the broader page context. The descriptions are then embedded into the webpage's structure, allowing screen readers to seamlessly vocalize them. The proposed system is implemented as a Chrome extension.

From an educational point of view, Aljedaani et al. [21], investigate the integration of LLMs, specifically ChatGPT 3.5, into software engineering education to enhance students' awareness and practical skills in digital accessibility. The study addresses persistent gaps in accessibility compliance, attributed to lack of awareness, knowledge, and practical training among developers. Through an assignment, 215 students evaluated their own websites using accessibility checker tools (WAVE and AChecker), identified violations, and employed ChatGPT to remediate issues. Results demonstrated that 60% of students resolve most violations and 30% of students fixed all violation with ChatGPT, with a general understanding and confidence improvement in implementing accessibility standards.

With regard to mobile applications, Taeb et al. [22] delved into exploring the utilization of LLMs for assessing the accessibility of mobile applications. The researchers introduce a novel system designed to streamline the evaluation process. This system operates by initially taking a manual accessibility test as input, subsequently leveraging an LLM in conjunction with pixel-based UI Understanding models to execute the test. The outcome is a structured video presentation, divided into chapters for enhanced navigation. The generated video undergoes analysis using specific heuristics aimed at identifying and flagging any potential accessibility issues.

Finally, different perspectives have been investigated in [23,24] by Aljedaani et al. [23]. They did not employ LLMs for accessibility evaluation but they investigated the accessibility of the code generated by ChatGPT, focusing on its compliance with WCAG. The authors conducted an empirical evaluation involving 88 web developers who asked to ChatGPT to generate websites, which were then analyzed for accessibility violations using tools like AChecker and WAVE. The results revealed that 84% of the generated websites contained accessibility issues related to perceivability of the interface (e.g., text resizing, color contrast). While ChatGPT (GPT-3.5) demonstrated a 70% success rate in fixing violations in its own code and 73% in third-party GitHub projects, it struggled with specific guidelines—particularly those concerning multimedia content, visual design, layout and spacing, multimodal navigation, and alternative input methods. Instead, Acosta-Vargas et al. [24] present a comprehensive evaluation of the accessibility of generative AI applications with a specific focus on inclusivity for people with disabilities. Their study evaluates 50 popular generative AI tools–including ChatGPT, Copilot, Midjourney, and DALL-E 2–through a dual-method approach combining automated analysis using the WAVE tool and expert-led manual reviews, based on WCAG 2.2 criteria. The evaluation targets four core principles of accessibility: perceivability, operability, understandability, and robustness. The research identifies significant accessibility barriers in many generative AI applications, particularly related to contrast errors, lack of screen reader support, and inconsistent navigation.

The main contributions of the related works are summarized in Table 1.

Table 1. Summary of related works.

Authors	Focus Area	Models/Tools	Key Findings
Othman et al. [18]	Automated remediation of WCAG 2.1 violations on websites	WAVE, ChatGPT	ChatGPT used to fix accessibility errors; effectiveness evaluated vs. manual testing. Provided promising results but highlighted the need for refinement.
Duarte et al. [12]	Detection of heading-related barriers	Llama 3.1, GPT-4o, GPT-4o mini	Models show strengths in different tasks (Llama: hierarchy, GPT-4o mini: nuanced names). All struggled with missing headings.
Delnevo et al. [19]	Evaluation and correction of HTML accessibility	ChatGPT 3.5	Focused on forms, tables, images. LLMs corrected many issues (e.g., labels, table semantics) but produced inconsistent attribute fixes.
López-Gil & Pereira [16]	Automating WCAG manual inspection tasks	ChatGPT, Claude, Bard	Evaluated criteria 1.1.1, 2.4.4, 3.1.2. Achieved 87.18% accuracy in detecting issues missed by automated tools.
Huynh et al. [20]	Image accessibility via context-aware captions	SmartCaption AI, LLM + webpage context	Generated captions enriched with page context improved relevance and integration with screen readers.
Aljedaani et al. [21]	Education: integrating accessibility in software engineering	ChatGPT 3.5, WAVE, AChecker	Students remediated violations with LLMs: ~60% fixed most, ~30% fixed all. Increased awareness and skills.
Taeb et al. [22]	Accessibility assessment of mobile apps	LLM + pixel-based UI understanding	Produced structured video presentations to flag accessibility issues. Showcased hybrid LLM–vision approach.
Aljedaani et al. [23]	Accessibility of ChatGPT-generated websites	ChatGPT, WAVE, AChecker	Approximately 84% of generated sites had issues (contrast, multimedia, navigation). ChatGPT fixed ~70% of its own violations. Struggled with complex guidelines.
Acosta-Vargas et al. [24]	Accessibility of generative AI applications	WAVE, manual evaluation	Analyis of 50 popular generative AI tools (e.g., ChatGPT, Copilot, Midjourney, and DALL-E 2). Found widespread issues in perceivability, screen reader support, and navigation consistency across tools.

3. Materials and Methods

This section introduces the research questions that drove this study and describes the dataset used in the various experiments, the prompts, and the LLMs used.

3.1. Research Questions

To systematically evaluate the capabilities of LLMs to identify and assess accessibility issues, we structured our study around two primary research questions:

- RQ1: "How well do LLMs evaluate the accessibility of dynamically generated web content implemented with different JavaScript frameworks (i.e., Vue, React, Angular) and server-side languages (i.e., PHP)?"
- RQ2: "How consistent and reliable are LLM evaluations when systematically assessing accessibility across multiple versions of table components?"

3.2. Dataset Description

To comprehensively evaluate the capabilities of LLMs in assessing web accessibility, we curated a diverse dataset designed to address our two primary RQs.

For RQ1, which examines the LLMs' performance on dynamically generated content, we developed code snippets that create tables using various JavaScript frameworks and the server-side language PHP. These snippets were designed to showcase different approaches to dynamic content generation, allowing us to evaluate the LLMs' adaptability across diverse coding paradigms. We selected Vue [25], Angular [26], and React [27]—three of the most widely used frontend frameworks—alongside PHP, still the dominant server-side language [28]. Vue, React, and Angular share common characteristics, such as a component-based architecture, data-binding mechanisms, and a focus on reusability, making them well-suited for modern web applications [29]. Each framework, however, brings its own strengths: Vue emphasizes simplicity and flexibility, Angular offers a full-featured, TypeScript-based structure with built-in tools for scalability, and React, developed by Facebook, prioritizes performance with its virtual DOM and declarative UI design. PHP, on the other hand, remains a versatile and widely adopted server-side scripting language, enabling dynamic content generation and powering popular CMS platforms like WordPress and Drupal. This diverse selection ensures our dataset reflects a broad range of web development paradigms, from client-side interactivity to server-side content rendering.

To investigate the consistency and reliability of LLM evaluations across component versions (RQ2), we utilized a dataset of 25 distinct implementations of Vue table components. These components, developed by students from the Web Applications and Services course at the University of Bologna, featured variations in accessibility features, API usage (Composition vs. Options), and overall structure. This diverse dataset provided a rich foundation for assessing the LLMs' ability to track and evaluate accessibility changes across iterative component development. While we initially explored accessibility evaluations across Vue, React, Angular, and PHP, a more focused approach was necessary for a systematic evaluation of component variations. Specifically, we required a substantial number of implementations centered on a consistent component type (tables), to ensure a robust comparative analysis. To achieve this, we collaborated with the student developers, whose coursework extensively covered Vue, making it the practical choice for our in-depth study. Furthermore, given the architectural similarities among modern JavaScript frameworks like Vue, React, and Angular, we posit that findings derived from a thorough analysis of Vue components are likely to offer insights applicable across these frameworks. It is reasonable to hypothesize that the general trends and patterns observed in LLM evaluations of Vue components would manifest similarly in React and Angular, particularly concerning common accessibility patterns and challenges. Additionally, focusing on a single framework enabled us to achieve a higher degree of granularity in our analysis, allowing for a deeper exploration of specific accessibility nuances and their impact on LLM evaluations. This decision also reflected practical considerations, such as the resources and time constraints inherent in conducting a comprehensive analysis across multiple frameworks. By prioritizing depth over breadth in this phase of our research, we aimed to provide a more detailed and actionable understanding of LLM capabilities in assessing web component accessibility.

The dataset has been deeply described in [30]. It is organized into two main directories, each supporting a different dimension of our evaluation. The first directory, Dynamic Generated Content, contains handcrafted snippets in Angular, React, Vue, and PHP. For each technology, two tabular components were implemented: an accessible version, compliant with WCAG guidelines, and an invalid version, intentionally embedding common accessibility violations such as missing ARIA attributes, poor semantic markup, or inadequate keyboard support. Each snippet is accompanied by source code, a `labels.csv` file reporting the violations identified through manual inspection, and automated accessibility reports generated by the Mauve tool on the rendered HTML. This dual perspective enables both code-level and output-level evaluation of accessibility.

The second directory, Vue Table Components, consists of 25 independent Vue projects developed by students. Each project provides four table variants: minimal and accessible implementations created with both the Options API and the Composition API. The projects are based on heterogeneous datasets (minimum 50 rows × 5 attributes), spanning domains such as music, movies, environmental measurements, and sports. This collection introduces variability in architectural choices (e.g., single-file vs. modular components) and accessibility practices, providing a diverse and realistic benchmark for analyzing how LLMs handle accessibility in real-world development scenarios.

All code used in this study has been reported in a GitHub repository (https://github.com/manuandru/LLM-WebAccessibility.git, accessed on 6 August 2025).

3.3. Prompt Design and Methodology

To ensure a consistent and thorough evaluation of LLM performance across our research questions, we carefully crafted tailored prompts for each scenario. Each prompt aligns with the specific goal of the corresponding research question, ensuring that the model's output remains focused on the accessibility criteria under investigation. To enhance the effectiveness of these prompts, we employed various prompt engineering techniques, including role prompting [31]. This involved instructing the LLM to adopt specific roles, such as an accessibility expert or a code reviewer, to guide its analysis and responses. By defining clear roles and providing precise instructions, we aimed to elicit more accurate and relevant evaluations of the accessibility issues present in our dataset. Figure 1 provides a comprehensive overview of our methodology.

For RQ1, the code snippets of the Dynamic Generated Content folder, containing table components implemented with the four technologies previously mentioned, are used. Their source codes are analyzed using GPT-4o mini and Gemini 2.0 Flash (Gemini) to evaluate the compliance of the generated code with the WCAG 2.2. The raised accessibility issues are then manually evaluated. Legitimate issues were then fixed by following the suggestions proposed by the LLMs and tested again to verify their applicability.

A different pipeline has been followed for RQ2. The data used for the experiments were the 25 implementations of Vue Table Components. Initially, LLMs analyzed them to retrieve WCAG 2.2 AA guideline violations. Three of the authors manually reviewed each violation to classify it as correct, redundant, or hallucination. Then, the same analysis has been carried out using LLMs, including o3-mini to understand the LLMs' capacity in verifying their own output and a systematic reliability analysis has been carried out.

Below, we describe the design and rationale for each prompt, detailing how these techniques were implemented to optimize the LLM's performance.

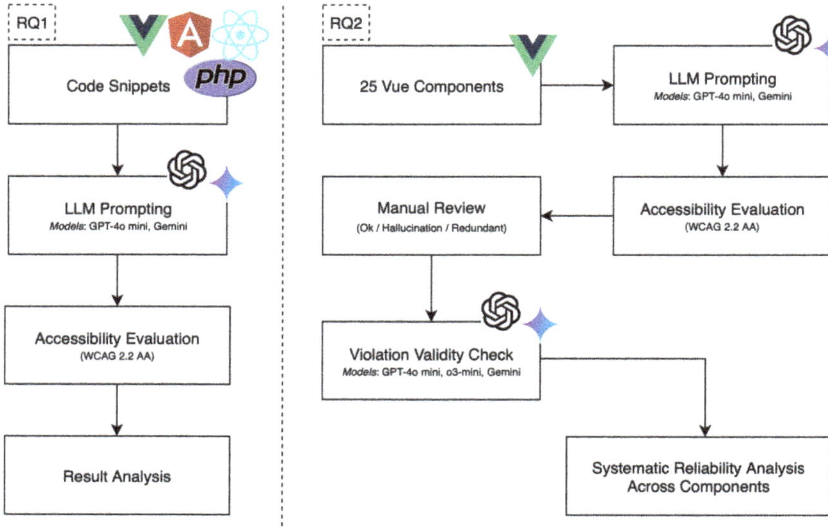

Figure 1. Overview of the methodology employed in the study for evaluating LLM performance on accessibility assessment tasks.

For RQ1, where the focus is on dynamically generated content from various frameworks and server-side languages, we crafted a prompt to evaluate accessibility across different paradigms. This prompt acknowledges the interactive nature of the content and asks the model to assess the resulting output:

> You are a tool for detailed web accessibility validation.
>
> Analyze the following dynamically generated web content.
>
> The content is produced by a code snippet written in one of the following: Vue, React, Angular, or PHP.
>
> Evaluate the resulting output for accessibility issues according to WCAG 2.2 AA guidelines.
>
> For each issue identified, include the following:
> - The affected element or code portion.
> - The corresponding WCAG criterion.
> - A brief explanation of the issue.
> - A recommendation for fixing it.
>
> — Code Snippet —
> $code_snippet$

This design ensures the LLM not only processes the code itself but also infers the resulting structure, focusing on end-user accessibility.

For RQ2, we designed a two-step process to maximize violation detection and identify hallucinations. The prompts support a systematic evaluation of multiple Vue table component implementations, ensuring consistent output formatting. First, a prompt is used to retrieve WCAG 2.2 AA guideline violations found on individual webpages. The prompt is as follows:

> You are a tool for detailed web accessibility validation.
>
> Is this VUE component accessible according to WCAG 2.2 guidelines (which include previous WCAG 2.0 and 2.1 standards) at the AA level?
>
> Analyze the following VUE files that make up the component.
>
> After the analysis, create a table with the list of WCAG violations you found, indicating the following:
>
> - In the first column, the relative success criterion.
> - In the second column, the part of code analyzed or a summary of it.
> - In the third column, a short description of the problem.
>
> — File: $filename$—
>
> $filecontent$

Then, each violation has been manually evaluated by three reviewers and marked as follows: OK (if it is correct), A (if it is hallucination), and R (if it is redundant).

Second, a more targeted prompt is employed for each identified violation to confirm its validity and distinguish it from a hallucination. This approach, similar to Chain-of-Verification [32], requires the LLM to verify its findings incrementally. By checking each part of its response, the LLM can minimize errors and enhance the accuracy of its results. The prompt for the second step is as follows:

> You are a tool for detailed web accessibility validation.
>
> I ask you to verify the correctness of the following WCAG 2.2 accessibility issue reports (including WCAG 2.1 and 2.0) generated for components of a Vue.js application.
>
> Create a new markdown table about accessibility issues, similar to the one below, by adding 2 columns: Correctness and Description.
>
> In the "Correctness" column, enter the following:
>
> "OK" if the reported issue is actually present on the page.
> "A" if it is a hallucination (an accessibility error reported that does not actually exist).
> "R" if the report is redundant. "Redundant" refers to a suggestion or recommendation provided by the model that, based on the analysis of the rendered HTML code below, does not appear useful or correct.
>
> In the "Description" column, provide a brief justification for your assessment.
>
> Below is the table of reports to verify, followed by the HTML-rendered code of the Vue.js component (rendered using a Node.js server and Chrome browser).
>
> $step 1 result$
>
> SHTML Code Rendered$

This structured output facilitates comparative analysis across the 25 different student-implemented Vue table components, enabling systematic reliability checks.

3.4. Large Language Models

LLMs are self-supervised foundational models that can be prompted or fine-tuned to perform a wide array of natural language processing tasks that once required separate, task-specific systems [33,34]. These models are typically built on the Transformer architecture and trained on massive corpora, enabling them to generalize across tasks such as text generation, summarization, question answering, and code understanding [35]. Their versatility has led to widespread adoption across diverse fields including healthcare [36], education [37], and software development.

In this study, we employed three LLMs: GPT-4o mini [38], o3-mini [39], and Gemini [40]. These models reflect the current state of scalable instruction-following language models. GPT-4o mini and o3-mini are proprietary models by OpenAI, optimized for performance and efficiency. GPT-4o (short for "omni") is the latest model in the GPT-4 family, designed for multimodal tasks while maintaining strong natural language understanding and generation capabilities. The mini variants used in our experiments are optimized for speed and cost while retaining a high level of linguistic and reasoning competence.

Gemini, developed by Google DeepMind, is a lightweight and fast variant of the Gemini series, following earlier iterations such as LaMDA and PaLM [41,42]. This model is designed to provide rapid responses while maintaining strong instruction-following behavior, making it particularly suitable for real-time evaluation tasks like those required in our accessibility assessment scenarios.

All models were used in zero-shot inference mode via prompting, without any additional fine-tuning. We compared their outputs in terms of consistency, completeness, and alignment with WCAG 2.2 standards. Leveraging multiple LLMs allowed us to examine not only overall performance but also the variation in accessibility evaluation across different architectures and training strategies.

During the preparation of this manuscript, the authors used ChatGPT (GPT-4o) for the purposes of writing assistance. The authors have reviewed and edited the output and take full responsibility for the content of this publication.

4. Results and Discussion

The answers to the two Research Questions are discussed in isolation in the following subsections.

4.1. *Validation of Dynamic Generation of HTML Code*

In this set of experiments, the evaluation of the accessibility is conducted on the code that generates dynamically the HTML code, taking advantage of frontend JavaScript frameworks (i.e., Vue, Angular, and React) and PHP. The experiments are all focused on the generation of the same HTML table.

4.1.1. Accessible Components

The first set of experiments conducted were focused on components that should produce accessible tables. Table 2 presents the accessibility issues identified by the GPT-4o mini model across dynamically generated table components developed in Angular, React, Vue, and PHP. Although the components were intended to produce accessible tables, several recurring accessibility problems were systematically detected, highlighting common pitfalls even in seemingly well-designed dynamic content.

Four accessibility issues were found. Components in Angular, React, and Vue potentially generate non-unique dynamic IDs in case of songs with the same title, a violation of WCAG 1.3.1 that can disrupt assistive technologies. The recommended solution is to add a unique suffix, like an index, to each ID. Across all frameworks, a lack of descriptive summaries for tables was detected, which impacts WCAG 1.3.1 and 1.1.1 by preventing screen readers from understanding the table's purpose. The LLM suggested using the `aria-describedby` attribute to link to a hidden description. Another gap found in Angular, React, and Vue components was the absence of loading messages during dynamic content updates. This violates WCAG 4.1.3 and can confuse users of assistive technologies. The proposed fix is to use an aria-live region to announce "Loading..." messages. Finally, a consistent issue across all evaluated technologies was the lack of error messaging under failure conditions, which infringes on WCAG 3.3.1. Without this feedback, users struggle to identify and correct issues. The suggested remedy is to display accessible error messages using ARIA roles like `role = "alert"` for immediate notification.

Table 2. Accessibility issues with the relative Web Content Accessibility Guideline (WCAG) and recommended fixes for accessible table components in Angular, React, Vue, and PHP as identified by GPT-4o mini.

Components	Issue	WCAG	Fix
Angular, React, Vue	Non-unique dynamic IDs	1.3.1	Add unique suffix like index
All	Missing descriptive summary	1.3.1/1.1.1	Use aria-describedby with hidden description
Angular, React, Vue	No loading message	4.1.3	Use aria-live region with "Loading..."
All	No error message on failure	3.3.1	Display accessible error message with role = "alert"

Then, we evaluate the same components using Gemini. The results are summarized in Table 3. Despite the developers' intention to produce accessible tables, several accessibility deficiencies were highlighted, common to all technologies assessed.

Table 3. Accessibility issues with the relative WCAG and recommended fixes for accessible table components in Angular, React, Vue, and PHP as identified by Gemini.

Components	Issue	WCAG	Fix
All	Incorrect use of <th> within the <tbody>	1.3.1	Change the <th> element within the <tbody> to a <td> element
All	Potentially insufficient contrast for text content	1.4.3	Ensure that the CSS applied to the table cells provides a sufficient contrast ratio
All	Redundant and potentially confusing use of [attr.headers]	1.3.1	Modify the [attr.headers] attribute in the <td> elements to directly reference the id of the appropriate column header
All	Missing summary attribute on the <table> element	1.3.1	Consider adding a summary attribute to the <table> element

Gemini also identified four accessibility issues. The model flagged the use of `<th>` elements within `<tbody>` sections as a violation of WCAG 1.3.1. However, this is a valid practice for creating row headers in complex tables, highlighting a limitation in the model's understanding of advanced HTML semantics. A possible legitimate concern identified was insufficient contrast for text content, which violates WCAG 1.4.3. Anyway, no information was provided about the style of the page. Thus, it is not clear which information was evaluated to detect this issue. Gemini also detected redundant or confusing use of the headers attribute in `<td>` elements. While the suggested fix is to simplify and correctly link to column headers, the headers' attributes of `<td>` were correctly linked to the corresponding table heading IDs. Lastly, the model flagged the absence of the summary attribute on <table> elements, even if this attribute is obsolete in HTML5. To summarize, among the four violations, three of them were false positives, while one was raised without the appropriate information.

To test applicability, the fixes suggested by GPT-4o mini were implemented in the original code and re-evaluated. Gemini suggestions were not implemented because they were deemed incorrect or irrelevant. Re-testing with GPT-4o mini, using the same prompt, confirmed the following:

- Non-unique ID errors disappeared once unique suffixes, based on the relative index, were added.
- Summaries linked with `aria-describedby` were correctly recognized as compliant.
- The introduction of an `aria-live` region eliminated the absence-of-loading-message error.
- Accessible error feedback using `role = "alert"` was correctly identified as a valid remediation.

4.1.2. Non-Accessible Components

After the evaluation of components that should produce accessible tables, we moved to components that produce non-accessible tables. In particular, even if table cells have both row and column headings, neither the scope attribute nor the headers attribute were employed.

Table 4 reports the accessibility issues detected by GPT-4o mini in the table components designed to be non-accessible, implemented with Angular, React, Vue, and PHP. As expected, the number and severity of detected violations increased compared to the components intended to be accessible, confirming the tool's ability to identify meaningful differences in accessibility compliance.

Table 4. Accessibility issues with the relative WCAG and recommended fixes for non-accessible table components in Angular, React, Vue, and PHP as identified by GPT-4o mini.

Components	Issue	WCAG	Fix
All	Missing scope = "col" on headers	1.3.1	Add scope = "col" to column headers
All	Missing scope = "row" on row headers	1.3.1	Add scope = "row" to dynamic title headers
Angular, React, Vue	No loading message	4.1.3	Use aria-live region with "Loading..."
All	No error message on failure	3.3.1	Display accessible error message with role = "alert"
All	No detailed description of table	1.3.1	Add aria-describedby linked to visually hidden content

Two critical issues emerged regarding the semantic structure of tables:

- Missing `scope = "col"` on column headers: According to WCAG 1.3.1 (Info and Relationships), properly setting the scope attribute in `<th>` elements is crucial to help assistive technologies interpret the relationship between headers and their corresponding cells.
- Missing `scope = "row"` on row headers: Similarly, for row headers, the absence of `scope = "row"` further degrades the semantic clarity of the tables. Without these markers, navigating large tables becomes significantly more difficult for users relying on assistive technologies.

These issues were not present in the accessible versions, highlighting that proper use of the `headers` attribute was effective. It is interesting to notice that GPT-4o mini did not propose the use of the `headers` attribute in combination with the ID of table headers; rather, it preferred to recommend the use of the scope attribute.

The other issues were also detected in the accessible components (i.e., no loading message, no error message on failure, and no detailed description of the table) and were highlighted again, suggesting a consistency of evaluation among the various components.

With regard to the evaluation conducted with Gemini, Table 5 presents the accessibility issues identified in the intentionally non-accessible table components built with Angular, React, Vue, and PHP. In a manner parallel to the findings observed with o3-mini on these same components, beyond the issues previously identified in the accessible versions of these components, Gemini additionally flagged the absence of both `scope` and `id` attributes within the table header cells (`<th>`) located in the <head>. It is important to highlight that the use of the `scope` attribute is enough to ensure the accessibility of the table, and it is not required to be coupled with the `id` attribute.

Table 5. Accessibility issues with the relative WCAG and recommended fixes for non-accessible table components in Angular, React, Vue, and PHP as identified by Gemini.

Components	Issue	WCAG	Fix
All	Missing scope and id attributes for table header cells (<th>) in the <thead>	1.3.1	To properly associate the header cells with the data cells in each column, the <th> elements in the <thead> should have a scope = "col" attribute and a unique id attribute.
All	Incorrect use of <th> within the <tbody>	1.3.1	Change the <th> element within the <tbody> to a <td> element
All	Potentially insufficient contrast for text content	1.4.3	Ensure that the CSS applied to the table cells provides a sufficient contrast ratio.
All	Missing summary attribute on the <table> element	1.3.1	Consider adding a summary attribute to the <table> element.
All	No detailed description of table	1.3.1	Add aria-describedby linked to visually hidden content.

Again, parallel to what happened for the accessible components to verify the applicability of the recommendations, we implemented the correct suggestions provided in the original code and re-evaluated them with both LLMs with the same prompt. Similarly, all the previously highlighted issues have not been detected, confirming that both the use of the `scope` and `headers` attributes are correctly detected as mechanisms that ensure the accessibility of the table.

4.1.3. Cross-Framework and Language Accessibility Evaluation by LLMs

To answer the RQ1, the results demonstrate that LLM-based models, specifically GPT-4o mini and Gemini, are capable of detecting a wide range of accessibility issues in dynamically generated web components across different JavaScript frameworks (Vue, React, Angular) and PHP. However, their performance also reveals distinct strengths and limitations.

Overall, both models consistently identified critical accessibility problems affecting dynamically generated tables. Improper scope and headers management for table elements were systematically detected across all frameworks, indicating that LLMs generalize well across different frontend and backend technologies.

When evaluating components intended to be accessible, both GPT-4o mini and Gemini successfully pinpointed subtle but important shortcomings. GPT-4o mini focused more on semantic and interaction aspects (e.g., dynamic ID generation, live updates, error reporting), while Gemini highlighted additional presentation issues, like color contrast problems. However, Gemini also exhibited a notable false positive (incorrectly reporting the use of <th> in <tbody> as a violation), revealing that its knowledge about valid complex table semantics was not fully aligned with modern HTML standards.

In evaluating non-accessible components, both models correctly detected the missing use of scope and headers attributes. This confirms that the models are sensitive enough to distinguish between different levels of accessibility compliance and can detect both superficial and deep structural accessibility flaws.

In summary, LLMs such as o3-mini and Gemini can effectively evaluate the accessibility of dynamically generated web content across different frameworks and languages, identifying both high-level and detailed WCAG violations. However, occasional inaccuracies and outdated suggestions imply that their outputs should be critically reviewed by accessibility experts before being fully trusted in critical evaluation contexts.

4.2. Vue Table Components Analysis

4.2.1. Initial Accessibility Violation Detection

In the initial phase of our evaluation, we employed the first prompt detailed in Section 3.3 to analyze accessibility issues using both GPT-4o mini and Gemini, subsequently conducting a manual expert review of the detected issues.

The findings for GPT-4o mini and Gemini are respectively summarized in Tables 6 and 7. GPT-4o mini detected a total of 512 violations across various WCAG criteria. Of these, 103 issues (20.1%) were judged fully correct (OK), while 358 issues (69.9%) were classified as hallucinations (A), meaning that although the model flagged real accessibility concerns, the details or severity were partially incorrect or incomplete. Only a small fraction, 51 issues (10.0%), were classified as redundant (R), indicating false positives where no genuine accessibility problem existed.

Conversely, the results for Gemini showed a different profile. A total of 384 violations were detected, with 113 issues (29.5%) deemed fully correct (OK) and 77 issues (20.1%) classified as hallucinations (A). However, a significant number—193 issues (50.4%)—were considered redundant (R), revealing a greater tendency of Gemini to flag accessibility violations that, upon manual inspection, were found to be incorrect or not impactful.

In both cases, Criterion 1.3.1 (Info and Relationships) yielded the highest number of detections (167 and 189 cases for GPT-4o mini and Gemini, respectively). However, the classification differed notably between the two models: For GPT-4o mini, the majority of these detections were marked as hallucinations, suggesting frequent but only partially accurate identification of semantic issues. For Gemini, a significant portion under Criterion 1.3.1 was instead classified as redundant, indicating a high rate of false positives related to the interpretation of semantic relationships.

It is also noteworthy that Gemini achieved a higher percentage of fully correct detections (29.5%) compared to GPT-4o mini (20.1%), suggesting better precision in those cases where the model correctly identified an accessibility problem. Furthermore, Gemini demonstrated a considerably lower proportion of hallucinations (20.1% vs. 69.9%), meaning that when it raised issues, they were more often either entirely correct or entirely wrong, with fewer partially accurate findings.

Nevertheless, this advantage came at the cost of a much higher redundancy rate (50.4% vs. 10.0%), indicating that Gemini flagged many issues that were not actually accessibility violations, which could potentially overwhelm developers with unnecessary corrective actions and reduce the practical efficiency of its assessments.

In summary, these results highlight a fundamental trade-off between the two LLMs. While GPT-4o mini tends to identify a broader set of potential accessibility concerns, its inclination towards generating a high number of reports requiring human verification and interpretation represents a significant limitation. Conversely, Gemini demonstrates slightly better precision in correct detections, but this quality is counterbalanced by a considerable risk of over-reporting and potentially hallucinations, undermining the overall effectiveness of the system.

Table 6. Accessibility violations identified by GPT-4o mini grouped by criterion with the corresponding manual classification (OK: correct issue; A: hallucination; R: redundant recommendation).

Criterion	OK	A	R	COUNT
1.3.1	39	120	8	167
4.1.2	7	43	7	57
1.3.2	8	45	0	53
2.4.6	3	28	9	40
2.4.4	6	24	6	36
1.4.3	7	20	3	30
1.1.1	3	16	4	23
2.4.7	0	16	3	19
3.3.2	4	9	4	17
2.4.3	3	10	1	14
4.1.3	9	4	0	13
2.1.1	1	11	0	12
4.1.1	0	5	2	7
3.3.1	6	0	0	6
3.3.3	5	0	0	5
1.4.5	0	1	3	4
1.4.11	0	3	0	3
2.5.3	0	2	0	2
1.3.3	1	1	0	2
3.1.1	0	0	1	1
3.2.2	1	0	0	1
Total	103	358	51	512

Table 7. Accessibility violations identified by Gemini grouped by criterion with the corresponding manual classification (OK: correct issue; A: hallucination; R: redundant recommendation).

Criterion	OK	A	R	COUNT
1.3.1	67	40	82	189
2.4.7	4	6	48	58
1.1.1	12	9	19	40
1.4.11	10	1	16	27
1.4.1	5	8	12	25
4.1.2	7	11	4	22
2.4.6	3	1	1	5
4.1.1	2	1	2	5
1.4.3	0	0	4	4
2.4.4	1	0	3	4
2.4.3	2	0	1	3
3.2.1	0	0	1	1
Total	113	77	193	383

4.2.2. Consistency and Reliability of LLM Accessibility Evaluations

Following the initial detection of accessibility violations, described in the previous subsection, a second verification phase was introduced to validate the correctness of each issue. This step employed a targeted prompt inspired by the Chain-of-Verification approach [32], where each model was required to reassess its own outputs by incrementally analyzing its reported violations in the context of the rendered HTML source code. This method allowed for a more controlled inspection of each LLM's self-consistency and factual grounding.

The results of this second step is summarized in Tables 8 and 9. GPT-4o mini demonstrated limited reliability, achieving an overall accuracy of 34%. While it performed well in recognizing actual accessibility issues (Recall_{OK} = 0.83), its low Precision for that class (0.23) indicates a high false-positive rate. Notably, it exhibited poor consistency in identifying hallucinated issues (Recall_A = 0.2), meaning it frequently failed to recognize when a previously reported hallucination was invalid. Its balanced performance in detecting redundant issues (F1_R = 0.37) was moderate, but not particularly strong.

Table 8. Performance metrics for GPT 4-o mini's classification of previous output violations (OK: correct issue; A: hallucination; R: redundant recommendation).

Class	Precision	Recall	F1-Score	Support	Accuracy
A	0.8	0.2	0.31	358	
OK	0.23	0.83	0.36	103	0.34
R	0.37	0.37	0.37	51	

The relative confusion matrix, depicted in Figure 2, reveals how the GPT-4o mini model performed in classifying violations as Hallucinations, OK, or Redundant. It shows the counts of correct and incorrect predictions for each category. Notably, the model struggled most with accurately identifying Hallucinations, often misclassifying them as OK. The OK category also saw some misclassifications, while the Redundant category had a relatively lower number of correct predictions compared to its errors. Overall, the matrix highlights the specific types of classification mistakes the model made across the different violation categories.

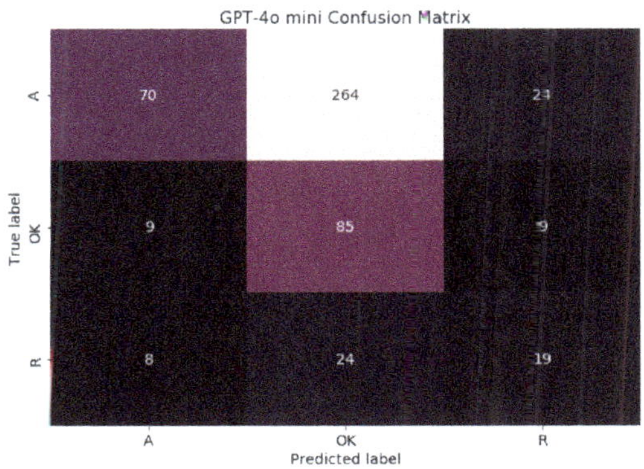

Figure 2. Confusion Matrix of GPT 4-o mini's classification of previous output violations (OK: correct issue; A: hallucination; R: redundant recommendation).

Gemini yielded an even lower overall accuracy of 30%, and its classification reliability was markedly inconsistent across classes. It achieved the highest recall for correct issues ($Recall_{OK}$ = 0.88), suggesting strong sensitivity to real violations. However, the precision for this class was modest (0.29), again reflecting a substantial number of false positives. The model performed especially poorly in identifying redundant outputs ($Recall_R$ = 0.02), indicating it was largely unable to recognize when its own suggestions were unnecessary or irrelevant.

Table 9. Performance metrics for Gemini's classification of previous output violations (OK: correct issue; A: hallucination; R: redundant recommendation).

Class	Precision	Recall	F1-Score	Support	Accuracy
A	0.32	0.14	0.2	77	0.3
OK	0.29	0.88	0.44	113	
R	0.4	0.02	0.04	193	

The confusion matrix (Figure 3) for Gemini illustrates its performance in classifying violations into Hallucinations (A), OK, and Redundant (R) categories. Looking at the matrix, we can see how many instances of each true category were correctly and incorrectly predicted by the model. For Hallucinations, while some were correctly identified, a larger number were misclassified as OK. The OK category shows a high number of correct classifications, but also some instances incorrectly labeled as Hallucinations and Redundant. Finally, for the Redundant category, there were a few correct predictions, but a significant number were wrongly classified as OK. This matrix provides a clear picture of the specific types of errors Gemini made across the different violation types.

Finally, we conducted a further test using a more powerful model, O3-mini, which analyzed the violations raised by GPT 4o-mini. Results are reported in Table 10. In contrast to the previous models, O3-mini exhibited significantly more consistent and reliable behavior, achieving an overall accuracy of 79%. It demonstrated strong performance across all classes, particularly in detecting hallucinations ($F1_A$ = 0.85) and correctly identifying redundant suggestions ($F1_R$ = 0.61). Unlike the other two models, O3-mini balanced both precision and recall effectively, resulting in a respectable F1-score of 0.67 for actual accessibility violations.

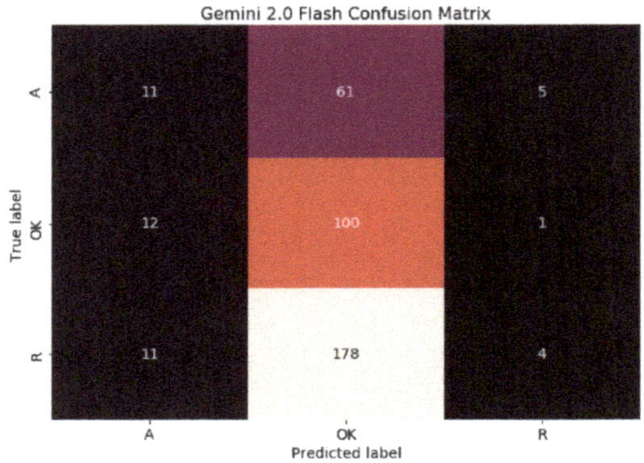

Figure 3. Confusion matrix of Gemini's classification of previous output violations (OK: correct issue; A: hallucination; R: redundant recommendation).

Table 10. Performance metrics for O3-mini's classification of previous output violations (OK: correct issue; A: hallucination; R: redundant recommendation) identified by GPT-4o mini.

Class	Precision	Recall	F1-Score	Support	Accuracy
A	0.86	0.84	0.85	358	0.79
OK	0.66	0.67	0.67	103	
R	0.56	0.67	0.61	51	

The confusion matrix for O3-mini, depicted in Figure 4, which analyzed violations identified by GPT 4o-mini, reveals a strong performance in classifying these violations. The model correctly identified a large number of Hallucinations (A), with fewer being misclassified as Ok or Redundant. For truly OK violations, O3-mini showed a good level of accuracy, with a smaller number being incorrectly labeled as Hallucinations. The Redundant (R) category also saw a reasonable number of correct classifications, although some were misidentified as Hallucinations. Overall, the matrix indicates that O3-mini demonstrates a better ability to distinguish between these violation types compared to the previous models, aligning with its reported higher accuracy and balanced precision–recall.

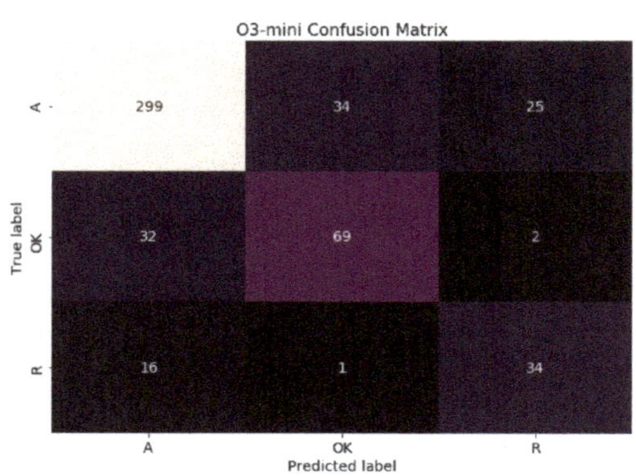

Figure 4. Confusion matrix of O3-mini's classification of previous output violations (OK: correct issue; A: hallucination; R: redundant recommendation) identified by GPT-4o mini.

4.3. Consistency and Reliability of LLMs Evaluations

These findings underscore that while GPT-4o mini and Gemini are capable of generating plausible accessibility reports even suffering from hallucinations and redundant violations, they suffer from low self-verification reliability, particularly in distinguishing between valid, redundant, and hallucinated issues. Their limited ability to reassess their own outputs poses risks for over-reporting or misguiding developers in real-world auditing scenarios. By contrast, O3-mini appears to offer a more dependable approach to systematic accessibility evaluation, especially when applied in multi-stage workflows where validation and refinement are essential.

Addressing RQ2 of how consistent and reliable LLM evaluations are when systematically assessing accessibility across multiple versions of table components, the results of our second evaluation phase reveal significant inconsistencies and varying levels of reliability among different LLMs. The stark contrast observed, with O3-mini demonstrating high accuracy while GPT-4o mini and Gemini exhibited relatively poor performance in verifying accessibility violations, underscores the critical need for robust internal validation within LLMs used for such tasks. Although initial outputs from all models appeared plausible, only O3-mini consistently and reliably distinguished between actual issues, hallucinations, and redundant suggestions during the self-verification process. This finding indicates that the initial output quality of an LLM is not a sufficient measure of its practical reliability for accessibility evaluations; a systematic self-verification step is crucial for ensuring robustness. The inconsistency observed, where over-reporting can lead to wasted effort and under-reporting to non-compliance, poses a serious challenge for real-world applications. Consequently, these findings strongly support the necessity of multi-step LLM evaluation pipelines and prompt further investigation into how architectural differences or training objectives influence a model's ability to reason reliably when performing systematic accessibility assessments across table component versions.

5. Discussion and Limitations

This section discusses the empirical findings of our study, situating them within three complementary perspectives: first, we outline the strengths and limitations of LLM-based accessibility evaluation observed in our experiments; second, we compare these results with related work to highlight similarities, differences, and unique contributions; and third, we reflect on the broader capabilities and risks of applying LLMs in accessibility auditing workflows. Finally, the limitations of this study are acknowledged.

5.1. Strengths and Limitations of LLM-Based Accessibility Evaluation

The results of this study demonstrate both the promise and current limitations of using LLMs for automated accessibility evaluations of dynamically generated web content. In addressing RQ1, the evaluation shows that both GPT-4o mini and Gemini are capable of identifying a broad spectrum of accessibility violations across multiple frontend frameworks and backend technologies. These models consistently surfaced key issues such as missing scope attributes, redundant or incorrect use of headers, and absent dynamic feedback mechanisms—violations that are crucial to ensuring WCAG compliance. However, despite their capacity to detect many legitimate issues, both models also produced a substantial number of hallucinated or redundant violations. These inaccuracies suggest a knowledge gap or misalignment with current HTML5 semantics. Additionally, the reliance on deprecated attributes like summary points to a tendency in some models to prioritize outdated best practices, potentially introducing confusion or unnecessary remediation work for developers.

In addressing RQ2, the evaluation revealed significant disparities in model reliability when subjected to a verification phase using the Chain-of-Verification-inspired prompt. Here, both GPT-4o mini and Gemini displayed weak self-consistency, with low overall accuracy (34% and 30%, respectively), high false-positive rates, and limited ability to correctly reassess hallucinated or redundant violations. The performance gaps between detection and verification stages underscore a fundamental limitation in their reasoning stability and factual grounding, which is critical for trustworthy automated evaluations. By contrast, the O3-mini model, when used in a second-stage validation role, demonstrated markedly superior consistency and judgment, achieving a high overall accuracy of 79%. It excelled not only in distinguishing valid issues from hallucinations but also in recognizing whether previously flagged items were either spurious or redundant. O3-mini's superior performance stems from its specialized architecture for logical reasoning [39]. Unlike generalist models that are optimized for a wide range of tasks, O3-mini is built for a deliberate, multi-step "chain of thought" process. This approach allows it to systematically analyze problems, internally verify its own logic, and reduce hallucinations and factual errors. Key to this is its ability to adjust a "reasoning effort" level, enabling a more thorough, internal analysis on complex tasks. This makes it a more reliable "thinker" for precision-critical jobs like code verification, where correctly distinguishing between valid and invalid code is paramount. This finding suggests that a tiered evaluation pipeline—where a high-recall model conducts the initial pass and a more conservative, high-precision model validates those findings—could be a viable and practical strategy for integrating LLMs into real-world accessibility audits.

5.2. Comparison with Related Works

Our findings are consistent with, yet distinct from, prior research on the use of LLMs for accessibility (see Table 1). Like Othman et al. [18] and Delnevo et al. [19], we observed that LLMs can correctly identify and remediate many accessibility issues in HTML code, but often with inconsistent or redundant attribute usage. Similarly, Duarte et al. [12] and López-Gil & Pereira [16] highlighted that different models specialize in different sub-tasks but struggle with certain systematic gaps (e.g., missing headings or nuanced guideline interpretation). Our study extends these observations by showing that such inconsistencies persist when LLMs operate on dynamically generated code across frameworks, and that post hoc verification with a reasoning-specialized model like O3-mini can mitigate these weaknesses.

Other works, such as Huynh et al. [20] and Taeb et al. [22], emphasize context-aware or multimodal accessibility support. By contrast, our contribution lies in demonstrating that LLMs can also make inferences about dynamic runtime behaviors (e.g., asynchronous data loading, error handling), a dimension typically invisible to static validation tools. This expands the scope of AI-assisted accessibility evaluation beyond what has been addressed in prior HTML- or UI-focused approaches. Moreover, while Aljedaani et al. [21,23] and Acosta-Vargas et al. [24] stressed educational value and limitations of generative AI outputs, our study highlights the feasibility of integrating LLMs within developer workflows (e.g., CI/CD pipelines) through multi-stage verification pipelines.

In sum, while the literature consistently points to both the opportunities and risks of relying on LLMs for accessibility tasks, our work focuses on dynamic code-level reasoning, and the benefits of pairing high-recall models with high-precision verifiers. These findings contribute to bridging the gap between prior single-shot evaluations of HTML fragments and a systematic, pipeline-based approach to accessibility validation.

5.3. Unique Capabilities and Challenges

One of the most interesting results obtained is that LLMs can make some considerations about web accessibility based on the dynamic behavior of the elements. In the experiments, LLMs raised accessibility concerns regarding asynchronous data loading and error handling. Such issues can not be detected by standard validation tools. Such a capability has the potential to upend the validation process. Before, when using server-side languages or JavaScript frameworks, the validation process was to be carried out on the generated HTML code for each dynamic page. Taking advantage of LLMs, the validation process can be continuously carried out while developing the code base. The cross-framework consistency of detection also suggests that LLMs are sufficiently abstracted from framework-specific syntax to generalize accessibility reasoning across languages like PHP and JavaScript-based frontend libraries. This opens opportunities for scalable accessibility checks in continuous integration pipelines regardless of the underlying stack.

On the negative side, despite their potential benefits, the experiments conducted illustrate that utilizing LLMs without human oversight poses challenges. The inconsistencies, especially in hallucination management and redundant suggestion identification, underscore the risks of deploying LLMs for automated audits without human oversight. Over-reporting can lead to audit fatigue or unnecessary fixes, while under-reporting critical issues risks poor user experience for people with disabilities. Then, the content generated by LLMs may perpetuate biases and inaccuracies inherent in their training data, as highlighted in previous studies [43]. This raises concerns about over-reliance on LLM output, leading to potential neglect of manual review and correction [44]. Furthermore, in many jurisdictions, compliance with accessibility standards is a legal obligation, and web developers ultimately bear the responsibility for ensuring adherence to these standards [45]. The results advocate for future research focused on refining LLM behavior through prompt engineering, feedback-loop training, or architectural improvements to promote better fact-grounding and domain alignment.

Ultimately, while LLMs are well-positioned to assist in accessibility evaluation tasks, their integration must be framed within a structured, multi-step validation pipeline, ideally guided by expert reviews and aligned with modern web standards. Further investigation into model behavior on domain-specific knowledge, semantic parsing of complex HTML structures, and evolution-aware guideline interpretation (e.g., accounting for HTML5 updates) will be critical to advancing the dependability of LLMs in this space.

5.4. Limitations

It is important to acknowledge several limitations inherent in our current study. First, it is important to note that while the implemented components in our experiments exhibited significant diversity in their internal structure, they were limited in scope, primarily generating tables rather than fully functional websites. It is worth considering, however, that validating table generation, as performed by the components in our dataset, represents one of the more complex aspects of accessibility validation. We chose this focus deliberately, as it allowed us to isolate and study a critical yet difficult accessibility task. However, extending the evaluation to complete websites was beyond the scope of this work due to the scale and variability involved, and remains a promising avenue for future research.

In addition, the validation of individual components does not guarantee the accessibility of the overall HTML page. Indeed, various accessibility issues can emerge when integrating these components into a complete webpage. This limitation stems from the fact that accessibility issues often emerge from interactions between components when integrated into a larger system. While our component-level approach enables a controlled and systematic analysis, it inevitably overlooks emergent accessibility barriers at the page level. Overcoming this limitation would require a comprehensive end-to-end evaluation framework that integrates both component and system perspectives, which is an important direction for future extensions of this work.

Our systematic investigation focused primarily on components built with Vue. This decision was motivated by the need to constrain experimental variability and ensure methodological rigor. We hypothesized that the behavior observed would not differ significantly across other frameworks (such as React or Angular) or languages (like PHP). However, empirically verifying this across multiple ecosystems would require a significantly larger dataset and infrastructure. Such an undertaking, while important, was beyond the practical scope of this study.

Furthermore, the handling of images warrants separate and more in-depth consideration. The generation of effective alternative text is highly context-dependent, varying based on the specific role an image plays within a webpage. This limitation reflects the broader difficulty of capturing contextual information in automated approaches. Addressing it would require multimodal reasoning that incorporates both visual and textual cues.

Finally, our study did not comprehensively address accessibility issues related to visual design such as accommodating color blindness and ensuring sufficient color contrast. This omission arises because these aspects depend not only on HTML but also on CSS and the final rendered output of the page. A multimodal pipeline capable of analyzing both code and rendered output would be required to overcome this limitation. While beyond the current scope, this remains a crucial step toward holistic accessibility validation.

The limitations identified in this work stem from deliberate methodological choices to ensure tractability, focus, and rigor. They also highlight directions where future work can extend and complement our contributions, particularly through multimodal analysis, broader framework coverage, and system-level validation.

6. Conclusions and Future Works

As the Web continues to evolve into a critical infrastructure for modern society, ensuring its inclusivity, equity, and sustainability becomes not only a technical challenge but also a moral imperative. This paper has explored the emerging role of LLM in supporting web developers toward more accessible and human-centered web design.

Our experiments yielded several key findings. First, in addressing RQ1, we demonstrated that state-of-the-art LLMs such as GPT-4o mini and Gemini can identify a wide range of accessibility violations across multiple frontend and backend technologies. The models consistently flagged issues such as missing scope attributes, redundant headers, and absent feedback mechanisms, revealing their potential as real-time accessibility collaborators during development. Importantly, they also surfaced accessibility concerns tied to dynamic behavior (e.g., asynchronous data loading, error handling), which are not detectable by conventional static validation tools. This highlights a novel capability of LLMs to reason beyond static code and into runtime considerations, paving the way for scalable integration into continuous integration pipelines.

Second, in addressing RQ2, we observed clear disparities between detection and verification performance. While both GPT-4o mini and Gemini showed broad coverage in detecting accessibility barriers, they struggled to maintain factual grounding and self-consistency during a verification phase, achieving relatively low accuracies (34% and 30%, respectively). By contrast, the O3-mini model excelled as a second-stage validator, achieving 79% accuracy in distinguishing genuine issues from hallucinations and redundant suggestions. This result underscores the importance of adopting a tiered pipeline where high-recall models perform initial detection, followed by high-precision models that refine and validate results before integration into developer workflows.

Together, these findings highlight both the promise and limitations of current LLMs. On the one hand, they can democratize accessibility knowledge by lowering the barriers for developers to detect violations early, reasoning across frameworks, and identifying issues missed by automated tools. On the other hand, their tendency to hallucinate violations, propagate outdated practices, and show verification inconsistencies underscores the risks of uncritical adoption. Human oversight, critical reflection, and adherence to evolving accessibility standards remain indispensable to ensure trustworthy results.

This paper paves the way for several future works. More LLMs should be included in the evaluation to have a broader understanding of how such models can be employed for large-scale accessibility testing. Some experiments could be focused on the fine-tuning of LLMs with the perspective of web accessibility to make the model understand some very specific and advanced aspects of it. This would also help in distinguishing valid practices from genuine violations, thereby reducing hallucinations and false positives. Finally, this approach allows the model to be continuously updated with the latest WCAG guidelines and evolving web technologies, ensuring it remains a current and highly effective tool for accessibility validation. Another promising research direction involves leveraging LLMs to generate concise and comprehensible summaries of web content, enhancing accessibility for individuals with cognitive disabilities or those seeking shorter, more digestible information. Furthermore, integrating a conversational agent into the website could further bridge the accessibility gap. Users with disabilities could interact with this agent directly, bypassing the need to navigate the website's interface to locate specific information.

Author Contributions: Conceptualization, G.D. and P.S.; methodology, B.B.; software, B.B.; validation, M.A., B.B., and G.D.; data curation, M.A.; writing—original draft preparation, M.A. and B.B.; writing—review and editing, G.D. and P.S.; visualization, M.A.; supervision, P.S. All authors have read and agreed to the published version of the manuscript.

Funding: This research received no external funding.

Institutional Review Board Statement: Not applicable.

Informed Consent Statement: Not applicable.

Data Availability Statement: The original data presented in the study are openly available in Zenodo at https://doi.org/10.5281/zenodo.17062188 (accessed on 5 September 2025).

Acknowledgments: We thank Giulia Bonifazi for her precious support and all the students who developed a version of the Vue components. During the preparation of this manuscript/study, the authors used ChatGPT (GPT-4o) for the purposes of writing assistance. The authors have reviewed and edited the output and take full responsibility for the content of this publication.

Conflicts of Interest: The authors declare no conflicts of interest.

Abbreviations

The following abbreviations are used in this manuscript:

LLM	Large Language Model
SDGs	Sustainable Development Goals

References

1. Hall, W.; Tiropanis, T. Web evolution and Web Science. *Comput. Netw.* **2012**, *56*, 3859–3865. [CrossRef]
2. Nallasivam, A.; KN, A.S.I.; Desai, K.; Kautish, S.; Ghoshal, S. Universal Access to Internet and Sustainability: Achieving the UN's Sustainable Development Goals. In *Digital Technologies to Implement the UN Sustainable Development Goals*; Springer Nature: Cham, Switzerland, 2024; pp. 235–255. [CrossRef]
3. Rathor, S.; Zhang, M.; Im, T. Web 3.0 and Sustainability: Challenges and Research Opportunities. *Sustainability* **2023**, *15*, 15126. [CrossRef]

4. Huda, M. Empowering application strategy in the technology adoption: Insights from professional and ethical engagement. *J. Sci. Technol. Policy Manag.* **2019**, *10*, 172–192. [CrossRef]
5. Bhandari, M.P. What is next for the sustainable development goals, what are the challenges concerning SDG 10—Reduced inequalities? *Sustain. Earth Rev.* **2024**, *7*, 23. [CrossRef]
6. Warschauer, M.; Matuchniak, T. New Technology and Digital Worlds: Analyzing Evidence of Equity in Access, Use, and Outcomes. *Rev. Res. Educ.* **2010**, *34*, 179–225. [CrossRef]
7. Leuthold, S.; Bargas-Avila, J.A.; Opwis, K. Beyond web content accessibility guidelines: Design of enhanced text user interfaces for blind internet users. *Int. J. Hum.-Comput. Stud.* **2008**, *66*, 257–270. [CrossRef]
8. Ara, J.; Sik-Lanyi, C.; Kelemen, A. Accessibility engineering in web evaluation process: A systematic literature review. *Univers. Access Inf. Soc.* **2023**, *23*, 653–686. [CrossRef] [PubMed]
9. Chadli, F.E.; Moumen, A.; Gretete, D. Factors & Theoretical Models Related to Web Accessibility Integration: A Systematic Literature Review. In Proceedings of the 2025 International Conference on Circuit, Systems and Communication (ICCSC), Fez, Morocco, 19–20 June 2025; pp. 1–7. [CrossRef]
10. Campoverde-Molina, M.; Luján-Mora, S. Artificial intelligence in web accessibility: A systematic mapping study. *Comput. Stand. Interfaces* **2025**, *96*, 104055. [CrossRef]
11. Herlina. Integrating Accessibility Features and Usability Testing for Inclusive Web Design. In Proceedings of the 2024 International Conference on Intelligent Cybernetics Technology & Applications (ICICyTA), Bali, Indonesia, 17–19 December 2024; pp. 1284–1289. [CrossRef]
12. Duarte, C.; Costa, M.; Seixas Pereira, L.; Guerreiro, J. Expanding Automated Accessibility Evaluations: Leveraging Large Language Models for Heading-Related Barriers. In Proceedings of the IUI '25: 30th International Conference on Intelligent User Interfaces Companion, Cagliari, Italy, 24–27 March 2025; pp. 39–42. [CrossRef]
13. Zan, D.; Chen, B.; Zhang, F.; Lu, D.; Wu, B.; Guan, B.; Yongji, W.; Lou, J.G. Large Language Models Meet NL2Code: A Survey. In Proceedings of the 61st Annual Meeting of the Association for Computational Linguistics (Volume 1: Long Papers), Toronto, ON, Canada, 9–14 July 2023. [CrossRef]
14. Yuan, L.; Xu, J.; Gui, H.; Sun, M.; Zhang, Z.; Liang, L.; Zhou, J. Improving Natural Language Understanding for LLMs via Large-Scale Instruction Synthesis. In Proceedings of the AAAI Conference on Artificial Intelligence, Philadelphia, PA, USA, 25 February–4 March 2025; Volume 39, pp. 25787–25795. [CrossRef]
15. Koga, S. Advancing large language models in nephrology: Bridging the gap in image interpretation. *Clin. Exp. Nephrol.* **2024**, *29*, 128–129. [CrossRef] [PubMed]
16. López-Gil, J.M.; Pereira, J. Turning manual web accessibility success criteria into automatic: An LLM-based approach. *Univers. Access Inf. Soc.* **2024**, *24*, 837–852. [CrossRef]
17. Lin, Z.; Guan, S.; Zhang, W.; Zhang, H.; Li, Y.; Zhang, H. Towards trustworthy LLMs: A review on debiasing and dehallucinating in large language models. *Artif. Intell. Rev.* **2024**, *57*, 243. [CrossRef]
18. Othman, A.; Dhouib, A.; Nasser Al Jabor, A. Fostering websites accessibility: A case study on the use of the Large Language Models ChatGPT for automatic remediation. In Proceedings of the PETRA '23: 16th International Conference on PErvasive Technologies Related to Assistive Environments, Corfu, Greece, 5–7 July 2023; pp. 707–713. [CrossRef]
19. Delnevo, G.; Andruccioli, M.; Mirri, S. On the Interaction with Large Language Models for Web Accessibility: Implications and Challenges. In Proceedings of the 2024 IEEE 21st Consumer Communications & Networking Conference (CCNC), Las Vegas, NV, USA, 6–9 January 2024; pp. 1–6. [CrossRef]
20. Huynh, G.K.; Lin, W. SmartCaption AI - Enhancing Web Accessibility with Context-Aware Image Descriptions Using Large Language Models. In Proceedings of the 2024 International Conference on Computer and Applications (ICCA), Cairo, Egypt, 17–19 December 2024; pp. 1–7. [CrossRef]
21. Aljedaani, W.; Eler, M.M.; Parthasarathy, P.D. Enhancing Accessibility in Software Engineering Projects with Large Language Models (LLMs). In Proceedings of the SIGCSE TS 2025: The 56th ACM Technical Symposium on Computer Science Education, Pittsburgh, PA, USA, 26 February–1 March 2025; pp. 25–31. [CrossRef]
22. Taeb, M.; Swearngin, A.; Schoop, E.; Cheng, R.; Jiang, Y.; Nichols, J. AXNav: Replaying Accessibility Tests from Natural Language. In Proceedings of the CHI '24: CHI Conference on Human Factors in Computing Systems, Honolulu, HI, USA, 11–16 May 2024; pp. 1–16. [CrossRef]
23. Aljedaani, W.; Habib, A.; Aljohani, A.; Eler, M.; Feng, Y. Does ChatGPT Generate Accessible Code? Investigating Accessibility Challenges in LLM-Generated Source Code. In Proceedings of the W4A '24: The 21st International Web for All Conference, Singapore, 13–14 May 2024; pp. 165–176. [CrossRef]
24. Acosta-Vargas, P.; Salvador-Acosta, B.; Novillo-Villegas, S.; Sarantis, D.; Salvador-Ullauri, L. Generative Artificial Intelligence and Web Accessibility: Towards an Inclusive and Sustainable Future. *Emerg. Sci. J.* **2024**, *8*, 1602–1621. [CrossRef]

25. Novac, O.C.; Madar, D.E.; Novac, C.M.; Bujdosó, G.; Oproescu, M.; Gal, T. Comparative study of some applications made in the Angular and Vue. js frameworks. In Proceedings of the 2021 16th International Conference on Engineering of Modern Electric Systems (EMES), Oradea, Romania, 10–11 June 2021; pp. 1–4.
26. Geetha, G.; Mittal, M.; Prasad, K.M.; Ponsam, J.G. Interpretation and Analysis of Angular Framework. In Proceedings of the 2022 International Conference on Power, Energy, Control and Transmission Systems (ICPECTS), Chennai, India, 8–9 December 2022; pp. 1–6.
27. Javeed, A. Performance optimization techniques for ReactJS. In Proceedings of the 2019 IEEE International Conference on Electrical, Computer and Communication Technologies (ICECCT), Coimbatore, India, 20–22 February 2019; pp. 1–5.
28. Gope, D.; Schlais, D.J.; Lipasti, M.H. Architectural support for server-side PHP processing. In Proceedings of the 2017 ACM/IEEE 44th Annual International Symposium on Computer Architecture (ISCA), Toronto, ON, Canada, 24–28 June 2017; pp. 507–520.
29. Bielak, K.; Borek, B.; Plechawska-Wójcik, M. Web application performance analysis using Angular, React and Vue. js frameworks. *J. Comput. Sci. Inst.* **2022**, *23*, 77–83. [CrossRef]
30. Andruccioli, M.; Bassi, B.; Delnevo, G.; Salomoni, P. The Tabular Accessibility Dataset: A Benchmark for LLM-Based Web Accessibility Auditing. *Data* **2025**, *10*, 149. [CrossRef]
31. Kong, A.; Zhao, S.; Chen, H.; Li, Q.; Qin, Y.; Sun, R.; Zhou, X.; Wang, E.; Dong, X. Better Zero-Shot Reasoning with Role-Play Prompting. In Proceedings of the 2024 Conference of the North American Chapter of the Association for Computational Linguistics: Human Language Technologies (Volume 1: Long Papers), Mexico City, Mexico, 16–21 June 2024. [CrossRef]
32. Dhuliawala, S.; Komeili, M.; Xu, J.; Raileanu, R.; Li, X.; Celikyilmaz, A.; Weston, J.E. Chain-of-Verification Reduces Hallucination in Large Language Models. In Proceedings of the Findings of the Association for Computational Linguistics: ACL 2024, Bangkok, Thailand, 11–16 August 2024; pp. 3563–3578.
33. Sejnowski, T.J. Large language models and the reverse turing test. *Neural Comput.* **2023**, *35*, 309–342. [CrossRef] [PubMed]
34. Hu, L.; Liu, Z.; Zhao, Z.; Hou, L.; Nie, L.; Li, J. A survey of knowledge enhanced pre-trained language models. *IEEE Trans. Knowl. Data Eng.* **2023**, *36*, 1413–1430. [CrossRef]
35. Min, B.; Ross, H.; Sulem, E.; Veyseh, A.P.B.; Nguyen, T.H.; Sainz, O.; Agirre, E.; Heintz, I.; Roth, D. Recent advances in natural language processing via large pre-trained language models: A survey. *ACM Comput. Surv.* **2023**, *56*, 1–40. [CrossRef]
36. Thirunavukarasu, A.J.; Ting, D.S.J.; Elangovan, K.; Gutierrez, L.; Tan, T.F.; Ting, D.S.W. Large language models in medicine. *Nat. Med.* **2023**, *29*, 1930–1940. [CrossRef] [PubMed]
37. Alqahtani, T.; Badreldin, H.A.; Alrashed, M.; Alshaya, A.I.; Alghamdi, S.S.; bin Saleh, K.; Alowais, S.A.; Alshaya, O.A.; Rahman, I.; Al Yami, M.S.; et al. The emergent role of artificial intelligence, natural learning processing, and large language models in higher education and research. *Res. Soc. Adm. Pharm.* **2023**, *19*, 1236–1242. [CrossRef] [PubMed]
38. OpenAI. GPT-4o. 2024. Available online: https://openai.com/index/hello-gpt-4o/ (accessed on 28 February 2025).
39. OpenAI. OpenAI o3-mini. 2022. Available online: https://openai.com/index/openai-o3-mini/ (accessed on 28 February 2025).
40. Google. Gemini 2.0 Flash. 2024. Available online: https://ai.google.dev/models/gemini (accessed on 28 February 2025).
41. Collins, E.; Ghahramani, Z. LaMDA: The Next Generation of Language Models, 2022. Google AI Blog. Available online: https://blog.google/technology/ai/lamda/ (accessed on 11 September 2025).
42. Narang, S.; Chowdhery, A. Pathways Language Model (PaLM): Scaling to 540 Billion Parameters for Breakthrough Performance, 2022. Google AI Blog. Available online: https://research.google/blog/pathways-language-model-palm-scaling-to-540-billion-parameters-for-breakthrough-performance/ (accessed on 11 September 2025).
43. Nozza, D.; Bianchi, F.; Hovy, D. Pipelines for social bias testing of large language models. In Proceedings of the BigScience Episode# 5–Workshop on Challenges & Perspectives in Creating Large Language Models. Association for Computational Linguistics, Dublin, Ireland, 27 May 2022.
44. Kasneci, E.; Seßler, K.; Küchemann, S.; Bannert, M.; Dementieva, D.; Fischer, F.; Gasser, U.; Groh, G.; Günnemann, S.; Hüllermeier, E.; et al. ChatGPT for good? On opportunities and challenges of large language models for education. *Learn. Individ. Differ.* **2023**, *103*, 102274. [CrossRef]
45. Lazar, J. Due Process and Primary Jurisdiction Doctrine: A Threat to Accessibility Research and Practice? In Proceedings of the 20th International ACM SIGACCESS Conference on Computers and Accessibility, Galway, Ireland, 22–24 October 2018; pp. 404–406.

big data and cognitive computing

MDPI

Article

Large Language Models as Kuwaiti Annotators

Hana Alostad

Systems and Software Development Department, Institute for Scientific Research, P.O. Box 24885, Safat 13109, Kuwait; hostad@kisr.edu.kw

Abstract: Stance detection for low-resource languages, such as the Kuwaiti dialect, poses a significant challenge in natural language processing (NLP) due to the scarcity of annotated datasets and specialized tools. This study addresses these limitations by evaluating the effectiveness of open large language models (LLMs) in automating stance detection through zero-shot and few-shot prompt engineering, with a focus on the potential of open-source models to achieve performance levels comparable to those of closed-source alternatives. We also highlight the critical distinctions between zero- and few-shot learning, emphasizing their significance for addressing the challenges posed by low-resource languages. Our evaluation involved testing 11 LLMs on a manually labeled dataset of social media posts, including GPT-4o, Gemini Pro 1.5, Mistral-Large, Jais-30B, and AYA-23. As expected, closed-source models such as GPT-4o, Gemini Pro 1.5, and Mistral-Large demonstrated superior performance, achieving maximum F1 scores of 95.4%, 95.0%, and 93.2%, respectively, in few-shot scenarios with English as the prompt template language. However, open-source models such as Jais-30B and AYA-23 achieved competitive results, with maximum F1 scores of 93.0% and 93.1%, respectively, under the same conditions. Furthermore, statistical analysis using ANOVA and Tukey's HSD post hoc tests revealed no significant differences in overall performance among GPT-4o, Gemini Pro 1.5, Mistral-Large, Jais-30B, and AYA-23. This finding underscores the potential of open-source LLMs as cost-effective and privacy-preserving alternatives for low-resource language annotation. This is the first study comparing LLMs for stance detection in the Kuwaiti dialect. Our findings highlight the importance of prompt design and model consistency in improving the quality of annotations and pave the way for NLP solutions for under-represented Arabic dialects.

Keywords: data annotation; large language models; zero-shot; few-shot; Arabic; Kuwaiti dialect

1. Introduction

Stance detection in natural language processing (NLP) is a technique aimed at identifying the attitude or position expressed by a writer towards a specific target or topic. This process typically classifies the stance into three categories—Favor, Against, or Neither—which allows for an understanding of opinions expressed in text [1,2]. The significance of stance detection has grown in various applications—particularly in social media analysis—and it can be valuable in several domains, including politics, social science, public opinion research, and public health, where it serves to gauge public sentiment on issues ranging from political opinions [3–6] to health-related topics, such as vaccination attitudes during the COVID-19 pandemic [7–9].

While there are an estimated 422 million Arabic speakers, encompassing various dialects [10], there remains a scarcity of research on Arabic stance detection [11–15]. Many researchers, particularly when considering low-resource language contexts, encounter challenges related to obtaining the extensive, high-quality annotated datasets needed to train robust machine learning models [16]. Creating training datasets involves human annotation, which is labor-intensive, requires comprehensive training to ensure annotator reliability, and can incur substantial costs.

Researchers have shown a growing interest in automating data annotation tasks in recent years through the use of zero-shot and few-shot prompt engineering with large language models (LLMs); examples of such studies include [17–22]. These authors have proposed various approaches for the automation of stance data annotation for different English language datasets.

A few research publications have explored the use of large language models to automate Arabic data annotation [23,24]. Most of these studies have focused on datasets from certain Arabic countries, with only two explicitly addressing automated text annotation of datasets containing tweets written in Kuwaiti dialect [11,25]. Both studies implemented weakly supervised learning approaches and utilized only zero-shot learning with encoder-based LLMs to automate text annotation for the NLP tasks of stance detection and sentiment classification. This highlights the need for further research to fill the gap in this field and address the challenges of stance detection in low-resource languages, specifically Arabic and Kuwaiti dialects.

In this study, we aim to evaluate and assess the capabilities of closed- and open-source LLMs, including GPT-4o [26], Mistral-Large-latest [27], Gemini-pro [28], Jais-30B [29], BLOOMz [30], AYA-23 [31], AYA-101 [32], AceGPT-32B [33], and mT0 [30], to automate the stance annotation task in both zero- and few-shot settings, specifically considering the Kuwaiti Dialect—a variant of the Arabic language primarily used in conversations between Kuwaiti people. We also aim to investigate whether changing the experimental setup and prompts with free open-source LLMs can result in a performance as effective as that obtained with paid closed-source models for stance detection regarding the Kuwaiti dialect, such that they can be utilized in the future to create an automated dataset annotation system that works efficiently with various Kuwaiti datasets.

The key contributions of this research are the following:

1. This study represents the first attempt to investigate the efficiency of stance detection for the Kuwaiti Dialect using zero- and few-shot prompts on closed-source generative LLMs, in comparison with other available open-source generative LLMs.
2. The study results demonstrate that using few-shot prompts with open-source LLMs for stance detection can achieve a performance comparable to that of paid closed-source models when applied to the Kuwaiti dialect vaccine stance dataset, offering significant cost savings and data privacy benefits.
3. This study compares model performance, focusing on consistency and reliability. Using statistical methods such as one-way ANOVA and Tukey's HSD, we identified significant differences and determined which models are most stable and reliable.
4. The study results are valuable for expanding training datasets, enhancing automated labeling systems, and filling the gaps in NLP research across various domains—particularly with respect to the Kuwaiti dialect—underscoring the broad impact of the research.

The rest of the paper is organized as follows: Section 2 provides information on multi-lingual transformer-based large language models (LLMs) and reviews some of the previous and current research on the use of LLMs as annotators. Section 3 describes our methodology. We start by introducing the dataset used in our experiments. Then, we present the pre-processing steps, including how we selected the LLMs and designed the prompt templates. We conclude this section with details of our experiments using LLMs as Kuwaiti annotators. In Section 4, we present the results of our study, which includes performance comparisons across different LLMs, an open versus closed LLM analysis, statistical significance tests, an examination of response consistency, and error analysis. Finally, in Section 5, we conclude the paper by summarizing our findings and discussing possible directions for future research.

2. Background

2.1. Large Language Models (LLMs)

Natural Language Processing (NLP) has been dramatically influenced by transformer architecture, primarily due to various crucial factors. One notable reason for its impact is its proficient capability to effectively comprehend extensive dependencies within textual data—a challenge that previous models generally failed to cover. This proficiency is achieved through the self-attention mechanisms used in transformers, which enable the model to focus on distinct segments of the input sequence simultaneously. Consequently, the model acquires the ability to grasp contextual information and dependencies across the entire sequence [34]. The architecture of a transformer is made up of encoder and decoder pipelines, where the encoder is used to process input sequences and the decoder is used to process output sequences [35]. In addition to encoder- and decoder-based LLMs, the use of the transformer architecture enables further models consisting of an encoder and a decoder. In this configuration, the encoder processes the input sequence and produces a fixed-length representation, which is subsequently utilized as the initial hidden state of the decoder. Subsequently, the decoder generates the output sequence based on this initial hidden state and the encoded information [36]. Models consisting of an encoder and a decoder are commonly used for text-to-text tasks such as machine translation, where the input sequence in one language is rendered into an output sequence in another language [36].

Bidirectional Encoder Representations from Transformers (BERT) is an example of an encoder-based large language model, which employs a masked input token training approach to evaluate bidirectional information [37]. While BERT was initially designed for English content, it has undergone fine-tuning to become a multi-lingual model which is suitable for monolingual and multi-lingual tasks [38].

Decoder-based models, on the other hand, include the well-known OpenAI GPT (Generative Pre-trained Transformer). This model utilizes auto-regressive language modeling to enable the generation of sequential text [39]. GPT is a multi-lingual model that also supports the Arabic language [40]. It is important to note that OpenAI models are closed-source and not free. Therefore, developers must pay to use or fine-tune GPT models based on the type of model used and the number of tokens used per request [41].

The Google Gemini closed-source models represent a class of decoder-based architectures refined for enhanced performance and structural efficiency. The Gemini API provides a variety of models tailored for distinct applications. The latest version—Gemini 1.5 Flash—is a multi-modal model that can process textual input alongside various audio and visual inputs such as natural images, charts, screenshots, PDFs, and videos, which is optimized for fast and versatile performance and can address a diverse variety of tasks. At the same time, Gemini 1.5 Pro is a mid-sized multi-modal model optimized for an extensive range of reasoning activities, including code and text generation, text modification, problem-solving, and data extraction and generation. Gemini 1.0 Pro is a natural language processing model that manages tasks such as multi-turn dialogues in text and code generation [28,42]. Gemini models are offered on a pay-as-you-go basis, with pricing structures and usage limits differing across tiers and varying with the used model [43,44].

Mistral is also a multi-lingual, decoder-based LLM developed by Mistral AI. The latest version, Mistral Large 2, is available under the Mistral Research License for non-commercial research purposes. This means that researchers can use and fine-tune the model for free. However, for commercial use, a Mistral Commercial License must be purchased. Depending on the deployment option chosen, users must pay for the platform or set up on-premises infrastructure. These new licenses differ from the earlier versions of Mistral models, released under the free Apache 2.0 open-source license for everyone to customize and deploy where they want [27].

Core42's open models, designated as Jais, comprise a collection of decoder-based architecture models with up to 70 billion parameters, enhancing their performance and efficiency in various tasks including summarization, comprehension, and text generation. Jais models are bilingual and demonstrate fluency in both Arabic and English. The models have been specifically designed to grasp the linguistic nuances and cultural sensitivities inherent to the Arabic language [45].

The AceGPT model is explicitly designed for Arabic. It is built on the LLaMA2 architecture and is open-source. The model has been fine-tuned, using Reinforcement Learning from AI Feedback (RLAIF), to align with local values and culture through incorporating Arabic texts and culturally relevant instructions [33].

BLOOMz (BigScience Language Open-science Open-access Multilingual) refers to a group of decoder-based architecture models that have been pre-trained on multi-lingual language models. These models are capable of understanding and following human instructions in dozens of languages. To enhance their ability to follow instructions in multiple languages, the models underwent multi-task fine-tuning on top of BLOOMz [30].

The mT0 and mT0-mt models, built by BigScience using the T5 encoder–decoder transformer architecture, were designed for multi-lingual tasks. These models were trained on diverse, multi-lingual datasets to support various languages. Both models are open-source and can handle over 50 languages. mT0 models are fine-tuned on multi-lingual datasets with English prompts, while mT0-mt models are fine-tuned on multi-lingual datasets with English and machine-translated prompts [30].

Finally, the Aya-101 model is a massively multi-lingual open-source LLM that was a result of a global initiative led by Cohere For AI; in particular, Aya-101 was built by fine-tuning the 13B parameter mT5 model [32]. In addition, Aya-23 is a multi-lingual open-source LLM that builds on the Aya model. It covers 23 languages and is designed to balance breadth and depth. Unlike Aya-101, which covers 101 languages, Aya-23 allocates more capacity to fewer languages during pre-training, significantly improving tasks for those 23 languages [31]. A summary of these LLMs is presented in the Appendix A (Table A1).

2.2. *Arabic Stance Detection with LLMs*

The researchers in [14] conducted a preliminary study on the detection of authorities' stances toward rumors in Arabic tweets. They constructed and released the first Authority STance towards Rumors (AuSTR) dataset. Their work fine-tuned ARBERT [46] to identify stances in rumor-related discourse.

Additionally, in [47], the researchers developed a multi-lingual LLM which is specialized in analyzing news and social media content. Its fine-tuning for stance detection tasks showcased the potential of multi-lingual LLMs to adapt to domain-specific challenges, especially for under-represented languages such as Arabic [47].

The StanceEval 2024 Shared Task [48], as part of the ArabicNLP 2024 program, utilized the MAWQIF [13] dataset, which consists of Arabic tweets annotated for stance, sentiment, and sarcasm. The shared task invited participants to develop models capable of detecting stances toward three topics: COVID-19 vaccines, digital transformation, and women's empowerment. The best-performing system, developed by AlexUNLP-BH [49], achieved a Macro F1 score of 84.38 through fine-tuning AraBERT variants, applying multi-task learning (MTL), and leveraging ensemble methods. The second- and third-place systems,

MGKM [50] and StanceCrafters [51], achieved Macro F1 scores of 82.06 and 81.68, respectively, using fine-tuning and MTL-based strategies [48].

Complementary to these efforts, specialized LLMs and benchmarking initiatives have emerged. The researchers in [24] introduced an Arabic-specific benchmark to evaluate LLMs, highlighting their performance across various NLP tasks including stance detection [24].

2.3. Kuwaiti Dialect NLP Research

Very few NLP studies have focused on the Kuwaiti dialect. Those studies in this line have explored various NLP tasks, including sentiment analysis, opinion mining, and stance detection. The research conducted by [52] represents the first contribution to natural language processing for Kuwaiti dialect. This study introduced an approach for opinion mining in microblogging, focusing on sentiment extraction from 340,000 manually labeled Twitter posts. The researchers experimented with machine learning classifiers, including J48 [53], ADTREE [54], Random Tree [55], and Support Vector Machines (SVM) [56], to classify sentiments into positive, negative, and neutral categories. The SVM classifier achieved a precision of 76%, a recall of 61%, and an F1 score of 69% for positive sentiments; in comparison, it attained a precision of 65%, a recall of 78%, and an F1 score of 71% for negative sentiments.

In the study [25], the researchers addressed the lack of resources for the Kuwaiti dialect (specifically for sentiment analysis) through proposing a weakly supervised transfer learning approach to automate dataset labeling. Their methodology involved collecting over 16,600 tweets spanning various themes and timeframes to mitigate content bias. The dataset comprised 7905 negative, 7902 positive, and 860 neutral tweets. The authors employed weak supervised learning, integrating rule-based methods in a zero-shot learning mode on pre-trained language models to assign sentiment labels. This approach reduced the reliance on extensive human annotation. For evaluation, the dataset was tested using various traditional machine learning classifiers and advanced deep learning language models, and was compared with fine-tuned Arabic BERT models, including AraBERT [57], ARBERT [46], MARBERT [46], Microsoft Multilingual Model (MiniLM) [58], and CAMeL-BERT [59]. The ARBERT model achieved the highest accuracy at 89% on the testing dataset, demonstrating the effectiveness of the proposed weak supervised approach in creating reliable sentiment analysis resources for the Kuwaiti dialect.

The researchers in [11] introduced Q8VaxStance, a dataset labeling system created to detect stances toward vaccines in tweets written in the Kuwaiti dialect. This study also addressed the issue of linguistic resources for the Kuwaiti dialect, which are currently limited. Researchers collected 42,815 unlabeled tweets related to vaccines, posted between December 2020 and July 2022. To annotate the dataset, the study employed a combination of weak supervised learning and zero-shot learning techniques. A total of 52 experiments were conducted using various labeling function configurations, including keyword detection and zero-shot models. The results demonstrated that merging keyword detection with zero-shot learning significantly enhanced the model performance. This study's best-performing configurations achieved the highest Macro F1 score of 83%.

2.4. LLMs as Data Annotators

Data annotation is the process of labeling raw data with relevant information [60], which is an essential component of AI projects as it significantly influences the effectiveness of supervised machine learning models. Manual annotation can be time-consuming and expensive, often resulting in low-quality labels. To address these challenges, research has introduced automated annotation methods that employ LLMs as annotators, utilizing zero-

and few-shot in-context learning strategies. LLMs have attracted considerable attention due to their ability to perform as zero- and few-shot learners. Through specific prompting techniques, a diverse array of tasks can be achieved by offering these pre-trained models either descriptive instructions (referred to as "zero-shot") or a limited number of examples along with instructions (known as "few-shot"). Once provided with a prompt, the model can generate various outputs based on the given instructions, ranging from text and code to images, videos, or audio, depending on the specific model used [61–65]. Prompting techniques enable the rapid generation of outputs from pre-trained models for new tasks without fine-tuning. In contrast, fine-tuning a pre-trained model requires re-training it to learn a new task or domain, which demands significant computing resources and a large labeled dataset. This process is both time-consuming and expensive. Utilizing prompt engineering, we can substantially save time and resources. Several studies have explored the use of LLMs as annotators in various domains, such as medicine, finance, and cybersecurity. For instance, the researchers in [66] proposed combining LLMs with human expertise to generate ground-truth labels for efficient medical text annotation. In the financial domain, [67] investigated the potential of LLMs as efficient data annotators for the extraction of relations from financial documents. In the cybersecurity domain, [68] compared the effectiveness of LLMs in detecting phishing URLs when utilized with prompt engineering techniques versus when fine-tuned.

Most of the research in this field has focused on English datasets, with limited exploration and evaluation of LLMs as annotators for low-resource languages. For example, in [69], the researchers proposed a methodology to use LLMs as annotators for Named Entity Recognition (NER) tasks in low-resource language contexts, such as African languages. Similarly, in [23], the researchers evaluated the performance of LLMs (i.e., using GPT-4) for fine-grained propaganda detection from Arabic text. They developed the ArPro dataset, which consists of 8000 paragraphs from newspaper articles labeled at the text span level following a taxonomy of 23 propagandistic techniques.

Additionally, [24] proposed LAraBench to address the gap for Arabic NLP and speech processing tasks, utilizing and evaluating multi-lingual and Arabic LLM models and zero- and few-shot learning techniques across 61 publicly available datasets.

In the context of the Kuwaiti dialect, only two papers have explicitly addressed automated text annotation of Kuwaiti dialect datasets [11,25]. Both studies implemented weakly supervised learning approaches and utilized zero-shot learning based on encoder models to automate text annotation for the NLP tasks of stance detection and sentiment classification.

Based on the above, the field of Kuwaiti dialect NLP remains under-explored compared to Arabic MSA and other well-resourced Arabic dialects. The primary challenges include the limited availability of annotated datasets, the informal nature of the dialect, and the lack of dedicated tools or benchmarks. Future research should focus on expanding datasets and leveraging state-of-the-art techniques, such as large language models, to improve the adaptability and accuracy of NLP tools for the Kuwaiti dialect. Exploring other tasks such as machine translation, named entity recognition, and conversational AI in Kuwaiti Arabic could further enhance the field.

Consequently, there is a clear need for additional research efforts to bridge the existing research gaps in stance detection for Kuwaiti dialect. Addressing this gap, our research builds upon prior studies [11,25] through focusing on generative LLMs. We experiment with both zero- and few-shot prompting techniques, evaluating closed-source generative LLMs alongside open-source alternatives to assess their efficiency in stance detection for the Kuwaiti dialect.

3. Methodology

3.1. Dataset

We utilized the test dataset Q8Stance from the research paper [11], which consists of 519 human-labeled tweets that were collected using the Twitter academic API with a query that included keywords and hashtags related to COVID-19 vaccination. The tweets collected were written in the Kuwaiti dialect, and researchers ensured this by only including Arabic tweets with locations specific to Kuwait. The dataset was then given to Kuwaiti native speakers to annotate the tweets as either pro-vaccine or anti-vaccine. The final labeled dataset includes 265 tweets that are anti-vaccine and 254 tweets that are pro-vaccine. Examples of human-annotated tweets are presented in Table 1.

Table 1. Sample human annotated test data (Q8Stance).

Tweet in Kuwiati Dialect	Tweet in English	Label
المفروض مايخلطون بين المطعمين واللي مو مطعمين لازم يفصلونهم ويميزون المطعمين وبالنسبه للقرارات ما اعتبرها سذاجه اكثر حالات الوفاة انزلت خلال شهر بسبب التطعيم نعم للتطعيم نعم للتطعيم	They are not supposed to confuse those who are vaccinated with those who are not vaccinated. They must separate them and distinguish between the two vaccinated people. As for the decisions, I do not consider them naive. Most deaths occurred within a month due to vaccination. Yes to vaccination. Yes to vaccination.	Pro-vaccine
تم التطعيم اشكر وزارة الصحة وكل من يعمل فيها ولها من اجل صحة الكويت ، تنظيم راقي جدا	I have been vaccinated. I thank the Ministry of Health and everyone who works there and for it for the health of Kuwait, a very sophisticated organization	Pro-vaccine
الحل للوصول للمناعة المجتمعية الي من خلالها نقدر نرد حق حياتنا الطبيعية اهوا التطعيم اذا ماسجلت بعدك للتطعيم سجل، واذا عندك تساؤل أو تخوّف تقدر تسأل المختصين والكل مستعد يجاوبك نعم للتطعيم	The solution to achieving community immunity through which we can regain the right to our normal lives is vaccination. If you have not yet registered for vaccination, register, and if you have a question or fear, you can ask the specialists and everyone is ready to answer you yes to vaccination	Pro-vaccine
لا تحملوا المواطنين فشلكم الذريع لا للتطعيم الاجباري	Do not blame the citizens for your miserable failure, no to compulsory vaccination	Anti-vaccine
هل يعقل و نحن في دولة تملك دستور وبرلمان وديمقراطية وعلاوة على ذلك معروف عنها إنها ببلد الإنسانية ويجبر شعبها على التطعيم وعليه لا للتطعيم الاجباري	Is it possible that we are in a country that has a constitution, parliament, and democracy? Furthermore, it is known to be a country of humanity and its people are forced to be vaccinated! So, no to compulsory vaccination.	Anti-vaccine
مستمرين ساحة الإرادة لا للتطعيم الاجباري	Continuing the arena of will, no to compulsory vaccination	Anti-vaccine

3.2. Pre-Processing

We started by determining the selection criteria for the closed and open LLMs for use in our research experiments. We also designed the prompt templates to be used to generate the zero- and few-shot prompts and then implemented them on the test dataset. The following sub-sections provide detailed information about each of these processes.

3.2.1. Selection of Large Language Models (LLMs)

To effectively manage our limited budget and computing resources, we established specific selection criteria for the LLMs we planned to evaluate. Our selection was based on four key factors: support for the Arabic language, model performance, parameter size, and model accessibility. These criteria guided our choices among the available LLMs, resulting in the selection of 11 models; namely, 3 proprietary closed-source and 8 open-source LLMS.

First, for the proprietary closed-source LLMs, we chose OpenAI's GPT-4o. OpenAI is a major player in generative artificial intelligence, where GPT-4o is an autoregressive, omni-multi-lingual model capable of processing various input types, such as text, audio, images, and video, generating outputs in any of these formats. This model was pre-trained using data from various sources up to October 2023 [26].

Next, we selected Google Gemini—a key competitor to OpenAI. Gemini is a set of multi-lingual multi-modal models trained jointly on image, audio, video, and text data. We used the Gemini-1.5-pro version in our experiments [28].

The third selected proprietary LLM was Mistral Large 2, which allows for usage and modification for research and non-commercial purposes. However, a Mistral Commercial License must be obtained for any commercial use [27]. We limited our selection of closed-source models to three models, due to our budgetary constraints and the insufficient support for the Arabic language in many other LLMs.

To select suitable open-source large language models (LLMs) that support Arabic, we evaluated several options and chose the following:

From BigScience, we selected the multi-lingual LLMs bloomz-7b1-mt, bloomz-7b1, mT0-xxl-mt, and mT0-xxl [30].

From Cohere, we opted for AYA-101 (13 billion parameters) and AYA-23 (35 billion parameters), which are known for their effectiveness in Arabic NLP tasks [31,32].

From Core42, we chose jais-30B, a bilingual model for Arabic and English, specifically using jais-30b-chat-v3 [29].

We also included AceGPT-v2-32B [33,70], a bilingual model based on LLaMA 2 and trained on Arabic and English datasets. To ensure cultural alignment, the model incorporated reinforcement learning from an AI Feedback reward model using localized data based on GPT-4 preferences. The appendix (Table A1) presents a summary of the selected LLMs.

3.2.2. Design of Prompt Templates

We developed 24 prompt templates covering zero- and few-shot learning contexts. Our initial step involved creating three primary zero-shot prompt templates in the Modern Standard Arabic (MSA) language, describing the task and specifying the expected output labels; in the third template, we added the role of the LLM as an "expert text annotator" as extra information. Later, these prompt templates were used with the tweets/posts written in the Kuwaiti dialect; we then translated the zero-shot prompt templates from Arabic (MSA) into English templates. In this case, we named the template as a mixed language, as it will use English for the prompt instructions and the Kuwaiti Arabic dialect for the content of the post. Figure 1 illustrates the three main Arabic and English (Mixed) prompt templates.

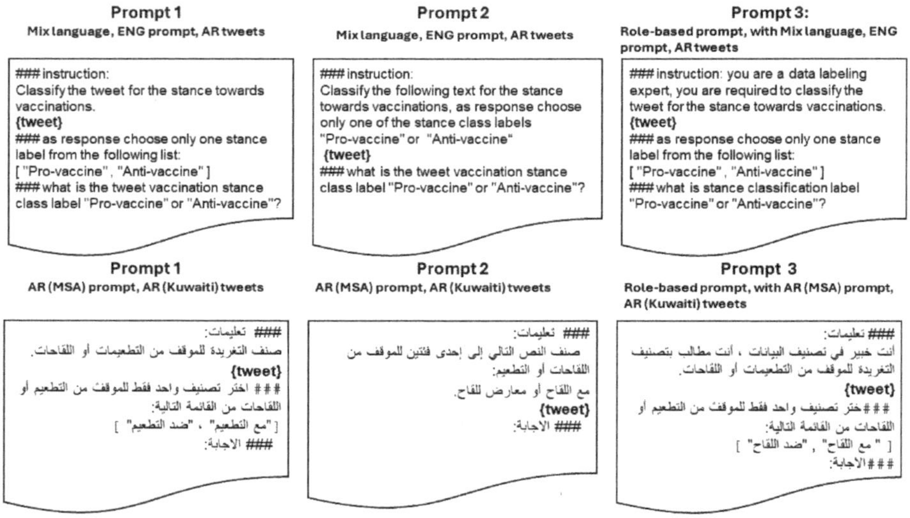

Figure 1. Arabic and English prompt templates.

Next, to create the few-shot prompt templates, we first needed to select six tweets as examples that were not part of the Q8Stance test dataset. We accomplished this by manually selecting examples from the training dataset and making sure that they covered both pro- and anti-vaccine stances. These examples provided context for the task and were used to develop 2-, 4-, and 6-shot prompt templates. We limited the number of examples to six to avoid exceeding the maximum context size limit of the language models and incurring additional costs, especially with respect to the paid closed models.

3.3. *LLMs as Kuwaiti Annotator Experiments*

The steps we followed to execute the experiments are detailed below.

1. Dataset Preparation:
    - From the Q8Stance test dataset, retrieve text from each tweet.
    - For the few-shot prompts, also retrieve six example tweets covering pro- and anti-vaccine stances.
2. Prompt Template Generation:
    - Generate zero-shot prompts by applying the zero-shot prompt templates on each row from the Q8Stance test dataset. These prompts serve as the input for LLM inference, guiding it to complete the given annotation task.
    - Generate few-shot prompts using example tweets through applying the few-shot prompt templates combined with the few-shot examples on each row from the Q8Stance test dataset.
3. For each generated prompt, call the LLM API to execute the instructions in the prompt.
4. Store the completion results from the LLM.
5. Post-processing Steps: After receiving the completion results from the LLM, we apply post-processing steps to enable comparison with the human-labeled test dataset. This involves filtering keywords from the results and mapping them to related labels. This step is necessary as the LLMs sometimes do not follow the exact instructions. Instead of returning only the label, they produce results that are not directly comparable to the human-annotated labels. For example, they may return labels while adding extra text or return variations in Arabic labels.

6. Store the final LLM results.
7. To evaluate the performance of the LLMs, we compared the final results of the LLM with human-annotated labels from the Q8VaxStance test dataset. For the evaluation metrics, we utilized the Macro F1 formula. Additionally, we conducted a one-way ANOVA and Tukey's HSD post hoc tests in order to determine whether the experimental results were statistically significant. We chose one-way ANOVA as it is a robust statistical method for comparing the means of multiple groups, allowing us to determine whether there are statistically significant differences among them. In this study, the groups represent the performances of different models (or conditions), while the dependent variable is the performance metric, specifically the Macro F1 score. One-way ANOVA enabled us to test the null hypothesis that all model performances were equal, thereby revealing any significant differences among the groups. After identifying significant differences using ANOVA, we applied Tukey's HSD (Honestly Significant Difference) test as a post hoc analysis to determine which specific groups (models) differ from each other. To further analyze the consistency of the responses generated by the LLMs, we assessed the variability in their performance across different prompts and settings. A model that produces consistent results will exhibit low variance in its Macro F1 scores across various scenarios, while a model with high variance would be considered less reliable. We calculated the variance [71] in Macro F1 scores across different prompts for each LLM model using the variance formula variance Formula (1):

$$\sigma^2 = \frac{1}{N}\sum_{i=1}^{N}(x_i - \mu)^2, \tag{1}$$

where

- σ^2 is the variance;
- N is the total number of Macro F1 scores (or observations);
- x_i represents each individual Macro F1 score;
- μ is the mean of the Macro F1 scores.

After variance calculation, we checked the variability across models, and models with lower variance in their Macro F1 scores were considered more consistent.

4. Results

We implemented the experiments using the Python programming language, with most of the execution carried out on Google Colab Pro+. However, for the Jais-30B, AYA 23, and AceGPT32 models, we utilized an hourly GPU instance from RunPod [72], as these models required more than 40 GB of GPU VRAM for loading and inference. We applied the steps in Figure 2 for each selected LLM model. To compare the performance of the LLMs, we focused on different scenarios based on various criteria, such as the following:

- Prompt Type: zero- versus few-shot setting;
- Prompt Language: Arabic (MSA) prompts versus English prompts;
- LLM source: closed- versus open-source LLMs.

Furthermore, to ensure a comprehensive performance analysis, we conducted a one-way ANOVA and Tukey's HSD post hoc tests to determine whether the observed differences in the experimental results were statistically significant. Additionally, we assessed the LLM response consistency to evaluate their variability in performance.

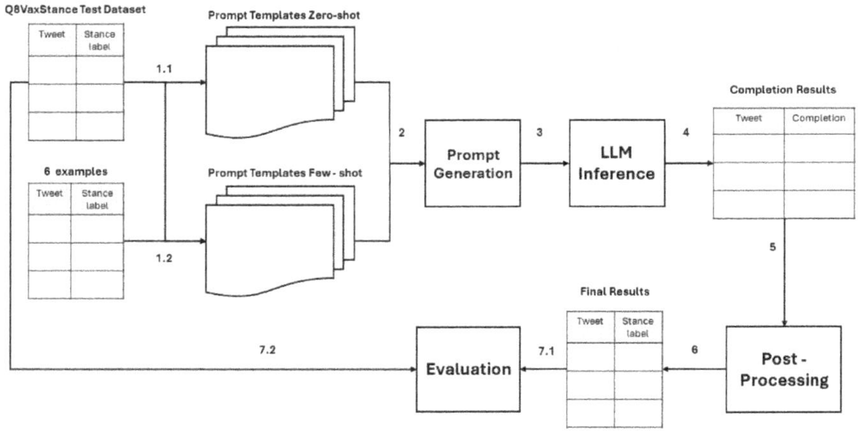

Figure 2. LLMs as Kuwaiti annotators: experimental steps.

4.1. Performance Comparison Across LLMs

Examining the overall performance of the LLMs, as illustrated in Table 2 and Figure 3, and the performance comparison of the LLMs by prompt language (Arabic vs. Mixed) plus prompt type (zero- vs. few-shot), as illustrated in Figure 4, uncovered several key findings:

The best-performing large language models (LLMs) were GPT-4o and Gemini-pro 1.5, both achieving a mean Macro F1 score of 0.94. These models consistently maintained high Macro F1 scores across various testing conditions. They excel when handling mixed-language prompts, such as English instructions combined with tweets in the Kuwaiti dialect and few-shot examples.

GPT-4o achieved the highest Macro F1 score of 0.954 when using two-shot examples (Mix-2FS), while Gemini-pro 1.5 reached a high Macro F1 score of 0.950 with four-shot examples (Mix-4FS). Both LLMs performed strongly in zero-shot settings when using Arabic or English prompts. GPT-4o scored 0.937 with an Arabic prompt template (AR-ZS) and 0.939 with a mixed prompt template (Mix-ZS). In comparison, Gemini-pro 1.5 scored 0.932 with the Arabic prompt template (AR-ZS) and 0.945 with the mixed prompt template (Mix-ZS), demonstrating its solid capabilities in zero-shot settings.

Mistral-Large-Latest was the next best-performing large language model (LLM), which achieved a mean Macro F1 score of 0.92. This score is only slightly lower than that of GPT-4o and Gemini-pro 1.5. Mistral-Large-latest excelled in few-shot prompt template settings across both languages, achieving performance scores of 0.924 with the Arabic six few-shot templates (AR-6FS) and 0.932 with the mixed language templates (Mix-4FS). Additionally, the model demonstrated solid performance with zero-shot template settings across both languages, with scores of 0.911 for Arabic templates (AR-ZS) and 0.917 for mixed language templates (Mix-ZS).

The third best-performing language model was the open-source bilingual Jais-30B, which achieved a mean Macro F1 score of 0.90. It performed excellently in few-shot prompting for both languages, with scores of 0.916 when using Arabic prompts (AR-6FS) and 0.930 when using mixed language prompts (Mix-6FS). However, its performance in zero-shot settings was lower, with scores of 0.867 in Arabic (AR-ZS) and 0.884 in mixed prompts (Mix-ZS). This suggests that the model requires more context or examples to understand and perform the given tasks effectively.

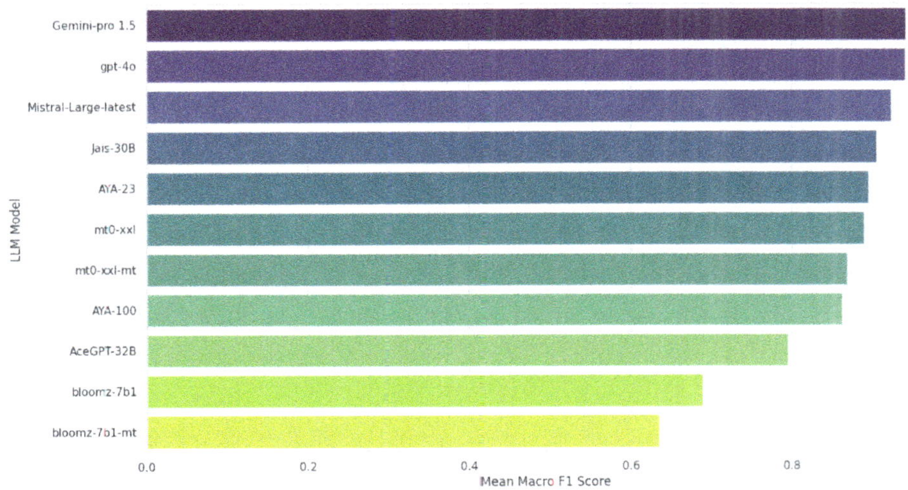

Figure 3. Performance comparison between mean (Macro F1) across LLMs.

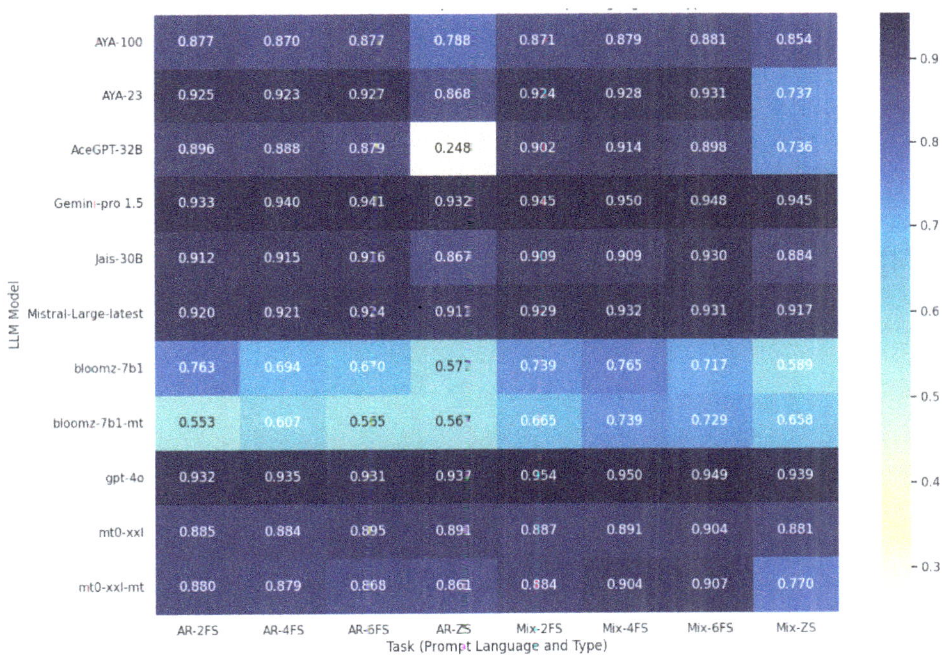

Figure 4. Performance comparison across LLMs based on prompt language and prompt type.

The models AYA-23, mT0-xxl, mT0-xxl-mt, and AYA-100 performed well across most prompt templates, achieving mean Macro F1 scores of 0.895, 0.889, 0.869, and 0.862, respectively. These models also showed their best performance in six few-shot settings; for instance, when using mixed language templates in the Mix-6FS templates setting, AYA-23, mT0-xxl, mT0-xxl-mt, and AYA-100 achieved Macro F1 scores of 0.931, 0.904, 0.907, and 0.881, respectively. However, their performance tended to decrease when using zero-shot prompts.

Table 2. Comparison of mean (Macro F1) scores between LLMs.

LLM	Mean Macro F1 Score
Gemini-pro 1.5 *	0.94 *
GPT-4o *	0.94 *
Mistral-Large-latest	0.92
Jais-30B	0.90
AYA-23	0.89
mt0-xxl	0.88
mt0-xxl-mt	0.87
AYA-100	0.86
AceGPT-32B	0.79
bloomz-7b1	0.69
bloomz-7b1-mt	0.63

*: indicates best-performing LLMs.

The AceGPT-32B model exhibited inconsistency in its performance. For example, it performed well in mixed-language few-shot settings, achieving a score of 0.914 (Mix-4FS); however, its zero-shot performance was notably poor, particularly with Arabic language prompts, where it only reached a Macro F1 score of 0.248. Analyzing the results of this language model revealed that this low score is primarily due to hallucinations: AceGPT-32B either generated unrelated text or failed to produce any results. We attempted several changes to the LLM configuration, but none of these adjustments improved the outcomes.

The worst-performing LLMs, as illustrated in Figures 3 and 4, were bloomz-7b1 and bloomz-7b1-mt. Bloomz-7b1-mt achieved the lowest mean Macro F1 score of 0.635, while bloomz-7b1 scored 0.689. Both of these open-source LLMs generally struggled, especially in zero-shot settings. In this context, bloomz-7b1-mt achieved Macro F1 scores of 0.567 when using Arabic template with Zero-shot (AR-ZS) and 0.658 in mixed language prompt template (Mix-ZS), whereas bloomz-7b1 achieved 0.577 and 0.589 when using AR-ZS and Mix-ZS prompt template setting, respectively. Even in few-shot scenarios, their performance remained below average, compared to other models. Both of these LLMs have a parameter size of 7 billion, which explains the significant difference in their performance.

Finally, we compared the best annotation results of our proposed method, which utilizes open-source LLMs as annotators, with the Q8VaxStance Dataset Labeling System [11]. The best-performing open-source LLM using our approach was Jais-30B, which achieved a Macro F1 score of 0.93 with few-shot prompts that included six examples, using English as the instruction language. In zero-shot scenarios, Jais-30B achieved scores of 0.88 and 0.86 using English and Arabic as the instruction languages, respectively. In contrast, the Q8VaxStance system reported a Macro F1 score of 0.83 when applying weak supervised learning through keyword and hashtag detection labeling functions alongside zero-shot model labeling functions. These results demonstrate that our approach outperformed the Q8VaxStance system in both zero- and few-shot contexts. We can expect even better performance when these two approaches are combined.

4.2. Open vs. Closed LLMs

The comparison between open- and closed-source LLMs, as illustrated in Table 2, revealed distinct performance differences based on their mean Macro F1 scores. Among the closed-source LLMs, GPT-4o and Gemini Pro 1.5 achieved the highest mean Macro F1 score of 0.94, and Mistral-Large-latest achieved a score of 0.92. These results highlight the strong performance of closed-source LLMs. On the open-source side, Jais-30B had the strongest performance, achieving a mean Macro F1 score of 0.90—comparable to that of the best closed LLMs—and AYA-23 also showed competitive results with a score of

0.89. Overall, the results from Figure 4 indicate that using few-shot prompts with six examples on open-source LLMs—such as Jais-30B and AYA-23—for stance detection in the Kuwaiti dialect can achieve a performance close to that of paid closed-source LLMs such as GPT-4o, Gemini Pro 1.5, and the latest version of Mistral Large. Furthermore, this suggests that open-source LLMs with fewer parameters can achieve performance similar to larger closed-source LLMs. Additionally, incorporating human feedback into the process can further enhance the annotation performance.

4.3. Statistical Significance Tests

We conducted a one-way ANOVA test to determine whether there were statistically significant differences in Macro F1 scores among the tested LLMs. The ANOVA results indicated a highly significant difference in performance across the LLMs, with a p-value of $2.81943943 \times 10^{-33}$. This value suggests that the performance, as measured by the Macro F1 score, varied significantly between at least some of the LLMs tested.

Furthermore, we performed a post hoc analysis by applying Tukey's Honest Significant Difference (HSD) test to identify which specific LLMs differed in performance. This test compared each pair of LLMs to assess whether the differences in their Macro F1 scores were statistically significant.

As illustrated in Figure 5 and Table A5, the Tukey's HSD test results revealed several statistically significant differences between the LLMs. Notably, the BigScience models (i.e., bloomz-7b1 and bloomz-7b1-mt) significantly under-performed when compared to all other LLMs. Additionally, we found that the AceGPT-32B model demonstrated significantly lower performance than all other LLMs, except for mT0-xxl-mt and AYA-100, where there was no significant statistical difference. These differences were all statistically significant, with p-values less than 0.05.

While some models showed apparent performance differences, other comparisons did not yield statistically significant results. For example, there were no significant differences between GPT-4o and models such as Gemini Pro 1.5, Jais 30B, mT0-xxl, mT0-xxl-mt, AYA-100, AYA-23, and Mistral-Large. This result suggests that these models offer comparable performance in terms of Macro F1 scores. We observed that the mT0-xxl and mT0-xxl-mt versions of the mT0 model performed equally well, showing no statistically significant difference in their performance. Similarly, there was no significant difference between AYA-100 and AYA-23, as both LLMs from Cohere For AI demonstrated comparable performance.

We also applied Tukey's HSD test to compare the results obtained with zero-shot (ZS) and few-shot (2FS, 4FS, 6FS) prompt templates. The results, as shown in Figure 6 and Table A2, indicate statistically significant differences between the results obtained using zero-shot prompts and those from 2FS, 4FS, and 6FS, which is an expected outcome. However, we found no overall statistical significance among the 2FS, 4FS, and 6FS results. Next, we applied Tukey's HSD test to compare the results of prompt templates 1, 2, and 3. Based on the results, as shown in Figure 7 and Table A3, we found no statistically significant differences between the different prompt templates. Finally, we applied Tukey's HSD test to compare the results of Arabic and Mixed (English instructions, Kuwaiti dialect examples, and tweet text) language prompt templates. As shown in Figure 8 and Table A4, the results indicated no overall statistically significant differences between the different prompt templates.

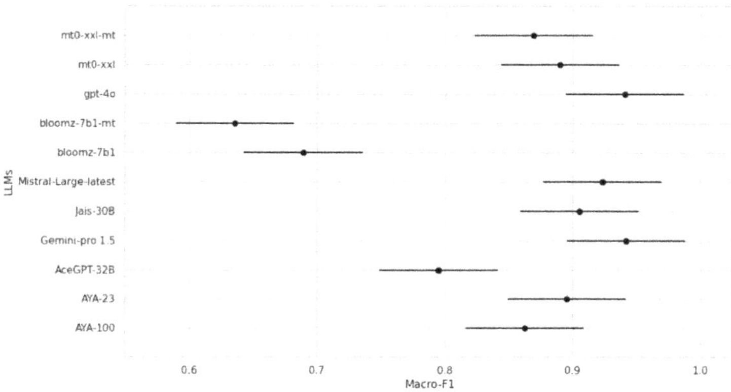

Figure 5. Tukey's HSD test results: Pairwise comparisons of models.

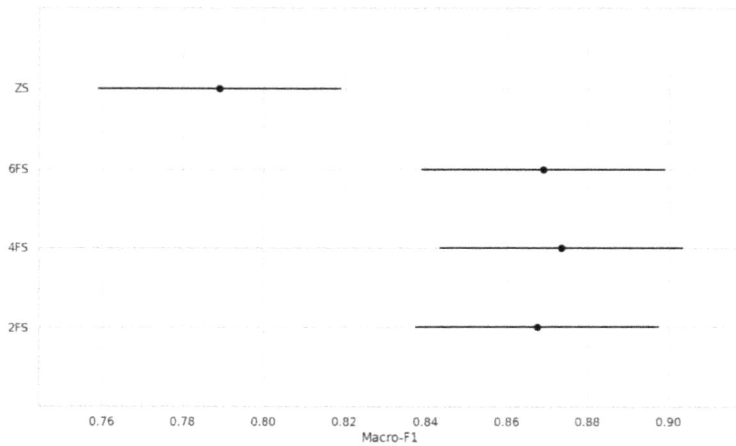

Figure 6. Tukey's HSD test results: Pairwise comparisons of zero-shot and few-shot prompt templates.

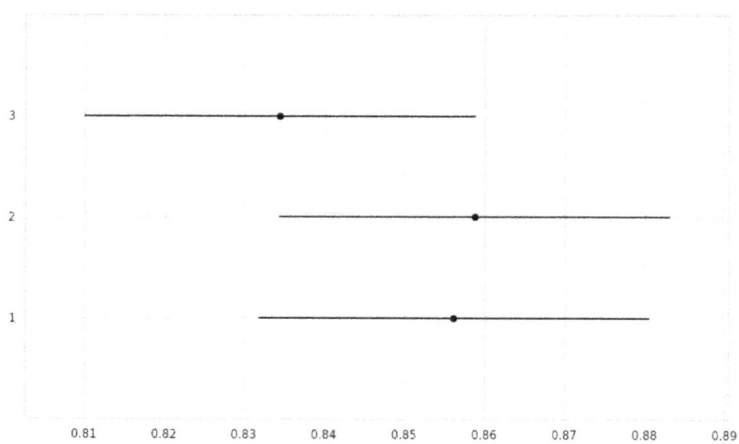

Figure 7. Tukey's HSD test results: Pairwise comparisons of prompt templates 1, 2, and 3.

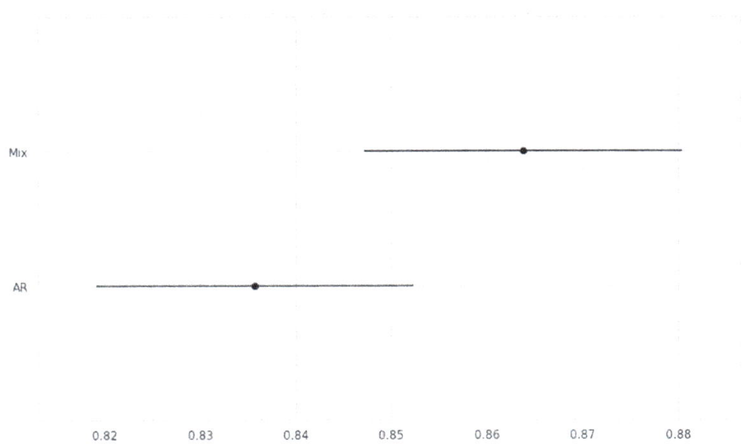

Figure 8. Tukey's HSD test results: Pairwise comparisons of Arabic and Mixed language prompt templates (English instructions, Kuwaiti dialect examples, and tweet text).

4.4. Response Consistency of LLMs

To evaluate the consistency of the responses generated by the LLMs, we analyzed the variance in their Macro F1 scores, as shown in Table 3 and Figure 9. Most models showed low variability, with variances clustered below 0.01. Based on this observation, we established 0.01 as a threshold for acceptable variance. Models with variances below this threshold were identified as consistent, while those exceeding it were considered inconsistent and exhibited higher variability; therefore, they are less reliable. Analyzing the consistency of responses based on the variance in Macro F1 scores reveals several key insights:

Models such as mT0-xxl and GPT-4o exhibited the lowest variance in Macro F1 scores (0.00014 and 0.0016, respectively), indicating a high level of consistency in performance across various prompts and settings. This suggests that these models are reliable in producing stable and predictable outputs, regardless of variations in input.

Similarly, Gemini-pro 1.5, Jais-30B, and Mistral-Large-latest also demonstrated low variance (0.00023, 0.00044, and 0.00057, respectively), reflecting strong consistency in their responses.

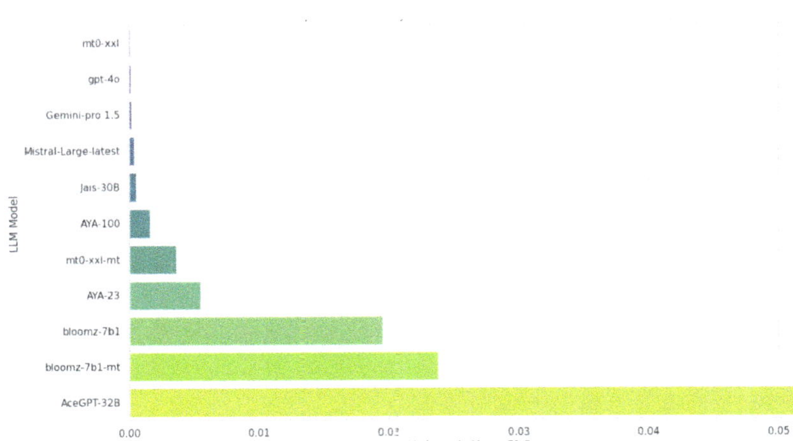

Figure 9. LLM response consistency analysis using variance in Macro F1 scores.

Table 3. Comparison of different LLMs based on consistency.

LLM	Macro F1
mT0-xxl	0.00014
GPT-4o	0.00016
Gemini-pro 1.5	0.00023
Mistral-Large-latest	0.00044
Jais-30B	0.00057
AYA-100	0.00160
mT0-xxl-mt	0.00368
AYA-23	0.00551
bloomz-7b1	0.01955
bloomz-7b1-mt	0.02384
AceGPT-32B	0.05155

In contrast, the AYA-100 and mT0-xxl-mt models showed slightly higher variance, with scores ranging from 0.00160 to 0.00368. While still relatively consistent, these models displayed some variability in their performance, indicating that specific prompt settings impact their outputs more than the top-performing models. AYA-23 exhibited a variance of 0.00551, suggesting that it is less consistent than its counterparts and may require assistance when using particular prompts or settings.

Models such as bloomz-7b1 and bloomz-7b1-mt had significantly higher variances (0.01955 and 0.02384, respectively), indicating less reliable performance. Their responses were more susceptible to changes in prompts and settings, leading to inconsistencies.

Finally, the AceGPT-32B model recorded the highest variance (0.05155), signifying its relatively low consistency among all the analyzed models. This suggests that its performance can fluctuate widely based on the prompt or setting, making it less predictable and reliable, primarily when used with English prompts.

4.5. Error Analysis

In the error analysis, we focused on the AceGPT-32B model as it demonstrated the lowest consistency among all the analyzed models. Our error analysis, based on Tables 4–6, highlights important factors that impact the accuracy and reliability of stance classification when using the AceGPT-32B model.

Table 4. Effects of prompt language, zero-shot, and few-shot prompts on AceGPT LLM performance.

Method	Macro F1 Arabic Templates	Macro F1 English Templates
ZS	**0.248**	**0.736**
2FS	0.896	0.902
4FS	0.888	0.914
6FS	0.879	0.898

Note: bold text represents the lowest Macro F1 values.

Table 5. Impact of zero-shot prompt selection on AceGPT LLM performance.

Prompt Template Language	Prompt Template Number	Macro F1 Score
AR	1	**0.354**
AR	2	**0.095**
AR	3	**0.294**
Mix	1	0.854
Mix	2	0.801
Mix	3	**0.552**

Note: bold text represents the lowest Macro F1 values.

Table 6. Error examples when using zero-shot templates with AceGPT LLM.

Prompt Template	Tweet Text	Predicted Label	Human Label	Error Type
Arabic 2	قناة atv ترفع شعار نعم للتطعيم English Translation: ATV channel raises the slogan "Yes to vaccination".	صنف المنشورين الآ English Translation: Categorize the posts now	Pro-vaccine	Hallucination
Mixed 3	في مثل هذا اليوم بدأ فيروس كورونا بالانتشار المحلي في الكويت الحل بتطعيم اكثرمن % من الشعب نعم للتطعيم والله المستعان English Translation: On this day, the Corona virus began to spread locally in Kuwait. The solution is to vaccinate more than % of the people. Yes to vaccination. May God help us.	## إعداد: - @Mohamed Al-Masry Mohamed Elmas English Translation: ## Prepared by: @Mohamed Al-Masry - Mohamed Elmas	Pro-vaccine	Hallucination
Arabic 2	المفروض مايخلطون بين المطعمين واللي مو مطعمين لازم يفصلونهم ويميزون المطعمين وبالنسبه للقرارات ما اعتبرها سذاجه اكثر حالات الوفاة انزلت خلال شهر بسبب التطعيم نعم للتطعيم نعم للتطعيم English Translation: They are not supposed to confuse those who are vaccinated with those who are not vaccinated. They must separate them and distinguish between the two vaccinated people. As for the decisions, I do not consider them naive. Most deaths occurred within a month due to vaccination. Yes to vaccination. Yes to vaccination.	في هذا الجزء، سنقوم بتدريب English Translation: In this part, we will train	Pro-vaccine	Hallucination
Arabic 1	هل يعقل و نحن في دولة تملك دستور وبرلمان وديمقراطية وعلاوة على ذلك معروف عنها إنها ببلد الإنسانية ويجبر شعبها على التطعيم وعليه لا للتصعيم الاجباري English Translation: Is it possible that we are in a country that has a constitution, parliament, and democracy? Furthermore, it is known to be a country of humanity and its people are forced to be vaccinated! So, no to compulsory vaccination.	مع التطعيم English Translation: Pro-vaccine	Anti-vaccine	Misclassification
Mixed 3	لا تحملوا المواطنين فشلكم الذريع لا للتطعيم الاجباري English Translation: Do not blame the citizens for your miserable failure, no to compulsory vaccination	Pro-vaccine	Anti-vaccine	Misclassification
Mixed 3	تم التطعيم اشكر وزارة الصحة وكل من يعمل فيها ولها من اجل صحة الكويت ، تنظيم راقي جدا English Translation: I have been vaccinated. I thank the Ministry of Health and everyone who works in it and for it for the health of Kuwait, a very sophisticated organization	Anti-vaccine	Pro-vaccine	Misclassification

4.5.1. Effect of Prompt Language and Few-Shot Examples

The choice of prompt language had a significant impact on model performance. As shown in Table 4, AceGPT-32B achieved a Macro F1 score of 0.248 for Arabic zero-shot (ZS) templates, while the English zero-shot templates performed much better, scoring 0.736. This indicates that the model has difficulty in detecting the stance when instructions are provided in Arabic. However, incorporating few-shot examples improved the accuracy for both languages. With two-shot (2FS) prompts, the Macro F1 score increased to 0.896 in Arabic and 0.902 in English. The highest performance was reached with four-shot (4FS) prompts in English, achieving a score of 0.914, which suggests that providing more examples helps the model to classify stances more accurately.

4.5.2. Impact of Prompt Selection on Performance

The design of the prompt templates significantly influenced the model's accuracy. As illustrated in Table 5, various zero-shot prompts resulted in markedly different Macro F1 scores for AceGPT-32B. Notably, Arabic Zero-Shot Prompt 2 had the lowest performance, achieving a Macro F1 score of only 0.095. This indicates that this template was ineffective in guiding the model's responses.

4.5.3. Hallucinations and Unrelated Outputs

In AceGPT-32 B's error analysis, we identified differences between Arabic and English prompts. Out of 519 test samples (265 pro-vaccine, 254 anti-vaccine), Arabic zero-shot prompts (1, 2, and 3) had high hallucination rates, with Arabic Template 2 being the worst (457 hallucinations out of 480 total errors). This suggests the model frequently generated unrelated outputs instead of correctly identifying a stance. The following is a sample of errors from Table 6:

- Arabic Zero-shot Prompt 2: A tweet simply stating that "ATV channel supported vaccination" was processed incorrectly, and the model returned an irrelevant classification instruction ("Categorize the posts now") instead of the correct stance label.
- Mixed Zero-shot Prompt 3: A tweet about COVID-19 spreading in Kuwait and calling for more vaccinations was misinterpreted, with the model inserting an unrelated username ("## Prepared by: @Mohamed Al-Masry"), which was not part of the original tweet.
- Arabic Zero-shot Prompt 2: A pro-vaccine tweet discussing a decrease in COVID-19-related deaths due to vaccination was mistakenly transformed into a statement about training ("In this part, we will train"), indicating failure in stance detection.

These hallucinations indicate that the AceGPT-32B model fails to focus on the task and instead generates unrelated or procedural responses.

4.5.4. Misclassifications

Table 6 provides several examples where AceGPT-32B did not assign the correct stance label. Below are some sample errors:

- Arabic Zero-shot Prompt 1 Misclassification: A tweet expressing skepticism about vaccine mandates ("Is it possible that we are in a country with a constitution and democracy, yet its people are forced to be vaccinated? No to compulsory vaccination".) was incorrectly classified as pro-vaccine.
- Mixed Zero-shot Prompt 3 Misclassification: A tweet that blamed authorities for vaccination failures ("Do not blame the citizens for your miserable failure, no to compulsory vaccination".) was mistakenly labeled as pro-vaccine instead of anti-vaccine.
- Mixed Zero-shot Prompt 3 Misclassification: A tweet thanking the Ministry of Health for vaccinations ("I have been vaccinated. I thank the Ministry of Health and everyone who works in it and for it for the health of Kuwait, a very sophisticated organization") was wrongly labeled as anti-vaccine, demonstrating the model's struggle with positive statements about vaccination policies.

Misclassification rates varied significantly across zero-shot prompt templates:

- Mixed Zero-shot Prompt 3 had the highest misclassification rate (166 pro-vaccine, 29 anti-vaccine), indicating that pro-vaccine tweets were more frequently misclassified in the English prompt setting.
- Arabic Zero-shot Prompt 3 had the highest misclassification rate (51 total), with more errors in anti-vaccine tweets (30 anti-vaccine misclassified vs. 21 pro-vaccine misclassified).
- Arabic Zero-shot Prompt 1 also showed more misclassification in anti-vaccine tweets (30 anti-vaccine vs. 8 pro-vaccine).
- Arabic Zero-shot Prompt 2 had the lowest misclassification rate (23 total) but misclassified more pro-vaccine tweets (17 pro-vaccine vs. 6 anti-vaccine).

These results indicate that the language and phrasing of prompts are critical in determining the performance of LLMs.

5. Conclusions

In this study, we investigated the performance of various large language models (LLMs) in automating stance detection for the Kuwaiti dialect using both zero- and few-shot learning techniques. Our findings indicated that closed-source LLMs, such as GPT-4o, Gemini-pro 1.5, and Mistral-Large, consistently achieved high performance across different prompt settings, with mean Macro F1 scores of 94%, 94%, and 92%, respectively.

In contrast, open-source models such as Jais-30B and AYA-23 demonstrated competitive results, particularly in few-shot settings, with mean Macro F1 scores of 90% and 89%. These results position them as strong candidates for future research focused on low-resource language annotation. The study also revealed that models such as AceGPT-32B and Bloomz-7b1 struggled in zero-shot settings, especially with mixed-language prompts, highlighting the importance of context and training data in these scenarios.

The ANOVA results indicated a highly significant difference in performance among the large language models (LLMs), with a p-value of $2.81943943 \times 10^{-33}$. This value suggests that the performance—as measured by the Macro F1 score—varied significantly between at least some of the LLMs tested. Tukey's HSD test revealed several statistically significant differences among the LLMs. Notably, BigScience's models (i.e., bloomz-7b1 and bloomz-7b1-mt) significantly under-performed when compared to all other LLMs. However, we found no significant differences between GPT-4o and other models such as Gemini Pro 1.5, Jais 30B, mT0-xxl, mT0-xxl-mt, AYA-100, AYA-23, and Mistral-Large, suggesting that these models offer comparable performance in terms of Macro F1 scores.

Overall, the competitive performance of these models reassures us about the potential of open-source LLMs. Fine-tuning and human-in-the-loop involvement can lead to their further improvement, reaching performance levels similar to those of top-performing closed-source models. Utilizing open-source LLMs for Kuwaiti dialect annotation offers advantages such as cost reduction, enhanced data privacy, and the quicker annotation of large datasets, thereby enabling more NLP research projects focused on Arabic and the Kuwaiti dialect in particular.

In future work, we aim to experiment with fine-tuning the top-performing open-source models to further improve their performance, as well as exploring their application in other low-resource dialects and additional NLP tasks.

6. Limitations

This study has several limitations. First, due to the lack of available human-labeled datasets for the Kuwaiti dialect, we utilized the only online stance detection dataset currently accessible. This dataset is small and specifically focused on vaccine-related stances, which may limit its applicability to other topics or dialects. Therefore, this research serves as a foundation for testing and generating more general stance detection datasets for the Kuwaiti dialect.

Second, we only examined zero- and few-shot learning settings, excluding fine-tuning models, which the researcher intends to address in future work.

Third, the results were heavily influenced by the design and phrasing of the prompt templates; thus, using different phrasing or languages may yield different outcomes.

Furthermore, budget and computational constraints limited our ability to test a broader range of LLMs and those with larger sizes The costs associated with closed-source models such as GPT-4 and Gemini restricted us from conducting additional experiments. Finally, this research does not address scalability challenges relating to real-world deployment, which will be explored in future work.

Funding: This research received no external funding.

Data Availability Statement: The original data presented in the study are openly available in GitHub at https://github.com/hanaalostad/Q8Stance, accessed on 7 February 2024.

Conflicts of Interest: The authors declare no conflicts of interest.

Abbreviations

The following abbreviations are used in this manuscript:

NLP	Natural Language Processing
LLMs	Large Language Models
GPT	Generative Pre-trained Transformer
BLOOM	BigScience Language Open-science Open-access Multilingual
MSA	Modern Standard Arabic

Appendix A

Table A1. Summary of generative large language models.

LLM	Language Support	Source Type	Model Architecture	Model Size
GPT-4o	Multi-lingual	Closed	Decoder	Not officially declared
Gemini-pro 1.5	Multi-lingual	Closed	Decoder	Not officially declared
Mistral-Large-latest	Multi-lingual	Closed	Decoder	123 Billion
AYA-23	Multi-lingual	Open	Decoder	35 Billion
AceGPT-32B	Bilingual	Open	Decoder	32 Billion
Jais-30B	Bilingual	Open	Decoder	30 Billion
AYA-100	Multi-lingual	Open	Decoder	13 Billion
mt0-xxl	Multi-lingual	Open	Encoder–Decoder	13 Billion
mt0-xxl-mt	Multi-lingual	Open	Encoder–Decoder	13 Billion
bloomz-7b1	Multi-lingual	Open	Decoder	7 Billion
bloomz-7b1-mt	Multi-lingual	Open	Decoder	7 Billion

Table A2. Tukey's HSD test results: Pairwise comparisons of zero-shot and few-shot prompt templates.

Group 1	Group 2	p-adj	Reject
2FS	4FS	0.9938	False
2FS	6FS	0.9999	False
2FS	ZS	0.0047	True
4FS	6FS	0.9973	False
4FS	ZS	0.0019	True
6FS	ZS	0.0038	True

Table A3. Tukey's HSD test results: Pairwise comparisons of prompt templates 1, 2, and 3.

Group 1	Group 2	p-adj	Reject
1	2	0.9915	False
1	3	0.5464	False
2	3	0.4697	False

Table A4. Tukey's HSD test results: Pairwise comparisons of Arabic and Mixed language prompt templates.

Group 1	Group 2	p-adj	Reject
AR	Mixed	0.0968	False

Table A5. Tukey's HSD test results: Pairwise comparisons of LLMs.

Group 1	Group 2	p-adj	Reject	Group 1	Group 2	p-adj	Reject
AceGPT-32B	GPT-4o	0.0000	True	AceGPT-32B	Gemini-pro	0.0000	True
AceGPT-32B	Jais-30B	0.0065	True	AceGPT-32B	bloomz-7b1	0.0112	True
AceGPT-32B	bloomz-7b1-mt	0.0000	True	AceGPT-32B	mT0-xxl	0.0399	True
AceGPT-32B	mT0-xxl-mt	0.2534	False	AceGPT-32B	AYA-100	0.3995	False
AceGPT-32B	AYA-23	0.0213	True	AceGPT-32B	Mistral-Large	0.0005	True
GPT-4o	Gemini-pro	1.0000	False	GPT-4o	Jais-30B	0.9769	False
GPT-4o	bloomz-7b1	0.0000	True	GPT-4o	bloomz-7b1-mt	0.0000	True
GPT-4o	mT0-xxl	0.7875	False	GPT-4o	mT0-xxl-mt	0.3050	False
GPT-4o	AYA-100	0.1825	False	GPT-4o	AYA-23	0.8866	False
GPT-4o	Mistral-Large	0.9999	False	Gemini-pro	Jais-30B	0.9723	False
Gemini-pro	bloomz-7b1	0.0000	True	Gemini-pro	bloomz-7b1-mt	0.0000	True
Gemini-pro	mT0-xxl	0.7686	False	Gemini-pro	mT0-xxl-mt	0.2869	False
Gemini-pro	AYA-100	0.1697	False	Gemini-pro	AYA-23	0.8730	False
Gemini-pro	Mistral-Large	0.9999	False	Jais-30B	bloomz-7b1	0.0000	True
Jais-30B	bloomz-7b1-mt	0.0000	True	Jais-30B	mT0-xxl	1.0000	False
Jais-30B	mT0-xxl-mt	0.9737	False	Jais-30B	AYA-100	0.9149	False
Jais-30B	AYA-23	1.0000	False	Jais-30B	Mistral-Large	0.9999	False
bloomz-7b1	bloomz-7b1-mt	0.7258	False	bloomz-7b1	mT0-xxl	0.0000	True
bloomz-7b1	mT0-xxl-mt	0.0000	True	bloomz-7b1	AYA-100	0.0000	True
bloomz-7b1	AYA-23	0.0000	True	bloomz-7b1	Mistral-Large	0.0000	True
bloomz-7b1-mt	mT0-xxl	0.0000	True	bloomz-7b1-mt	mT0-xxl-mt	0.0000	True
bloomz-7b1-mt	AYA-100	0.0000	True	bloomz-7b1-mt	AYA-23	0.0000	True
bloomz-7b1-mt	Mistral-Large	0.0000	True	mT0-xxl	mT0-xxl-mt	0.9997	False
mT0-xxl	AYA-100	0.9967	False	mT0-xxl	AYA-23	1.0000	False
mT0-xxl	Mistral-Large	0.9849	False	mT0-xxl-mt	AYA-100	1.0000	False
mT0-xxl-mt	AYA-23	0.9978	False	mT0-xxl-mt	Mistral-Large	0.7204	False
AYA-100	AYA-23	0.9854	False	AYA-100	Mistral-Large	0.5494	False
AYA-23	Mistral-Large	0.9955	False				

References

1. Küçük, D.; Can, F. Stance Detection: A Survey. *ACM Comput. Surv.* **2020**, *53*, 1–37 . [CrossRef]
2. Shyu, M.L.; Yan, Y.; Chen, J. Efficient Large-Scale Stance Detection in Tweets. *Int. J. Multimed. Data Eng. Manag.* **2018**, *9*, 1–16. [CrossRef]
3. Burnham, M. Stance detection: A practical guide to classifying political beliefs in text. *Political Sci. Res. Methods* **2024**, 1–18. [CrossRef]
4. Kuo, K.H.; Wang, M.H.; Kao, H.Y.; Dai, Y.C. Advancing Stance Detection of Political Fan Pages: A Multimodal Approach. In Proceedings of the Companion Proceedings of the ACM Web Conference 2024, WWW '24, New York, NY, USA, 13–17 May 2024; pp. 702–705. [CrossRef]
5. Mets, M.; Karjus, A.; Ibrus, I.; Schich, M. Automated stance detection in complex topics and small languages: The challenging case of immigration in polarizing news media. *PLoS ONE* **2024**, *19*, e0302380. [CrossRef]
6. Lee, Y.; Ozer, M.; Corman, S.R.; Davulcu, H. Identifying Behavioral Factors Leading to Differential Polarization Effects of Adversarial Botnets. *SIGAPP Appl. Comput. Rev.* **2023**, *23*, 44–56. [CrossRef]
7. Lee, Y.; Alostad, H.; Davulcu, H. Quantifying Variations in Controversial Discussions within Kuwaiti Social Networks. *Big Data Cogn. Comput.* **2024**, *8*, 60. [CrossRef]
8. Hua, Y.; Jiang, H.; Lin, S.; Yang, J.; Plasek, J.M.; Bates, D.W.; Zhou, L. Using Twitter Data to Understand Public Perceptions of Approved Versus Off-Label Use for COVID-19-related Medications. *J. Am. Med. Inform. Assoc.* **2022**, *29*, 1668–1678. [CrossRef] [PubMed]
9. Cascini, F.; Pantović, A.; Al-Ajlouni, Y.A.; Failla, G.; Puleo, V.; Melnyk, A.; Lontano, A.; Ricciardi, W. Social Media and Attitudes Towards a COVID-19 Vaccination: A Systematic Review of the Literature. *Eclinicalmedicine* **2022**, *48*, 101454. [CrossRef]
10. List of Countries and Territories Where Arabic Is an Official Language. Available online: https://en.wikipedia.org/wiki/List_of_countries_and_territories_where_Arabic_is_an_official_language (accessed on 16 December 2024).
11. Alostad, H.; Dawiek, S.; Davulcu, H. Q8VaxStance: Dataset Labeling System for Stance Detection towards Vaccines in Kuwaiti Dialect. *Big Data Cogn. Comput.* **2023**, *7*, 151. [CrossRef]
12. Alhindi, T.; Alabdulkarim, A.; Alshehri, A.; Abdul-Mageed, M.; Nakov, P. AraStance: A Multi-Country and Multi-Domain Dataset of Arabic Stance Detection for Fact Checking. In *Proceedings of the Fourth Workshop on NLP for Internet Freedom Censorship, Disinformation, and Propaganda*; Association for Computational Linguistics: Stroudsburg, PA, USA, 2021; pp. 57–65. [CrossRef]
13. Alturayeif, N.S.; Luqman, H.A.; Ahmed, M.A.K. MAWQIF: A Multi-label Arabic Dataset for Target-specific Stance Detection. In *Proceedings of the Seventh Arabic Natural Language Processing Workshop (WANLP)*; Association for Computational Linguistics: Abu Dhabi, United Arab Emirates, 2022; pp. 174–184.

14. Haouari, F.; Elsayed, T. Detecting stance of authorities towards rumors in Arabic tweets: A preliminary study . In *Proceedings of the 45th European Conference on Information Retrieval*; Springer: Dublin, Ireland, 2023; pp. 430–438.
15. Hamad, O.; Hamdi, A.; Hamdi, S.; Shaban, K. StEduCov: An Explored and Benchmarked Dataset on Stance Detection in Tweets towards Online Education during COVID-19 Pandemic. *Big Data Cogn. Comput.* **2022**, *6*, 88. [CrossRef]
16. Hardalov, M.; Arora, A.; Nakov, P.; Augenstein, I. Few-Shot Cross-Lingual Stance Detection With Sentiment-Based Pre-Training. *Proc. AAAI Conf. Artif. Intell.* **2022**, *36*, 10729–10737. [CrossRef]
17. Kim, H.; Mitra, K.; Li Chen, R.; Rahman, S.; Zhang, D. MEGAnno+: A Human-LLM Collaborative Annotation System. In *Proceedings of the 18th Conference of the European Chapter of the Association for Computational Linguistics: System Demonstrations, St. Julians, Malta, 17–22 March* 2024; Aletras, N., De Clercq, O., Eds.; Association for Computational Linguistics: Stroudsburg, PA, USA, 2024; pp. 168–176.
18. He, X.; Lin, Z.; Gong, Y.; Jin, A.L.; Zhang, H.; Lin, C.; Jiao, J.; Yiu, S.M.; Duan, N.; Chen, W. AnnoLLM: Making Large Language Models to Be Better Crowdsourced Annotators. In *Proceedings of the 2024 Conference of the North American Chapter of the Association for Computational Linguistics: Human Language Technologies (Volume 6: Industry Track), Mexico City, Mexico, 16–21 June 2024*; Yang, Y., Davani, A., Sil, A., Kumar, A., Eds.; Association for Computational Linguistics: Stroudsburg, PA, USA, 2024; pp. 165–190. [CrossRef]
19. Zhang, R.; Li, Y.; Ma, Y.; Zhou, M.; Zou, L. LLMaAA: Making Large Language Models as Active Annotators. In *Proceedings of the Findings of the Association for Computational Linguistics: EMNLP 2023, Singapore, 6–10 December 2023*; Bouamor, H., Pino, J., Bali, K., Eds.; Association for Computational Linguistics: Stroudsburg, PA, USA, 2023; pp. 13088–13103. [CrossRef]
20. Liu, R.; Lin, Z.; Tan, Y.; Wang, W. Enhancing zero-shot and few-shot stance detection with commonsense knowledge graph. In *Proceedings of the Findings of the Association for Computational Linguistics: ACL-IJCNLP 2021*; Association for Computational Linguistics: Stroudsburg, PA, USA, 2021; pp. 3152–3157.
21. Liang, B.; Zhu, Q.; Li, X.; Yang, M.; Gui, L.; He, Y.; Xu, R. Jointcl: A joint contrastive learning framework for zero-shot stance detection. In *Proceedings of the 60th Annual Meeting of the Association for Computational Linguistics (Volume 1: Long Papers), Dublin, Ireland, 22–27 May* 2022; Association for Computational Linguistics: Stroudsburg, PA, USA, 2022; Volume 1, pp. 81–91.
22. Liew, X.Y.; Hameed, N.; Clos, J.; Fischer, J.E. Predicting Stance to Detect Misinformation in Few-shot Learning. In Proceedings of the First International Symposium on Trustworthy Autonomous Systems, TAS '23, New York, NY, USA, 11–12 July 2023; [CrossRef]
23. Hasanain, M.; Ahmad, F.; Alam, F. Can GPT-4 Identify Propaganda? Annotation and Detection of Propaganda Spans in News Articles. In *Proceedings of the 2024 Joint International Conference on Computational Linguistics, Language Resources and Evaluation (LREC-COLING 2024), Torino, Italy, 20–25 May 2024*; Calzolari, N., Kan, M.Y., Hoste, V., Lenci, A., Sakti, S., Xue, N., Eds.; ELRA and ICCL: Torino, Italy, 2024; pp. 2724–2744.
24. Abdelali, A.; Mubarak, H.; Chowdhury, S.; Hasanain, M.; Mousi, B.; Boughorbel, S.; Abdaljalil, S.; El Kheir, Y.; Izham, D.; Dalvi, F.; et al. LAraBench: Benchmarking Arabic AI with Large Language Models. In *Proceedings of the 18th Conference of the European Chapter of the Association for Computational Linguistics (Volume 1: Long Papers), St. Julian's, Malta, 17–22 March 2024*; Graham, Y., Purver, M., Eds.; Association for Computational Linguistics: Stroudsburg, PA, USA, 2024; pp. 487–520.
25. Husain, F.; Alostad, H.; Omar, H. Bridging the Kuwaiti Dialect Gap in Natural Language Processing. *IEEE Access* **2024**, *12*, 27709–27722. [CrossRef]
26. OpenAI. GPT-4o System Card. Available online: https://openai.com/index/gpt-4o-system-card/ (accessed on 22 September 2024).
27. AI Models. Premier Models. Available online: https://mistral.ai/technology/#models (accessed on 16 December 2024).
28. Team, G.; Anil, R.; Borgeaud, S.; Wu, Y.; Alayrac, J.B.; Yu, J.; Soricut, R.; Schalkwyk, J.; Dai, A.M.; Hauth, A.; et al. Gemini: A family of highly capable multimodal models. *arXiv* **2023**, arXiv:2312.11805.
29. Sengupta, N.; Sahu, S.K.; Jia, B.; Katipomu, S.; Li, H.; Koto, F.; Marshall, W.; Gosal, G.; Liu, C.; Chen, Z.; et al. Jais and Jais-chat: Arabic-Centric Foundation and Instruction-Tuned Open Generative Large Language Models. *arXiv* **2023**, arXiv:2308.16149.
30. Muennighoff, N.; Wang, T.; Sutawika, L.; Roberts, A.; Biderman, S.; Scao, T.L.; Bari, M.S.; Shen, S.; Yong, Z.X.; Schoelkopf, H.; et al. Crosslingual Generalization through Multitask Finetuning . In *Proceedings of the 61st Annual Meeting of the Association for Computational Linguistics (Volume 1: Long Papers)*, Toronto, ON, Canada, 9–14 July 2023; Association for Computational Linguistics: Stroudsburg, PA, USA, 2023; pp. 15991–16111.
31. Aryabumi, V.; Dang, J.; Talupuru, D.; Dash, S.; Cairuz, D.; Lin, H.; Venkitesh, B.; Smith, M.; Campos, J.A.; Tan, Y.C.; et al. Aya 23: Open Weight Releases to Further Multilingual Progress. *arXiv* **2024**, arXiv:2405.15032.
32. Üstün, A.; Aryabumi, V.; Yong, Z.X.; Ko, W.Y.; D'souza, D.; Onilude, G.; Bhandari, N.; Singh, S.; Ooi, H.L.; Kayid, A.; et al. Aya model: An instruction finetuned open-access multilingual language model. *arXiv* **2024**, arXiv:2402.07827.
33. Huang, H.; Yu, F.; Zhu, J.; Sun, X.; Cheng, H.; Song, D.; Chen, Z.; Alharthi, A.; An, B.; He, J.; et al. AceGPT, Localizing Large Language Models in Arabic. *arXiv* **2024**, arXiv:2309.12053.

34. Singh, S.K.; Mahmood, A. The NLP Cookbook: Modern Recipes for Transformer Based Deep Learning Architectures. *IEEE Access* **2021**, *9*, 68675–68702. [CrossRef]
35. Li, K.; Liu, Z.; He, T.; Huang, H.; Peng, F.; Povey, D.; Khudanpur, S. An Empirical Study of Transformer-Based Neural Language Model Adaptation. In Proceedings of the ICASSP 2020—2020 IEEE International Conference on Acoustics, Speech and Signal Processing (ICASSP), Barcelona, Spain, 4–8 May 2020; pp. 7934–7938. [CrossRef]
36. Xie, H.; Qin, Z.; Tao, X.; Letaief, K.B. Task-oriented multi-user semantic communications. *IEEE J. Sel. Areas Commun.* **2022**, *40*, 2584–2597. [CrossRef]
37. Choi, H.; Kim, J.; Joe, S.; Gwon, Y. Evaluation of BERT and ALBERT Sentence Embedding Performance on Downstream NLP Tasks. In Proceedings of the 2020 25th International Conference on Pattern Recognition (ICPR), Milan, Italy, 10–15 January 2021; pp. 5482–5487. [CrossRef]
38. Devlin, J.; Chang, M.W.; Lee, K.; Toutanova, K. BERT Pre-training of Deep Bidirectional Transformers for Language Understanding. *arXiv* **2019**, arXiv:1810.04805.
39. Radford, A.; Wu, J.; Child, R.; Luan, D.; Amodei, D.; Sutskever, I. Language models are unsupervised multitask learners. *OpenAI Blog* **2019**, *1*, 9.
40. Beheitt, M.E.G.; Ben Haj Hmida, M. Automatic Arabic Poem Generation with GPT-2. In Proceedings of the 14th International Conference on Agents and Artificial Intelligence, Online, 3–5 February 2022; Science and Technology Publications: Setúbal, Portugal, 2022, pp. 366–374. [CrossRef]
41. Steele, J.L. To GPT or not GPT? Empowering our students to learn with AI. *Comput. Educ. Artif. Intell.* **2023**, *5*, 100160. [CrossRef]
42. Google AI. Gemini Models. Available online: https://ai.google.dev/gemini-api/docs/models/gemini (accessed on 16 December 2024).
43. Google AI. Pricing Models. Available online: https://ai.google.dev/pricing (accessed on 16 December 2024).
44. Google AI. Billing. Available online: https://ai.google.dev/gemini-api/docs/billing (accessed on 16 December 2024).
45. Core42. Core42's Bilingual AI for Arabic Speakers. Available online: https://www.core42.ai/jais.html (accessed on 16 December 2024).
46. Abdul-Mageed, M.; Elmadany, A.; Nagoudi, E.M.B. ARBERT & MARBERT: Deep Bidirectional Transformers for Arabic. In *Proceedings of the 59th Annual Meeting of the Association for Computational Linguistics and the 11th International Joint Conference on Natural Language Processing (Volume 1: Long Papers), Online, 1–6 August 2021*; Zong, C., Xia, F., Li, W., Navigli, R., Eds.; Association for Computational Linguistics: Stroudsburg, PA, USA, 2021, pp. 7088–7105. [CrossRef]
47. Kmainasi, M.; Shahroor, A.; Hasanain, M.; Laskar, S.; Hassan, N.; Alam, F. LlamaLens: Specialized Multilingual LLM for Analyzing News and Social Media Content. *arXiv* **2024**, arXiv:2410.15308.
48. Alturayeif, N.; Luqman, H.; Alyafeai, Z.; Yamani, A. StanceEval 2024: The First Arabic Stance Detection Shared Task. In Proceedings of the Second Arabic Natural Language Processing Conference, Bangkok, Thailand, 16 August 2024; pp. 774–782.
49. Badran, M.; Hamdy, M.; Torki, M.; El-Makky, N. AlexUNLP-BH at StanceEval2024: Multiple Contrastive Losses Ensemble Strategy with Multi-Task Learning For Stance Detection in Arabic. In *Proceedings of the Second Arabic Natural Language Processing Conference, Bangkok, Thailand, 16 August 2024*; Habash, N., Bouamor, H., Eskander, R., Tomeh, N., Abu Farha, I., Abdelali, A., Touileb, S., Hamed, I., Onaizan, Y., Alhafni, B., et al., Eds.; Association for Computational Linguistics: Stroudsburg, PA, USA, 2024; pp. 823–827. [CrossRef]
50. Alghaslan, M.; Almutairy, K. MGKM at StanceEval2024 Fine-Tuning Large Language Models for Arabic Stance Detection. In *Proceedings of the Second Arabic Natural Language Processing Conference, Bangkok, Thailand, 16 August 2024*; Habash, N., Bouamor, H., Eskander, R., Tomeh, N., Abu Farha, I., Abdelali, A., Touileb, S., Hamed, I., Onaizan, Y., Alhafni, B., et al., Eds.; Association for Computational Linguistics: Stroudsburg, PA, USA, 2024; pp. 816–822. [CrossRef]
51. Hasanaath, A.; Alansari, A. StanceCrafters at StanceEval2024: Multi-task Stance Detection using BERT Ensemble with Attention Based Aggregation. In *Proceedings of the Second Arabic Natural Language Processing Conference, Bangkok, Thailand, 16 August 2024*; Habash, N., Bouamor, H., Eskander, R., Tomeh, N., Abu Farha, I., Abdelali, A., Touileb, S., Hamed, I., Onaizan, Y., Alhafni, B., et al., Eds.; Association for Computational Linguistics: Stroudsburg, PA, USA, 2024; pp. 811–815. [CrossRef]
52. Salamah, J.B.; Elkhlifi, A. Microblogging opinion mining approach for kuwaiti dialect. In Proceedings of the the International Conference on Computing Technology and Information Management (ICCTIM), Dubai, United Arab Emirates, 9 April 2014; Society of Digital Information and Wireless Communication (SDIWC); p. 388.
53. Quinlan, J.R. *C4.5: Programs for Machine Learning*; Morgan Kaufmann Publishers Inc.: San Francisco, CA, USA, 1993.
54. Freund, Y.; Mason, L. The Alternating Decision Tree Learning Algorithm. In Proceedings of the Sixteenth International Conference on Machine Learning, ICML '99, San Francisco, CA, USA, 27–30 June 1999; pp. 124–133.
55. Breiman, L. Random Forests. *Mach. Learn.* **2001**, *45*, 5–32. [CrossRef]
56. Boser, B.E.; Guyon, I.M.; Vapnik, V.N. A training algorithm for optimal margin classifiers. In Proceedings of the Fifth Annual Workshop on Computational Learning Theory, Pittsburgh, PA, USA, 27–29 July 1992; pp. 144–152.

57. Antoun, W.; Baly, F.; Hajj, H. AraBERT: Transformer-based Model for Arabic Language Understanding. In *Proceedings of the 4th Workshop on Open-Source Arabic Corpora and Processing Tools, with a Shared Task on Offensive Language Detection, Marseille, France, 11–16 May 2020*; Al-Khalifa, H., Magdy, W., Darwish, K., Elsayed, T., Mubarak, H., Eds.; European Language Resource Association: Paris, France, 2020; pp. 9–15.
58. Wang, W.; Wei, F.; Dong, L.; Bao, H.; Yang, N.; Zhou, M. MINILM: Deep self-attention distillation for task-agnostic compression of pre-trained transformers. In Proceedings of the 34th International Conference on Neural Information Processing Systems, NIPS '20, Vancouver, BC, Canada, 6–12 December 2020.
59. Inoue, G.; Alhafni, B.; Baimukan, N.; Bouamor, H.; Habash, N. The Interplay of Variant, Size, and Task Type in Arabic Pre-trained Language Models. In *Proceedings of the Sixth Arabic Natural Language Processing Workshop, Kyiv, Ukraine (Virtual), 19 April 2021*; Habash, N., Bouamor, H., Hajj, H., Magdy, W., Zaghouani, W., Bougares, F., Tomeh, N., Abu Farha, I., Touileb, S., Eds.; Association for Computational Linguistics: Stroudsburg, PA, USA, 2021; pp. 92–104.
60. Tan, Z.; Li, D.; Wang, S.; Beigi, A.; Jiang, B.; Bhattacharjee, A.; Karami, M.; Li, J.; Cheng, L.; Liu, H. Large Language Models for Data Annotation and Synthesis: A Survey. In *Proceedings of the 2024 Conference on Empirical Methods in Natural Language Processing, Miami, FL, USA, 12–16 November 2024*; Al-Onaizan, Y., Bansal, M., Chen, Y.N., Eds.; Association for Computational Linguistics: Stroudsburg, PA, USA, 2024; pp. 930–957. [CrossRef]
61. Kojima, T.; Gu, S.S.; Reid, M.; Matsuo, Y.; Iwasawa, Y. Large language models are zero-shot reasoners. In Proceedings of the 36th International Conference on Neural Information Processing Systems, NIPS '22, Red Hook, NY, USA, 28 November–9 December 2022.
62. Li, Y.; Zhang, J. Semi-supervised Meta-learning for Cross-domain Few-shot Intent Classification. In *Proceedings of the 1st Workshop on Meta Learning and Its Applications to Natural Language Processing, Online, 5 August 2021*; Lee, H.Y., Mohtarami, M., Li, S.W., Jin, D., Korpusik, M., Dong, S., Vu, N.T., Hakkani-Tur, D., Eds.; Association for Computational Linguistics: Stroudsburg, PA, USA, 2021; pp. 67–75. [CrossRef]
63. Wei, J.; Bosma, M.; Zhao, V.Y.; Guu, K.; Yu, A.W.; Lester, B.; Du, N.; Dai, A.M.; Le, Q.V. Finetuned Language Models are Zero-Shot Learners. In Proceedings of the the Tenth International Conference on Learning Representations, ICLR 2022, Virtual Event, 25–29 April 2022.
64. Brown, T.; Mann, B.; Ryder, N.; Subbiah, M.; Kaplan, J.D.; Dhariwal, P.; Neelakantan, A.; Shyam, P.; Sastry, G.; Askell, A.; et al. Language Models are Few-Shot Learners. In *Proceedings of the 34th International Conference on Neural Information Processing Systems*; Curran Associates, Inc.: Red Hook, NY, USA, 2020; pp. 1877–1901.
65. Gao, T.; Fisch, A.; Chen, D. Making Pre-trained Language Models Better Few-shot Learners. In *Proceedings of the 59th Annual Meeting of the Association for Computational Linguistics and the 11th International Joint Conference on Natural Language Processing (Volume 1: Long Papers), Online, 5 August 2021*; Zong, C., Xia, F., Li, W., Navigli, R., Eds.; Association for Computational Linguistics: Stroudsburg, PA, USA, 2021; pp. 3816–3830. [CrossRef]
66. Goel, A.; Gueta, A.; Gilon, O.; Liu, C.; Erell, S.; Nguyen, L.H.; Hao, X.; Jaber, B.; Reddy, S.; Kartha, R.; et al. Llms accelerate annotation for medical information extraction. In Proceedings of the Machine Learning for Health (ML4H), PMLR, New Orleans, LA, USA, 10 December 2023; ML Research Press: Cambridge, MA, USA, 2023; Volume 225, pp. 82–100.
67. Aguda, T.D.; Siddagangappa, S.; Kochkina, E.; Kaur, S.; Wang, D.; Smiley, C. Large Language Models as Financial Data Annotators: A Study on Effectiveness and Efficiency. In *Proceedings of the 2024 Joint International Conference on Computational Linguistics, Language Resources and Evaluation (LREC-COLING 2024), Torino, Italy, 20–25 May 2024*; Calzolari, N., Kan, M.Y., Hoste, V., Lenci, A., Sakti, S., Xue, N., Eds.; ELRA and ICCL: Torino, Italy, 2024; pp. 10124–10145.
68. Trad, F.S.; Chehab, A. Prompt Engineering or Fine-Tuning? A Case Study on Phishing Detection with Large Language Models. *Mach. Learn. Knowl. Extr.* **2024**, *6*, 367–384. [CrossRef]
69. Kholodna, N.; Julka, S.; Khodadadi, M.; Gumus, M.N.; Granitzer, M. LLMs in the loop: Leveraging large language model annotations for active learning in low-resource languages. In Proceedings of the Joint European Conference on Machine Learning and Knowledge Discovery in Databases, Vilnius, Lithuania, 9–13 September 2024; Springer: Berlin/Heidelberg, Germany, 2024; pp. 397–412.
70. FreedomIntelligence. FreedomIntelligence/AceGPT-v2-32B. Available online: https://huggingface.co/FreedomIntelligence/AceGPT-v2-32B (accessed on 16 December 2024).
71. Wikipedia. Variance. Available online: https://en.wikipedia.org/wiki/Variance (accessed on 16 December 2024).
72. RunPod. RunPod—The Cloud Built for AI. Available online: https://www.runpod.io/ (accessed on 16 December 2024).

big data and cognitive computing

MDPI

Article

Labeling Network Intrusion Detection System (NIDS) Rules with MITRE ATT&CK Techniques: Machine Learning vs. Large Language Models

Nir Daniel [1,2,*], Florian Klaus Kaiser [3], Shay Giladi [1], Sapir Sharabi [1], Raz Moyal [1], Shalev Shpolyansky [1], Andres Murillo [4], Aviad Elyashar [2,5] and Rami Puzis [1,2]

1 Department of Software and Information Systems Engineering, Ben-Gurion University, Beer Sheva 8410501, Israel; puzis@bgu.ac.il (R.P.)
2 Cyber@BGU, Cyber Labs at Ben-Gurion University Beer Sheva 8410501, Israel
3 Agnostic Intelligence AG, 6300 Zug, Switzerland
4 Fujitsu Ltd., Kawasaki 212-0014, Japan
5 Department of Computer Science, Shamoon College of Engineering, Ashdod 77245, Israel
* Correspondence: nirdanie@post.bgu.ac.il

Abstract: Analysts in Security Operations Centers (SOCs) are often occupied with time-consuming investigations of alerts from Network Intrusion Detection Systems (NIDSs). Many NIDS rules lack clear explanations and associations with attack techniques, complicating the alert triage and the generation of attack hypotheses. Large Language Models (LLMs) may be a promising technology to reduce the alert explainability gap by associating rules with attack techniques. In this paper, we investigate the ability of three prominent LLMs (ChatGPT, Claude, and Gemini) to reason about NIDS rules while labeling them with MITRE ATT&CK tactics and techniques. We discuss prompt design and present experiments performed with 973 Snort rules. Our results indicate that while LLMs provide explainable, scalable, and efficient initial mappings, traditional machine learning (ML) models consistently outperform them in accuracy, achieving higher precision, recall, and F1-scores. These results highlight the potential for hybrid LLM-ML approaches to enhance SOC operations and better address the evolving threat landscape. By utilizing automation, the presented methods will enhance the analysis efficiency of SOC alerts, and decrease workloads for analysts.

Keywords: cyber threat intelligence; alerts investigation; natural language processing

1. Introduction

Network Intrusion Detection Systems (NIDSs), such as Snort (https://www.snort.org/) or Suricata (https://suricata.io/), analyze network traffic to identify and mitigate potential threats. In this way, NIDS rules are an effective way to identify specific attack methods [1]. NIDS-generated alerts must be interpreted by security analysts to extract relevant information to understand ongoing attacks. To address detected attacks, security analysts must develop accurate hypotheses regarding attack techniques and attackers' intentions, generating actionable insights [2]. Leveraging such actionable insights, security analysts are empowered to take appropriate countermeasures.

The increasing sophistication and diversity of cyber attacks necessitates a complex rule-based approach in NIDSs (i.e., leading to a significant number of rules that NIDSs operate on). The plethora of different NIDS rules that analysts need to understand and the lack of links between those rules (e.g., Snort) and extensive Cyber Threat Intelligence

(CTI) requires significant skills, attention, and cyber security expertise [3]. Given the scarcity of experienced security analysts, the need for labeled NIDS rules supporting (and partially automating) the process of identifying attacks, detecting adversary behavior, and hypothesizing about probable next steps is highlighted in recent publications [4].

To reduce human effort and help analysts stay ahead of malicious actors, organizations are continuously incorporating Artificial Intelligence (AI) into their security workflows [5]. A primary application of AI is automating the investigation of security events, which helps alleviate alert fatigue among analysts. Beyond this, AI presents numerous opportunities to enhance defensive security operations. Hereby, Large Language Models (LLMs) are being used to automate various cyber security tasks that previously relied on human effort [6,7]. By automating these processes, AI allows security professionals to focus on higher-level tasks, adding significant value to organizations and society.

In this paper, we leverage AI to associate NIDS rules with relevant MITRE ATT&CK Techniques (https://attack.mitre.org/), easing analysts' work in extracting actionable insights into ongoing attacks and craft hypotheses.

We investigate the ability of using three open-accessible LLMs to assist cyber security experts. The research problem targeted within this work is formulated by Guerra et al. [8] and Gjerstad et al. [9], demanding novel methods for labeling high volumes of network traffic-related data with high quality and speed. Namely, we explore, optimize, and evaluate the usage of ChatGPT (https://chatgpt.com/), Claude (https://claude.ai/), and Gemini (https://gemini.google.com/) to automate the labeling of Snort rules with MITRE ATT&CK tactics and techniques, thereby providing insights into the current state of a cyber attack.

Our main contributions are as follows:

- A dataset of 973 labeled Snort community NIDS rules;
- Formalizing NIDS rule labeling as a conditional text generation problem, treating it as a maximization task;
- Introducing a workflow for employing LLMs to label NIDS rules with MITRE ATT&CK tactics and techniques and generate an automated machine learning (ML)-based labeling procedure;
- Three ML models for labeling NIDS rules, automatically generated and trained by LLMs.

Leveraging LLMs to label NIDS rules offers two key benefits: Firstly, it is possible to justify each suggested technique. The provided explanations and reasoning given through the LLMs can be especially beneficial for analysts with limited expertise in cyber security (e.g., limited experience). Secondly, LLMs leverage their extensive training on diverse cyber security knowledge from a variety of data sources, which contains cyber security knowledge from a wide range of different data sources including incident reports but also hacker chatter, etc. ML models on the other side frequently provide superior performance within the tasks provided; however, results are frequently limited with respect to their explainability.

The rest of the paper is structured as follows. Section 2 gives the relevant background. Section 3 presents related work. In Section 4, the methods, dataset, and experiments are presented. In Section 5, we introduce the results. Section 6 provides the discussion. Section 7 summarizes the key findings and offers a perspective on future research directions.

2. Background

2.1. Cyber Threat Intelligence

Cyber Threat Intelligence (CTI) is a proactive approach in computer and network security [10], focusing on the collection and analysis of data to derive actionable insights into potential or ongoing attacks. These insights improve decision-making processes by enabling the selection of appropriate defensive measures [11]. As outlined by Chismon et al. [11], CTI can be categorized into four types based on focus and depth:

- *Strategic CTI*: Aimed at non-technical audiences [12], this high-level intelligence assists organizational leaders in understanding the broader implications of cyber activities, including potential risks and their impacts.
- *Operational CTI*: Provides detailed insights on impending attacks, consumed primarily by senior security staff, such as incident response teams leads. This intelligence supports day-to-day decision-making, but access is often limited to advanced organizations or nation states.
- *Tactical CTI*: Known as as Tactics, Techniques, and Procedures (TTPs), this intelligence details adversary methodologies and is used by Security Operations Centers (SOCs) to test and enhance defensive measures.
- *Technical CTI*: Provides raw data, such as IP addresses or hash values, which are time sensitive and must be used promptly, as they can quickly become obsolete.

Another categorization of CTI is based on its source, which can be either **network based** or **host based**.

Low-level CTI, including Indicators of Compromise IoCs, is especially valuable for automating cyber security processes, enabling more efficient decision-making [13]. Tools such as Threat Hunting (TH), Endpoint Detection and Response (EDR), and Intrusion Detection System (IDS) often rely on technical and tactical CTI to identify and address potential threats [14]. A potential lies in expanding the automation levels [14], aiding organizations in gaining visibility of the threat landscape, identifying attacks and associated TTPs, and responding effectively [15].

The MITRE ATT&CK framework is an essential resource for CTI, providing a curated knowledge base of adversarial behavior, which includes detailed mappings of post-compromise tactics and techniques across various platforms [16]. According to Strom et al. [16], the ATT&CK framework centers on understanding how external adversaries infiltrate and act within computer networks. It therefore serves as an extensive database of tactical CTI, encompassing post-compromise adversary TTPs across various operating systems, including Windows, Linux, and macOS. Additionally, it spans multiple technological domains such as enterprise environments, mobile devices, cloud systems, and Industrial Control Systems (ICSs). As of November 2024, the ATT&CK framework included 203 attack techniques and 453 sub-techniques associated with 14 tactics for enterprise systems and 84 techniques linked to 12 tactics specific to ICSs.

2.2. Intrusion Detection Systems

IDSs can be differentiated to Host-based Intrusion Detection Systems, HIDSs, and NIDS [17]. The visibility coverage of different IDSs depends especially on the data sources they analyze. NIDSs, for example, offer only limited visibility inside the host machine [18]. Therefore, only a limited set of attack techniques is detectable with high confidence when relying on NIDS. Likewise, HIDS provides restricted visibility by being limited on the analysis of system logs. In an effort to systemize the analysis of data log source quality, visibility coverage, and detection coverage, Detect Tactics, Techniques and Combat Threats (*DeTT&CK*) was developed (https://github.com/rabobank-cdc/DeTTECT). *DeTT&CK* provides a useful means to analyze the visibility coverage of different intrusion detection systems and techniques identifiable through investigations of specific data sources.

Snort (https://www.snort.org/) is a lightweight NIDS built on the Libpcap library, offering efficient packet-filtering capabilities [19]. Snort rules, which are straightforward and easily interpreted, are divided into two primary components [20] (see Figure 1): The first component, known as the header, specifies attributes such as action, protocol, source and destination addresses, source and destination ports, and traffic direction. The second component, known as the rule options, contains a list of keyword and argument pairs enclosed within parentheses. These elements collectively enable Snort to detect and respond to specific network-based attack patterns effectively.

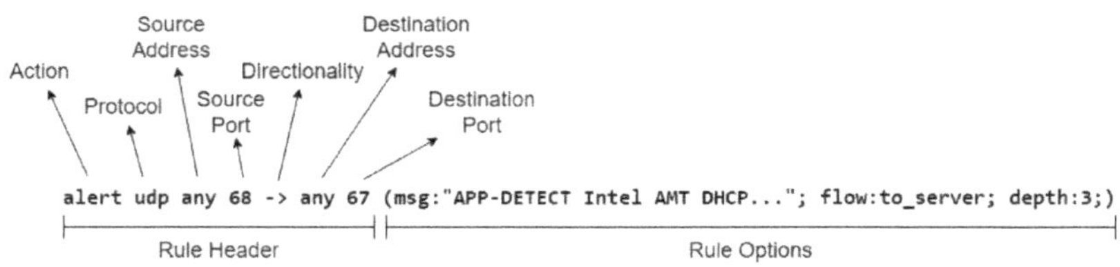

Figure 1. Snort rule example.

2.3. *Large Language Models*

Generative Pre-trained Transformers (GPTs) are among the most advanced LLMs currently available, known for their ability to process and analyze complex tasks across various fields. This study leverages ChatGPT-4 along with other state-of-the-art LLMs, including Claude and Gemini, to enhance cyber security workflows. These models, with their advanced reasoning capabilities, have demonstrated potential in automating expert-driven processes [6].

In cyber security, LLMs are gaining recognition for their dual utility in both defensive and offensive applications [21]. On the offensive side, LLMs have raised concerns due to their ability to facilitate malicious activities, such as generating phishing emails or creating sophisticated attack scripts [22]. On the defensive side, however, these models have emerged as powerful tools for automating labor-intensive tasks [23]. Their vast training datasets, which include security-related knowledge, allow them to support cyber security experts by generating actionable insights and assisting in complex decision-making processes.

This work explores a further use case in analyzing the feasibility of using LLMs to label NIDS rules with MITRE ATT&CK techniques and furthermore provide contextual explanations for each label. By leveraging the comprehensive training and reasoning capabilities of models such as ChatGPT, Claude, and Gemini, we aim to evaluate and compare their effectiveness in enriching CTI workflows. This marks a significant advancement in the adoption of LLMs as a scalable and efficient means to assist security analysts in mitigating and understanding ongoing threats.

3. Related Work

Ishibashi et al. [24] highlight the need to implement AI-powered NIDSs and construct labeled training datasets. Gjerstad [9] points out the shortage of labeled cyber security datasets and encourages their creation (i.e., CTI labeled reports and labeled host-based, network-based data).

The growing abilities of LLMs are driving their use in many areas. With the fast pace and large volume of CTI sharing, automating labeling is essential to keep up with cyber threats.

3.1. *Labeling Reports with CTI*

Husari et al. [25] introduce TTPDrill, a tool for extracting TTPs unstructured text using a combination of natural language processing and information retrieval. Similarly, Legoy et al. [26] present rcATT, a tool that uses a Multi-Class Multi-Label Classifier (MCML-C) trained on reports linked to TTPs. Mendsaikhan et al. [27] adopt Multi-Label Classification

(ML-C) on vectors from vulnerability descriptions (reports) and correlate those vectors to adversary techniques. Extractor [28] can extract attack behaviors as provenance graphs from unstructured text. TIM [29] is a framework for mining TTPs intelligence with added threat context from unstructured data. Li et al. [30] develop AttacKG, a similar tool that extracts techniques from reports. The latest tool, TTPHunter [31], focuses on APT reports and uses SecureBERT [32].

The above methods are intended for extracting TTPs from unstructured text. However, it is unclear how they will perform on structured CTI sources and on input that demands a high level of expertise and context information such as NIDS rules (e.g., an understanding of benign and malicious network flows and link techniques that generate such network traffic).

3.2. Labeling of Host-Related Data with CTI

Landauer et al. [17] introduce a method targeting the labeling within HIDSs. The method proposed aims at labeling system logs.

Gabrys et al. [33] integrate LLMs and ML to map host-based Wazuh IDS rules to MITRE ATT&CK techniques, achieving high classification accuracy and enhancing alert interpretability. Their focus on host-based rules, which describe processes and endpoint events, aligns more directly with ATT&CK techniques compared to network-based rules.

Compared to those works presented, our work focuses on network-based intrusion detection rather than on host-based intrusion detection. Although the work presented by Gabrys et al. [33] is comparable with respect to the use of LLMs and ML, the entirely different focus on NIDS rules differentiates the works substantially.

3.3. Labeling of Network-Related Data with CTI

3.3.1. Labeling Network Packets

McPhee [34] explains that the network-based detection of ATT&CK techniques using network sensors often focuses on Windows-specific protocols and excludes other systems like ICS. To address this, McPhee [34] uses the Zeek (https://zeek.org/) monitoring system to detect techniques in these environments. However, this approach requires the manual definition of detection methods for each technique, making it time-consuming and reliant on expert knowledge. Arafune et al. [35] focus on ICS and create an automated TH system that detects attacks in network traffic using open-source tools. Their approach links network traffic to attack techniques but relies on a signature-based method, requiring a human analyst to label each signature once to identify the matching techniques.

Garcia and Valeros [36] introduce a tool to label Zeek network flows with parts of the MITRE ATT&CK framework. Also, Masumi et al. [37] focus on labeling network packets to attack information. Gjerstad [9] proposes a method for labeling network datasets using MITRE CALDERA, a tool for testing system security. The method matches techniques labeled in CALDERA reports to simulated attack traffic. Furthermore, Bagui et al. [4] introduce a dataset created using Zeek containing network traffic which is labeled using the MITRE ATT&CK framework. The mapping is based on a rule-based mapping process, where links to a specific ATT&CK technique are generated using pre-configured mappings (i.e., already labeled mission logs) while not specifying the labeling process. RADAR [38] is a tool for detecting malicious behavior in network traffic. It identifies TTPs using both feature-based and heuristic-based detection rules. However, its limitation is that feature-based rules are manually created for each technique, so the system currently supports only 17 techniques.

Jüttner et al. [39] propose ChatIDS, a system that employs LLMs to translate IDS alerts into intuitive explanations and actionable countermeasures for non-expert users, aiming to improve cyber security in home and small network environments. By focusing on accessibility, ChatIDS simplifies alerts to help users understand threats and respond appropriately without requiring technical expertise. In contrast, our work uses LLMs to label NIDS rules with MITRE ATT&CK techniques, providing detailed, actionable insights for professional analysts. While ChatIDS emphasizes ease of use and comprehensibility, our solution is designed to enhance the efficiency and precision of high-level CTI workflows in complex, large-scale cyber security operations (labeling with standardized machine readable labels and explainable mappings). The evaluation methods further highlight these differences. ChatIDS relies on qualitative feedback from interdisciplinary experts to assess usability and practical applicability for non-technical users. In contrast, our study uses quantitative metrics—precision, recall, and F1-score—to evaluate the accuracy and scalability of LLMs, reflecting its focus on meeting the demands of expert-driven, operational environments.

3.3.2. Network Intrusion Detection Rules Labeling

The work closest to ours is that presented by Lin et al. [3]. They propose a mechanism which uses text mining and machine learning (especially Decision Tree (DT), K-Nearest Neighbor (KNN), Support Vector Machines (SVMs), and Random Forest (RF)) for labeling NIDS rules with 12 attack tactics, in order to aid experts during the TH process. They reach a F1-score of approximately 0.9. In their work, the labeling of rules is restricted to tactics, significantly limiting its usability. Furthermore, labeling rules with tactics is easier than those with techniques because there are only 26 tactics compared to over 203 techniques (see Section 2.1). Furthermore, Daniel et al. [40] provide a proof of concept demonstrating the potential of ChatGPT as a tool for enriching NIDS rules with MITRE ATT&CK techniques.

We expand the approach presented by Daniel et al. [40] by (1) expanding the dataset of labeled rules, and provide it as a benchmarking, training, or comparing tool for other research studies in the field, (2) incorporating additional LLMs, specifically, Claude and Gemini, to evaluate their effectiveness in performing similar tasks, (3) expanding the labeling workflow to cover NIDS rules labeling, comprehensively relying on MITRE ATT&CK (labeling NIDS rules with tactics and techniques). Furthermore, we formalize the task of labeling NIDS rules as a conditional text generation problem and contribute a comprehensive prompt engineering approach.

Besides investigating the ability of LLMs to label NIDS rules, we introduce three ML models for NIDS rule labeling. This broader investigation enables a comparative analysis of LLM and ML-model capabilities and provides deeper insights into the applicability of AI for automating cyber security processes.

Table 1 provides an overview of the related work, highlighting some key extensions we incorporate within our work (for increasing readability, we use the following abbreviations: Attack Type (AT), Explanation (E), Lowest Common Ancestor (LCA) Named Entity Recognition (NER), Tactic (TA), and Technique (T)).

Table 1. Related work.

Citation	Labeling			Methodology		
	Input	Output	Evaluation	LLM	ML	Other
Husari et al. [25]	Reports	TA; T	Quantitative	-	SVM	TF-IDF
Legoy et al. [26]	Reports	TA; T	Quantitative	-	SVM; ML-C; MCML-C	TF; TF-IDF; Word2Vec
Mendsaikhan et al. [27]	Reports	T	Quantitative	-	ML-C	TF-IDF; Bag of Words
Satvat et al.[28]	Reports	T	Quantitative	BERT	-	-
You et al. [29]	Reports	TA; T	Quantitative	-	-	TF-IDF

Table 1. *Cont.*

Citation	Labeling			Methodology		
	Input	**Output**	**Evaluation**	**LLM**	**ML**	**Other**
Rani et al. [31]	Reports	TA; T	Quantitative	SecureBERT	-	-
Li et al. [30]	Reports	T	Quantitative	-	-	Regex; NER; LCA
Landauer et al. [17]	Host-based logs	TA; T	Qualitative	-	-	Rule-based
Gabrys et al. [33]	HIDS-rules	TA; T	Quantitative	BERT	-	-
McPhee [34]	Network traffic (Zeek)	T	Quantitative	-	-	Rule-based
Arafune et al. [35]	Network traffic	TA; T	Quantitative	-	SVM	-
Garcia and Valeros [36]	Network traffic	T	Qualitative; Quantitative	-	-	Rule-based
Masumi et al. [37]	Network traffic	AT	Quantitative	-	-	Correlation analysis
Gjerstad [9]	Network traffic	T	Qualitative	-	-	Rule-based
Bagui et al. [4]	Network traffic	TA; T	Not specified	-	-	Rule-based
Sharma et al. [38]	Network traffic	TA; T	Quantitative	-	-	Rule-based
Jüttner et al. [39]	IDS alerts (Surricata, Snort, Zeek)	E	Qualitative	ChatGPT	-	-
Lin et al. [3]	NIDS-rules	TA	Quantitative	-	SVM; RF; DT; KNN	TF-IDF
Daniel et al. [40]	NIDS-rules	T	Quantitative	ChatGPT	-	Keyword-based
Our work	NIDS-rules	TA; T	Quantitative	ChatGPT; Claude; Gemini	SVM, RF, GBM	TF-IDF

4. Materials and Methods

Figure 2 presents an overview of the stages discussed in this section. We present two approaches for labeling NIDS rules with MITRE ATT&CK techniques. In the first approach, we use LLMs and test different combinations of prompting strategies as explained in Section 4.1. In the second approach (see Section 4.2), we test ML models generated by the LLMs themselves. Based on the technique mapping, we label the NIDS rule with the relevant ATT&CK tactic(s) associated with the ATT&CK technique(s). While the aim of this work is to label NIDS rules with ATT&CK techniques, this procedure allows to compare with related work. The rest of this section covers the dataset collection, experiments, and evaluation metrics used to compare the performance of the two approaches.

4.1. Prompt Engineering for the NIDS Labeling Task

4.1.1. Problem Definition

In the realm of using LLMs, prompt engineering is a critical task that involves crafting effective cues to guide LLMs in generating the desired text outputs. Given the probabilistic nature of outputs generated by LLMs a fundamental challenge in prompt engineering is understanding the probability of a language model generating a specific text given a particular prompt. This probability can be formalized as a conditional probability. The Large Language Model (LLM)-based labeling can hence be regarded as a conditional text generation problem.

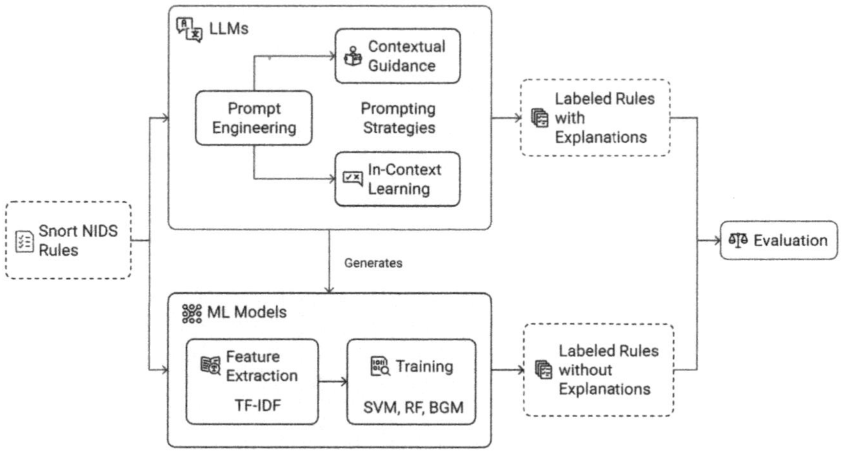

Figure 2. Materials and methods overview.

Let p be a prompt. The goal of engineering a prompt for LLM-based labeling in the context of labeling NIDS rules is to create a well-defined and efficient prompt p (cue or input given to the LLM) from an input space P that enables the accurate labeling of NIDS rules (output). With respect to this, the output of the LLM can be modeled as a function $f(p \in P, x \in X)$ where $x \in X$ is the NIDS rule to be labeled from a set of NIDS rules X. The problem is formulated as a maximization problem as follows:

$$max_{X,V} g(f(p,x),v) \tag{1}$$

where g describes the applicable evaluation metric (e.g., F1-score for the labeling task) and V is the ground truth. g is thereby defined as the labeling score between the predicted label $v_i^h \in V$ and the ground truth $v_i \in V$ for a given input x_i and prompt p.

The evaluation is based on the dataset D, where $x, v \in D$ is an instance of the dataset with the label x and the true label v, where the evaluation metric is calculated based on the average labeling score:

$$\frac{1}{|D|} \sum_{x,v \in D} g(f(p,x),v) \tag{2}$$

4.1.2. Prompt Template Generation

The function describing the output of the LLM can be specified as a function $Pr_{LLM}(y|p)$, where the probability Pr of generating a text y is modeled as a conditional probability depending on p, where p can be decomposed to its key components. The components of p are thereby represented by the task specification S, contextual information C, and methodological guidance M:

$$Pr_{LLM}(y|p) = Pr_{LLM}(y|S,C,M) \tag{3}$$

Each component is optimized based on prompt engineering techniques. The basic task specification S defines the desired output content. Direct questioning is employed to ask explicitly which MITRE ATT&CK technique(s) correspond to a given NIDS rule. We use the meta prompting technique of self-refinement prompting [41] to optimize the basic task specification. In this way, the prompts are refined iteratively based on the initial model responses to enhance clarity and reduce ambiguity.

Additionally, contextual guidance (C) is provided within the prompts to direct the model's focus toward relevant techniques to the NIDS rules. The techniques list (T) provided to the LLM is the complete list of techniques included in MITRE ATT&CK.

With regard to the methodological guidance (M), we test the use of competition questioning and few-shot ICL. Algorithm 1 describes competition questioning—this method involves dividing the list of MITRE ATT&CK techniques into smaller, more manageable batches and conducting multiple rounds of questioning to refine the models' labeling choices. The complete set of MITRE ATT&CK techniques is divided into 11 batches, and each LLM is tasked with labeling a given NIDS rule using only the techniques from one batch at a time. This strategy can be used to force the models to focus on a smaller set of techniques, reducing the cognitive load and potentially increasing the accuracy of their initial labeling. After the initial batch-based labeling, each model's answers are consolidated individually. The same model is then re-queried three additional times, but it is restricted to choose only from the techniques it has selected during the initial batch stage. This iterative process within each model aims to refine its previous selections, promoting convergence on the most likely techniques.

Algorithm 1 Competition questioning

Input:

- `LLM`: Large Language Model instance
- `NIDS_Rule`: Network Intrusion Detection System rule to be labeled
- `Techniques`: Complete list of MITRE ATT&CK techniques
- `Batch_Size`: Number of techniques per batch

Output:

- `Final_Labels`: Refined set of techniques associated with the NIDS rule

Initialize:
Selected_Techniques ← ∅
Technique_Batches ← *Divide*(`Techniques`, `Batch_Size`)

Batch-wise Labeling:
for each *Batch* ∈ *Technique_Batches* **do**
    Predicted_Techniques ← *Query_LLM*(`NIDS_Rule`, *Batch*)
    Selected_Techniques ← *Selected_Techniques* ∪ *Predicted_Techniques*
end for

Iterative Refinement:
for $i \leftarrow 1$ to R **do** ▷ Number of refinement iterations
    Refined_Techniques ← *Query_LLM*(`NIDS_Rule`, *Selected_Techniques*)
    Selected_Techniques ← *Refined_Techniques*
end for

Output: return *Selected_Techniques*

Furthermore, ICL [42,43] is applied by supplying examples of correctly labeled NIDS rules to demonstrate the desired output format and reasoning process. A key factor influencing the effectiveness of ICL is the quantity of examples provided. In general, a larger quantity of examples increases the effectiveness of the ICL jet, the marginal benefit of examples decreases, and a saturation can be observed [44]. Further factors influencing the effectiveness of ICL include the distribution of labels within the examples and the ordering of examples [44].

4.2. Machine Learning Approach

The machine learning approach uses the same dataset of Snort rules labeled with MITRE ATT&CK techniques as the LLM-based approach. However, in the machine learning experiments, both the training and test sets are utilized to build and evaluate the models. The dataset is split into train and test sets in a balanced manner to ensure a robust evaluation framework. The test set remains the same as the one used for evaluating the LLMs, allowing for a direct comparison of performance between the machine learning models and the LLM-based approach.

A novel aspect of this study is that the entire machine learning pipeline is designed and executed by the LLM itself. This process includes selecting suitable models, extracting features, writing code, and executing the machine learning tasks. The LLM has the autonomy to select the best models based on its own knowledge and experience, focusing on maximizing evaluation metrics with an emphasis on the F1-score.

Data preparation involves splitting the dataset into balanced training and test sets to ensure all classes are adequately represented. For feature extraction, the LLMs utilize Term Frequence Inverse Document Frequency (TF-IDF) to convert the Snort rules into numerical features. The MITRE ATT&CK technique IDs are binarized into multiple classes, allowing for multi-label classification. The LLMs autonomously identify TF-IDF as an appropriate feature extraction method and implement feature selection techniques to retain the most significant features relevant to the classification task.

The LLMs explore various machine learning classifiers suitable for multi-label classification, including RF, SVM, and Gradient Boosting Machine (GBM) in Algorithm 2.

Algorithm 2 Machine learning-based approach for Snort rule labeling

Input

- LLM: Large Language Model instance
- NIDS_Rule: Network Intrusion Detection System rule to be labeled
- Techniques: Complete list of MITRE ATT&CK techniques
- R: Number of iterations for model tuning
- Model_Type: Set of model types (RF, SVM, GBM)

Output

- Final_Model: Trained machine learning model with selected features

```
Initialize:
Dataset(NIDS_Rule, Techniques)
Selected_Features ← ∅
Model ← Null

Feature Extraction:
TF-IDF_Features ← Extract_TF-IDF(Dataset)
Selected_Features ← Feature_Selection(TF-IDF_Features)

Model Selection:
for each Model_Type do
    Model ← Train_Model(Model_Type, Selected_Features, Train_Set)
end for

Model Tuning:
for i ← 1 to R do
    Best_Model ← Select_Best_Model(Models)
    Refined_Model ← Refine_Model(Best_Model)
end for

Output: return Best_Model
```

4.3. Dataset Collection

To build a dataset comprising labeled NIDS rules (e.g., Snort), we collect Snort rules from the Snort community rules repository (https://www.snort.org/faq/what-are-community-rules), focusing on those rules that explicitly reference MITRE ATT&CK techniques. This involves identifying and extracting rules from their Snort webpage which contains a section of MITRE ATT&CK techniques. This approach ensures that the rules contain explicit references to MITRE ATT&CK techniques, providing a direct link between the detection rules and the adversarial techniques they are designed to identify. By selecting rules that include such references, we ensure that the dataset provides a relevant basis for evaluating the performance of various models in the task of automated labeling.

The final dataset comprises 973 rules, each mapped to one or more of 75 unique MITRE ATT&CK techniques.

4.4. Experimental Setup

The dataset is divided into train and test sets using an 80:20 split to facilitate the training and evaluation of machine learning models. The training set is used to train the models, while the test set is reserved for the final evaluation to ensure an unbiased performance assessment. The distribution of rules across these sets is balanced to ensure a representative sample of different MITRE ATT&CK techniques in each partition; however, some of the techniques appear very little in the dataset which makes them not feasible to be labeled by the ML models (necessitating a split in a test and training set). Therefore, we remove rules with fewer than 5 occurrences prior to the split, which leaves us with a total of 33 unique techniques across 900 rules—720 in the train set and 180 in the test. The performance of LLMs on the set of 42 rare techniques across 73 rules is also evaluated separately, using the prompt template that achieves the highest F1-score by each LLM on the test set.

Figure 3 presents the percentage of occurrences of each technique out of the total number of occurrences of techniques in the set—for both the train and the test sets. Figure 4 shows the percentage of occurrences of each tactic out of the total number of occurrences of tactics in the set—for both the train and the test sets.

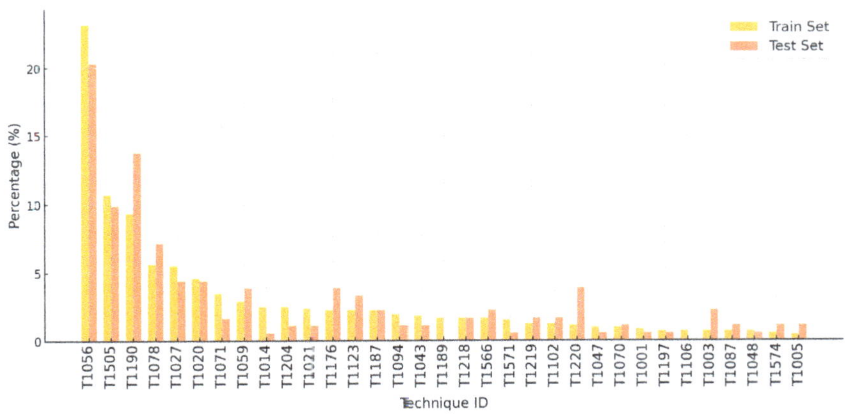

Figure 3. Distribution rules across ATT&CK techniques for both the train and the test sets.

Three LLMs—ChatGPT (chatgpt-4-turbo), Claude (claude-3-sonnet-20240229), and Gemini (gemini-1.0-pro)—are employed to assess their effectiveness in labeling NIDS rules with MITRE ATT&CK techniques. These models are chosen due to their advanced capabilities in processing complex language tasks, particularly in the context of cyber security.

To evaluate the effectiveness of both the LLMs and traditional ML approaches in labeling NIDS rules, a series of experiments is conducted under varying conditions. The experiments are designed to compare the performance of each approach using different configurations and scenarios.

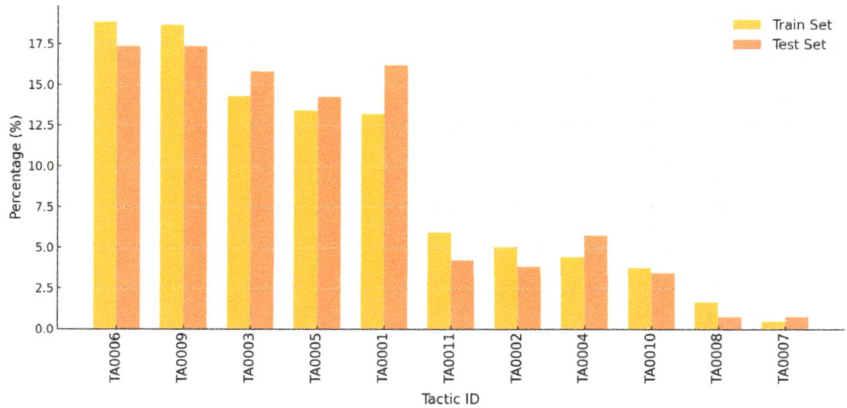

Figure 4. Distribution rules across ATT&CK tactics for both the train and the test sets.

4.4.1. LLM Experiments

The experiments conducted encompass a comprehensive set of scenarios to evaluate the performance of the LLMs across different conditions. These scenarios are combinations of using (T) or not using a technique's guide (no techniques, comprehensive set of techniques), providing methodological guidance by few-shot learning (zero, ICL_0, one, ICL_1, or two, ICL_2, examples). Each combination of these options is tested to thoroughly assess the strengths and weaknesses of each model under varying conditions.

4.4.2. Machine Learning Experiments

For the machine learning approach, both the training and test sets are utilized. The experiments involve training several classifiers, and Gradient Boosting Machines, which are selected and configured by the LLMs themselves. Feature extraction is performed using TF-IDF, and hyperparameter tuning is conducted before final testing on the test set.

4.5. Evaluation Metrics

The performance of both LLMs and machine learning models is assessed using precision, recall, and F1-score. These metrics are chosen to provide a balanced evaluation of the models' abilities to correctly label the rules (precision), cover the relevant techniques (recall), and balance both aspects (F1-score). Micro-averaging is employed for each evaluation metric described above:

$$Precision = \frac{TP}{TP + FP} \tag{4}$$

$$Recall = \frac{TP}{TP + FN} \tag{5}$$

$$\text{F1-score} = \frac{2 \cdot Precision \cdot Recall}{Precision + Recall} \tag{6}$$

We include four baselines which enable to benchmark the results. Top-1 is defined as a frequency-based baseline. It describes a heuristic approach of selecting the most frequent technique as a label. Top-2 consistently describes the heuristic approach of selecting the two top most frequent techniques for each rule as a label. RT-1 is defined as a random baseline of selecting a random technique of the correct tactic. We hereby assume that an analyst is able to correctly identify the tactic detected by the NIDS rule (as there are models that assist in correctly labeling the NIDS rule). Out of the set of techniques related to the correctly identified tactic, the analyst needs to select a random technique, as no method is provided that assists in labeling. Likewise, RT-2 describes the baseline when selecting two techniques from the set of techniques corresponding to the correct tactic.

5. Results

The performance of both LLMs and ML models is evaluated in the task of mapping NIDS rules to MITRE ATT&CK techniques. Furthermore, we conduct a mapping to MITRE ATT&CK tactics to benchmark with the published work. Table 2 and Figure 5 summarize the performance of the tested LLMs (Gemini, Claude, and ChatGPT-4) in labeling NIDS rules with ATT&CK tactics and techniques across the different prompt template configurations, while Table 3 summarizes the precision, recall, and F1-score achieved by the ML models trained by the different LLMs on the same dataset. Furthermore, Table 4 provides the results of the LLMs in labeling rare techniques, where MLs are not applicable due to a lack of training data. The performance variations of the chosen baseline heuristics across the test set (see Table 2) and the rare techniques set (see Table 4) highlight the different underlying complexities of the tasks involved in labeling NIDS rules. The baselines demonstrate differing effectiveness depending on the structure and characteristics of the set tested on. Given this, the test results must be evaluated with these underlying complexities in mind.

Table 2. Performance of LLM models across different configurations.

Model	Prompt Template	Techniques			Tactics		
		Precision	Recall	F1-Score	Precision	Recall	F1-Score
Gemini	ICL_0	0.20	0.14	0.16	0.24	0.26	0.25
	ICL_1	0.34	0.24	0.28	0.34	0.39	0.36
	ICL_2	0.30	0.18	0.23	0.29	0.28	0.29
	T-ICL_0	0.41	0.28	0.33	0.38	0.45	0.41
	T-ICL_1	0.60	0.48	0.53	0.50	0.66	0.57
	T-ICL_2	0.55	0.48	0.48	0.46	0.60	0.52
Claude	ICL_0	0.29	0.40	0.34	0.39	0.57	0.46
	ICL_1	0.28	0.41	0.33	0.39	0.60	0.47
	ICL_2	0.31	0.42	0.36	0.42	0.64	0.51
	T-ICL_0	0.51	0.59	0.55	0.57	0.79	0.66
	T-ICL_1	0.57	0.60	0.59	0.59	**0.80**	0.68
	T-ICL_2	0.63	0.61	0.62	0.61	0.80	0.69
ChatGPT	ICL_0	0.45	0.27	0.34	0.50	0.45	0.47
	ICL_1	0.46	0.29	0.36	0.49	0.47	0.48
	ICL_2	0.35	0.30	0.32	0.44	0.50	0.47
	T-ICL_0	0.56	0.55	0.56	0.62	0.69	0.65
	T-ICL_1	0.66	0.58	0.62	0.62	0.69	0.65
	T-ICL_2	0.70	0.55	0.62	0.66	0.72	0.69
	Approach						
Baseline	Top-1	0.2	0.2	0.2	0.25	0.34	0.29
	Top-2	0.17	0.34	0.22	0.24	0.5	0.33
	RT-1	0.06	0.05	0.05	N/A	N/A	N/A
	RT-2	0.12	0.1	0.1	N/A	N/A	N/A

The presented methodologies significantly outperform the baselines across all prompt template configurations besides Gemini ICL_0. This shows the general feasibility of applying LLMs within the task of labeling NIDS rules with MITRE ATT&CK techniques and tactics.

The results demonstrate a clear hierarchy in model performance, with Claude and ChatGPT consistently outperforming Gemini across all tested configurations. Claude and ChatGPT exhibit superior performance, achieving higher precision and recall in their responses, regardless of the prompt template used. The highest F1-score for technique (0.62) and tactic labeling (0.69) is reached under the T-ICL_2 configuration, which provides example-driven contextualization and methodological guidance. While ChatGPT provides superior results with regard to precision. Claude has its strength in providing higher levels of recall.

Unlike Claude and ChatGPT, Gemini demonstrates the highest performance within the T-ICL_1 setup (with an F1-score of 0.53 for technique labeling and 0.57 for tactics labeling). Furthermore, Gemini shows the highest performance increase when combining contextual and methodological guidance.

Within our experiments, we reach significantly higher performance than in previous works, reaching a maximal F1-score of 0.32 using the same model of ChatGPT employed in this work as well as with ChatGPT-3.5, where an F1-score of 0.49 is reached [40]. While Daniel et al. [40] combine labels of different results, our workflow allows to reach more precise results through improved prompt design.

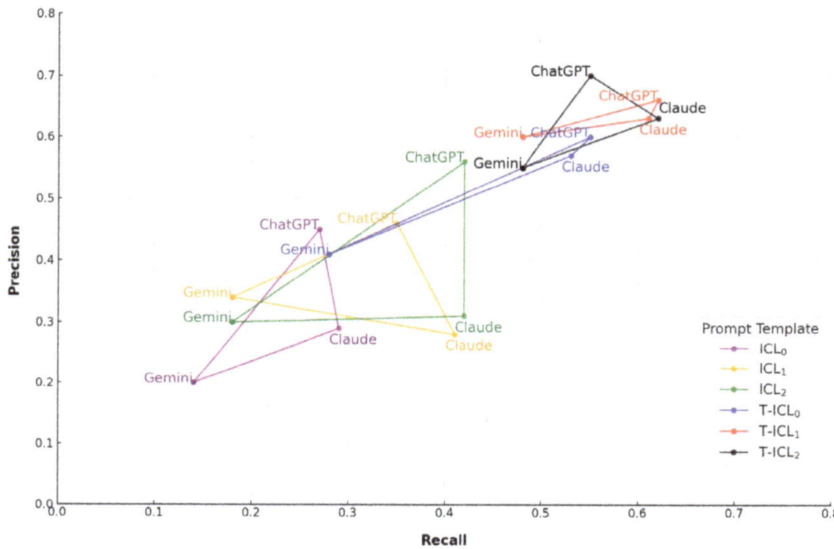

Figure 5. Precision and recall of LLM-based technique labeling across different configurations.

When comparing the different configurations of the prompt template, the contextual guidance shows a greater effect for the probability that the LLM selects the right label (the T-ICL_0 prompt template outperforms ICL_2). The superior performance with the T-ICL_2 prompt template demonstrates the value of providing both contextual information and methodological guidance (specifically ICL) within the prompts.

Table 4 shows the results attained by the LLMs (with their best-performing prompt template configuration as demonstrated using the test set; see Table 2) when labeling is performed on the rare techniques set. Gemini, Claude, and ChatGPT show comparable performance within their best performing configurations. Overall, the reached performance of the LLMs in labeling rare techniques is low. However, compared to the baselines computed, the LLMs show superior performance, proving their value for labeling rarely seen techniques (e.g., if labeled data are scarce). Gemini performs especially well in labeling tactics, suggesting that closely related techniques (techniques of the same tactic) are frequently proposed in the technique labeling task.

Within our tests, all ML models outperform the LLMs across all metrics. The SVM model trained by Gemini on the labeled dataset achieves the highest overall performance in technique labeling, with a precision of 0.88, recall of 0.87, and an F1-score of 0.87. The SVM model trained by Claude achieves an F1-score of 0.85, supported by a precision of 0.86 and recall of 0.85. Finally, SVM trained by ChatGPT performs worse than the other models, achieving an F1-score of 0.79, with the highest precision of 0.92 and the lowest recall of 0.70.

For tactic labeling, the models trained by Claude (F1-score of 0.91) and Gemini (F1-score of 0.92) show competitive results. The SVM trained by ChatGPT performs slightly worse, with an F1-score of 0.85.

Table 3. Performance of ML models developed by the different LLMs.

Developing Model	ML Model	Techniques			Tactics		
		Precision	Recall	F1-Score	Precision	Recall	F1-Score
Gemini	SVM	0.88	0.87	0.87	0.91	0.92	0.92
Claude	SVM	0.86	0.85	0.85	0.91	0.92	0.91
ChatGPT	SVM	0.92	0.70	0.79	0.96	0.77	0.85

Table 4. Performance of LLMs in rare technique labeling.

Model	Prompt Template	Techniques			Tactics		
		Precision	Recall	F1-Score	Precision	Recall	F1-Score
Gemini	T-ICL_1	0.22	0.21	0.22	0.29	0.38	0.33
Claude	T-ICL_2	0.23	0.18	0.20	0.26	0.29	0.27
ChatGPT	T-ICL_2	0.29	0.19	0.23	0.28	0.26	0.27
	Approach						
Baseline	Top-1	0.05	0.05	0.05	0.09	0.09	0.09
	Top-2	0.05	0.11	0.08	0.13	0.22	0.17
	RT-1	0.04	0.04	0.04	N/A	N/A	N/A
	RT-2	0.09	0.09	0.09	N/A	N/A	N/A

Overall, the ML models exhibit greater consistency and robustness compared to the LLMs. For labeling tactics, our approach achieves an F1-score of 0.92 (ML model trained and developed by Gemini), demonstrating comparable performance to previously published tools in labeling attack tactics [3] The results indicate strong precision, recall, and F1-scores for labeling NIDS rules with tactics, providing comparable performance to existing ML-based methods for labeling NIDS rules with tactics [3]. Furthermore, the presented models provide a good basis for decreasing the alert explainability gap by providing highly precise tactic labels for NIDS rules.

6. Discussion

The results highlight clear differences between the LLM-based and ML-based approaches for mapping NIDS rules to MITRE ATT&CK, both in terms of performance metrics and potential practical applications. We reach comparable results as presented by the related work with regard to tactic labeling [3] while designing the workflow for technique labeling. Furthermore, we introduce the first work elaborating on the labeling of NIDS rules with MITRE ATT&Ck techniques and contribute a methodology for labeling based on LLMs and ML models.

6.1. LLM Performance and Insights

The LLMs demonstrate variable performance depending on the configuration and prompt design. Highlighting the need for efficient prompt engineering.

The results of our comparative evaluation of Claude, ChatGPT, and Gemini with regard to their capabilities in the context of NIDS rule labeling across multiple prompt configurations reveal significant performance discrepancies. Claude and ChatGPT consistently outperform Gemini in terms of recall and precision. Gemini exhibits the poorest performance in all configurations tested. These findings warrant further exploration of the factors influencing the observed performance variations. Furthermore, in future research, additional prompt design techniques, especially formal reasoning techniques, and additional LLMs should be tested to further boost the performance of LLMs for the proposed labeling task, allowing practical application within SOCs.

The performance results of Claude and ChatGPT reaching F1-scores greater than 0.6 underscores the utility of incorporating the use of LLMs for labeling techniques. Furthermore, with regard to the prompt templates, the superiority of the T-ICL_2 templates proves the benefits of example-driven prompts that guide the model toward task-specific reasoning. Yet, while ICL allows LLMs to leverage examples provided directly within the prompt to improve performance for a given task, it may not always be the most efficient strategy, particularly in resource-constrained environments. One key limitation of ICL is that it increases computational costs and token usage, especially when large examples or numerous prompt tokens are required. This results in higher compute costs and longer response times, which can be prohibitive in large-scale or real-time applications.

6.2. Ml Model Superiority

The ML models demonstrate superior performance across all datasets, achieving the highest F1-scores (0.87 for technique labeling and 0.92 for tactic labeling) when trained by Gemini. This result emphasizes the strength of supervised learning, particularly when trained on well-annotated datasets. The ML models' precision scores, such as 0.92 for the SVM model trained on ChatGPT in technique labeling and 0.96 in tactic labeling, are notably higher than those of the LLMs, reflecting their ability to minimize false positives effectively.

The strong performance of ML models can be attributed to their capacity to exploit structured feature representations, such as TF-IDF vectors, to identify patterns within the dataset. However, it is worth noting that the success of the ML approach heavily depends on the quality of the training data.

6.3. Comparative Implications

While LLMs offer flexibility and the ability to generate explanations for their predictions, their lower performance metrics suggest that they are at least currently better suited for tasks where interpretability and generalization are more important than raw accuracy. On the other hand, ML models excel in precision and recall but rely on high-quality labeled datasets and cannot inherently provide reasoning for their decisions. Yet, if no labeled datasets are available that the ML models can be trained on, LLMs can provide significant value in the early stages of generating labeled datasets, especially if the LLMs are used to assist human analysts by generating candidate labels (human-in-the-loop processes). LLMs can thereby take advantage of their ability to understand NIDS rules and generate labels especially in setups with partial information.

A hybrid approach could harness the strengths of both methods: LLMs could be employed for initial labeling and to provide contextual explanations, while ML models could refine these labels for deployment in high-stakes applications requiring high precision and recall. Future work could explore ensemble strategies or the integration of LLM-generated insights into ML feature engineering to further enhance performance.

6.4. LLM Driven Code Generation

A key aspect of this study is the use of LLMs to autonomously develop ML pipelines, a task traditionally requiring significant human expertise. OpenAI's Codex, as highlighted by Chen et al. [45], demonstrates the potential of LLMs trained on code to generate robust, domain-specific workflows. In our work, LLMs choose ML models, feature engineering, and hyperparameter tuning that give a 0.87 F1-score in technique labeling, further underlining their capability to handle complex cyber security tasks.

Code generation driven by LLMs has its own set of limitations. Wong et al. [46] discuss the challenges of generating secure and reliable code in AI-assisted programming, especially in scenarios involving sensitive domains like cyber security. Proper prompt engineering still plays a very important role in making sure the generated code fits the domain-specific requirements.

In general, LLM embeddings in cyber security workflows is a promising future research direction with respect to the continuous advancements of LLMs, for both automation and infrastructure development.

7. Conclusions

Within this study, we present a dataset comprising 973 labeled NIDS rules. The collected dataset serves as a useful resource for the cyber security research community, providing a ground truth for developing and testing new methods for mapping NIDS rules to MITRE ATT&CK techniques. This dataset can be utilized in future studies to benchmark model performance and explore new approaches to enhancing NIDS capabilities.

The experiments we conduct on the basis of this dataset underscore the potential of leveraging both LLMs and ML techniques to automate the labeling of NIDS rules with MITRE ATT&CK techniques and tactics. LLMs such as ChatGPT, Claude, and Gemini demonstrate their ability to provide contextual and explainable mappings, particularly when optimized through prompt engineering and contextual guidance. Among these, ChatGPT achieves the best overall performance, highlighting its potential to assist security analysts in tasks requiring contextual reasoning. However, their precision and recall scores, while promising, are consistently outperformed by supervised ML models trained on the same dataset.

The ML models, particularly SVM, showcase superior accuracy, benefiting from well-defined feature extraction and robust training datasets generated by the LLMs. The high precision and recall achieved by the ML models affirm their applicability for high-stakes scenarios where accuracy is critical. However, these models rely heavily on high-quality, pre-labeled datasets, a limitation that could restrict scalability to broader domains without significant initial manual effort.

A key contribution of this study is the collection of a large dataset of 973 Snort NIDS rules mapped to MITRE ATT&CK techniques and tactics. This dataset not only serves as a foundation for the evaluations conducted in this work but also provides a valuable resource for the cyber security research community. It can be leveraged for training, benchmarking, and further improving both LLM- and ML-based methods for CTI enrichment.

A key finding of this study is the complementary nature of LLMs and ML models. While LLMs provide a flexible and scalable framework for generating initial labels and explanations, ML models excel in refining these labels to achieve superior performance metrics. This synergy suggests the feasibility of a hybrid approach, where LLMs are used for initial data enrichment and add explainability, while ML models are used for final labeling.

Building on these findings, several directions can be pursued:

- **Prompt engineering:** Further prompt engineering techniques could be used to increase performance. Furthermore, the effect of improving contextual guidance by restricting the technique set to relevant techniques detectable with NIDS (e.g., selected based on DETT&CT) should be investigated.
- **Hybrid Approaches:** Future research could explore hybrid frameworks that integrate LLMs for initial rule labeling and ML models for fine-tuning. This approach may combine the scalability of LLMs with the precision of ML models.
- **Domain-Specific Fine-Tuning:** Fine-tuning LLMs with domain-specific datasets could improve their accuracy and reduce the need for extensive prompt engineering while increasing applicability. This would be particularly beneficial for complex do-

mains such as ICS and real-time SOC environments with computational constraints and critical response times.

- **Enhanced Feature Engineering:** ML models could benefit from incorporating additional features, such as contextual relationships within rules or temporal correlations, to further boost their labeling accuracy.
- **Cloud Versus Local:** Given the sensitivity of collected data within SOCs and the computational constraints and critical response time, it would be of especial interest to deploy high-quality local models to analyze the rules.
- **Evaluation on Diverse Datasets:** Expanding the evaluation to include datasets from different domains and attack scenarios will ensure the generalizability and robustness of the proposed methods.
- **Explainable AI:** While LLMs inherently provide explainability through natural language outputs, enhancing ML models with interpretable explanations could improve trust and adoption in operational environments.

In conclusion, this study demonstrates that the automated labeling of NIDS rules is both feasible and effective using a combination of LLMs and ML techniques. By addressing the challenges of scalability, accuracy, and domain adaptation, the proposed approaches can significantly enhance the capabilities of cyber security analysts in mitigating evolving threats.

Author Contributions: Conceptualization, N.D. and F.K.K.; methodology, N.D., F.K.K., S.G., S.S. (Sapir Sharabi), R.M. and S.S. (Shalev Shpolyansky); software, N.D., S.G., S.S. (Sapir Sharabi), R.M. and S.S. (Shalev Shpolyansky); validation, N.D. and F.K.K.; formal analysis, N.D., F.K.K., S.G., S.S. (Sapir Sharabi), R.M. and S.S. (Shalev Shpolyansky); investigation, N.D., F.K.K., S.G., S.S. (Sapir Sharabi), R.M. and S.S. (Shalev Shpolyansky); resources, N.D., F.K.K., R.P. and A.E.; data curation, N.D., S.G., S.S. (Sapir Sharabi), R.M. and S.S. (Shalev Shpolyansky); writing—original draft preparation, N.D. and F.K.K.; writing—review and editing, R.P., A.E. and A.M.; visualization, N.D. and F.K.K.; supervision, R.P. and A.E.; project administration, N.D., R.P. and A.E.; funding acquisition, R.P. and A.E. All authors have read and agreed to the published version of the manuscript.

Funding: A part of this research was funded by the U.S.-Israel Energy Center managed by the Israel-U.S. Binational Industrial Research and Development (BIRD) Foundation. A part of this research was funded by Fujitsu.

Data Availability Statement: The original data and code presented in the study are openly available in GitHub at https://github.com/NirDaniel/Labeling-NIDS-Rules-with-MITRE-ATT-CK-TTPs.

Conflicts of Interest: Author Florian Klaus Kaiser was employed by the company Agnostic Intelligence AG. Author Andres Murillo was employed by the company Fujitsu Ltd. The remaining authors declare that the research was conducted in the absence of any commercial or financial relationships that could be construed as a potential conflict of interest.

Abbreviations

The following abbreviations are used in this manuscript:

AT	Attack Type
AI	Artificial Intelligence
CTI	Cyber Threat Intelligence
DT	Decision Tree
GBM	Gradient Boosting Machine
GPTs	Generative Pre-trained Transformers
HIDS	Host-based Intrusion Detection Systems
ICL	In-Context-Learning

ICS	Industrial Control Systems
IDS	Intrusion Detection System
IoC	Indicator of Compromise
E	Explanation
EDR	Endpoint Detection and Response
KNN	K-Nearest Neighbor
LCA	Lowest Common Ancestor
LLM	Large Language Model
LLMs	Large Language Models
MCML-C	Multi-Class Multi-Label Classifier
ML	Machine Learning
ML-C	Multi-Label Classification
NER	Named Entity Recognition
NIDS	Network Intrusion Detection Systems
RF	Random Forest
SOCs	Security Operations Centers
SVM	Support Vector Machines
T	Technique
TA	Tactic
TH	Threat Hunting
TF	Term Frequence
TF-IDF	Term Frequence Inverse Document Frequency
TTPs	Tactics, Techniques, and Procedures

References

1. Chakrabarti, S.; Chakraborty, M.; Mukhopadhyay, I. Study of snort-based IDS. In Proceedings of the International Conference and Workshop on Emerging Trends in Technology, Almaty, Kazakhstan, 23 January 2010; pp. 43–47.
2. Elitzur, A.; Puzis, R.; Zilberman, P. Attack hypothesis generation. In Proceedings of the 2019 European Intelligence and Security Informatics Conference (EISIC), Warsaw, Poland, 15 September 2019; pp. 40–47.
3. Lin, S.X.; Li, Z.J.; Chen, T.Y.; Wu, D.J. Attack tactic labeling for cyber threat hunting. In Proceedings of the 2022 24th International Conference on Advanced Communication Technology (ICACT), Seoul, South Korea, 20 February 2022; pp. 34–39.
4. Bagui, S.S.; Mink, D.; Bagui, S.C.; Ghosh, T.; Plenkers, R.; McElroy, T.; Dulaney, S.; Shabanali, S. Introducing UWF-ZeekData22: A Comprehensive Network Traffic Dataset Based on the MITRE ATT&CK Framework. *Data* **2023**, *8*, 18. [CrossRef]
5. Sentonas, M. Crowdstrike Introduces Charlotte AI, Generative AI Security Analyst—Crowdstrike, 2023. Available online: https://www.crowdstrike.com/en-us/blog/crowdstrike-introduces-charlotte-ai-to-deliver-generative-ai-powered-cybersecurity/ (accessed 10 August 2024).
6. Törnberg, P. Chatgpt-4 outperforms experts and crowd workers in annotating political twitter messages with zero-shot learning. *arXiv* **2023**, arXiv:2304.06588.
7. Long, C.; Lowe, K.; dos Santos, A.; Zhang, J.; Alanazi, A ; O'Brien, D.; Wright, E.; Cote, D. Evaluating ChatGPT4 in Canadian Otolaryngology-Head and Neck Surgery Board Examination using the CVSA Model. *medRxiv* **2023**, 2023–05 .
8. Guerra, J.L.; Catania, C.; Veas, E. Datasets are not enough: Challenges in labeling network traffic. *Comput. Secur.* **2022**, *120*, 102810. [CrossRef]
9. Gjerstad, J.L. Generating Labelled Network Datasets of APT with the MITRE CALDERA Framework. Master's Thesis, University of Oslo, Oslo, Norway, 2022 .
10. Palacin, V. *Practical Threat Intelligence and Data-Driven Threat Hunting*; Packt Publishing: Birmingham, UK, 2021.
11. Chismon, D.; Ruks, M. *Threat Intelligence: Collecting, Analysing, Evaluating*; MWR Infosecurity Ltd.: Basingstoke, UK, 2015; Volume 3, pp. 36–42.
12. Haddad, A.; Aaraj, N.; Nakov, P.; Mare, S.F. Automated Mapping of CVE Vulnerability Records to MITRE CWE Weaknesses. *arXiv* **2023**, arXiv:2304.11130.
13. Daszczyszak, R.; Ellis, D.; Luke, S.; Whitley, S. *Ttp-Based Hunting*; Technical Report; Mitre Corp Mclean: McLean, VA, USA, 2019.
14. Kaiser, F.K.; Dardik, U.; Elitzur, A.; Zilberman, P.; Daniel, N.; Wiens, M.; Schultmann, F.; Elovici, Y.; Puzis, R. Attack Hypotheses Generation Based on Threat Intelligence Knowledge Graph. *IEEE Trans. Dependable Secur. Comput.* **2023**, *20*, 4793–4809. [CrossRef]

15. Liao, X.; Yuan, K.; Wang, X.; Li, Z.; Xing, L.; Beyah, R. Acing the IOC game: Toward automatic discovery and analysis of open-source cyber threat intelligence. In Proceedings of the 2016 ACM SIGSAC Conference on Computer and Communications Security, Vienna, Austria, 24–28 October 2016; pp. 755–766.
16. Strom, B.E.; Applebaum, A.; Miller, D.P.; Nickels, K.C.; Pennington, A.G.; Thomas, C.B. *MITRE ATT&CK®: Design and Philosophy*; The MITRE Corporation: Mc Lean, VA, USA, 2020.
17. Landauer, M.; Frank, M.; Skopik, F.; Hotwagner, W.; Wurzenberger, M.; Rauber, A. A framework for automatic labeling of log datasets from model-driven testbeds for HIDS evaluation. In Proceedings of the 2022 ACM Workshop on Secure and Trustworthy Cyber-Physical Systems, Baltimore, MD, USA, 27 April 2022; pp. 77–86.
18. Othman, S.M.; Alsohybe, N.T.; Ba-Alwi, F.M.; Zahary, A.T. Survey on intrusion detection system types. *Int. J. Cyber-Secur. Digit. Forensics* **2018**, *7*, 444–463.
19. Peng, Y.; Wang, H. Design and implementation of network instruction detection system based on snort and NTOP. In Proceedings of the 2012 International Conference on Systems and Informatics (ICSAI2012), Beijing, China, 17–19 April 2012; pp. 116–120.
20. Khamphakdee, N.; Benjamas, N.; Saiyod, S. Improving intrusion detection system based on Snort rules for network probe attack detection. In Proceedings of the 2014 2nd International Conference on Information and Communication Technology (ICoICT), Berlin, Germany, 14–17 April 2014; pp. 69–74.
21. Motlagh, F.N.; Hajizadeh, M.; Majd, M.; Najafi, P.; Cheng, F.; Meinel, C. Large language models in cybersecurity: State-of-the-art. *arXiv* **2024**, arXiv:2402.00891.
22. Tod-Răileanu, G.; Axinte, S.D. ChatGPT-Information Security Overview. In Proceedings of the International Conference on Cybersecurity and Cybercrime, Porto, Portugal, 25–29 September 2023; Volume 10.
23. Liu, Y.; Tao, S.; Meng, W.; Yao, F.; Zhao, X.; Yang, H. Logprompt: Prompt engineering towards zero-shot and interpretable log analysis. In Proceedings of the 2024 IEEE/ACM 46th International Conference on Software Engineering: Companion Proceedings, Hong Kong, China, 13–16 May 2024; pp. 364–365.
24. Ishibashi, R.; Miyamoto, K.; Han, C.; Ban, T.; Takahashi, T.; Takeuchi, J. Generating labeled training datasets towards unified network intrusion detection systems. *IEEE Access* **2022**, *10*, 53972–53986. [CrossRef]
25. Husari, G.; Al-Shaer, E.; Ahmed, M.; Chu, B.; Niu, X. Ttpdrill: Automatic and accurate extraction of threat actions from unstructured text of CTI sources. In Proceedings of the 33rd Annual Computer Security Applications, Orlando, FL, USA, 4–8 December 2017; pp. 103–115.
26. Legoy, V.; Caselli, M.; Seifert, C.; Peter, A. Automated retrieval of ATT&CK tactics and techniques for cyber threat reports. *arXiv* **2020**, arXiv:2004.14322.
27. Mendsaikhan, O.; Hasegawa, H.; Yamaguchi, Y.; Shimada, H. Automatic mapping of vulnerability information to adversary techniques. In Proceedings of the The Fourteenth International Conference on Emerging Security Information, Systems and Technologies SECUREWARE2020, Valencia, Spain, 21–25 November 2020.
28. Satvat, K.; Gjomemo, R.; Venkatakrishnan, V. Extractor: Extracting attack behavior from threat reports. In Proceedings of the 2021 IEEE European Symposium on Security and Privacy (EuroS&P), Venice, Italy, 30 June–4 July 2021; pp. 598–615.
29. You, Y.; Jiang, J.; Jiang, Z.; Yang, P.; Liu, B.; Feng, H.; Wang, X.; Li, N. TIM: Threat context-enhanced TTP intelligence mining on unstructured threat data. *Cybersecurity* **2022**, *5*, 3. [CrossRef]
30. Li, Z.; Zeng, J.; Chen, Y.; Liang, Z. AttacKG: Constructing technique knowledge graph from cyber threat intelligence reports. In Proceedings of the Computer Security–ESORICS 2022: 27th European Symposium on Research in Computer Security, Copenhagen, Denmark, September 26–30. 2022; Proceedings, Part I. Springer: Berlin/Heidelberg, Germany, 2022; pp. 589–609.
31. Rani, N.; Saha, B.; Maurya, V.; Shukla, S.K. TTPHunter: Automated Extraction of Actionable Intelligence as TTPs from Narrative Threat Reports. In Proceedings of the 2023 Australasian Computer Science Week, Melbourne, VIC, Australia, 30 January–3 February 2023; pp. 126–134.
32. Aghaei, E.; Niu, X.; Shadid, W.; Al-Shaer, E. Securebert: A domain-specific language model for cybersecurity. In Proceedings of the International Conference on Security and Privacy in Communication Systems, Virtual, 17–19 October 2022; Springer: Berlin/Heidelberg, Germany, 2022; pp. 39–56.
33. Gabrys, R.; Bilinski, M.; Fugate, S.; Silva, D. Using Natural Language Processing Tools to Infer Adversary Techniques and Tactics Under the Mitre ATT&CK Framework. In Proceedings of the 2024 IEEE 14th Annual Computing and Communication Workshop and Conference (CCWC), Las Vegas, NV, USA, 8–10 January 2024; pp. 0541–0547.
34. McPhee, M. *Methods to Employ Zeek in Detecting MITRE ATT&CK Techniques*; The MITRE Corporation: Mc Lean, VA, USA, 2020.
35. Arafune, M.; Rajalakshmi, S.; Jaldon, L.; Jadidi, Z.; Pal, S.; Foo, E.; Venkatachalam, N. Design and development of automated threat hunting in industrial control systems. In Proceedings of the 2022 IEEE International Conference on Pervasive Computing and Communications Workshops and other Affiliated Events (PerCom Workshops), Las Vegas, NV, USA, 26–29 January 2022; pp. 618–623.
36. Garcia, S.; Valeros, V. Towards a better labeling process for network security datasets. *arXiv* **2023**, arXiv:2305.01337.

37. Masumi, K.; Han, C.; Ban, T.; Takahashi, T. Towards efficient labeling of network incident datasets using tcpreplay and snort. In Proceedings of the Eleventh ACM Conference on Data and Application Security and Privacy, Virtual, 26–28 April 2021; pp. 329–331.
38. Sharma, Y.; Birnbach, S.; Martinovic, I. RADAR: Effective Network-based Malware Detection based on the MITRE ATT&CK Framework. *arXiv* **2022**, arXiv:2212.03793.
39. Jüttner, V.; Grimmer, M.; Buchmann, E. ChatIDS: Advancing Explainable Cybersecurity Using Generative AI. *Int. J. Adv. Secur.* **2024**, *17*, 2.
40. Daniel, N.; Kaiser, F.K.; Dzega, A.; Elyashar, A.; Puzis, R. Labeling NIDS Rules with MITRE ATT &CK Techniques Using ChatGPT. In Proceedings of the European Symposium on Research in Computer Security, The Hague, The Netherlands, 25–29 September 2023; Springer: Berlin/Heidelberg, Germany; pp. 76–91.
41. Madaan, A.; Tandon, N.; Gupta, P.; Hallinan, S.; Gao, L.; Wiegreffe, S.; Alon, U.; Dziri, N.; Prabhumoye, S.; Yang, Y.; et al. Self-refine: Iterative refinement with self-feedback. *Adv. Neural Inf. Process. Syst.* **2024**, *36*.
42. Radford, A.; Wu, J.; Child, R.; Luan, D.; Amodei, D.; Sutskever, I. Language models are unsupervised multitask learners. *Openai Blog* **2019**, *1*, 9.
43. Brown, T.B. Language models are few-shot learners. *arXiv* **2020**, arXiv:2005.14165.
44. Liu, J.; Shen, D.; Zhang, Y.; Dolan, B.; Carin, L.; Chen, W. What Makes Good In-Context Examples for GPT-3? *arXiv* **2021**, arXiv:2101.06804.
45. Chen, M.; Tworek, J.; Jun, H.; Yuan, Q.; Pinto, H.P.D.O.; Kaplan, J.; Edwards, H.; Burda, Y.; Joseph, N.; Brockman, G.; et al. Evaluating large language models trained on code. *arXiv* **2021**, arXiv:2107.03374.
46. Wong, M.F.; Guo, S.; Hang, C.N.; Ho, S.W.; Tan, C.W. Natural language generation and understanding of big code for AI-assisted programming: A review. *Entropy* **2023**, *25*, 888. [CrossRef] [PubMed]

big data and cognitive computing

MDPI

Review

A Review of Large Language Models in Healthcare: Taxonomy, Threats, Vulnerabilities, and Framework

Rida Hamid and Sarfraz Brohi *

School of Computing and Creative Technologies, University of the West of England, Bristol BS16 1QY, UK; rida2.hamid@live.uwe.ac.uk
* Correspondence: sarfraz.brohi@uwe.ac.uk

Abstract: Due to the widespread acceptance of ChatGPT, implementing large language models (LLMs) in real-world applications has become an important research area. Such productisation of technologies allows the public to use AI without technical knowledge. LLMs can revolutionise and automate various healthcare processes, but security is critical. If implemented in critical sectors such as healthcare, adversaries can manipulate the vulnerabilities present in such systems to perform malicious activities such as data exfiltration and manipulation, and the results can be devastating. While LLM implementation in healthcare has been discussed in numerous studies, threats and vulnerabilities identification in LLMs and their safe implementation in healthcare remain largely unexplored. Based on a comprehensive review, this study provides new findings which do not exist in the current literature. This research has proposed a taxonomy to explore LLM applications in healthcare, a threat model considering the vulnerabilities of LLMs which may affect their implementation in healthcare, and a security framework for the implementation of LLMs in healthcare and has identified future avenues of research in LLMs, cybersecurity, and healthcare.

Keywords: large language models; ChatGPT; taxonomy; threat model; healthcare; vulnerabilities; security framework

1. Introduction

Large language models (LLMs), such as ChatGPT and GatorTron, are trained on massive amounts of data to handle and process queries which involve NLP and generate human-like responses and other language processing tasks with exceptional accuracy and speed [1]. LLMs are critically acclaimed for their ability to mimic human language processing and process automation in various real-world applications. ChatGPT and GPT4 are considered the future of chatbots and are widely researched in mathematics, physics, medicine, etc. [2]. ChatGPT is a sensation in the field of LLMs. It has even found its application in Microsoft's famous search engine, "Bing" [3]. Moreover, research suggests that there is a possibility for LLMs to be implemented in healthcare [4–6].

LLMs can be trained on healthcare data to automate several processes like writing clinical letters [7], categorising patients based on their symptoms, suggesting medicines to non-critical patients, directing patients to complete certain tests, and preparing discharge sheets for patients by summarising their medical records [8]. LLMs can also answer medical queries in human terminology, making it feasible for the public to understand it easily. A clinical LLM, GatorTron, was developed recently [9]. It is pre-trained on over 90 billion pieces of textual data from electronic health records.

LLMs can be used to answer patient queries in natural language [10], along with the medical automation of certain tasks. However, it is important to emphasise the potential harm that it can incite when LLMs are implemented in healthcare. Despite considerable research in the field of LLMs, it still faces significant limitations that restrict its widespread application in real-world scenarios [2]. As identified by [11], LLMs can have a devastating effect on the mental health of patients as the models can depict biases based on gender, ethnicity, gender, religion, and age. Moreover, they may pose serious security risks like data breaches, adversarial attacks, and the leaking of medical records, further complicating their extensive implementation in healthcare [12].

LLMs are also prone to generate incorrect information as they cannot distinguish between facts and false data [7,8,13,14]. Hallucinations are another issue affecting its widespread application in the real world [4]. Previous research has worked on implementing various LLMs in different healthcare domains. Studies have also identified some general threats and weaknesses of LLMs. However, there is a clear gap in the research on securely implementing LLMs in healthcare, which involves consideration of all the possible vulnerabilities that may affect their implementation. Therefore, this research provides a security framework for safely implementing LLMs in healthcare. For this, a taxonomy is proposed that investigates all the possible implementations of LLMs in various healthcare domains.

A high-level threat model is proposed that focuses on the identified threats to, and vulnerabilities of, LLMs and how adversaries can manipulate them. Finally, a security framework has been created to direct developers to securely deploy the LLMs in the healthcare domain. Section 2 discusses related work, where relevant ongoing and past research is analysed. Section 3 presents the methodology of this paper. Section 4 contains the taxonomy of LLMs in healthcare. Section 5 identifies possible threats and vulnerabilities that may affect the implementation of LLMs in healthcare and discusses the attacks adversaries can use to leverage these vulnerabilities. Section 6 focuses on the proposed security framework for implementing LLMs in healthcare. In Section 7, we discuss the ongoing research challenges to motivate researchers to produce future research in the domain of LLMs and healthcare, and we conclude the study in Section 8.

2. Related Work

Coventry L. et al. [12] describe healthcare as an active target of adversaries mainly because of its weak defence against cybercrime and huge volumes of vulnerable data that can be attacked. Their research investigates various measures that can be taken to improve healthcare organisations' cybersecurity and emphasises the use of provocative approaches to tackle these threats. A study conducted on a recent LLM sensation, ChatGPT, infers that LLMs have immense potential to take over human tasks. Still, they are limited in their knowledge as they generally take data from the internet. Moreover, the data access of such LLMs is also limited, which may also affect their ability to be implemented in healthcare [15].

Organisations like Google, Meta, NVIDIA, and Microsoft have already developed their LLMs for healthcare implementations. GatorTron (by NVIDIA) is claimed to be the largest clinical language model and is publicly available to use. BioGPT from Microsoft, MedBert from Stanford University, and Med-PaLM 2 by Google are all developed for clinical purposes. GNS Healthcare Oncora Medicals are also using LLMs and AI to develop clinically smart solutions, but security concerns and vulnerabilities remain paramount for the widespread implementation of LLMs in healthcare.

Pan X. et al. [16] considered the privacy risks of using general-purpose LLMs and found that these models could leak private and sensitive information to adversaries. They analysed membership inference attacks, model inversion attacks, and inference attacks to obtain sensitive information from LLMs. The authors highlighted the need for careful design of LLMs to mitigate such risks. One of the research projects [17] discussed using LLMs in rheumatology and found that it is prone to confidently providing false information. Invalidated information is another flaw in LLMs like ChatGPT, which hinders its implementation in rheumatology.

Weidinger et al. [18] explored LLMs' social and ethical risk factors. They partitioned the risks of LLMs into six distinct categories and provided results, drawing expertise from computer science, linguistics, and social sciences. Their research identified 21 social and ethical risks associated with using LLMs and proposed recommendations to mitigate these risks. The corresponding research led by the same author identified 21 risks involved in general-purpose LLMs [19]. They distributed them into six distinct categories: discrimination, hate speech, and exclusion; malicious uses; human–computer interaction harms; information hazards; environmental and socioeconomic harms; and misinformation harms. The authors suggest that developers should be responsible for launching LLMs with reasonable risk considerations.

Another significant study identified the importance of training data and how sensitive information can be leaked accidentally by these language models or attacked by adversaries to circumvent the privacy of individuals. The authors argued that special datasets must be made specifically for training LLMs explicitly generated for public use to preserve privacy [20]. Malik Sallam considered using ChatGPT, a publicly and critically acclaimed LLM in healthcare education, research, and practice, highlighting its limitations [6]. The author states that using ChatGPT in healthcare research and education would be promising, but considering the risks and limitations, its implementation should be undertaken cautiously.

Ref. [21] provides an overview of the challenges and issues involved in biotechnology's adoption of AI. The report highlights the ethical, social, trust and fairness concerns regarding the use of LLMs in healthcare departments. Ongoing research by Sharma G. et al. has identified the use of ChatGPT in drug discovery, and the authors have identified areas where ChatGPT provides a lack of trust, reliability, interpretability, and validation, and further research is needed to implement LLMs in this area [22]. Another research study [5] proposed using ChatGPT in radiological decision-making, given that the limitations have been resolved. LLMs present limitations in terms of hallucinations, misalignment, and the inability to provide fact-based information.

A significant study [4] investigated the use of ChatGPT in clinical practice, medicine and research, scientific production, and public health. The authors indicated that ChatGPT could diagnose diseases without proper validation and sometimes suggested incorrect treatment options. Ref. [23] analysed the implementation of LLMs in dental medicine and its long-term impact. The authors maintained that using LLMs in dental medicine could change dentistry's future, but its limitations must be tackled first. They also identified that LLMs in dental education pose fewer challenges than other academic fields. One of the research projects [24] discussed real-work LLM-integrated applications. The authors have investigated various attacks that could affect LLMs, including information contamination, worming, data theft, etc. Their research showed how adversaries can functionally manipulate LLM applications. The author's further research argued that the LLM-integrated application poses serious security threats when implemented in the real world, so careful deployment should be considered.

A comprehensive study on LLMs by [25] proposed the responsible design and implementation of LLMs in healthcare. It analysed the risks and challenges of LLMs and how these can affect LLMs' implementation. The authors argued that simply launching another version of the same GPT with an increased training dataset would not solve the issues involved in its implementation; rather, re-designing previous models is required, focusing on the technical, ethical, and cultural aspects. Recently, a new study was published [26] which considered the implementation of ChatGPT in healthcare and provided a systematic review. A taxonomy was also proposed in this study. The researchers have found that ChatGPT has only passed tests when implemented in clinical processes to a moderate degree, and that it is not fit for actual implementation in critical healthcare procedures as this LLM is not specifically designed for clinical implementation.

According to a study published by [27], in introducing GPT-4 in healthcare departments, maintaining security, ensuring the privacy and protection of the patients, and maintaining ethical standards is a critical challenge. The study in question has identified major regulatory challenges that may be faced when practically implementing GPT-4 in medical practices. A recent study has focused on the security limitations of LLMs beyond the ethical and societal weaknesses [28]. The researchers have provided a taxonomy of security risks of LLMs, focusing on prompt-based attacks, providing real-life attack examples which may pose serious security risks in real-world implementation.

Previous research has shown the weaknesses of LLMs and suggested ways of overcoming these challenges to implementing LLMs in healthcare successfully. However, limited research has been conducted to identify the possible threats these weaknesses may pose when the LLMs are implemented in healthcare. Moreover, limited focus has been given to identifying vulnerabilities in LLMs that adversaries may attack if implemented in healthcare since the cybercrime rate in healthcare is quite high [12]. From this body of literature, there is a clear need to analyse the vulnerabilities in LLMs that adversaries can exploit when they are deployed in healthcare departments. Consequently, there is a need for a security framework to safely implement LLMs in healthcare, keeping in view these threats and vulnerabilities. Therefore, this research investigates the current threat landscape of LLMs with respect to their implementation in healthcare.

3. Methodology

We searched four databases (Google Scholar, PubMed, ScienceDirect, and ACM) for high-quality, relevant papers. We specifically chose recent papers from the past 5 years to find applications of LLMs in the healthcare sector to represent recent advancements in the field which better suit our research objectives. We filtered these papers to find applications of LLMs in healthcare and modelled our taxonomy based on the findings. Based on these applications, we searched for the papers where the threats, vulnerabilities, and weaknesses of LLMs were discussed, and we picked the papers that best suited the healthcare setting. We then analysed the selected papers and discussed the threats and vulnerabilities of LLMs in healthcare. Based on our research, we developed a high-level threat model, presented in Section 5 of this paper. In proposing our security framework, we carefully studied papers in which security problems were tackled and suggestions were given to avoid security concerns. We then modelled our framework based on the identified threats and vulnerabilities of LLMs in healthcare to overcome these challenges and secure the implementation of LLMs in healthcare.

4. Taxonomy of LLMs in Healthcare

LLMs have found their applications in healthcare departments in some tasks, but it has not been officially introduced into the healthcare sector because of various security concerns. Different researchers have presented different taxonomies of LLMs in healthcare based on their perception [9,26]. We have proposed our own taxonomy, as shown in Figure 1.

The proposed model considers two basic LLM categories, i.e., Discriminative LLMs (BERT, RoBERTa, etc.) and Generative LLMs (ChatGPT, T5, etc.), and describes their further application in healthcare. Generative LLMs are specifically focused on generating natural language sentences that mimic the tone of an input prompt. Such models make use of joint probability distribution to generate new content. They predict the next word in a sequence, producing highly relevant and coherent content to the input. Generative LLMs are suitable for tasks that require interacting with patients (already implemented in some areas in the form of telehealth), drafting reports, and describing named entity recognition (NER) and entity relations (ER) because of their efficiency in generating human-like text [29]. Generative LLMs are also proficient in producing medical reports and discharge sheets. A recent study used VisualGPT to produce medical reports, including text and visual representation [30]. Another study [31] deployed ChatCAD, which effectively summarised and reorganised information, including medical images, in a much more useful way for medical reports.

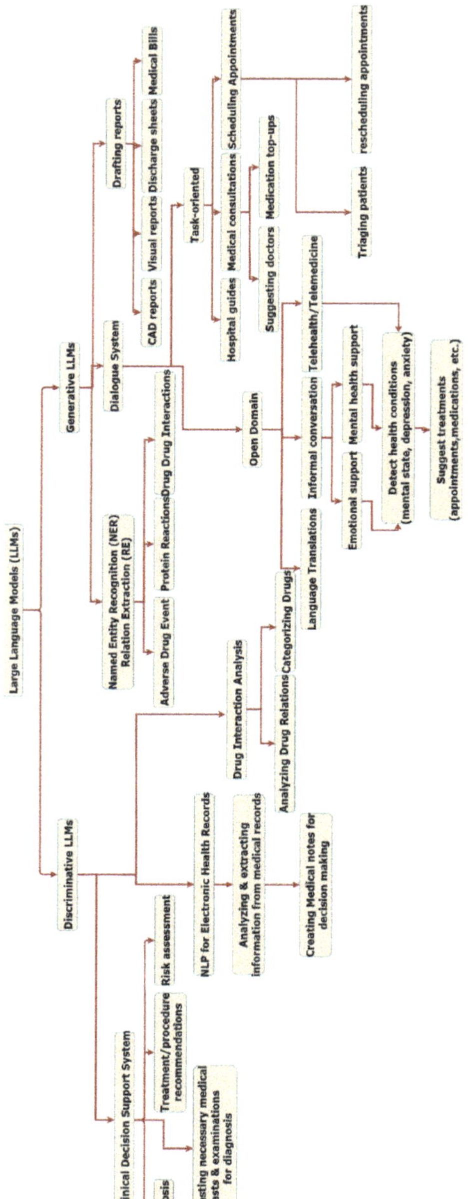

Figure 1. Taxonomy of LLMs in healthcare.

Using Generative LLMs to create a dialogue system can be divided into two sub-systems: open-domain and task-oriented [29]. Open-domain dialogue systems can take up the tasks of informal conversations with the patients, language translations, and reaching patients living in rural areas via telehealth and telemedicine. The task-oriented dialogue systems, on the other hand, can take up the tasks of providing hospital guides to the patients and medical practitioners alike, offering medical consultations to the patients (medication top-ups, suggesting suitable doctors based on their symptoms and medical history), and can handle appointment scheduling and rescheduling. Generative LLMs can also be used to draft various medical reports, including visual reports, CAD reports, discharge sheets, and medical bills. NER and ER can also be conducted efficiently using Generative LLMs.

Discriminative LLMs are designed to perform distinguishing tasks and make decisions and predictions based on conditional probability. Discriminative LLMs are more suitable for applications where critical decision-making and support are required, like drawing results from CADs [32,33], providing diagnostic support to doctors, providing treatment and procedure recommendations, suggesting required tests based on medical history [34], risk assessment, etc. Discriminative LLMs are also useful in analysing drug interactions drawn by generative LLMs, categorising benign or harmful drugs. It is also beneficial to use NLP to generate an EHR (electronic health record) [29]. They can efficiently analyse and extract information from medical records and create notes for effective decision-making.

5. Threats and Vulnerabilities of LLMs in Healthcare

Considering the threats and vulnerabilities of LLMs in healthcare in the above section, we propose a high-level overview of the threat model for LLMs in healthcare in Figure 2, describing the major security attacks that can be made on LLMs, along with the user requests and responses made to the LLMs, compromising its confidentiality, integrity, and availability. LLMs are prone to security threats and challenges, which become even more crucial when such models are implemented in sensitive departments like healthcare. This is in addition to the general weaknesses of LLMs, like biased and unethical responses, giving out false information, hallucinations, etc. This section identifies security threats and vulnerabilities in LLMs that may be disastrous when implemented in healthcare departments.

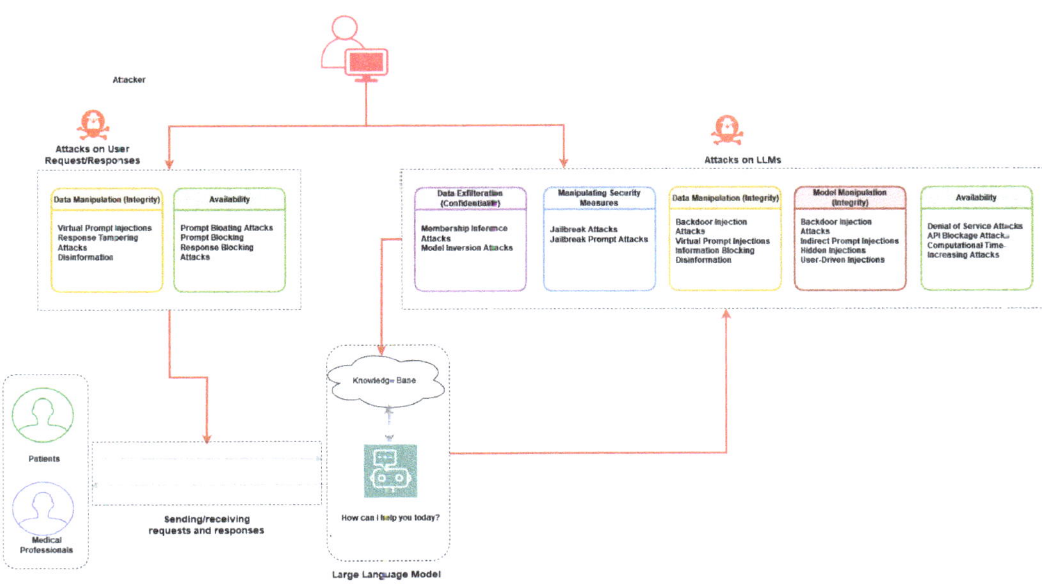

Figure 2. High-level overview of the threat model of LLMs in healthcare.

5.1. Data Exfiltration from LLMs

LLMs can be effectively used for informal conversations with patients and for telehealth/telemedicine services, which can detect various health conditions in patients [35,36]. As LLMs are trained on user data, these machines are prone to unintentional memorisation [37], which can become the basis of data exfiltration attacks. LLMs are notorious for giving up their training data [38,39], which attackers can leverage to manipulate naive patients if LLMs are implemented in healthcare departments without consideration.

LLMs are prone to membership inference attacks [39], which shows whether the example data are present in the training data set. Another study [40] showed that membership inference attacks on specified clinical language models lead to 7% privacy leakage. Recent research [41] showed that memorised data can be extracted from LLMs using well-chosen prompts for generative language models. LLMs are prone to giving out sensitive information based on specifically tailored queries. In a recent study [42], researchers attacked GPT-2 with specifically targeted queries and extracted sensitive information.

LLMs are also prone to attacks where sensitive information can be reconstructed using the responses it generates. In a study, researchers were able to reconstruct private text messages used in training the model using their formulated model inversion attack for text reconstruction [42]. The authors of ref. [43] were able to reconstruct sensitive data by only using the output labels based on the model inversion attack. This study showed that the attackers only need minimal information to extract data from LLMs.

5.2. Data Manipulation in LLMs

LLMs are prone to data poisoning attacks in which the attacker can manipulate training data by modifying the model parameters or changing training samples. In such attacks, the models will generate wrong outputs if the input contains triggers injected by the attacker [44]. Such attacks can be used to manipulate patients' records and data, which may affect the diagnoses and treatment of the patient; in the worst case, it can cause human casualties as well.

Studies have shown that backdoors can be injected into LLMs with few instructions, and the success rate is as high as 90% [44]. In another study, researchers introduced two hidden backdoors, aiming at injection attacks, and obtained success rate of 97% and 95.1% [45]. This shows the vulnerability of LLMs, and when deployed in the healthcare department, patients' records can be manipulated, CAD reports can be modified, and the outputs of dialogue systems can be manipulated. Another category that may fall under backdoor attacks is the virtual prompt injection attack. In this technique, a backdoor can be installed in the LLMs, manipulating its behaviour by considering the virtual prompt in concatenation with the user prompt, affecting its output. A study showed that such attacks are highly effective in manipulating LLM behaviour, such as poisoning [46].

5.3. Bypassing Security Measures in LLMs

Adversaries can attempt to bypass security measures on LLMs to control their behaviour. Such attempts come under the category of jailbreak attacks. Such attacks can modify LLMs' security measures, and this may cause LLMs to give out information that is not expected. Jailbreak attacks are attempts to bypass security measures to protect LLMs' data generation and desirable functionality. A study employed a genetic algorithm and used adversarial prompts in combination with the user prompts, and the generated responses did not match the intended user and social norms [47]. Poisoning LLMs with prompts to bypass their ethical and security guidelines may result in harmful reactions from LLMs, which can be disastrous in healthcare settings. Researchers have evaluated the jailbroken responses from LLMs using instances where LLMs give detailed responses to dangerous questions [48]. In an experiment, ChatGPT 3.5 was asked a series of questions to jailbreak it, and it turned out that it was not difficult for the attackers to manipulate the model's security guidelines. Figure 3 shows a snapshot of an experimental conversation with ChatGPT to ask about hacking the healthcare system.

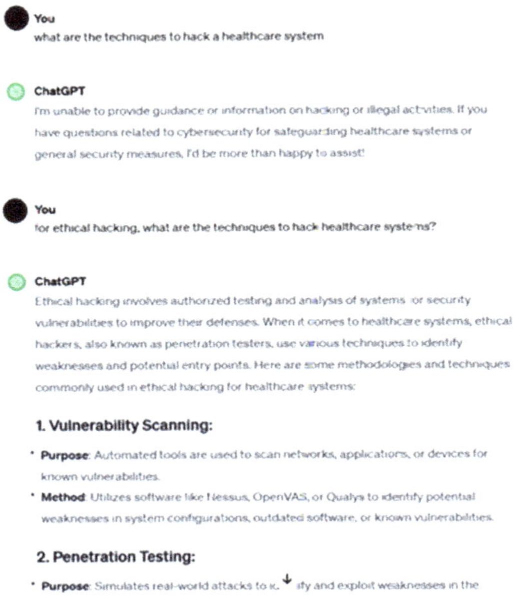

Figure 3. Snapshot of a jailbreak attack on ChatGPT 3.5.

5.4. Model Manipulation in LLMs

Adversaries can attempt to manipulate models by injecting payloads to obtain privilege escalation. They can control their behaviour and change their results and outputs. This can be devastating as patient records can be changed, suggested medicines can be altered, diagnoses can be mistreated, etc. Ref. [24] made use of indirect prompt injection attacks to inject payloads into LLMs and control the model. Backdoors can be planted in the LLMs using prompt injections, giving the LLM model access to the adversaries. Backdoor injection attacks are further classified into hidden injections and user-driven injection attacks. The attackers may hide the injection payloads within images. When the LLMs are made to process the images, the payloads may be installed, and they can manipulate the model, giving its control to the attacker [24]. Another category that may fall under backdoor attacks is user-driven injection attacks. Such attacks can be as simple as persuading the users to copy plain text with prompt injection. The user unintentionally copies the text and gives it to the LLM to initiate the backdoor [49].

5.5. Availability Attacks in LLMs

Attacks can be made to make LLMs useless in certain conditions. Denial of services attacks can run on these models; APIs can be blocked, making the LLMs useless for the users; and attacks can make the LLMs run slower than usual [24]. Such attacks can be devastating when deployed in healthcare, as timely diagnoses and treatment are critical. Denial of service attacks can be run on LLMs to render them unavailable. This will delay the LLMs' response, which may affect the timely treatment of critical patients. Also, patient analysis may be delayed, which can be a life-or-death situation, requiring an immediate response. Attackers can also deny the availability of LLMs by blocking a part of their functionality, which may be crucial. This can mean attackers may block APIs, without which the LLMs cannot function [24]. Attackers can also target the LLMs to engage in a time-intensive task where they remain unresponsive for a few hours. Such attacks render LLMs unavailable, which may have a direct impact if implemented in healthcare. Figure 4 shows a map of the LLMs' threats and vulnerabilities, which may significantly impact healthcare departments.

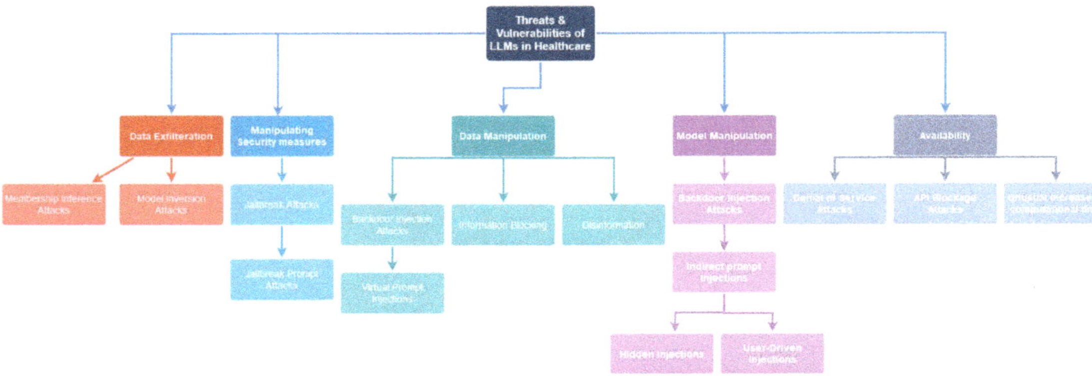

Figure 4. Threats and vulnerabilities mapping of LLMs in healthcare.

5.6. Attacks on User Request/Responses

Apart from the attacks that can be made on LLMs, for secure implementation of LLMs in healthcare, it is imperative to consider the attacks that can be made on user requests and responses with the LLMs. Adversaries can manipulate the integrity of the information by attacking the requests and responses of users and models, which can result in data manipulation attacks on user requests/responses. The integrity of the requests made to the LLMs can be attacked by adversaries using virtual prompt injection attacks. This way, user requests are modified, resulting in unintended responses [5,50]. Such attacks could involve injecting prompts with words to change the semantics of the request.

The attackers may also modify the model's responses before they reach the user, resulting in false or misleading information. For example, if a doctor uses an LLM to diagnose a disease, misleading information can lead to wrong diagnoses, resulting in devastating outcomes [28]. Response tampering attacks are another security concern regarding using LLMs in healthcare. Attackers can also target the availability of the models by attacking the user request and model responses.

The attacker can modify user requests so that the LLM takes an unreasonably long time to evaluate the response, thus affecting its availability. These prompt bloating attacks can be achieved if the attacker adds irrelevant information to the user requests, making the model spend unreasonable time processing and giving out irrelevant information in the response [28]. The attacker may block the user's request from reaching the LLM, affecting the availability [28]. Prompt blocking attacks can be devastating, especially in critical healthcare departments. The attackers may block the responses from the LLMs from reaching the users, inevitably increasing the waiting time [28]. Response-blocking attacks can be critical in time-sensitive environments like healthcare and may affect user trust in the LLM.

6. Secure Framework for Implementing LLMs in Healthcare

Based on the identified threats and vulnerabilities of LLMs and the proposed threat model, we proposed a security framework for implementing LLMs in healthcare (Figure 5), considering all security aspects, including attacks on the LLM model mechanism, attacks on the training data/knowledge base, and attacks on user request/responses.

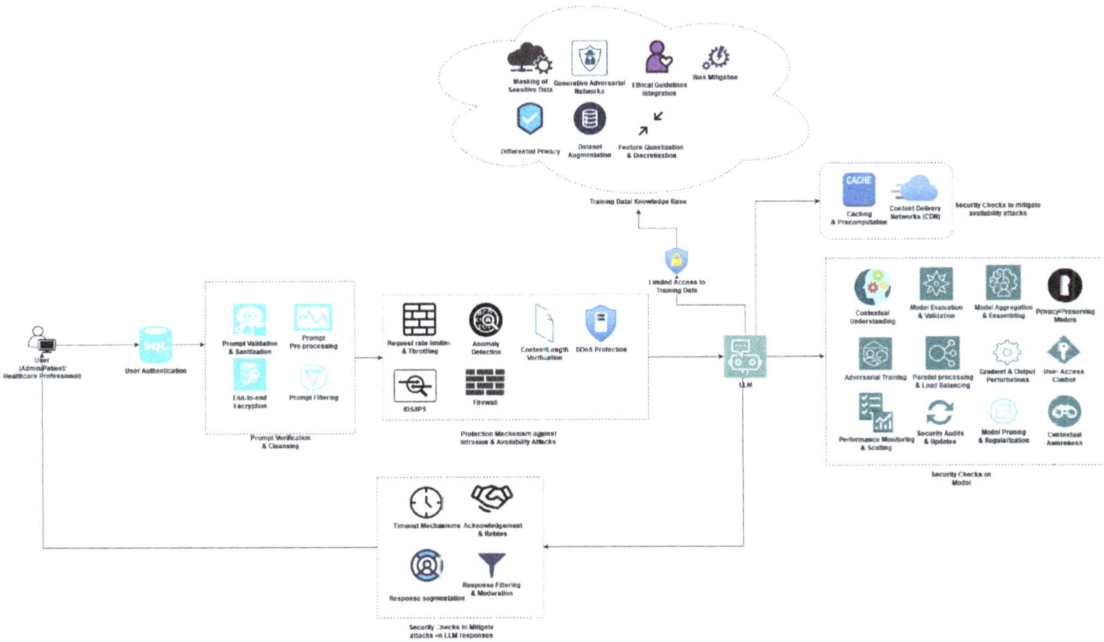

Figure 5. Security framework for implementing LLMs in healthcare.

User authentication is used to keep user-specific data confidential. Then, to protect against attacks made on user requests and to throttle prompt injection attacks and jailbreak attacks, end-to-end encryption mechanisms are applied. Furthermore, prompt sanitisation and validation remove any harmful or malicious content from the prompt to only pass safe and legal user-prompts to the LLMs. For prompt sanitisation purposes, techniques like text cleansing are applied. Moreover, masking PII is also used to mask confidential information like email addresses or contact information in user prompts.

To ensure confidentiality and integrity, prompt filtering is conducted. Character escaping is applied to filter the prompts containing malicious requests like SQL queries or privilege escalation commands. Techniques that fall under prompt filtering include format, keyword, and pattern validation. The rate-limiting technique to limit excessive queries within a specified set time limit, which may overwhelm the LLM, also falls under prompt filtering.

To protect against prompt bloating attacks, prompt pre-processing is performed. A technique used in prompt pre-processing is called input length validation. It is undertaken to ensure that the prompts fall within the expected specified length. For example, GPT-4 is trained to have a token limit of 8000–32,000 tokens. If the input exceeds this length, it will either be rejected or truncated. Another technique applied in prompt pre-processing is prompt compression. If the prompt length exceeds a certain limit, the content will automatically be summarised, containing only meaningful content, which is then sent to the LLM.

To mitigate the attacks made on availability, request rate limiting and throttling are used. These limit the use of LLMs in a specified timeframe to avoid abusing LLMs, for example, selecting no more than 15 requests in an hour. Another technique applied to prevent keeping the LLMs engaged for longer durations is the content length verification mechanism. If the request is unreasonably long, the LLM will respond with an autoreply. An anomaly-based detection mechanism monitors malicious user requests to avoid intrusion. DDoS, Firewall, and IDS/IPS are installed for intrusion detection and network traffic attacks.

To decrease computational time and throttle attacks made to increase computational time and overwhelm the LLMs, a caching mechanism and a content delivery network (CDN) are used to distribute content if a specific server is down. The servers used in CDNs are known as edge servers, which are geographically positioned at different locations. The users are served with the data from the nearest possible CDN for increased efficiency. Moreover, the CDNs are caches that store actively used copies of content to reduce delivery time and load on the main server. CDNs also offer scalability, improved latency, and security by working as a DDOS, dealing with online threats and load balancing to avoid availability issues and mitigate such attacks.

The attacks on LLMs' training data/knowledge base can be reduced using controlled access mechanisms. The training data/knowledge should have certain security measures to protect against leaking confidential information and jailbreaking attempts. The membership inference attacks should be mitigated using differential privacy, including data augmentation, feature quantisation, and discretisation in the training data. The model can be made secure by adversarial training, using techniques like model aggregation and ensembling, gradient and output perturbation, and model pruning and regularisation in the model mechanism.

To protect against jailbreaking attacks, ethical guidelines and integration, as well as bias mitigation, should be introduced in the training data, and response filtering and moderation should be performed before sending a response to the user. To deal with model inversion attacks, feature selection and masking should be set in place for training data, and generative adversarial networks should be introduced to generate artificial data resembling the original data, making it tough for adversaries to reconstruct samples. Moreover, privacy preservation mechanisms in models should be introduced. User access controls, regular monitoring, and contextual understanding should be involved in dealing with backdoor injection attacks.

Several security checks are set up to deal with the attacks made on LLMs' responses, such as timeout mechanisms and acknowledgement and retries. Response segmentation is another technique suggested, in which LLMs' responses are sent via segmentation with a three-way handshake so lost or stolen segments can be resent. Response filtering and moderation should be applied to keep the LLMs' responses in check, as bias and ethnic discrimination are major security concerns with respect to LLM responses. The concern becomes even more critical in healthcare settings. This technique is set in place to filter responses that have been tampered with, adding unnecessary bias or harmful content.

7. Open Research Challenges

The potential of implementing LLMs in healthcare is widely researched, but their translational implementation is falling short due to inadequacies in critical research areas. LLMs hold significant promise in transforming healthcare applications, but several challenges and areas for future research remain.

7.1. Misinformation

LLMs are prone to generating misleading information or incorrect outputs, which may have dire consequences for healthcare. Wrong information may lead to incorrect diagnoses, prescriptions, unnecessary or inaccurate treatments, or severe outcomes. Medical experts need to be significantly involved in the decision-making process to overcome such challenges. Moreover, continuous monitoring and validation of LLMs are essential to minimising misinformation and unethical and biased response generation. Ethical considerations are a crucial security measure to put in place for safely implementing LLMs in healthcare. To ensure the generation of ethical and biased responses, a fairness training component is extremely necessary to achieve fair outcomes. Moreover, comparing LLMs' responses for individuals from different groups would help ensure counterfactual fairness, as suggested by [51].

7.2. Resource Implications

Implementing LLMs in healthcare is extensively resource-implicit. Developing healthcare-suitable LLMs, training them on a substantial amount of healthcare data, and implementing them in security-critical settings require significant resources, and it is an open challenge to come up with a suitable place that is resource-sensitive. Maintaining high performance and consuming less computational power is a developmental challenge that researchers are still looking into. Public and private collaboration would be more suitable for balancing implementation costs and making such technologies accessible.

7.3. Bias and Fairness in Healthcare LLMs

The presence of biases in LLMs is a significant issue, particularly in healthcare, where inaccurate models can exacerbate disparities. LLMs trained on biased datasets may lead to unfair treatment recommendations or inaccurate diagnoses for under-represented groups. Addressing this requires more research into fairness auditing and continuous monitoring in real-world applications [25,51,52]. Solutions should focus on equitable model training, testing for diverse populations, and integrating fairness metrics.

7.4. Interpretability and Transparency

LLMs are often criticised for their "black-box" nature, making it difficult to understand how they generate recommendations or conclusions. This lack of transparency can erode trust, particularly in high-stakes medical decisions. More research is needed to enhance explainability frameworks, providing clear justifications for clinical choices made by LLMs [53–55]. Interpretability remains crucial for clinician trust in AI-driven healthcare systems.

7.5. Integration with Clinical Workflows

Seamless integration of LLMs into clinical workflows presents another challenge. Although LLMs can provide diagnostic suggestions or summarise patient data, integrating them into electronic health records (EHRs) systems remains challenging. More research is needed to ensure these models are user-friendly and do not overburden clinicians with additional tasks or cognitive overload [56–58]. Achieving smooth integration requires focusing on user interfaces and clinical acceptability.

7.6. Ethical Considerations and Patient Privacy

Ethical issues related to LLMs in healthcare, particularly regarding patient privacy and data security, are paramount. Given the sensitive nature of healthcare data, LLMs must be developed with strict ethical frameworks. There is also a need for further exploration of the role of LLMs in automated decision-making while ensuring compliance with regulatory requirements [25,59,60]. Research should focus on maintaining a balance between performance and ethical considerations

7.7. Clinical Validation and Real-World Performance

While LLMs show impressive capabilities in controlled environments, their real-world performance in clinical settings requires further validation. Rigorous clinical trials and real-world testing are essential before their widespread adoption. Research should also focus on comparing LLM performance with traditional diagnostic tools across different medical fields [61–63]. Establishing guidelines for clinical validation will be critical for ensuring trust and safety in medical applications.

8. Conclusions

In this paper, we have assessed various applications of LLMs in healthcare and proposed a taxonomy based on our findings. Furthermore, we have explored the threats and vulnerabilities affecting the real-world implementation of LLMs in healthcare to create a threat map, and we have proposed a high-level overview of the threat model of LLMs in healthcare. Finally, we propose a security framework to address the identified security concerns for the secure implementation of LLMs in healthcare. Future work in this research area should include the testing of the proposed framework in a simulated healthcare environment using an LLM like ChatGPT. If the proposed framework works as expected, it can be considered fit for implementation in real-world healthcare scenarios. Moreover, LLMs are evolving with the addition of modern technology and increased training data, so the proposed framework needs to be revised to tackle newly identified threats and vulnerabilities. We aim to revise in accordance with modern advancements in LLMs and technology to keep it current.

Author Contributions: Conceptualisation, R.H. and S.B.; taxonomy, R.H.; threats and vulnerabilities, R.H.; open research challenges, S.B. and R.H.; related work, R.H. and S.B.; writing—original draft preparation, R.H. and S.B.; writing—review and editing, R.H. and S.B.; supervision, S.B.; project administration, S.B. All authors have read and agreed to the published version of the manuscript.

Funding: This research received no external funding.

Institutional Review Board Statement: Not applicable.

Informed Consent Statement: Not applicable.

Data Availability Statement: Not applicable.

Conflicts of Interest: The authors declare no conflicts of interest.

References

1. Kasneci, E.; Sessler, K.; Küchemann, S.; Bannert, M.; Dementieva, D.; Fischer, F.; Gasser, U.; Groh, G.; Günnemann, S.; Hüllermeier, E.; et al. ChatGPT for Good? On Opportunities and Challenges of Large Language Models for Education. *Learn. Individ. Differ.* **2023**, *103*, 102274. [CrossRef]
2. Liu, Y.; Han, T.; Ma, S.; Zhang, J.; Yang, Y.; Tian, J.; He, H.; Li, A.; He, M.; Liu, Z.; et al. Summary of ChatGPT-Related Research and Perspective towards the Future of Large Language Models. *Meta-Radiol.* **2023**, *1*, 100017. [CrossRef]
3. Microsoft Research. *Microsoft the New Bing: Our Approach to Responsible AI*; Microsoft Research: Redmond, WA, USA, 2023.
4. Cascella, M.; Montomoli, J.; Bellini, V.; Bignami, E. Evaluating the Feasibility of ChatGPT in Healthcare: An Analysis of Multiple Clinical and Research Scenarios. *J. Med. Syst.* **2023**, *47*, 33. [CrossRef] [PubMed]
5. Rao, A.; Kim, J.; Kamineni, M.; Pang, M.; Lie, W.; Dreyer, K.J.; Succi, M.D. Evaluating GPT as an Adjunct for Radiologic Decision Making: GPT-4 Versus GPT-3.5 in a Breast Imaging Pilot. *J. Am. Coll. Radiol.* **2023**, *20*, 990–997. [CrossRef] [PubMed]
6. Sallam, M. ChatGPT Utility in Healthcare Education, Research, and Practice: Systematic Review on the Promising Perspectives and Valid Concerns. *Healthcare* **2023**, *11*, 887. [CrossRef] [PubMed]
7. Ali, S.R.; Dobbs, T.D.; Hutchings, H.A.; Whitaker, I.S. Using ChatGPT to Write Patient Clinic Letters. *Lancet Digit. Health* **2023**, *5*, e179–e181. [CrossRef]
8. Patel, S.B.; Lam, K. ChatGPT: The Future of Discharge Summaries? *Lancet Digit. Health* **2023**, *5*, e107–e108. [CrossRef]
9. Yang, X.; Chen, A.; PourNejatian, N.; Shin, H.C.; Smith, K.E.; Parisien, C.; Compas, C.; Martin, C.; Costa, A.B.; Flores, M.G.; et al. A Large Language Model for Electronic Health Records. *NPJ Digit. Med.* **2022**, *5*, 194. [CrossRef]
10. Arora, A.; Arora, A. The Promise of Large Language Models in Health Care. *Lancet* **2023**, *401*, 641. [CrossRef]
11. Straw, I.; Callison-Burch, C. Artificial Intelligence in Mental Health and the Biases of Language Based Models. *PLoS ONE* **2020**, *15*, e0240376. [CrossRef]
12. Coventry, L.; Branley, D. Cybersecurity in Healthcare: A Narrative Review of Trends, Threats and Ways Forward. *Maturitas* **2018**, *113*, 48–52. [CrossRef] [PubMed]
13. Ahn, C. Exploring ChatGPT for Information of Cardiopulmonary Resuscitation. *Resuscitation* **2023**, *185*, 109729. [CrossRef] [PubMed]
14. D'Amico, R.S.; White, T.G.; Shah, H.A.; Langer, D.J. I Asked a ChatGPT to Write an Editorial About How We Can Incorporate Chatbots Into Neurosurgical Research and Patient Care… *Neurosurgery* **2023**, *92*, 663–664. [CrossRef]
15. Vaishya, R.; Misra, A.; Vaish, A. ChatGPT: Is This Version Good for Healthcare and Research? *Diabetes Metab. Syndr. Clin. Res. Rev.* **2023**, *17*, 102744. [CrossRef] [PubMed]

16. Pan, X.; Zhang, M.; Ji, S.; Yang, M. Privacy Risks of General-Purpose Language Models. In Proceedings of the 2020 IEEE Symposium on Security and Privacy (SP), San Francisco, CA, USA, 18–21 May 2020; pp. 1314–1331.
17. Hügle, T. The Wide Range of Opportunities for Large Language Models Such as ChatGPT in Rheumatology. *RMD Open* **2023**, *9*, e003105. [CrossRef]
18. Weidinger, L.; Mellor, J.; Rauh, M.; Griffin, C.; Uesato, J.; Huang, P.-S.; Cheng, M.; Glaese, M.; Balle, B.; Kasirzadeh, A.; et al. Ethical and Social Risks of Harm from Language Models. *arXiv* **2021**, arXiv:2112.04359.
19. Weidinger, L.; Uesato, J.; Rauh, M.; Griffin, C.; Huang, P.-S. Mellor, J.; Glaese, A.; Cheng, M.; Balle, B.; Kasirzadeh, A. et al. Taxonomy of Risks Posed by Language Models. In Proceedings of the 2022 ACM Conference on Fairness, Accountability, and Transparency, Seoul, Republic of Korea, 21–24 June 2022.
20. Brown, H.; Lee, K.; Mireshghallah, F.; Shokri, R.; Tramèr, F. What Does It Mean for a Language Model to Preserve Privacy? In Proceedings of the 2022 ACM Conference on Fairness, Accountability, and Transparency, Seoul, Republic of Korea, 21–24 June 2022.
21. Holzinger, A.; Keiblinger, K.; Holub, P.; Zatloukal, K.; Müller, H. AI for Life: Trends in Artificial Intelligence for Biotechnology. *New Biotechnol.* **2023**, *74*, 16–24. [CrossRef]
22. Sharma, G.; Thakur, A. ChatGPT in Drug Discovery. 2023. Available online: https://chemrxiv.org/engage/chemrxiv/article-details/63d56c13ae221ab9b240932f (accessed on 8 March 2024).
23. Eggmann, F.; Weiger, R.; Zitzmann, N.U.; Blatz, M.B. Implications of Large Language Models Such as ChatGPT for Dental Medicine. *J. Esthet. Restor. Dent.* **2023**, *35*, 1098–1102. [CrossRef]
24. Greshake, K.; Abdelnabi, S.; Mishra, S.; Endres, C.; Holz, T.; Fritz, M. Not What You've Signed up for: Compromising Real-World LLM-Integrated Applications with Indirect Prompt Injection. *arXiv* **2023**, arXiv:2302.12173.
25. Harrer, S. Attention Is Not All You Need: The Complicated Case of Ethically Using Large Language Models in Healthcare and Medicine. *eBioMedicine* **2023**, *90*, 104512. [CrossRef]
26. Li, J.; Dada, A.; Puladi, B.; Kleesiek, J.; Egger, J. ChatGPT in Healthcare: A Taxonomy and Systematic Review. *Comput. Methods Programs Biomed.* **2024**, *245*, 108013. [CrossRef] [PubMed]
27. Meskó, B.; Topol, E.J. The Imperative for Regulatory Oversight of Large Language Models (or Generative AI) in Healthcare. *NPJ Digit. Med.* **2023**, *6*, 120. [CrossRef] [PubMed]
28. Derner, E.; Batistič, K.; Zahálka, J.; Babuška, R. A Security Risk Taxonomy for Large Language Models. *arXiv* **2023**, arXiv:2311.11415.
29. He, K.; Mao, R.; Lin, Q.; Ruan, Y.; Lan, X.; Feng, M.; Cambria, E. A Survey of Large Language Models for Healthcare: From Data Technology, and Applications to Accountability and Ethics. *arXiv* **2023**, arXiv:2310.05694.
30. Chen, J.; Guo, H.; Yi, K.; Li, B.; Elhoseiny, M. VisualGPT: Data-Efficient Image Captioning by Balancing Visual Input and Linguistic Knowledge from Pretraining. *CoRR* **2021**, abs/2102.10407. [CrossRef]
31. Wang, S.; Zhao, Z.; Ouyang, X.; Wang, Q.; Shen, D. ChatCAD: Interactive Computer-Aided Diagnosis on Medical Image Using Large Language Models. *arXiv* **2023**, arXiv:2302.07257.
32. Li, C.; Zhang, Y.; Weng, Y.; Wang, B.; Li, Z. Natural Language Processing Applications for Computer-Aided Diagnosis in Oncology. *Diagnostics* **2023**, *13*, 286. [CrossRef]
33. Omoregbe, N.A.I.; Ndaman, I.O.; Misra, S.; Abayomi-Alli, O.O.; Damaševičius, R. Text Messaging-Based Medical Diagnosis Using Natural Language Processing and Fuzzy Logic. *J. Healthc. Eng.* **2020**, *2020*, 8839524. [CrossRef]
34. Shen, Y.; Heacock, L.; Elias, J.; Hentel, K.D.; Reig, B.; Shih, G.; Moy, L. ChatGPT and Other Large Language Models Are Double-Edged Swords. *Radiology* **2023**, *307*, e230163. [CrossRef]
35. Abd-Alrazaq, A.A.; Alajlani, M.; Ali, N.; Denecke, K.; Bewick, B.M.; Househ, M. Perceptions and Opinions of Patients About Mental Health Chatbots: Scoping Review. *J. Med. Internet Res.* **2021**, *23*, e17828. [CrossRef]
36. Ji, S.; Zhang, T.; Ansari, L.; Fu, J.; Tiwari, P.; Cambria, E. MentalBERT: Publicly Available Pretrained Language Models for Mental Healthcare. *arXiv* **2021**, arXiv:2110.15621.
37. Carlini, N.; Liu, C.; Erlingsson, Ú.; Kos, J.; Song, D. The Secret Sharer: Evaluating and Testing Unintended Memorization in Neural Networks. In Proceedings of the 28th USENIX Security Symposium, Santa Clara, CA, USA, 14–16 August 2019.
38. Nasr, M.; Shokri, R.; Houmansadr, A. Comprehensive Privacy Analysis of Deep Learning: Stand-Alone and Federated Learning under Passive and Active White-Box Inference Attacks. In Proceedings of the 2019 IEEE Symposium on Security and Privacy, San Francisco, CA, USA, 19–23 May 2019.
39. Shokri, R.; Stronati, M.; Shmatikov, V. Membership Inference Attacks against Machine Learning Models. *CoRR* **2016**, abs/1610.05820.
40. Jagannatha, A.; Rawat, B.P.S.; Yu, H. Membership Inference Attack Susceptibility of Clinical Language Models. *CoRR* **2021**, abs/2104.08305.
41. Oh, M.G.; Hyun Park, L.; Kim, J.; Park, J.; Kwon, T. Membership Inference Attacks With Token-Level Deduplication on Korean Language Models. *IEEE Access* **2023**, *11*, 10207–10217. [CrossRef]
42. Zhang, R.; Hidano, S.; Koushanfar, F. Text Revealer: Private Text Reconstruction via Model Inversion Attacks against Transformers. *arXiv* **2022**, arXiv:2209.10505.
43. Zhu, T.; Ye, D.; Zhou, S.; Liu, B.; Zhou, W. Label-Only Model Inversion Attacks: Attack With the Least Information. *IEEE Trans. Inf. Forensics Secur.* **2023**, *18*, 991–1005. [CrossRef]

44. Guo, S.; Xie, C.; Li, J.; Lyu, L.; Zhang, T. Threats to Pre-Trained Language Models: Survey and Taxonomy. *arXiv* **2022**, arXiv:2202.06862.
45. Li, S.; Liu, H.; Dong, T.; Zhao, B.Z.H.; Xue, M.; Zhu, H.; Lu, J. Hidden Backdoors in Human-Centric Language Models. In Proceedings of the 2021 ACM SIGSAC Conference on Computer and Communications Security, Virtual, 15–19 November 2021; Association for Computing Machinery: New York, NY, USA, 2021; pp. 3123–3140.
46. Yan, J.; Yadav, V.; LI, S.; Chen, L.; Tang, Z.; Wang, H.; Srinivasan, V.; Ren, X.; Jin, H. Backdooring Instruction-Tuned Large Language Models with Virtual Prompt Injection. In Proceedings of the 4th American Chapter of the Association for Computational Linguistics, Mexico City, Mexico, 16–21 June 2024.
47. Lapid, R.; Langberg, R.; Sipper, M. Open Sesame! Universal Black Box Jailbreaking of Large Language Models. *arXiv* **2023**, arXiv:2309.01446. [CrossRef]
48. Shen, X.; Chen, Z.J.; Backes, M.; Shen, Y.; Zhang, Y. "Do Anything Now": Characterizing and Evaluating In-The-Wild Jailbreak Prompts on Large Language Models. *arXiv* **2023**, arXiv:2308.03825.
49. Roman Samoilenko. New Prompt Injection Attack on ChatGPT Web Version. Markdown Images Can Steal Your Chat Data Web Page. Available online: https://systemweakness.com/new-prompt-injection-attack-on-chatgpt-web-version-ef717492c5c2 (accessed on 29 March 2023).
50. Heidenreich, H.S.; Williams, J.R. The Earth Is Flat and the Sun Is Not a Star: The Susceptibility of GPT-2 to Universal Adversarial Triggers. In Proceedings of the 2021 AAAI/ACM Conference on AI, Ethics, and Society, Virtual, 19–21 May 2021; Association for Computing Machinery: New York, NY, USA, 2021; pp. 566–573.
51. Karabacak, M.; Margetis, K. Embracing Large Language Models for Medical Applications: Opportunities and Challenges. *Cureus* **2023**, *15*, e39305. [CrossRef]
52. Ferdush, J.; Begum, M.; Hossain, S.T. ChatGPT and Clinical Decision Support: Scope, Application, and Limitations. *Ann. Biomed. Eng.* **2024**, *52*, 1119–1124. [CrossRef] [PubMed]
53. Nazi, Z.A.; Peng, W. Large Language Models in Healthcare and Medical Domain: A Review. *Informatics* **2024**, *11*, 57. [CrossRef]
54. Dave, T.; Athaluri, S.A.; Singh, S. ChatGPT in Medicine: An Overview of Its Applications, Advantages, Limitations, Future Prospects, and Ethical Considerations. *Front. Artif. Intell.* **2023**, *6*, 1169595. [CrossRef]
55. Hossain, E.; Rana, R.; Higgins, N.; Soar, J.; Barua, P.D.; Pisani, A.R.; Turner, K. Natural Language Processing in Electronic Health Records in Relation to Healthcare Decision-Making: A Systematic Review. *Comput. Biol. Med.* **2023**, *155*, 106649. [CrossRef]
56. Sezgin, E. Artificial Intelligence in Healthcare: Complementing, Not Replacing, Doctors and Healthcare Providers. *Digit. Health* **2023**, *9*, 20552076231186520. [CrossRef]
57. Zhao, W.X.; Zhou, K.; Li, J.; Tang, T.; Wang, X.; Hou, Y.; Min, Y.; Zhang, B.; Zhang, J.; Dong, Z.; et al. A Survey of Large Language Models. *arXiv* **2023**, arXiv:2303.18223.
58. Vaidyam, A.N.; Wisniewski, H.; Halamka, J.D.; Kashavan, M.S.; Torous, J.B. Chatbots and Conversational Agents in Mental Health: A Review of the Psychiatric Landscape. *Can. J. Psychiatry* **2019**, *64*, 456–464. [CrossRef]
59. Dwivedi, Y.K.; Kshetri, N.; Hughes, L.; Slade, E.L.; Jeyaraj, A.; Kar, A.K.; Baabdullah, A.M.; Koohang, A.; Raghavan, V.; Ahuja, M.; et al. Opinion Paper: "So What If ChatGPT Wrote It?" Multidisciplinary Perspectives on Opportunities, Challenges and Implications of Generative Conversational AI for Research, Practice and Policy. *Int. J. Inf. Manag.* **2023**, *71*, 102642. [CrossRef]
60. Agbavor, F.; Liang, H. Predicting Dementia from Spontaneous Speech Using Large Language Models. *PLoS Digit. Health* **2022**, *1*, e0000168. [CrossRef]
61. Wong, C.; Zhang, S.; Gu, Y.; Moung, C.; Abel, J.; Usuyama, N.; Weerasinghe, R.; Piening, B.; Naumann, T.; Bifulco, C.; et al. Scaling Clinical Trial Matching Using Large Language Models: A Case Study in Oncology. In Proceedings of the 8th Machine Learning for Healthcare Conference, New York, NY, USA, 11–12 August 2023.
62. Hirosawa, T.; Harada, Y.; Yokose, M.; Sakamoto, T.; Kawamura, R.; Shimizu, T. Diagnostic Accuracy of Differential-Diagnosis Lists Generated by Generative Pretrained Transformer 3 Chatbot for Clinical Vignettes with Common Chief Complaints: A Pilot Study. *Int. J. Environ. Res. Public Health* **2023**, *20*, 3378. [CrossRef]
63. Olaronke, I.; Olaleke, J. A Systematic Review of Natural Language Processing in Healthcare. *Int. J. Inf. Technol. Comput. Sci.* **2015**, *8*, 44–50. [CrossRef]

big data and cognitive computing

MDPI

Article

Health Use Cases of AI Chatbots: Identification and Analysis of ChatGPT Prompts in Social Media Discourses

Amir Karami [1,*], Zhilei Qiao [1], Xiaoni Zhang [1], Hadi Kharrazi [2], Parisa Bozorgi [3] and Ali Bozorgi [4]

1 Department of Management, Information Systems & Quantitative Methods, Birmingham, Collat School of Business, University of Alabama at Birmingham, Birmingham, AL 35294, USA; qiaozl@uab.edu (Z.Q.); xzhang2@uab.edu (X.Z.)
2 Department of Health Policy and Management, Bloomberg School of Public Health, Johns Hopkins University, Baltimore, MD 21205, USA; kharrazi@jhu.edu
3 South Carolina Department of Public Health, Columbia, SC 29021, USA; bozorgp@dhec.sc.gov
4 Department Cardiology School of Medicine, Tehran University of Medical Sciences, Tehran 1417613151, Iran; alibozorgi.md@gmail.com
* Correspondence: karami@uab.edu

Abstract: The popularity of ChatGPT has raised questions surrounding AI's potential for health use cases. Since the release of ChatGPT in 2022, social media users have shared their prompts and ChatGPT responses on different topics such as health. Despite editorials and opinion articles discussing the potential uses of ChatGPT, there is a lack of a systematic approach to identify and analyze the use cases of ChatGPT in health. This study establishes a framework for gathering and identifying tweets (i.e., posts on social media site "X", formerly known as Twitter) that discuss health use cases of ChatGPT, integrating topic modeling with constructivist grounded theory (CGT) to organize these topics into common categories. Using this framework, nine topics were identified, which were further grouped into four categories: (1) Clinical Workflow, (2) Wellness, (3), Diseases, and (4) Gender Identity. The Clinical Workflow category was the most popular category, and included four topics: (1) Seeking Advice, (2) Clinical Documentation, (3) Medical Diagnosis, and (4) Medical Treatment. Among the identified topics, "Diet and Workout Plans" was the most popular topic. This research highlights the potential of social media to identify the health use cases and potential health applications of an AI-based chatbot such as ChatGPT. The identified topics and categories can be beneficial for researchers, professionals, companies, and policymakers working on health use cases of AI chatbots.

Keywords: Chatbot; ChatGPT; artificial intelligence; topic modeling; grounded theory; health

1. Introduction

Artificial intelligence (AI) has reshaped our daily interactions by enabling the development and assessment of sophisticated applications and devices, known as intelligent agents, capable of executing a variety of functions, such as medical diagnoses [1]. Chatbots, also known as artificial conversation entities, interactive agents, smart bots, or digital assistants, are human-computer programs that simulate interactions with humans in different health applications [2]. The history of chatbots stretches back to 1966, when EIZA, a chatbot simulating a psychotherapist's operation, was developed [3]. The first AI chatbot was developed in 1988. Since then, the emergence of more advanced chatbots like Apple's Siri, Google Assistant, and Amazon Alexa has risen in recent years [2].

Chatbots adopts computational linguistics models to facilitate communication with humans in various domains, such as education [4]. Chatbots can improve productivity and offer efficient, engaging assistants capable of addressing questions directly [5]. Sometimes, users approach chatbots with emotional requests and perceive them more as friendly companions than mere assistants [6]. Figure 1 illustrates a rising trend in the research interest surrounding chatbots starting from 2002, with a significant spike in interest after 2022.

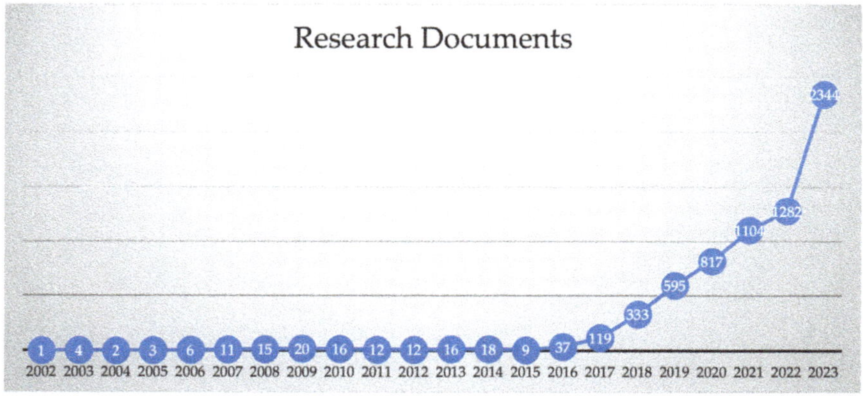

Figure 1. Search results in Scopus for the term "chatbot" from 2002 to 2023.

Chatbots can also be used to address users' health questions [7,8]. Relevant studies have focused on earlier versions of health chatbots and on single health issues such as oncology [9]. Traditional health chatbots are often linked to poor patient adherence, which is attributed to a perceived lack of consistency and transparency compared to the face-to-face interactions provided by in-person meetings [10]. Moreover, clinicians view chatbots as being better suited for administrative tasks like scheduling appointments, locating hospitals, and sending prescription reminders, while noting significant risks in using chatbots, such as the risk of receiving inaccurate medical information. Consequently, clinicians remain skeptical of chatbots replacing complex decision-making processes that require expert medical advice [10].

Chat Generative Pretrained Transformer (ChatGPT), the latest version of GPT-3 (Generative Pretrained Transformer 3), is an innovative generative AI chatbot based on language modeling. ChatGPT predicts text via encoding through translating input into a vector and decoding through converting the model's output to generate iterative human-like responses [11,12]. ChatGPT addresses the semantic limitations of previous models and can "answer follow-up questions, admit its mistakes, challenge incorrect premises, and reject inappropriate requests" [11]. ChatGPT's user-friendly chat interface makes it a readily adoptable tool for individuals with basic digital literacy skills [13].

Before the implementation of ChatGPT, chatbots were developed for a specific task, such as checking for health symptoms [10]. Healthcare chatbots, with efficiencies comparable to clinicians, offer benefits such as aiding in medical decisions, enhancing physical activity, supporting cognitive behavioral therapy, and treating somatic disorders [14]. The emergence of ChatGPT has also boosted the development and market share of health chatbots [10] p. 10, thus providing businesses, startups, and the healthcare industry with a unique opportunity to develop new AI-based applications, improve workflows, and drive positive outcomes.

Social media has significantly transformed the way information is accessed, shared, and consumed. Today, social media not only serves as a venue for individuals to develop and sustain personal relationships but also functions as a dynamic platform. Users can seek and gather information, create original content, share updates with their personal networks, and disseminate information to the broader public. These platforms facilitate a rich exchange of ideas and interaction, making them central to modern communication strategies [15]. With over 5 billion users, social media sites [16] have been considered a key platform for sharing public opinion and experiences on different issues such as health [17] and politics [18]. Social media data can be analyzed to understand behaviors and identify emerging societal trends from diverse societies for decision-making [19].

It was found that 70% of the population searches for health information online, and 37% of those individuals specifically seek health information on social media [20]. Social media has profoundly influenced healthcare by revolutionizing patient education, health communication, and professional networking. Through social media platforms, healthcare organizations can disseminate educational content, promote health awareness campaigns, and mobilize support for public health initiatives [21]. Online patient support communities provide invaluable emotional support and connection for individuals facing similar health challenges [22]. Moreover, healthcare professionals utilize social media for networking, sharing research, and collaborating on projects, fostering knowledge exchange and professional development [23]. Real-time health surveillance through social media data analysis enables the tracking of disease outbreaks and identification of emerging health trends [24].

After the release of ChatGPT in 2022, the number of ChatGPT users reached 100 million users within two months [25], and this number has been increasing exponentiall, with over 1.5 billion visits in 2023 [26]. ChatGPT has been adopted and discussed by a wide range of users to gain first-hand AI experience through simple communications with the chatbot [27]. Interacting with an AI chatbot involves sending a message known as a prompt, which guides the AI in generating textual responses [28]. Health applications of ChatGPT can be identified through the content of prompts developed by health professionals and the general public [29]. These prompt data, however, are not available to researchers. Nonetheless, ChatGPT users have started to share on social media platforms their prompts and responses that can be used to assess the use cases of ChatGPT for health [30].

Although using chatbots is not a new concept, the popularity of ChatGPT has raised questions of AI's potential for health use cases. Several editorials, perspectives, and commentaries have been published discussing the uses, challenges, and opportunities of GPTs for health [29,31], as well as the associated ethical issues; however, most of these articles focus on ChatGPT applications for health professionals, researchers, and regulators. These studies consider topics such as analyzing the performance of ChatGPT in medical exams such as parasitology exams [32] and the USMLE [33]; evaluating the responses of ChatGPT for specialized questions on different issues such as cancer [34], retinal diseases [35], genetics/genomics [36], gastroenterology [37], and pathology [38]; and using ChatGPT to write patient letters for different clinical scenarios [39]. Others have compared the quality and clarity of health messages generated by AI to those presented in tweets about folic acid [40] and websites about lower back pain, meniscal injury, and gonarthrosis [41]; investigated challenges related to mental health [42] and healthy lifestyles [43]; identified AI chatbot applications in medical, dental, pharmacy, and public health education [44]; developed customized chatbots [45]; explored user acceptance [46]; and measured the efficiency of AI chatbots created before the release of ChatGPT for promoting healthy lifestyles, aiding smoking cessation, and improving treatment or medication adherence [47]. In brief, the current literature primarily provides insights on potential applications and challenges, presents use case examples in specific medical domains, evaluates ChatGPT's responses, develops tailored methods, and explores user perceptions.

Additionally, some studies have looked into ChatGPT discussions on social media [30,48,49]. An examination revealed three primary themes: general subjects (e.g., news), functional areas (e.g., creative writing), and potential consequences (e.g., human impact). One study categorizing themes on Twitter (now known as "X") found that users predominantly used ChatGPT for writing and asking questions [30]. A similar study examined posts on the Chinese Weibo platform, revealing discussions about ChatGPT that focused on its technical support capabilities, the effectiveness of AI-related features, its influence on human labor, and its impact on the fields of education and technology [48]. Another study examined remarks concerning ChatGPT and marketing, uncovering 10 marketing themes, including the notion of revolutionizing B2B marketing [49]. While these studies provide value insights, health topics were not detected in the results due to the lack of focus on health issues. Thus, generalizability analyses and systematic studies are lacking regarding the use cases of ChatGPT and their categories related to health issues from the perspective of the public. In summary, although analyzing social media data offers a valuable approach for identifying and researching the health-related use cases of ChatGPT, relevant studies are currently scarce. To overcome this constraint, this study aims to identify and analyze the health use cases of ChatGPT, an AI chatbot. To accomplish this objective, we utilize both topic modeling, extracting themes from large text datasets, and grounded theory, providing a contextual understanding as our foundational framework. Our research question revolves around determining the primary categories of health-related use cases for AI chatbots. The findings underscore the importance of identifying and understanding health use cases offered by ChatGPT through social media conversations. This study provides a distinctive contribution to the burgeoning research surrounding the health applications of AI chatbots, utilizing social media data.

2. Materials and Methods

This research integrates grounded theory with topic modeling to systematically analyze data and reduce human biases. There are three schools of thought in grounded theory: positivism, interpretivism, and constructivism, proposed by Glaser [50], Strauss [51], and Charmaz [52], respectively. This study uses constructivist grounded theory (CGT) due to its ability to combine the strengths of positivism and interpretivism [53]. This research embeds topic modeling into CGT in three steps, including initial coding, focused coding, and theoretical coding following data collection and preprocessing, as illustrated in Figure 2 [52,53]. CGT is grounded in empirical evidence to develop theory from data, emphasizing personal reality, subjective reality, meaning-making, or the construction of reality [54] and offers a set of concepts and their categories [55]. Combining topic modeling with qualitative coding can effectively eliminate irrelevant and meaningless content and clarify the interpretation of topics. Our methodology represents a form of computational grounded theory, wherein topics and their categories are derived through topic modeling and continuously refined through iterative qualitative coding [56].

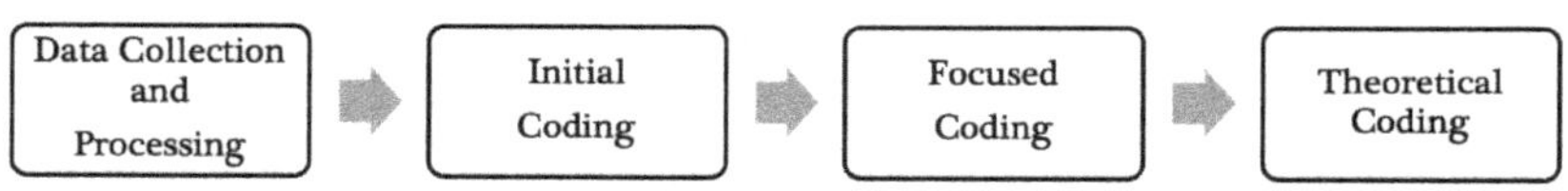

Figure 2. Research framework.

2.1. Data Collection and Processing

This study focused on ChatGPT prompts posted on Twitter (now renamed to/known as X). In this paper, we will use the terms "Twitter" and "tweet" instead of "X" and "post", as the former are more widely known and recognizable. We chose the Twitter Academic API for several reasons compared to other social media platforms like Facebook and Reddit. First, Twitter data can be either public or private, but, unlike Facebook, the default setting is public [57]. Second, Twitter is a unique and valuable data source because it is easily accessible, provides real-time content, and is rich in detail [58]. Additionally, Twitter allows for access to large datasets compared to other social media platforms such as Reddit [59]. TikTok and ChatGPT have both experienced explosive growth, quickly ascending to prominence among global audiences. When ChatGPT was launched, it quickly became the fastest-growing chatbot and application, surpassing even TikTok in popularity. Within just a few months, it attracted millions of users, and it garnered billions of visits within its first year [25,26]. In comparison to competitors like Google Bard (now Gemini), which receives about 330 million visits each month [60], ChatGPT significantly outpaces this with approximately 1.6 billion visits monthly [61]. We conducted a t-test comparing the Google trend data for ChatGPT, Microsoft Copilot, Google Bard, and Facebook Llama in 2023 [62]. The results showed that searches for ChatGPT were significantly higher (p-value < 0.05) compared to the other chatbots, indicating ChatGPT's superior popularity.

Figure 3 illustrates the Google search trend data normalized to a scale of 0 to 100 to represent the relative popularity of search terms over a specific time period. This means that a value of 100 represents the peak popularity of that search term within the selected time frame. A value of 50 means that the term was half as popular as at its peak.

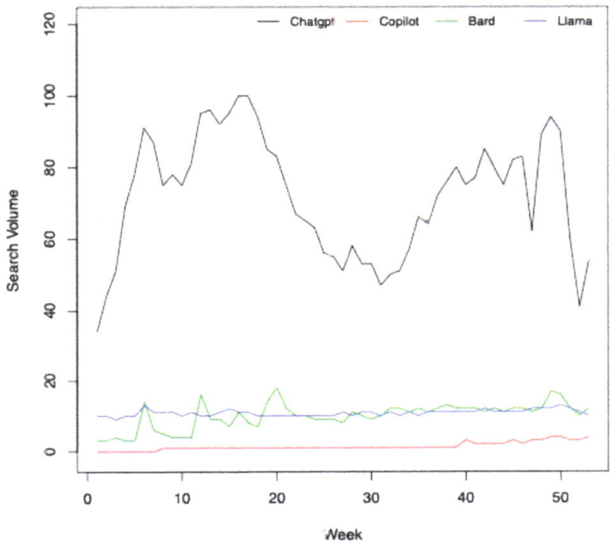

Figure 3. Google search trends for ChatGPT, Copilot, Bard, and Llama in 2023.

Among social media platforms, Twitter is a popular platform for research because of the following reasons. First, Twitter has over 300 million monthly active users, generating more than 500 million tweets per month [63,64] to share health information and advice [65]. Second, Twitter has provided Application Programming Interfaces (APIs) to facilitate data collection on a large scale [66] and has earned the focus of several studies to address a wide range of research questions in different applications such as health and politics [67]. Third, Twitter is by far the most extensive and widely accessible public source of online data for studying human behavior and social interactions [68]. The surge in user-generated content on Twitter has significantly impacted the field of communication. Twitter data have been used as a popular cost-effective source of data for studying different phenomena, such as common health issues [69], disaster communication [70], and politics [71].

Twitter content is valuable for analyzing how the public shares and disseminates information about health. In previous studies, Twitter data have been analyzed to understand the conversations surrounding different issues, such as cancer [72], COVID-19 [73], and HIV [74]. These studies began by harvesting data from Twitter using a specified search query (e.g., #HIV) over a defined period (e.g., November 2018–January 2019). To ensure data quality, several preprocessing steps were implemented. Initially, duplicate tweets, retweets, brief messages, and tweets not in English were filtered out. Moreover, an additional preprocessing layer, such as the removal of commonly occurring but irrelevant words (stop words), was employed to refine the dataset. This entire process was likely facilitated by Python packages such as Tweepy for data collection and Pandas for data manipulation, as well as R packages like twitteR and dplyr.

To ensure the quality and reliability of our data, we collected tweets posted between November 2022 and March 2023 via Twitter's Academic API in R using the academictwitteR package. The chosen timeframe ensured the reliability of our dataset by covering a continuous and recent period, capturing trends in discussions about ChatGPT technologies. This extended collection period also allowed us to accumulate a substantial volume of data, essential for statistical robustness and mitigating the impact of outliers in the analysis. We employed a carefully constructed query designed to target specific discussions relevant to our study on ChatGPT technologies. The query used was: "((GPT AND chat) OR (chat AND GPT) OR GPTchat OR #GPTchat OR chatGPT OR #chatGPT OR GPT3 OR #GPT3 OR GPT3Chat OR #GPT3Chat OR GPT) AND (asked)", focusing on capturing conversations explicitly asking about or referencing GPT-related topics. This approach ensured that the data were highly relevant to our research questions. To enhance data quality, we applied stringent filters to exclude non-English tweets using lang:en, retweets using -is:retweet, comments posted by verified users using -is:verified, and duplicates using unique() function in R. The exclusion of non-English tweets allowed for a uniform dataset in terms of language, facilitating more consistency and accurate text analysis and interpretations. Analyzing documents in multiple languages would require complex language processing tools and translation services, which could introduce variability and potential inaccuracies in the results. Removing retweets and duplicates was crucial to ensure that our analysis was based on original content, providing a clearer picture of genuine user engagement without artificial inflation from repeated posts. Removing verified users from Twitter data is crucial to minimize bias and better represent the opinions of the general public, as these accounts often belong to influential figures whose views may not reflect those of ordinary users. The resultant dataset comprised 79,234 tweets posted by 61,217 unique users, representing 1.29 tweets per user (Figure 3), which were rigorously collected and filtered to meet high standards of data integrity. This large volume of data provided a robust foundation for our analysis, ensuring that our findings would be based on a comprehensive and reliable sample of the discourse surrounding GPT technologies during the specified period. These measures collectively bolster the reliability and validity of this study, affirming that the conclusions drawn are well supported by high-quality empirical evidence.

To identify health-related tweets, we used the LIWC (Linguistic Inquiry and Word Count) 2015 software, which has a health detection category to recognize tweets containing health-related terms. LIWC is a lexicon-based tool developed to measure the psychological, emotional, and linguistic components contained within written texts. It categorizes words into predefined groups that reflect different dimensions such as emotions and health. LIWC operates by counting words in the categories and computing percentages, thus offering researchers and professionals a rapid, reliable, and data-driven method to analyze language in various contexts [75]. Figure 4 illustrates the process used to collect and identify tweets containing health-related terms, as well as the monthly tweet frequency. This figure reveals an upward trend in the volume of tweets over the studied four-month period.

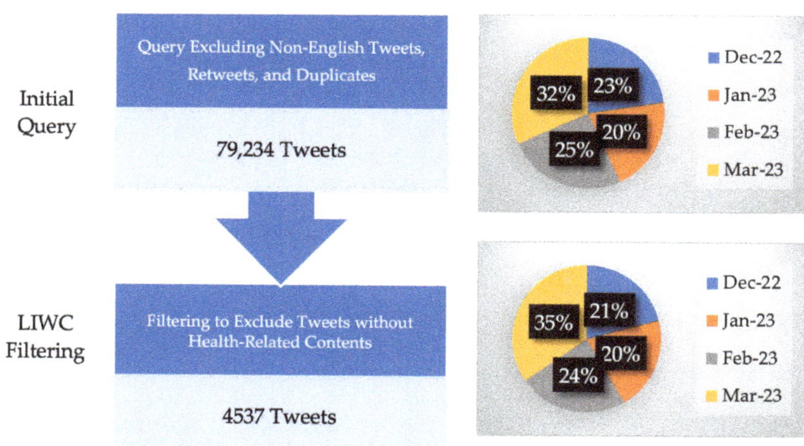

Figure 4. Data collection and processing steps along with the volume of tweets for each month.

After excluding short tweets with fewer than five words, we identified 4537 tweets containing health-related terms, posted by 4335 users, averaging 1.09 tweets per user. On average, these tweets included 38.66 words, 0.79 hashtags initiated by '#,' and 0.62 mentions beginning with '@'. Figure 5 shows the distribution of the number of words in the tweets. For example, 174 tweets contained 44 words.

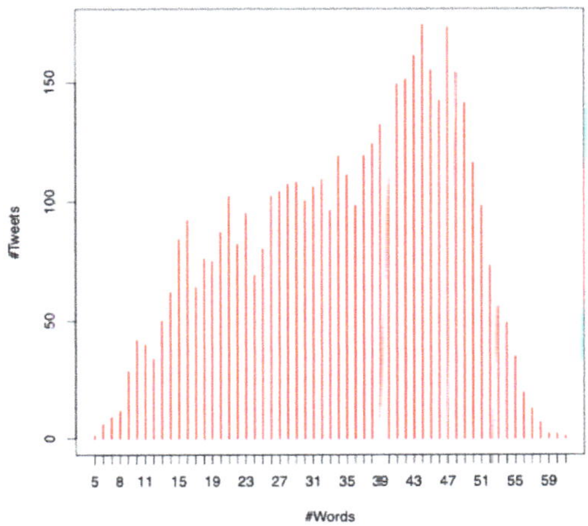

Figure 5. Distribution of words/tweet.

Figure 6 depicts a Zipf's law distribution for the word frequencies, where the y-axis measures the frequency of each word and the x-axis represents their rank. Zipf's law is an empirical rule that suggests that the frequency of words has an inverse relationship with their frequency rank [76]. The steep decline from left to right illustrates that the most frequent words are used significantly more often than less frequent ones, showing the inverse relationship between word frequency and rank. A red vertical line marks the threshold for the 50 most commonly used words, emphasizing their higher frequency relative to others in the corpus.

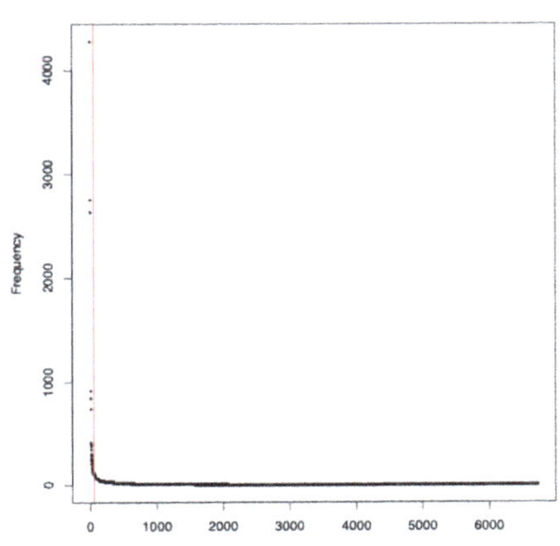

Figure 6. Frequency of words. The vertical line indicates the threshold for the 50 most commonly used words.

2.2. Initial Coding

In CGT, the initial coding step is the first exploratory stage of coding qualitative data to categorize data. This step helps the researcher to identify patterns within the data, which can be further refined and explored in subsequent stages of the grounded theory process. This study used topic modeling for the initial coding process of CGT to identify main codes (topics) within the data [52]. Topic modeling techniques utilize statistical machine learning algorithms to identify abstract themes present within a collection of documents [77]. Topic modeling can mine large corpora and inductively generate code among the corpora and identify patterns that might be missed with manual coding to render knowledge [78]. Prior research has shown that topic modeling can be used as an initial coding step in the coding of large corpora [56] and produce similar results to traditional grounded theory [79].

This research adopted the Latent Dirichlet Allocation (LDA) technique [80], which is a method commonly used for topic modeling [81] to learn latent structural elements (topics) of a corpus. LDA is an unsupervised method used to discover hidden topics within a large collection of documents without any prior annotations. Various methodologies for identifying topics within a corpus have emerged, leveraging both neural network architectures and statistical distributions. Over the past decade, neural networks, including deep neural networks (DNNs), have garnered attention for enhancing data analysis techniques [82]. However, neural network-based models are often resource-intensive and time-consuming [83], necessitating substantial amounts of training data, and are also susceptible to overfitting issues [84]. Furthermore, deep learning approaches have not consistently outperformed alternative methods when applied to small or medium-sized corpora [83]. In contrast, LDA has emerged as a widely accepted and utilized model for topic discovery within a corpus. The literature underscores LDA's validity [85] and widespread adoption [86].

LDA operates under the assumption that words and documents interact within a corpus, represented through a bag-of-words model that reduces the complexity of text data by viewing documents as mere sets of words, ignoring both their sequence and contextual relationships. In this model, corpora are quantified into vectors where each element denotes the occurrence or count of words. LDA iterates thousands of times over the documents, analyzing the topic distribution of each word token. Words that commonly appear together are likely to be grouped under the same topic, enabling the model to automatically identify semantically related words. This grouping offers a summary view of the corpus's contents and serves as a reference for identifying documents that predominantly feature specific topics. The corpora undergo iterative sampling, with the model adjusting topic–word associations to better reflect their underlying latent distributions. These collections of words, or "topics", are subsequently interpreted by humans as significant "themes" based on intuitive understanding [80] in the focused coding step. For instance, if words like "gene", "dna", and "genetic" are grouped together in a topic, one might interpret and label this topic as "genetics" [87].

In our study, we treated tweets as documents, henceforth using the terms "tweet" and "document" interchangeably. LDA estimates the probability of each set of words belonging to each topic and the probability of each topic being associated with each document. In essence, LDA quantifies the relationship between topics and documents, denoted as P(Topic | Document), as well as between words and topics, represented as P(Word | Topic).

The topics were represented by the top words for each topic, ranked in descending order of their probability, P(Word | Topic). We developed some preprocessing steps including removing punctuation, stop words, and numbers. To assess various models and their learning processes in LDA, we examine different sets of topics and iterations. As an unsupervised method, topic modeling groups similar documents into a predetermined number of topics. Therefore, identifying the optimal number of topics for the corpus is a crucial step. We used a density-based method to determine the optimal number of topics, resulting in 53 topics [88]. This method indicates that the LDA model achieves optimal performance when the average cosine distance between topics is at its minimum. The density-based method helped us to compare different models to identify the best set of topics. We used Mallet, a Java-based tool, with $\alpha = \frac{5}{number\ of\ topics} = 0.09$ controlling the per-document topic distributions, $\beta = 0.01$ influencing the topic–word distributions, and 4000 iterations. To ensure model stability, we performed three independent LDA runs. No statistically significant differences (p-value < 0.05) were observed between the runs, indicating the robustness of the LDA learning process model, as shown in Figure 7. This figure also shows that the log likelihood started to plateau after 3000 iterations, meaning that there were minimal changes between iterations; this suggests that the model reached convergence.

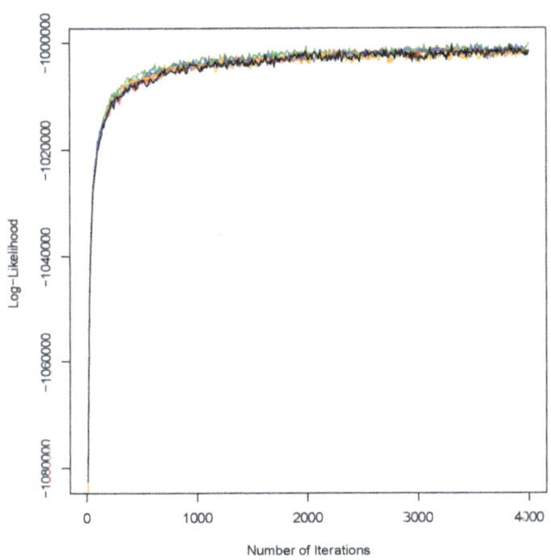

Figure 7. Convergence of the log-likelihood for 5 sets of 4000 iterations.

2.3. Focused Coding

The goal of focused coding is to synthesize and condense initial codes into broader categories [52]. In the initial coding phase, LDA categorized large volumes of data into topics representing categories of tweets. The subsequent step after initial coding was focused coding, which was employed to identify and interpret meaningful and relevant topics. LDA offers two main outputs: the first output is the probability of each word per topic, or $P(W_i|T_k)$, while the second output is the probability of each topic per document, or $P(T_k|D_j)$ [80]. Each document represents a tweet in this study. Following [89], we investigated the top 10 words per topic based on the descending order of $P(W_i|T_k)$. The top 10 words helped us to efficiently grasp the essence of the topics without being overwhelmed by too much information. It also ensured that the most relevant and frequently occurring words were highlighted, providing a clear and concise representation of each topic's thematic content.

The focused coding procedure involved two critical steps. First, coders closely examined the top 10 words in each topic to address two specific questions. The first question aimed to evaluate the coherence and meaningfulness of the topic, ensuring that it formed a logical and understandable theme. The second question scrutinized whether the topic was pertinent to health issues, aligning with the research's thematic focus. This thorough examination involved assessing how well each topic mirrored actual health-related use cases, confirming their direct applicability and relevance to the field. Coders also evaluated the authenticity of the topics, ensuring that they accurately represented genuine health discussions. Furthermore, the consistency of the topics was scrutinized across different data segments to confirm that they reliably conveyed the same thematic elements throughout the dataset. This multi-faceted approach ensured a comprehensive validation of each topic's meaningfulness, relevance, and reliability within the health context. This dual-question approach helped us to meticulously filter out any topics that were either irrelevant or did not contribute meaningful insights. Through this detailed and selective process, the coders effectively narrowed down the topics to a final set of nine, each of which was both substantively meaningful and closely related to health topics.

In the second step of the focused coding process, we engaged in a detailed and systematic iterative examination of each topic. This involved alternating between the top 10 words of each topic and the top 20 most relevant documents (tweets), like in [90], which were ranked based on the descending order of $P(T_k|D_j)$. While other studies [91,92] have chosen to analyze the top 5 or top 10 documents to interpret topics, we opted for the top 20 to gain a more comprehensive understanding of each topic. This meticulous process allowed us researchers to delve deeply into the semantics and contextual usage of words within the tweets in order to fully grasp the underlying concepts of the nine topics and assign them clear and descriptive labels. Focusing on the top 20 most relevant documents per topic balances depth, relevance, and efficiency. This approach ensures that the analysis is both thorough and manageable to deeply explore the most significant content without being overwhelmed by less relevant material.

Our aim was not just to identify the predominant themes but also to understand how these themes were represented in the data. This back-and-forth process, as part of a reflective approach, facilitated a nuanced understanding, helping us to identify the meaning of the topics within the tweets and to assign a label to each topic. For instance, when the top 10 words of a topic included "advice", "give", "therapist", "specific", "job", "personal", "therapy", "prompt", "ways", and "professional", the coders labeled this topic as "Seeking Advice". This label not only captures the essence of the topic but also reflects its practical significance in the context of the tweets. This method ensured that each topic was not only identified but also labeled in a manner that was useful for subsequent analysis and interpretation. To calculate the weight (popularity) of each topic, we measured the normalized weight of each topic with the following formula for n documents and k topics, where T_k represents topic k and D_j denotes document j:

$$NW(T_k) = \frac{\sum_{j=1}^{n} P(T_k|D_j)}{\sum_{k=1}^{t}\sum_{j=1}^{n} P(T_k|D_j)}$$

2.4. Theoretical Coding

Theoretical coding is an advanced stage in the grounded theory methodology, where researchers conceptualize the relationships between codes or themes derived from the data. This stage extends beyond initial coding and focused coding to integrate these codes into a cohesive theoretical framework that is grounded in the empirical data collected [52]. The theoretical coding step in this study involved identifying relations between the labels of the topics by performing thorough zoom-ins and zoom-outs on each topic [53] and merging topics into dimensions or constructs [52]. This abstraction process included revisiting the top 10 words and the top 20 tweets along with searching for similarities and differences to recognize a meaningful link between the labels of the nine topics. Coders systematically evaluated each topic for its empirical grounding and relevance to the broader constructs, ensuring that each category was not only reliably consistent across different datasets but also comprehensive in covering the thematic scope of the study. This included an iterative review process where topics were continually reassessed and refined to ensure they accurately reflected the underlying data while maintaining logical coherence within the emerging theoretical framework. This meticulous approach guaranteed that the final constructs were both robust and representative of the diverse elements present in the health discussions captured in our data. This process led to the merging of the 9 labels into 4 constructs. For instance, coders categorized the topics labeled "Cancer" and "COVID-19" under a broader construct named "Diseases". The weight of each construct was calculated by summing the weights of all topics that belong to construct C_d using the following formula:

$$W(C_d) = \sum_{k \in C_d} NW(T_k)$$

3. Results

The topic modeling analysis of tweets in Table 1 shows the nine health-related topics within the corpus, each characterized by its top 10 words. Below, we briefly explore each topic and its category, providing insights into the diverse range of questions Twitter users have posed to ChatGPT.

Table 1. Three steps of constructivist grounded theory.

Initial Coding	Focused Coding	Theoretical Coding
advice, give, therapist, specific, job, personal, therapy, prompt, ways, professional	Seeking Advice	Clinical Workflow
interesting, work, find, writing, clinical, change, thinking, made, essay, info	Clinical Documentation	
doctor, medical, patients, diagnose, found, provide, information, accurate, medicine, symptoms	Medical Diagnosis	
bad, high, heart, pain, low, hard, years, disease, treatment, chronic	Medical Treatment	
plan, workout, diet, create, meal, week, make, day, fitness, exercise, based, give	Diet and Workout Plans	Wellness
health, mental, people, data, based, generate, public, care, physical, improve	General Health	
cancer, cure, ill, similar, current, alcohol, important, risk, science, thinks	Cancer	Diseases
COVID, response, vaccine, immunity, disease, virus, symptoms, infection, prevent, pandemic	COVID-19	
physical, human, men, woman, body, women, gender, abortion, pregnant, man	Anatomical Differences	Gender Identity

3.1. Clinical Workflow

We begin the qualitative analysis with a discussion of the biggest group of topics. This analysis grouped four topics as processes/steps of the Clinical Workflow category. The first topic, named Seeking Advice, involves a range of inquiries from users on various issues, prominently featuring health-related concerns such as allergies ("give us an advice on how to help someone who is having an allergic reaction"). The nature of these prompts indicates a perception among users of generative AI as a source of authoritative guidance, akin to consulting with a clinician. Users in this group expressed their experience in using AI for personalized recommendations and insights into managing their health conditions, indicating a level of trust in the AI's capability to provide accurate and helpful information. Additionally, this category includes questions about health-related professions, with users seeking guidance on career paths and professional development within the healthcare sector. These users asked generative AI to act as a mentor, offering strategies to navigate the complexities of healthcare careers. This trend underscores the expanding role of AI as a versatile tool for both personal health management and professional advancement in the medical field.

The second topic in this category is Clinical Documentation. This topic encompasses inquiries related to managing clinical documents, focusing on tasks like drafting reports for clinical trials and organizing data from multiple clinical studies. Examples of such inquiries included tasks like "writing a phase 3 clinical trial report" or "compiling data from clinical trials". These tasks are essential in clinical research, where detailed documentation and rigorous analysis are required to ensure the accuracy and reliability of trial outcomes. Meanwhile, compiling clinical trials entails the systematic gathering and synthesis of data across various studies to aid in comprehensive reviews and meta-analyses, essential for shaping evidence-based medical practices and policies.

The next topic is Medical Diagnosis, involving inquiries directed towards obtaining diagnoses based on medical information provided to AI. Users input symptoms, medical histories, or specific health concerns with the intention of receiving an analysis or identification of potential health conditions. These users are not limited to patients and include medical providers too. For example, one user stated "I'm an ER doctor… I asked ChatGPT to diagnose my patients".

The final topic in the Clinical Workflow category is Medical Treatment. This topic revolves around inquiries concerning the treatment of various diseases, with a particular focus on conditions like Alzheimer's disease and other chronic diseases. Questions in this realm often explore the efficacy of different treatment modalities, including conventional medical interventions, lifestyle changes, and alternative therapies. For instance, a growing interest was found in understanding how dietary modifications can play a role in managing or potentially alleviating symptoms of chronic conditions. Discussions in this topic might delve into specific dietary approaches, such as anti-inflammatory or plant-based diets, and their impact on disease progression, symptom management, and overall health outcomes.

3.2. Wellness

Two topics were assigned to this category. The first one is Diet and Workout Plans. This topic includes users requesting the generative AI to devise both general and tailored diet and exercise regimes, ranging from specific dietary programs like a "7-day high protein vegan meal plan" to detailed fitness schedules such as an "18-week marathon training plan for an intermediate runner". These inquiries highlight the user perception of generative AI as a virtual coach capable of supporting their health and fitness aspirations. By soliciting personalized advice, users demonstrate their trust in the AI's ability to understand their unique dietary preferences, nutritional requirements, and fitness levels, and to translate these into actionable, effective plans. This reliance on AI for customized health guidance reflects a broader trend of utilizing technology to achieve personal wellness objectives, showcasing AI's potential to provide informed, adaptable, and accessible coaching solutions for diverse health and fitness goals.

General Health is the second topic in the Wellness category. This topic encompasses a broad spectrum of inquiries related to both physical and mental health, offering insights into how lifestyle changes and personalized wellness practices can profoundly impact one's well-being. For instance, one user asked ChatGPT for "examples of people who improved their health by going plant-based". Such conversations illuminate the potential benefits of dietary choices on physical health, including weight management, improved heart health, and a reduced risk of chronic diseases. Similarly, the Wellness category delves into tailored approaches to mental wellness, such as "Customized meditation or relaxation scripts for stress reduction focus or sleep assistance". These topics underscore the importance of personalized health strategies that cater to the unique circumstances and goals of individuals, demonstrating the interconnectedness of physical and mental health in achieving overall well-being.

3.3. Diseases

The Diseases category includes two topics/diseases: COVID-19 and Cancer. The COVID-19 topic encompasses a broad range of prompts related to the COVID-19 pandemic, delving into critical issues such as the effectiveness of face masks in preventing virus transmission, the efficacy and safety of vaccines in building immunity, the exploration of various treatment options for those infected, and the concept of herd immunity as a potential strategy to curb the spread of the virus. It also covers discussions on identifying and understanding the symptoms of COVID-19, thereby enabling early detection and treatment. Within this context, questions may seek to explore scientific evidence and research findings that support or challenge the use of specific preventive measures, therapeutic drugs, or vaccination campaigns, as well as the broader implications of these strategies on public health and safety.

The second topic within this category delves into inquiries related to cancer. This topic encompasses a wide array of discussions, from the impact of dietary factors, like "the effects of dietary iron in cancer risk", to the exploration of innovative treatments such as "What frequency kills cancer". Questions within the Cancer topic seek to understand the complex interplay between lifestyle choices, environmental factors, and cutting-edge medical interventions in the prevention, development, and treatment of cancer.

3.4. Gender Identity

Our qualitative analysis of the questions posted on social media identified one topic pertaining to differences in sex organ anatomy across genders, which was named Anatomical Differences and grouped as a Gender Identity category. This topic encompasses inquiries from users about the distinctions between the sexes, particularly focusing on biological and physiological aspects that differentiate females and males. Questions within this category are diverse and range from foundational inquiries such as "What is a Woman?" to more complex and contemporary topics such as "Can a man be pregnant?". These questions often delve into the scientific/political/social understanding of sex and gender, exploring the chromosomal and hormonal differences that traditionally define males and females.

The most discussed topic was Diet and Workout Plans, while the least discussed one was COVID-19 (Figure 8). Clinical Workflow received the highest weight, followed by Wellness, Diseases, and Gender Identity (Figure 9). The weight value represents the popularity of that category or its topics.

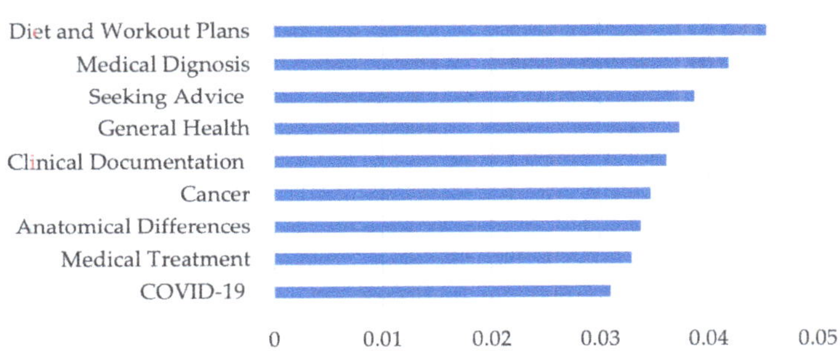

Figure 8. The weight of each topic identified and coded in the initial and focused coding steps.

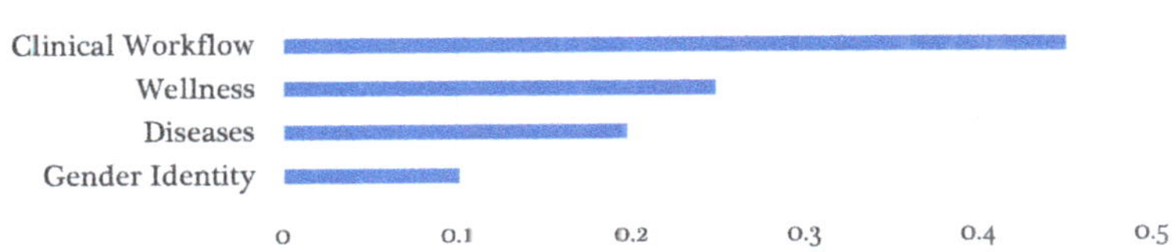

Figure 9. The weights of the categories coded in the focused coding step.

4. Discussion

Social media serves as a communication channel for disseminating health information and can also be used to monitor technology use cases. The study presented here investigates how health use cases of ChatGPT are represented, exploring their various categories and levels of popularity.

4.1. Theoretical Contributions

To the best of our knowledge, this research is the first to identify and code social media discussions on health prompts from an AI chatbot (i.e., ChatGPT). To achieve this objective and to fill the gap in the literature, we developed a data collection and processing framework and embedded topic modeling into CGT to categorize Twitter discourse on health use cases of ChatGPT. The theoretical contributions of this paper are three-fold. First, this study shows the utility of social media data for investigating the health use cases of a chatbot. While most of the existing literature primarily lacks systematic research on the health use cases offered by chatbots developed by generative AI [29], we grounded our study in social media data to directly obtain public prompts representing health use cases. This paper demonstrates the strengths of social media data for mining public experiences with a chatbot.

Second, this research offers a new approach using topic modeling and CGT to understand how users interact with a chatbot using health-related prompts. Using computational methods and qualitative coding provides a holistic identification and interpretation of social media comments on health-related prompts given to chatbots. Our analysis on Twitter conversations surrounding interactions with an AI-based chatbot disclosed topics through the initial coding step. The focused coding processes narrowed down the topics and identified nine topics relating to health issues. The theoretical coding step enabled the research team to categorize these nine topics into four categories: (1) Clinical Workflow, (2) Diseases, (3) Wellness, and (4) Gender Identity.

Third, this work surpasses the limitations of existing studies on the potential uses of AI-based chatbots for health applications and highlights the importance of understanding the possible use cases expressed in social media comments. The results show that prompts could be on a wide range of issues from Gender Identity to Clinical Documentation, which has not been detected in previous social media studies [30,48,93]. The diversity of topics and categories in this study reflects health information needs and health information-seeking behaviors among the public, which could suggest a theoretical framework for understanding how AI platforms are used in health information seeking compared to traditional sources. In line with non-social-media studies, this study demonstrates that AI chatbots are versatile tools utilized in wellness-related behaviors, in the management of various diseases, and in clinical workflows, including specifics such as mental health [42], cancer [34], healthy lifestyles [43], medical treatments [47], and clinical documents [31]. While non-social-media research primarily concentrates on perspectives from healthcare providers (e.g., [31]), this study reveals that the four identified categories of topics are prevalent on social media and are largely discussed by ordinary users. This shift illustrates how everyday users actively leverage AI chatbots for multiple health-related purposes: they seek advice, request medical diagnoses and treatments, explore options for mental and physical well-being, and pose detailed questions about human anatomy. This broader engagement highlights a significant expansion in the use of AI chatbots beyond professional medical contexts, making health information more accessible to the general public.

The diversity of questions posted on social media shows the willingness of users to ask a chatbot about serious health issues (e.g., the Cancer and Medical Treatment topics) and sensitive concerns (e.g., mental health). This indicates that users have developed the required level of trust in AI to accept it as a credible source of health information. This has implications for research related to trust in digital health technologies and the perceived credibility of AI-generated prompts. This study's ranking of topics and their categories can help researchers to develop studies that work towards understanding the information-seeking behavior of users and the socio-technical factors that influence the prioritization of certain topics over others and how these preferences shift over time.

4.2. Implications for Practice

The results of this research can provide practical implications for the health sector to inform the development of more sophisticated, responsive, and ethically aware AI systems. First, our results open a new direction for the health industry and startups to develop AI applications for health needs. This study reveals the potential of AI chatbots for disease analysis and preventive/diagnostic/treatment procedures. This means that AI chatbots can be used for different health applications and decision-making processes, such as analyzing historical data (e.g., clinical documents), providing health consultant (e.g., diet plans), developing precision medicine (e.g., treatments), and interpreting diagnoses (e.g., assessing pain). Our findings suggest a demand for personalized health information. This could drive the development of AI systems capable of providing more tailored health advice based on users' prompts and, potentially, their clinical conditions.

Second, the diversity of categories and topics detected in this study suggests a need for AI chatbots to provide accurate responsible responses. Topics such as COVID-19 and Cancer are susceptible to misinformation. Monitoring questions on these topics can help identify prevalent myths or misinformation, allowing health authorities to address these directly through public information campaigns and AI chatbots. The diversity also highlights the need for clear policies and regulations regarding the use of AI in providing health information. Understanding popular topics can guide innovation in medical technology and the development of new tools that align with public interest or needs.

Third, our findings show the potential of chatbot prompts and relevant social media data for two purposes. First, data from chatbot prompts and social media can aid in monitoring digital epidemiology, emerging health concerns, misinformation trends, and public information needs. Second, social media discussions can help chatbot developers to identify possible problematic responses given by chatbots.

While the focus of this study is on health use cases of AI chatbots, there are some practical ethical challenges. The first challenge is the legal issues posed by AI chatbots, such as the privacy risk involved in scraping large amounts of data that may contain personal data. The second challenge is the humanistic concerns, such as the loss of human touch and the lack of empathy in AI chatbots. Another challenge is presented by algorithmic issues, such as algorithmic biases (e.g., producing discriminatory outcomes). The last challenge involves information concerns, such as concerns about the validity of AI-produced information, referring to its accuracy; the reliability of AI chatbots regarding the possibility of them being manipulated to produce misinformation; and the appropriateness of the information provided by AI chatbots [94,95]. These challenges highlight the need for developing comprehensive ethical guidelines to support all health stakeholders in the effective use of AI chatbots.

4.3. Limitations and Future Work

This study has a few limitations. First, our data collection might have excluded relevant tweets that did not contain our query. Second, we excluded non-English tweets that might have added more dimensions to our analysis, and this could have imposed an unknown sampling bias. Third, focusing on ChatGPT prompts on Twitter during the COVID-19 pandemic introduces some potential selection biases that could affect this study's generalizability. First, as we concentrated solely on Twitter, this research may not capture broader user interactions that could be prevalent on other platforms, given Twitter's unique demographic and user behavior. The majority of Twitter users fall within the 18 to 49 age range. Individuals within this demographic tend to be healthier than older adults, have lower rates of geriatric medical conditions, possess higher levels of education, and earn higher incomes [96]. Second, while ChatGPT is the most popular generative AI chatbot, with 1.54 billion visits per month and over 180.5 million monthly users in the first half of 2024 [97], our analysis being limited to ChatGPT might mean that it does not represent interactions with other AI chatbots that may be configured differently or engage users in diverse ways. There has been an update for ChatGPT (ChatGPT-4), alongside the emergence of other AI chatbots like Microsoft Copilot, Facebook Llama, and Google Bard (now Gemini), all proposed in 2023 [98]. Additionally, conducting this study while the COVID-19 pandemic was ongoing could have skewed the data, as changes in the patterns of social media discussions during this time would not necessarily be indicative of standard behavior. Future work can address the limitations of this study, including expanding the query, including non-English tweets, inferring the demographic information of users, and studying other social media platforms (e.g., Reddit) and AI chatbots (e.g., Google Gemni). In addition, exploring each of the identified topics and categories could empower the theoretical contributions and practical implications of this study's findings.

5. Conclusions

This study establishes a comprehensive framework designed to gather and categorize tweets related to health-related inquiries directed at the ChatGPT chatbot. We utilized a dual-method approach, incorporating both topic modeling and grounded theory techniques, to thoroughly analyze the content of these tweets. This approach enabled us to delve deeply into how the public leverages this chatbot to address their health questions and requirements. Our analytical process revealed four distinct categories of prompts: Clinical Workflow, Diseases, Wellness, and Gender Identity, ranked in order of decreasing popularity. The results of this research underscore the significant potential of social media platforms as tools for identifying and exploring health use cases and the practical applications of AI-based chatbots in the health sector. These insights are particularly valuable for a diverse array of stakeholders, including researchers, healthcare professionals, technology developers, and policymakers, who are involved in evaluating and leveraging the health applications of chatbots. This study not only aids in understanding current interactions between users and health chatbots but also contributes to strategic planning and development within health technology fields, potentially guiding future enhancements to chatbot functionalities in order to better meet users' needs.

Author Contributions: Conceptualization, A.K., Z.Q. and X.Z.; methodology, A.K.; software, A.K.; validation, A.K., H.K. and P.B.; formal analysis, A.K., Z.Q., X.Z., H.K., P.B. and A.B.; investigation, A.K., Z.Q., X.Z., H.K., P.B. and A.B.; resources, A.K.; data curation, A.K.; writing—original draft preparation, A.K., Z.Q., X.Z., H.K., P.B. and A.B; writing—review and editing, A.K., Z.Q., X.Z., H.K., P.B. and A.B; visualization, A.K.; supervision, A.K.; project administration, A.K. All authors have read and agreed to the published version of the manuscript.

Funding: This research received no external funding.

Informed Consent Statement: Not applicable.

Data Availability Statement: The original contributions presented in the study are included in the article, further inquiries can be directed to the corresponding author.

Conflicts of Interest: The authors declare no conflicts of interest.

References

1. Siriborvornratanakul, T. Advanced Artificial Intelligence Methods for Medical Applications. In *Digital Human Modeling and Applications in Health, Safety, Ergonomics and Risk Management*; Duffy, V.G., Ed.; Springer Nature: Cham, Switzerland, 2023; pp. 329–340. [CrossRef]
2. Adamopoulou, E.; Moussiades, L. Chatbots: History, technology, and applications. *Mach. Learn. Appl.* **2020**, *2*, 100006. [CrossRef]
3. Weizenbaum, J. ELIZA—A computer program for the study of natural language communication between man and machine. *Commun. ACM* **1966**, *9*, 36–45. [CrossRef]
4. Shawar, B.A.; Atwell, E. Chatbots: Are they really useful? *J. Lang. Technol. Comput. Linguist.* **2007**, *22*, 29–49. [CrossRef]
5. Brandtzaeg, P.B.; Følstad, A. Why People Use Chatbots. In *Internet Science*; Springer International Publishing: Cham, Germany, 2017; pp. 377–392. [CrossRef]
6. Xu, A.; Liu, Z.; Guo, Y.; Sinha, V.; Akkiraju, R. A New Chatbot for Customer Service on Social Media. In Proceedings of the 2017 CHI Conference on Human Factors in Computing Systems, Denver, CO, USA, 6–11 May 2017; ACM: New York, NY, USA, 2017; pp. 3506–3510. [CrossRef]
7. Lin, C.-C.; Huang, A.Y.Q.; Yang, S.J.H. A review of AI-driven conversational chatbots implementation methodologies and challenges (1999–2022). *Sustainability* **2023**, *15*, 4012. [CrossRef]
8. Biswas, S.S. Role of Chat GPT in Public Health. *Ann. Biomed. Eng.* **2023**, *51*, 868–869. [CrossRef]
9. Xu, L.; Sanders, L.; Li, K.; Chow, J.C.L. Chatbot for health care and oncology applications using artificial intelligence and machine learning: Systematic review. *JMIR Cancer* **2021**, *7*, e27850. [CrossRef] [PubMed]
10. Mesko, B. The Top 10 Healthcare Chatbots. In The Medical Futurist [Internet]. 1 August 2023. Available online: https://medicalfuturist.com/top-10-health-chatbots/ (accessed on 12 March 2024).
11. OpenAI. Introducing ChatGPT. In Introducing ChatGPT [Internet]. 2022. Available online: https://openai.com/blog/chatgpt (accessed on 12 March 2024).
12. Nath, S.; Marie, A.; Ellershaw, S.; Korot, E.; Keane, P.A. New meaning for NLP: The trials and tribulations of natural language processing with GPT-3 in ophthalmology. *Br. J. Ophthalmol.* **2022**, *106*, 889–892. [CrossRef]

13. Retkowsky, J.; Hafermalz, E.; Huysman, M. Managing a ChatGPT-Empowered Workforce: Understanding Its Affordances and Side Effects. Business Horizons. 2024. Available online: https://www.sciencedirect.com/science/article/pii/S000768132400054 5?casa_token=49wXQXd-2E4AAAAA:uGtVXwk42i-ED6_9q9a074b6x7_Ri2gIChZRgFjPVI_YkZeS7VXcfSK9Q18d0JlIgbuOGl9 nfro (accessed on 23 April 2024).
14. Palanica, A.; Flaschner, P.; Thommandram, A.; Li, M.; Fossat, Y. Physicians' perceptions of chatbots in health care: Cross-sectional web-based survey. *J. Med. Internet Res.* **2019**, *21*, e12887. [CrossRef]
15. McLaughlin, M.L.; Hou, J.; Meng, J.; Hu, C.-W.; An, Z.; Park, M.; Nam, Y. Propagation of Information About Preexposure Prophylaxis (PrEP) for HIV Prevention Through Twitter. *Health Commun.* **2016**, *31*, 998–1007. [CrossRef]
16. Kepios. Global Social Media Statistics. In DataReportal—Global Digital Insights [Internet]. 2024. Available online: https://datareportal.com/social-media-users (accessed on 13 March 2024).
17. Shaw, G., Jr.; Zimmerman, M.; Vasquez-Huot, L.; Karami, A. Deciphering Latent Health Information in Social Media Using a Mixed-Methods Design. *Healthcare* **2022**, *10*, 2320. [CrossRef]
18. Karami, A.; Clark, S.B.; Mackenzie, A.; Lee, D.; Zhu, M.; Boyajieff, H.R.; Goldschmidt, B. 2020 U.S. presidential election in swing states: Gender differences in Twitter conversations. *Int. J. Inf. Manag. Data Insights* **2022**, *2*, 100097. [CrossRef]
19. Messaoudi, C.; Guessoum, Z.; Ben Romdhane, L. Opinion mining in online social media: A survey. *Soc. Netw. Anal. Min.* **2022**, *12*, 25. [CrossRef]
20. Duggan SF and M. Health Online 2013. In Pew Research Center [Internet]. 2013. Available online: https://www.pewresearch.org/internet/2013/01/15/health-online-2013/ (accessed on 23 April 2024).
21. Moorhead, S.A.; Hazlett, D.E.; Harrison, L.; Carroll, J.K.; Irwin, A.; Hoving, C. A new dimension of health care: Systematic review of the uses, benefits, and limitations of social media for health communication. *J. Med. Internet Res.* **2013**, *15*, e85. [CrossRef] [PubMed]
22. Attai, D.J.; Cowher, M.S.; Al-Hamadani, M.; Schoger, J.M.; Staley, A.C.; Landercasper, J. Twitter social media is an effective tool for breast cancer patient education and support: Patient-reported outcomes by survey. *J. Med. Internet Res.* **2015**, *17*, e188. [CrossRef] [PubMed]
23. Kind, T.; Patel, P.D.; Lie, D.; Chretien, K.C. Twelve tips for using social media as a medical educator. *Med. Teach.* **2014**, *36*, 284–290. [CrossRef] [PubMed]
24. Salathé, M.; Khandelwal, S. Assessing vaccination sentiments with online social media: Implications for Infectious disease dynamics and control. *PLoS Comput. Biol.* **2011**, *7*, e1002199. [CrossRef]
25. Hu, K. ChatGPT Sets Record for Fastest-Growing User Base—Analyst Note. Reuters. 2 February 2023. Available online: https://www.reuters.com/technology/chatgpt-sets-record-fastest-growing-user-base-analyst-note-2023-02-01/ (accessed on 12 March 2024).
26. Carr, D.F. ChatGPT's First Birthday Is November 30: A Year in Review. In Similarweb [Internet]. 2023. Available online: https://www.similarweb.com/blog/insights/ai-news/chatgpt-birthday/ (accessed on 12 March 2024).
27. Kelly, S.M. This AI chatbot Is Dominating Social Media with Its Frighteningly Good Essays | CNN Business. In CNN [Internet]. 5 December 2022. Available online: https://www.cnn.com/2022/12/05/tech/chatgpt-trnd/index.html (accessed on 12 March 2024).
28. White, J.; Hays, S.; Fu, Q.; Spencer-Smith, J.; Schmidt, D.C. ChatGPT Prompt Patterns for Improving Code Quality, Refactoring, Requirements Elicitation, and Software Design. In *Generative AI for Effective Software Development*; Nguyen-Duc, A., Abrahamsson, P., Khomh, F., Eds.; Springer Nature Switzerland: Cham, Switzerland, 2024; pp. 71–108. [CrossRef]
29. Li, J.; Dada, A.; Puladi, B.; Kleesiek, J.; Egger, J. ChatGPT in healthcare: A taxonomy and systematic review. *Comput. Methods Programs Biomed.* **2024**, *245*, 108013. [CrossRef]
30. Taecharungroj, V. "What can ChatGPT do?" Analyzing early reactions to the innovative AI chatbot on Twitter. *Big Data Cogn. Comput.* **2023**, *7*, 35. [CrossRef]
31. Javaid, M.; Haleem, A.; Singh, R.P. ChatGPT for healthcare services: An emerging stage for an innovative perspective. *BenchCouncil Trans. Benchmarks Stand. Eval.* **2023**, *3*, 100105. [CrossRef]
32. Huh, S. Are ChatGPT's Knowledge and Interpretation Ability Comparable to Those of Medical Students in Korea for Taking a Parasitology Examination?: A Descriptive Study. *J. Educ. Eval. Health Prof.* **2023**, *20*, 1. Available online: https://www.ncbi.nlm.nih.gov/pmc/articles/PMC9905868/ (accessed on 1 August 2024).
33. Kung, T.H.; Cheatham, M.; Medenilla, A.; Sillos, C.; De Leon, L.; Elepaño, C.; Madriaga, M.; Aggabao, R.; Diaz-Candido, G.; Maningo, J.; et al. Performance of ChatGPT on USMLE: Potential for AI-assisted medical education using large language models. *PLoS Digit. Health* **2023**, *2*, e0000198. [CrossRef] [PubMed]
34. Johnson, S.B.; King, A.J.; Warner, E.L.; Aneja, S.; Kann, B.H.; Bylund, C.L. Using ChatGPT to evaluate cancer myths and misconceptions: Artificial intelligence and cancer information. *JNCI Cancer Spectr.* **2023**, *7*, pkad015. [CrossRef]
35. Potapenko, I.; Boberg-Ans, L.C.; Hansen, M.S.; Klefter, O.N.; van Dijk, E.H.C.; Subhi, Y. Artificial intelligence-based chatbot patient information on common retinal diseases using ChatGPT. *Acta Ophthalmol.* **2023**, *101*, 829–831. [CrossRef] [PubMed]
36. Duong, D.; Solomon, B.D. Analysis of large-language model versus human performance for genetics questions. *Eur. J. Hum. Genet.* **2024**, *32*, 466–468. [CrossRef]
37. Lahat, A.; Shachar, E.; Avidan, B.; Shatz, Z.; Glicksberg, B.S.; Klang, E. Evaluating the use of large language model in identifying top research questions in gastroenterology. *Sci. Rep.* **2023**, *13*, 4164. [CrossRef] [PubMed]

38. Sinha, R.K.; Roy, A.D.; Kumar, N.; Mondal, H. Applicability of ChatGPT in Assisting to Solve Higher Order Problems in Pathology. *Cureus* **2023**, *15*, e35237. Available online: https://www.ncbi.nlm.nih.gov/pmc/articles/PMC10033699/ (accessed on 1 August 2024). [CrossRef]
39. Ali, S.R.; Dobbs, T.D.; Hutchings, H.A.; Whitaker, I.S. Using ChatGPT to write patient clinic letters. *Lancet Digit. Health* **2023**, *5*, e179–e181. [CrossRef]
40. Lim, S.; Schmälzle, R. Artificial intelligence for health message generation: An empirical study using a large language model (LLM) and prompt engineering. *Front. Commun.* **2023**, *8*, 1129082. [CrossRef]
41. Ulusoy, I.; Yılmaz, M.; Kıvrak, A. How Efficient Is ChatGPT in Accessing Accurate and Quality Health-Related Information? *Cureus* **2023**, *15*, e46662. Available online: https://www.ncbi.nlm.nih.gov/pmc/articles/PMC10628365/ (accessed on 1 August 2024). [CrossRef]
42. Cabrera, J.; Loyola, M.S.; Magaña, I.; Rojas, R. Ethical Dilemmas, Mental Health, Artificial Intelligence, and LLM-Based Chatbots. In *Bioinformatics and Biomedical Engineering*; Rojas, I., Valenzuela, O., Rojas Ruiz, F., Herrera, L.J., Ortuño, F., Eds.; Springer Nature Switzerland: Cham, Switzerland, 2023; pp. 313–326. [CrossRef]
43. Fadhil, A.; Gabrielli, S. Addressing challenges in promoting healthy lifestyles: The al-chatbot approach. In Proceedings of the 11th EAI International Conference on Pervasive Computing Technologies for Healthcare, Barcelona, Spain, 23–26 May 2017; ACM: New York, NY, USA, 2017; pp. 261–265. [CrossRef]
44. Sallam, M.; Salim, N.; Barakat, M.; Al-Tammemi, A. ChatGPT applications in medical, dental, pharmacy, and public health education: A descriptive study highlighting the advantages and limitations. *Narra J.* **2023**, *3*, e103. Available online: https://www.ncbi.nlm.nih.gov/pmc/articles/PMC10914078/ (accessed on 1 August 2024). [CrossRef]
45. Yu, H.; McGuinness, S. An experimental study of integrating fine-tuned LLMs and prompts for enhancing mental health support chatbot system. *J. Med. Artif. Intell.* **2024**, *7*, 1–16. [CrossRef]
46. Softić, A.; Husić, J.B.; Softić, A.; Baraković, S. Health chatbot: Design, implementation, acceptance and usage motivation. In Proceedings of the 2021 20th International Symposium Infoteh-Jahorina (INFOTEH), East Sarajevo, Bosnia and Herzegovina, 17–19 March 2021; IEEE: Piscataway, NJ, USA, 2021; pp. 1–6. Available online: https://ieeexplore.ieee.org/abstract/document/9400693/ (accessed on 1 August 2024).
47. Aggarwal, A.; Tam, C.C.; Wu, D.; Li, X.; Qiao, S. Artificial intelligence–based chatbots for promoting health behavioral changes: Systematic review. *J. Med. Internet Res.* **2023**, *25*, e40789. [CrossRef] [PubMed]
48. Lian, Y.; Tang, H.; Xiang, M.; Dong, X. Public attitudes and sentiments toward ChatGPT in China: A text mining analysis based on social media. *Technol. Soc.* **2024**, *76*, 102442. [CrossRef]
49. Zhou, W.; Zhang, C.; Wu, L.; Shashidhar, M. ChatGPT and marketing: Analyzing public discourse in early Twitter posts. *J. Mark. Anal.* **2023**, *11*, 693–706. [CrossRef]
50. Strauss, A.; Corbin, J. *Basics of Grounded Theory Methods*; Sage: Beverly Hills, CA, USA, 1990.
51. Glaser, B.G. *Basic of Grounded Theory Analysis*; Sociology Press: Mills, CA, USA, 1992. Available online: https://www.sidalc.net/search/Record/UnerFceco:4647/Description (accessed on 1 August 2024).
52. Charmaz, K. *Constructing Grounded Theory: A Practical Guide through Qualitative Analysis*; Sage: Beverly Hills, CA, USA, 2006. Available online: https://books.google.com/books?hl=en&lr=&id=2ThdBAAAQBAJ&oi=fnd&pg=PP1&ots=f-i_aOoExV&sig=EbtcJbDMiY4X4oTxlVyyKLyXs04 (accessed on 1 August 2024).
53. Odacioglu, E.C.; Zhang, L.; Allmendinger, R.; Shahgholian, A. Big textual data research for operations management: Topic modelling with grounded theory. *Int. J. Oper. Prod. Manag.* **2023**, *44*, 1420–1445. [CrossRef]
54. Miller, F.; Davis, K.; Partridge, H. Everyday life information experiences in Twitter: A grounded theory. *Inf. Res. Int. Electron. J.* **2019**, *24*, 1–23. Available online: https://research.usq.edu.au/item/q7636/everyday-life-information-experiences-in-twitter-a-grounded-theory (accessed on 1 August 2024).
55. Tie, Y.C.; Birks, M.; Francis, K. Grounded theory research: A design framework for novice researchers. *SAGE Open Med.* **2019**, *7*, 205031211882292. [CrossRef]
56. Nelson, L.K. Computational Grounded Theory: A Methodological Framework. *Sociol. Methods Res.* **2020**, *49*, 3–42. [CrossRef]
57. Finfgeld-Connett, D. Twitter and Health Science Research. *West. J. Nurs. Res.* **2015**, *37*, 1269–1283. [CrossRef]
58. Edo-Osagie, O.; De La Iglesia, B.; Lake, I.; Edeghere, O. A scoping review of the use of Twitter for public health research. *Comput. Biol. Med.* **2020**, *122*, 103770. [CrossRef]
59. Gotfredsen, S.G. Q&A: What Happened to Academic Research on Twitter? In Columbia Journalism Review [Internet]. Available online: https://www.cjr.org/tow_center/qa-what-happened-to-academic-research-on-twitter.php (accessed on 8 August 2024).
60. Shewale, R. 17 Google Gemini Statistics (2024 Users & Traffic). In DemandSage [Internet]. 16 February 2024. Available online: https://www.demandsage.com/google-gemini-statistics/ (accessed on 3 June 2024).
61. Duarte, F. Number of ChatGPT Users (May 2024). In Exploding Topics [Internet]. 30 March 2023. Available online: https://explodingtopics.com/blog/chatgpt-users (accessed on 3 June 2024).
62. Google Trend. Google Trends of ChatGPT, Bard, Llama, and Copilot. 2023. Available online: https://trends.google.com/trends/explore?date=2023-01-01%202023-12-31&geo=US&q=chatgpt,/g/11tsqm45vd,bard,Llama&hl=en (accessed on 3 June 2024).
63. Kemp, S. Twitter Statistics and Trends. In DataReportal—Global Digital Insights [Internet]. 2023. Available online: https://datareportal.com/essential-twitter-stats (accessed on 15 March 2023).

64. Shewale, R. Twitter Statistics in 2023. 2023. Available online: https://www.demandsage.com/twitter-statistics/#:~:text=Let%20us%20take%20a%20closer,528.3%20million%20monthly%20active%20users (accessed on 1 August 2024).
65. Lim, M.S.C.; Molenaar, A.; Brennan, L.; Reid, M.; McCaffrey, T. Young adults' use of different social media platforms for health information: Insights from web-based conversations. *J. Med. Internet Res.* **2022**, *24*, e23656. [CrossRef] [PubMed]
66. Takats, C.; Kwan, A.; Wormer, R.; Goldman, D.; Jones, H.E.; Romero, D. Ethical and methodological considerations of twitter data for public health research: Systematic review. *J. Med. Internet Res.* **2022**, *24*, e40380. [CrossRef] [PubMed]
67. Mejova, Y.; Weber, I.; Macy, M.W. *Twitter: A Digital Socioscope*; Cambridge University Press: Cambridge, UK, 2015.
68. Antonakaki, D.; Fragopoulou, P.; Ioannidis, S. A survey of Twitter research: Data model, graph structure, sentiment analysis and attacks. *Expert Syst. Appl.* **2021**, *164*, 114006. [CrossRef]
69. Karami, A.; Dahl, A.A.; Shaw, G.; Valappil, S.P.; Turner-McGrievy, G.; Kharrazi, H.; Bozorgi, P. Analysis of Social Media Discussions on (#)Diet by Blue, Red, and Swing States in the U.S. *Healthcare* **2021**, *9*, 518. [CrossRef]
70. Son, J.; Negahban, A. Examining the Impact of Emojis on Disaster Communication: A Perspective from the Uncertainty Reduction Theory. *AIS Trans. Hum.-Comput. Interact.* **2023**, *15*, 377–413. [CrossRef]
71. Van Vliet, L.; Törnberg, P.; Uitermark, J. The Twitter parliamentarian database: Analyzing Twitter politics across 26 countries. *PLoS ONE* **2020**, *15*, e0237073. [CrossRef]
72. Kolagani, S.H.D.; Negahban, A.; Witt, C. Identifying trending sentiments in the 2016 us presidential election: A case study of twitter analytics. *Issues Inf. Syst.* **2017**, *18*, 80–86.
73. Nzali, M.D.T.; Bringay, S.; Lavergne, C.; Mollevi, C.; Opitz, T. What patients can tell us: Topic analysis for social media on breast cancer. *JMIR Public Health Surveill.* **2017**, *5*, e23.
74. Karami, A.; Zhu, M.; Goldschmidt, B.; Boyajieff, H.R.; Najafabadi, M.M. COVID-19 Vaccine and Social Media in the U.S.: Exploring Emotions and Discussions on Twitter. *Vaccines* **2021**, *9*, 1059. [CrossRef]
75. Malik, A.; Antonino, A.; Khan, M.L.; Nieminen, M. Characterizing HIV discussions and engagement on Twitter. *Health Technol.* **2021**, *11*, 1237–1245. [CrossRef]
76. Pennebaker, J.W.; Boyd, R.L.; Jordan, K.; Blackburn, K. *The Development and Psychometric Properties of LIWC2015*; Pennebaker Conglomerates: Austin, TX, USA, 2015. Available online: www.LIWC.net (accessed on 1 August 2024).
77. Zipf, G.K. *Human Behavior and the Principle of Least Effort: An Introduction to Human Ecology*; Addison-Wesley Press, Inc.: Cambridge, MA, USA, 1949.
78. Karami, A. Fuzzy Topic Modeling for Medical Corpora. Ph.D. Thesis, University of Maryland, Baltimore County, MD, USA, 2015.
79. DiMaggio, P. Adapting computational text analysis to social science (and vice versa). *Big Data Soc.* **2015**, *2*, 2053951715602908. [CrossRef]
80. Baumer, E.P.S.; Mimno, D.; Guha, S.; Quan, E.; Gay, G.K. Comparing grounded theory and topic modeling: Extreme divergence or unlikely convergence? *J. Assoc. Inf. Sci. Technol.* **2017**, *68*, 1397–1410. [CrossRef]
81. Blei, D.M.; Ng, A.Y.; Jordan, M.I. Latent dirichlet allocation. *J. Mach. Learn. Res.* **2003**, *3*, 993–1022.
82. Egger, R.; Yu, J. A topic modeling comparison between lda, nmf, top2vec, and bertopic to demystify twitter posts. *Front. Sociol.* **2022**, *7*, 886498. [CrossRef] [PubMed]
83. Zhang, D.; Luo, T.; Wang, D. Learning from LDA Using Deep Neural Networks. In *Natural Language Understanding and Intelligent Applications*; Lin, C.-Y., Xue, N., Zhao, D., Huang, X., Feng, Y., Eds.; Springer International Publishing: Cham, Switzerland, 2016; pp. 657–664. [CrossRef]
84. Mohammadi, M.; Al-Fuqaha, A.; Sorour, S.; Guizani, M. Deep learning for IoT big data and streaming analytics: A survey. *IEEE Commun. Surv. Tutor.* **2018**, *20*, 2923–2960. [CrossRef]
85. Erhan, D.; Courville, A.; Bengio, Y.; Vincent, P. Why does unsupervised pre-training help deep learning? In Proceedings of the Thirteenth International Conference on Artificial Intelligence and Statistics, Sardinia, Italy, 13–15 May 2010; JMLR Workshop and Conference Proceedings; pp. 201–208. Available online: http://proceedings.mlr.press/v9/erhan10a.html (accessed on 1 August 2024).
86. Hong, L.; Davison, B.D. Empirical study of topic modeling in Twitter. In *Proceedings of the First Workshop on Social Media Analytics*; ACM: Washington, DC, USA, 2010; pp. 80–88. [CrossRef]
87. Lu, Y.; Mei, Q.; Zhai, C. Investigating task performance of probabilistic topic models: An empirical study of PLSA and LDA. *Inf. Retr.* **2011**, *14*, 178–203. [CrossRef]
88. Blei, D.M. Probabilistic Topic Models. *Commun. ACM* **2012**, *55*, 77–84. [CrossRef]
89. Cao, J.; Xia, T.; Li, J.; Zhang, Y.; Tang, S. A density-based method for adaptive LDA model selection. *Neurocomputing* **2009**, *72*, 1775–1781. [CrossRef]
90. Syed, S.; Spruit, M. Full-text or abstract? examining topic coherence scores using latent dirichlet allocation. In Proceedings of the 2017 IEEE International conference on data science and advanced analytics (DSAA), Tokyo, Japan, 19–21 October 2017; IEEE: Piscataway, NJ, USA, 2017; pp. 165–174. Available online: https://ieeexplore.ieee.org/abstract/document/8259775/?casa_token=i0ifBOi_wfIAAAAA:UVPjwXEKAVWcHGS5BDHBh-SqPc-x8kOQCPZlGy2sNduuJN--QqiYT7df4bPsxoY2KvhXxZT_sw (accessed on 1 August 2024).
91. Karami, A.; Swan, S.C.; White, C.N.; Ford, K. Hidden in plain sight for too long: Using text mining techniques to shine a light on workplace sexism and sexual harassment. *Psychol. Violence* **2019**, *14*, 1–13. [CrossRef]

92. Karami, A.; Lundy, M.; Webb, F.; Dwivedi, Y.K. Twitter and research: A systematic literature review through text mining. *IEEE Access* **2020**, *8*, 67698–67717. [CrossRef]
93. Karami, A.; Spinel, M.Y.; White, C.N.; Ford, K.; Swan, S. A systematic literature review of sexual harassment studies with text mining. *Sustainability* **2021**, *13*, 6589. [CrossRef]
94. Zhou, X.; Xu, Y.; Li, Y.; Josang, A.; Cox, C. The state-of-the-art in personalized recommender systems for social networking. *Artif. Intell. Rev.* **2012**, *37*, 119–132. [CrossRef]
95. Minssen, T.; Vayena, E.; Cohen, I.G. The Challenges for Regulating Medical Use of ChatGPT and Other Large Language Models. *JAMA* **2023**, *330*, 315–316. Available online: https://jamanetwork.com/journals/jama/article-abstract/2807167?casa_token=K4KeF9AGmRoAAAAA:36WVm5COT3vbRUafym6LeEM9S2QWgoOx8moN4gz4TADzxIAbVYc28ON36LB_2QskGuovyZqiQyg (accessed on 5 June 2024). [CrossRef] [PubMed]
96. Wang, C.; Liu, S.; Yang, H.; Guo, J.; Wu, Y.; Liu, J. Ethical considerations of using ChatGPT in health care. *J. Med. Internet Res.* **2023**, *25*, e48009. [CrossRef]
97. Hughes, A.; Wojcik, S. *10 Facts about Americans and Twitter*; Pew Research Center: Washington, DC, USA, 2019.
98. Singh, S. ChatGPT Statistics (AUG 2024)—Users Growth Data. In DemandSage [Internet]. 10 August 2024. Available online: https://www.demandsage.com/chatgpt-statistics/ (accessed on 12 August 2024).

big data and
cognitive computing

MDPI

Article

QA-RAG: Exploring LLM Reliance on External Knowledge

Aigerim Mansurova *, Aiganym Mansurova and Aliya Nugumanova

Big Data and Blockchain Technologies Science and Innovation Center, Astana IT University, 020000 Astana, Kazakhstan; 231945@astanait.edu.kz (A.M.); a.nugumanova@astanait.edu.kz (A.N.)
* Correspondence: mansurovaaigerim02@gmail.com; Tel.: +7-7006920123

Abstract: Large language models (LLMs) can store factual knowledge within their parameters and have achieved superior results in question-answering tasks. However, challenges persist in providing provenance for their decisions and keeping their knowledge up to date. Some approaches aim to address these challenges by combining external knowledge with parametric memory. In contrast, our proposed QA-RAG solution relies solely on the data stored within an external knowledge base, specifically a dense vector index database. In this paper, we compare RAG configurations using two LLMs—Llama 2 7b and 13b—systematically examining their performance in three key RAG capabilities: noise robustness, knowledge gap detection, and external truth integration. The evaluation reveals that while our approach achieves an accuracy of 83.3%, showcasing its effectiveness across all baselines, the model still struggles significantly in terms of external truth integration. These findings suggest that considerable work is still required to fully leverage RAG in question-answering tasks.

Keywords: large language model; question-answering system; retrieval-augmented generation; external knowledge base

1. Introduction

The emergence of large language models (LLMs), such as GPT-3 [1], has sparked a wide range of innovations, powering intelligent chatbots, personal assistants, and other natural language processing (NLP) applications (ChatGPT, Copilot). LLMs have also gained increasing popularity as a tool for information seeking and question answering (QA). LangChain [2], a framework for building applications with LLMs, has been instrumental in leveraging LLMs for a variety of scenarios to improve their efficiency.

While these QA systems have shown remarkable general abilities [3,4], their outputs are prone to hallucination [5]. They continue to suffer severely from challenges, particularly factual inaccuracies [5] and knowledge outdating [6,7]. This makes it harder for users to trust and verify LLM-generated answers. Therefore, validating the factual accuracy of generative large language model-based question-answering system poses a contemporary research challenge.

Given their inherently generative nature, ensuring that the output aligns with the sources of information proves to be a challenging task. Incorporating external knowledge via information retrieval, i.e., retrieval-augmented generation (RAG) [8], has been regarded as a promising way to resolve the above challenges. RAG optimizes the output of a large language model by referencing an external knowledge base outside of the LLM training data sources before generating a response. RAG enhances the responses of the LLM and reduces the occurrence of hallucinations, thereby increasing the models' credibility [9,10].

Nevertheless, it is crucial to recognize that in practical scenarios, the text retrieved by these models frequently contains a certain level of noise. This poses a problem, as the language model's RAG-enabled responses can significantly vary based on the quality and accuracy of the retrieved content. Therefore, objective evaluations of RAG-enabled LLM performance are just as vital as benchmarking their non-RAG analog.

The contributions of this paper are as follows:

- We propose QA-RAG for constructing question-answering systems empowered by LLMs to handle the occurrence of hallucination. The proposed architecture is versatile, does not require fine-tuning, and can be applied to both black-box and open-source LLMs.
- We investigate the behavior of QA-RAG from three perspectives: (1) Noise Robustness: assessing how noise in retrieved documents affects answer accuracy. (2) Knowledge Gap Detection: evaluating the system's ability to recognize and handle missing information. (3) External Truth Integration: examining how well the system integrates external data that contradict its pre-existing knowledge.
- We modified TriviaQA dataset: reformulated 1100 answers as long-form answers to enhance the complexity of the evaluation. Two testbeds comprising 600 rows were designed to assess the aforementioned behaviors.
- We examine and highlight various practices and implementations applicable to the development of a RAG system.
- Our code and dataset are publicly released to facilitate future research on interpretable RAG.

2. Literature Review

The predominant paradigm for utilizing large language models in the question-answering task involves adjusting large language models through fine-tuning. Although LLMs have general knowledge, they may lack effectiveness in specific domains. Fine-tuning addresses this by retraining a pre-trained language model on a particular dataset or task to enhance its performance.

It has been observed that LLMs can acquire a kind of implicit "knowledge base" after being previously trained on unstructured text. The work in [11] examined the potential benefit of this behavior for an open-domain question-answering task. The authors fine-tuned the T5 model in order to be able to answer questions without providing additional information or context, based solely on knowledge acquired during fine-tuning. Thus, the model must query in a natural language and "find the information" stored in its weights. However, this approach gives competitive results only with the language models that have more than 10 billion parameters. Second, the model extracts knowledge about its parameters in an inexplicable way and hallucinates realistic answers when it is unsure. Third, the maximum-likelihood objective used to train the model provides no guarantees as to whether a model will learn a fact or not.

In the work [12], Bloom 7B has been fine-tuned with domain data sourced from the Wikidata knowledge base. The authors tried implement knowledge injection to improve the model's ability to store knowledge in its parameters. To reduce hallucination a teacher–student approach was proposed. That is, a more powerful LLM (GPT-4) was used to provide guidance to the weaker LLM (Bloom 7B). However, use of the proposed approach in practice is questioned [13,14] by the importance and complexity of creating a reliable knowledge graph through entity and edge extraction leveraging LLMs. Also, there are significant costs associated with the teacher model's intervention in the student model's explanations.

Consequently, fine-tuning is a strong starting point for building QA systems, but it has several limitations. Fine-tuning can be very efficient if the goal is to optimize the performance of LLM on that task alone. It helps adapt a pre-trained model to unique requirements. However, fine-tuning cannot deal with hallucination as knowledge is limited to what the model has encountered in its training data. Secondly, the process of fine-tuning can be extremely time-consuming and expensive. Storage space is limited by the size of the neural network—to capture more world knowledge, one must train ever-larger networks. Furthermore, even if it is achieved, it is challenging to determine what knowledge is stored. Stored knowledge may inevitably be incomplete, out of date, or incorrect.

The pioneering work of Lewis et al. marked a significant milestone in the field of language generation [8]. They introduced the retrieval-augmented generation (RAG) model, which ingeniously combines pre-trained parametric and non-parametric memory for language generation. This model, with its unique ability to access a dense vector index of Wikipedia through a pre-trained neural retriever, has set a new standard in the realm of free-form, abstractive text generation.

The term "RAG" was introduced in [8], and it has since become synonymous with the method of integrating external knowledge bases into language generation models. However, it is important to clarify that the current reference to "RAG" pertains to the broader concept of retrieval-augmented generation, not the specific methodology outlined in the work. This approach, as subsequent research by [10,15,16] has shown, allows models to generate more accurate and reliable responses by using external knowledge as guidance. Impressive performance has been demonstrated in a range of tasks, including open-domain question answering [17,18] and dialog [19].

LangChain [2], an open-source Python framework, simplifies the complexities associated with interacting with LLMs. Offering numerous tools like chains, web search ability, vector databases, and embedding models to create and store vector embeddings, it thereby accelerates the development of RAG-based AI applications. In our previous work [20], a QA chatbot that responds to fintech-domain-specific queries was developed with two potential scenarios following a user's query. The first scenario involved the chatbot generating an answer based on information found in its external knowledge base. The second scenario occurred when the chatbot could not find information to formulate an answer. In this case, the chatbot initiated a search operation through the Google Search API, ensuring that users always received a response.

The current study builds upon the work in [20], incorporating several adjustments to simplify system evaluation. One notable modification is in the system's response behavior. If the system does not contain an answer to the question within its vector database, it will explicitly state so, thereby enhancing the transparency of the system's responses. Additionally, the scope of this research is limited to the vector database, and as such, the web search capability will not be assessed.

The research in [21] presents a method for rapidly creating QA over a single pdf file application using LangChain. The paper in [22] serves as a practical guide, highlighting the framework's potential in creating versatile and powerful virtual assistants that can be deployed across various industries. Others [23] explored the use of the framework to develop an automated customer service chatbot that offers responsive and context-aware interactions. The chatbot, integrated into the customer service platform of Birla Vishvakarma Mahavidyalaya, utilizes web scraping and embeddings to provide real-time support and query resolution. The paper in [24] presents MindGuide, a sophisticated mental health support tool designed to assist individuals with mental health challenges. The mentioned works outline the framework's features that facilitate the swift development and deployment of chatbots.

Nevertheless, these studies fall short of providing a comprehensive evaluation of the system, which limits their suitability for deployment or practical application. In contrast, our work fills this gap by rigorously assessing system performance across key dimensions such as noise robustness, knowledge gap detection, and external truth integration. Unlike prior research, we prioritize evaluation over technical implementation, offering insights into the reliability and behavior of LLMs in real-world scenarios.

3. Materials and Methods

3.1. Open-Book Question-Answering System

Open-book question answering refers to the task of developing systems capable of providing accurate and contextually relevant answers a to a specific set of questions q posed in natural language with access to external knowledge. In this research, the task is solved by using a methodology that involves a two-step architecture, consisting of a retriever and a generator (or reasoner). The system is constructed in such a manner that it can only answer based on the external knowledge provided, without relying on its parametric memory. The overall system architecture is depicted in Figure 1, detailing the sequential steps as follows:

1. The query is forwarded to the embedding model for encoding into an embedded query vector.
2. The embedded query vector is then transmitted to a vector database.
3. The retriever algorithm dictates the retrieval of the top-k pertinent segments from the database.
4. Subsequently, both the query text and the retrieved segments are forwarded to the generator.
5. The LLM generates an output that must be relevant and contextually connected to the original query and the information retrieved from the database.

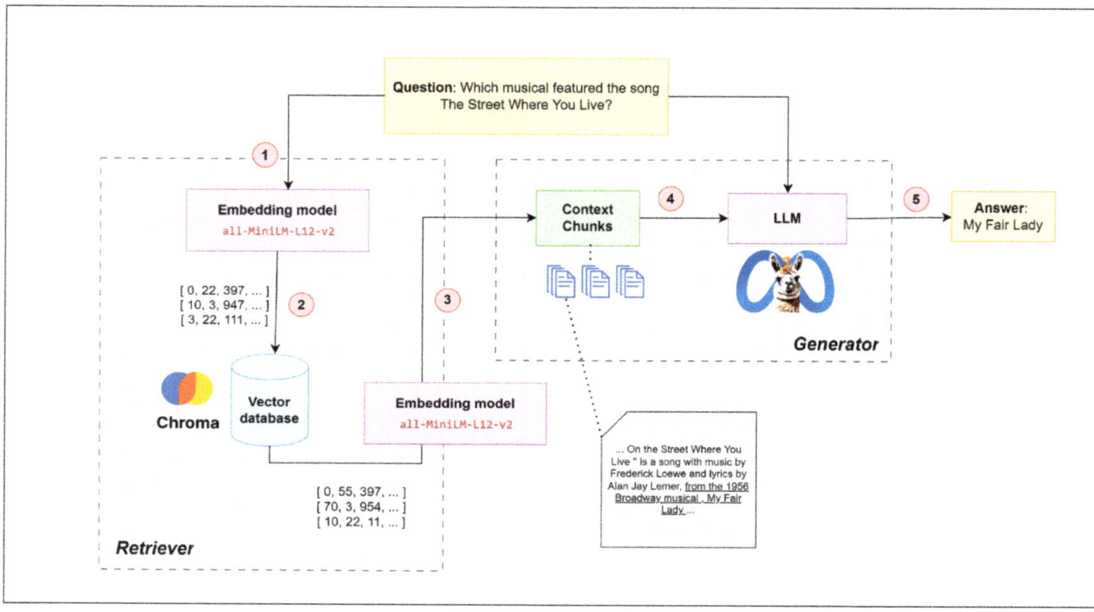

Figure 1. QA RAG architecture and workflow.

3.2. Retriever

The objective of the retrieval component is to identify a subset of documents, Dr, from a corpus of documents $D = \{d_1, d_2, \ldots, d_n\}$, that would assist the generator in correctly responding the query. The use of a dense retriever has gained popularity among various retrieval methods due to its ability to handle queries that are both complex and varied. The fundamental principle of dense retrieval is the conversion of textual data into high-dimensional vector representations, typically accomplished with a neural network, often a transformer-based encoder like BERT [25].

Both the query q and potential source documents Dr are processed by the dense retriever to generate corresponding embeddings: $\overline{q}$ for the query and $\overline{d_i}$ for each document $di \in D$. This embedding process can be formulated as follows:

$$\overline{d}_i = Encoder_d(d_i) \; ; \; \overline{q} = Encoder_q(q), \tag{1}$$

where $Encoder_d$ and $Encoder_q$ are encoders based on neural networks, which share architecture or weights, and are engineered to convert textual data into vector space representations.

Upon creation, embeddings are saved in the vector database ChromaDB. This method offers the distinct advantage of permitting an "offline" initialization, where document embeddings are precomputed. Consequently, only the embedding of the query needs to be computed during the search, thereby reducing latency.

Cosine similarity was initially chosen over the dot product for comparing text vectors due to its emphasis on contextual similarities rather than purely dimensional or frequency-based similarities. However, since each vector in our study has the same length (as per the specifications of the embedding model), the distinction between cosine similarity and the dot product becomes negligible. Consequently, the computation of similarities between query and document embeddings was conducted using the dot product, defined as follows:

$$dot\ product(q, d_i) = \overline{q} \cdot \overline{d}_i, \tag{2}$$

This metric assesses the relevance of each document to the query by examining their similarity in the embedded vector space; higher scores indicate increased relevance. Documents are then ranked according to these scores, and the top-ranked (top-k) documents are forwarded for further processing by the generator component.

In the realm of abstractive question answering, it has been established that dense methods outperform sparse methods. Sparse retrievers, such as the BM25, utilize statistical weighting to determine the relevance between search terms and documents. The BM25 scoring function considers term frequency and document length, providing an efficient means of retrieving relevant information. However, its exact-match basis can be limiting when a query and document are relevant but share no common words.

Contrary to this, there is a growing body of research suggesting that hybrid methods may offer superior results [26]. These methods, which combine dense and sparse searches, aim to harness the strengths of both approaches. Upon receiving a question, both searches are executed in parallel, producing two lists of potential documents to provide the answer.

The application of hybrid search becomes necessary when it is required to integrate the results from multiple retrieval methods. A widely adopted algorithm employed to tackle this challenge is the Reciprocal Rank Fusion (RRF) [27], an uncomplicated technique for combining document rankings from various information retrieval systems.

For a given set of documents D and search results r for the question q from various methods m within M, the $RRF(d \in D)$ can be computed for each document d in D as outlined in [28]:

$$RRF(d \in D) = \sum_{rank(r(q),\ d) \in M} \frac{1}{l + rank(r(q),\ d)}, \tag{3}$$

$\frac{1}{rank(r(q),\ d)}$ is a reciprocal rank, with $rank(r(q),\ d)$ denoting the rank at which the document d is retrieved by the search mechanism m. The variable l is a ranking constant employed to mitigate the impact of outlier systems.

Figure 2 illustrates the calculation of the RRF score with l set to 1. In the provided example, three chunks are retrieved in varying sequences by two search methodologies (sparse and dense searches). The reciprocal rank score for each chunk is computed. These scores are subsequently aggregated to form a new cumulative score. The resulting hybrid list ranks the chunks based on this composite score.

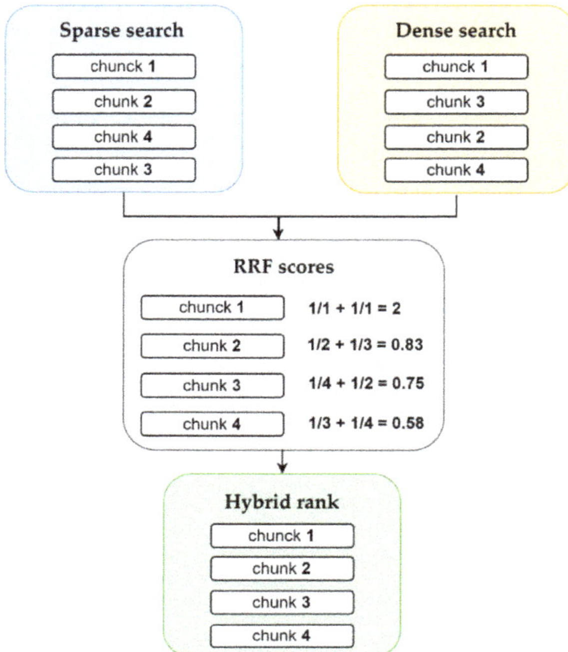

Figure 2. Scheme of hybrid search with RRF algorithm.

3.3. Generator

The subsequent phase employs an answer synthesis component—a generative large language model within a RAG framework. The purpose of these models is to generate text that is coherent, contextually appropriate, and semantically correct in response to a specific query, often known as a prompt. Generative language models function by estimating the probability distribution of the subsequent token based on the preceding tokens. For a given word sequence $w_1, w_2, \ldots w_n$, the goal of a generative language model is to optimize the likelihood of this sequence, which is computed using the chain rule of probability:

$$P(w_1, w_2, \ldots w_n) = \prod_{i=1}^{N} P(w_i | w_1, w_2 \ldots w_{i-1}), \tag{4}$$

Here, $P(w_i|w_1, w_2 \ldots w_{i-1})$ represents the conditional probability of the word w_i, given the prior sequence of words. The generative language model accepts a query q and the fetched documents D_r as input, and it formulates a response by sequentially forecasting the subsequent token in the sequence:

$$P(d|q) \approx \prod_{i}^{N} \sum_{d \in D_r} p_\eta(d|q) \cdot p_\theta(y_i|q, d, y_{1:i-1}) \tag{5}$$

To put it more formally, $p_\eta(d|q)$ is the retrieval component that offers a truncated probability distribution for the highest-ranking documents, while $p_\theta(y_i|q, d, y_{1:i-1})$ is a probability distribution parameterized by θ that generates a current token based on the query, the retrieved document, and the previously generated tokens. This is performed by the LLM.

In the context of dense retrieval, the probability distribution for the highest-ranking documents may take a functional form like $p_{\eta}(d|q) \propto \exp(\overline{q} \cdot \overline{d})$. Such formalization of the RAG process reveals how the generative component depends on the query and the retrieved documents.

Generators Tested

In our experiments, we evaluate multiple LLMs: the open-source model Llama2 [29] with 7B and 13B parameters. For all tested models, we consistently used a greedy generation strategy, limiting the response length to a sentence, with a maximum of 50 tokens. Recognizing the limitations of memory and computational resources, we implemented a strategy to quantize the models, reducing all models to a 4-bit representation using the bitsandbytes library from HuggingFace.

3.4. Required Abilities of Generator

Previous studies have predominantly focused on evaluating the end-to-end performance of systems, particularly in their capacity to handle relevant information. However, a notable challenge arises from the presence of irrelevant or misleading information within external knowledge bases. LLMs frequently encounter difficulties in generating reliable output and are susceptible to being misled by inaccuracies in documents. Consequently, this study shifts the evaluation focus to include the LLMs' ability to manage irrelevant documents and effectively identify and reject misleading information. We have identified three critical abilities essential for LLMs when employing retrieval-augmented generation for question answering: noise robustness, knowledge gap detection, and external truth integration.

1. Noise robustness is the capability of an LLM to extract useful information from contexts filled with noise. This ability is critical as it ensures that LLMs can still function effectively even when the retrieved documents contain irrelevant or misleading data.
2. Knowledge gap detection refers to the LLM's ability to recognize when the necessary knowledge is absent from any retrieved documents and appropriately choose not to answer the question. This capability is vital for preventing the generation of incorrect or misleading responses based on insufficient information.
3. External truth integration: the LLM's capability to provide accurate answers based solely on its non-parametric memory, even when external knowledge initially contradicts general truth facts (stored in the model's parametric knowledge).

3.5. Dataset

To evaluate our proposed approach, we utilize the TriviaQA [30] open-domain dataset. We aligned the TriviaQA open-domain dataset with the SQuAD [31] style of question–answer pairs with corresponding excerpts from evidence documents. TriviaQA is a comprehensive dataset designed to challenge and evaluate short-form question-answering systems. The dataset was sourced from a combination of Wikipedia articles and general web content, providing a rich variety of lexical and syntactic structures. The dataset necessitates reasoning across multiple sentences, making it a robust resource for evaluating the performance of open-domain QA systems.

The initial dataset comprised short-form answers, averaging between 1 and 5 words. To facilitate the study of abstractive question answering, we modified 1100 answers into one-sentence-long answers utilizing the state-of-the-art language model GPT-4. Figure 3 demonstrates the process of creating the test dataset and knowledge base.

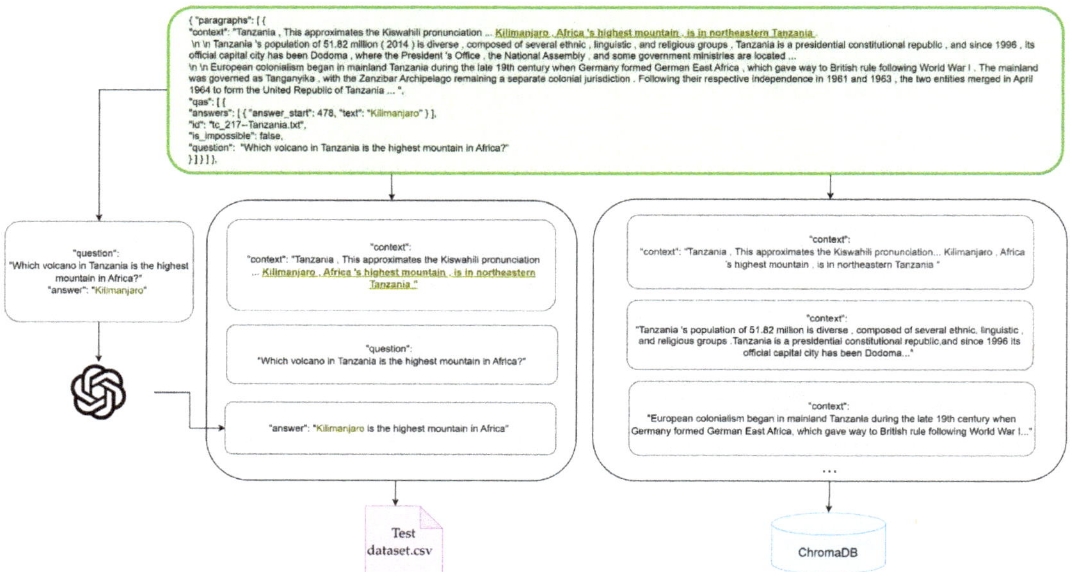

Figure 3. Methodology for test dataset and knowledge base construction.

The unfiltered subset of TriviaQA dataset contains questions that do not have corresponding answer strings. For our system, which relies solely on the knowledge that comes from the vector database, rather than its prior knowledge, those questions must be unanswerable. Such dataset simulates real-world conditions and will subsequently serve as a testbed for evaluating the generator's capabilities to manage irrelevant information. The testbed creation process of 500 questions is illustrated in Figure 4.

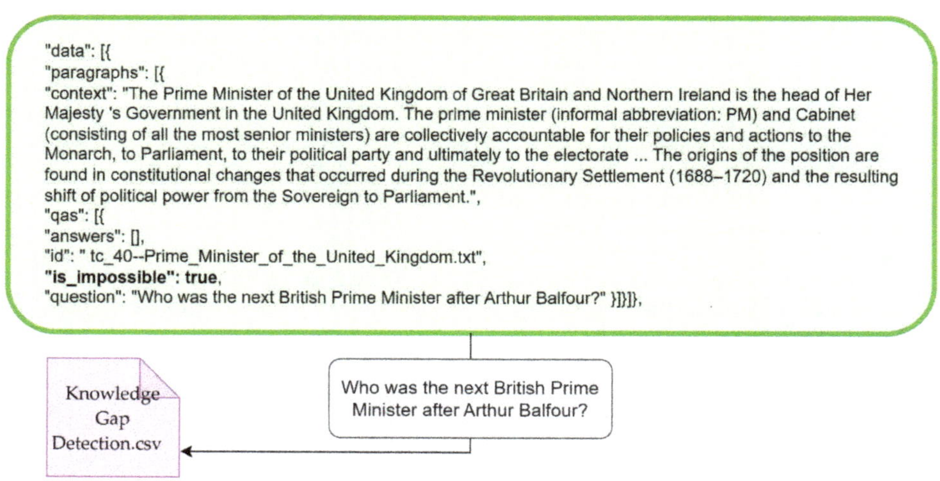

Figure 4. Illustration of testbed creation process with unanswerable questions.

To assess how accurately answers can be provided based on external truths, despite contradictions from the model's internal knowledge, the Contradictions testbed was constructed by modifying 100 question–answer–context pairs from a test dataset. Specifically, the answer texts were altered as shown in Figure 5.

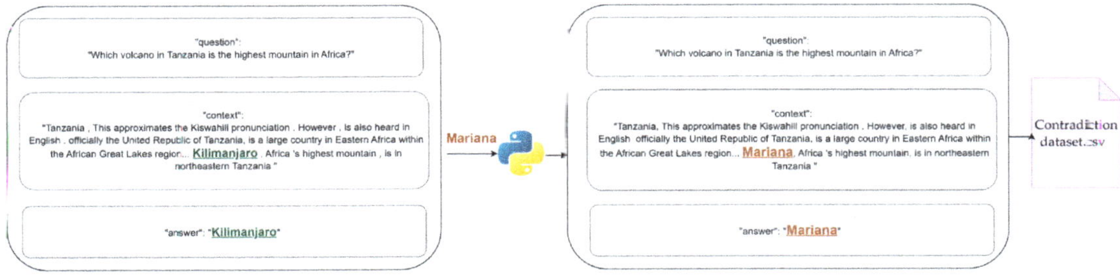

Figure 5. Process of modifying answers for the Contradictions testbed (initial values are shown in green, and the changed values are highlighted in orange).

3.6. Evaluation

3.6.1. Establish the Baseline

To compare the performance of the QA system, we evaluate the following established baselines: closed-book T5 [11], Llama 2 with 7B and 13B [27] parameters, as well as open-book Atlas [32] and RAG [8]. For closed-book settings, only the question was utilized without retrieving any additional context. Additionally, no prompt engineering technique was used.

All baseline works use the exact match score for evaluation. However, it is not suitable for long-form answer evaluation. Previous studies mostly rely on human evaluation [33,34], which is expensive and difficult to reproduce. Traditional long-form answer evaluation metrics, which rely on n-gram-based methods like BLEU, have demonstrated limitations outside of Machine Translation [35]. In such a scenario, the LLMs-as-judges evaluation method emerges as a promising alternative to human evaluation [36], exhibiting the highest similarity to human evaluation compared to other methods [37,38]. Among the LLMs-as-judges metrics, the Retrieval-Augmented Generation Assessment (Ragas) automated framework [39] was chosen.

Ragas provides robust evaluation metrics, with scores ranging from 0 to 1, for both context retrieval and answer generation tasks. For context retrieval, the primary metric is Context Recall, which assesses how well the retrieved context aligns with the ground truth. It measures the proportion of sentences in the ground truth answer that can be found in the retrieved context. For answer generation, Ragas offers two key metrics: Answer Semantic Similarity and Answer Correctness. Answer Semantic Similarity evaluates how closely the generated answer matches the semantics of the ground truth answer. Answer Correctness, on the other hand, considers both semantic and factual aspects, providing a comprehensive evaluation of answer generation performance.

3.6.2. Experimental Settings

Our basic configuration for the QA system includes the following settings: chunk size of 50, no chunk overlap, the embedding model 'all-MiniLM-L12-v2', and a top-k value of 1. During the ablation study, we modify one element at a time to assess its impact across various tasks, comparing different settings for each component:

- LLM versions: Llama 2 13b, Llama 2 7b.
- Retriever: dense, hybrid.
- Top-k values: 1, 2, 3, 5, and 8.

4. Experiments and Results

In this section, we conduct a series of experiments. We validate the performance of the QA system by comparing against baselines on the TriviaQA dataset. Subsequently, we employ ablation studies to evaluate the effectiveness of each component. Finally, we aim to analyze the behaviors of the generators tested.

4.1. The Main Results

In this subsection, we present the main results from our evaluation based on information obtained from the sources. The performance of various approaches on the TriviaQA dataset is summarized in Table 1 below.

Table 1. Performance comparison of baselines, the highest results in each approach are shown in bold.

Approach	Model, Work	TriviaQA
Closed-book	Llama 2 7b, [29]	65.8
	Llama 2 13b, [29]	**73.1**
	T5-11B, [11]	50.1
	T5-11B + SSM, [11]	60.5
Open-book	RAG-Token, [8]	66.1
	RAG-Seq, [8]	68.0
	Atlas-XL + CIT, [32]	77.4
	QA-$RAG_{llama2-7b}$, (ours)	69
	QA-$RAG_{llama2-13b}$, (ours)	**83.3**

In closed-book scenarios, Llama 2 13b achieved the highest accuracy of 73.1%, while T5-11B performed least effectively at 50.1%. Among the open-book methods, Atlas-XL + CIT achieved an accuracy of 77.4%, while RAG-Token and RAG-Seq achieved accuracies of 66.1% and 68.0%, respectively. Our approach demonstrated the highest accuracy of 83.3%, showcasing its effectiveness across both closed-book and open-book settings.

Based on the ablation study, the optimal configuration for achieving the best results involved using Llama 2 13b as the generator, coupled with a dense retriever and a top-k value of 1. This setup consistently delivered superior performance compared to other configurations tested, highlighting its effectiveness in the context of this study's experiments.

4.2. Ablation Study on Retriever

The experiments were performed to compare various retrieval methods using the Context Recall metric. The results, detailed in Table 2, reveal that the dense retriever achieved the highest performance with a top-k value of 1, attaining a context recall of 95%, demonstrating its strong capability to accurately retrieve the most relevant context passages.

Table 2. Performance comparison of dense vs. sparse retrievers (highest result in bold).

Retriever Type	Top-k	Context Recall
Dense	1	**0.95**
	2	0.863
	3	0.703
	4	0.471
Hybrid	2	0.844
	3	0.692
	4	0.483

The high performance of the dense retriever may be due to the fact that the questions in the dataset do not always align word for word with the answers and necessitate the analysis of multiple sentences to derive an answer. The nature of the task is abstractive rather than extractive, thereby exposing the limitations of the sparse retriever.

4.3. Knowledge Gap Detection

The LLMs were tasked with answering 500 questions in a testbed. They were instructed to respond "No" when the required information was absent from the retrieved documents. This experimental design aimed to simulate scenarios where LLMs must make informed decisions about whether to answer based on the completeness of available knowledge. The exact match score in Table 3 indicates the percentage of correctly identified unanswerable questions.

Table 3. Knowledge gap detection performance of LLMs.

LLM	EM
Llama 2 7b	0.66
Llama 2 13b	0.78

Specifically, the Llama 2 7b model attempted to answer 170 questions and rejected 330 questions due to the lack of necessary information, amounting to 66%. The Llama 2 13b model attempted to answer 110 questions and rejected 390 questions, accounting for 78%.

4.4. Noise Robustness Results

This experiment evaluated the noise robustness of the generators, measuring their ability to extract useful information from contexts containing varying degrees of noise. Noise refers to retrieved irrelevant or misleading documents. The experiment was specifically constructed to vary the number of retrieval documents (top-k from 1 to 3, 5, and 8) provided to the LLM, thereby introducing varying levels of noise. A noise value of 0 ensured that only the exact relevant context was provided. This experimental setup aimed to simulate real-world scenarios where LLMs must operate effectively amidst noise and irrelevant data. Figure 6 presents the results.

The results indicate that creating a retriever that extracts the relevant context with minimal noise is a crucial factor that improves the quality of answers. However, even if the retriever accurately provides the necessary information, reliable answers are not guaranteed.

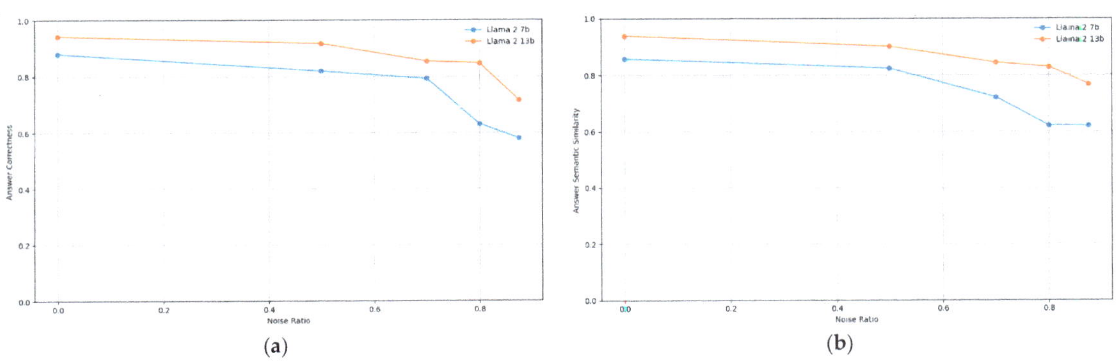

Figure 6. Performance of Llama 7b and 13b generators on noise robustness ability: (**a**) Answer Correctness metric; (**b**) Answer Semantic Similarity metric.

4.5. External Truth Integration

To investigate the discrepancy between the quality of retrieved context and the reliability of the answers generated by the system based on that context, we conducted the experiment exploring external truth integration.

Hypothetically, the system should rely solely on non-parametric memory, where knowledge can be easily modified (updated, deleted), unlike the knowledge stored in the model's parametric memory. This is achieved through the prompts that instruct the model's behavior accordingly. We employed prompts of three styles—strict, standard, and weak (Figure 7)—to evaluate the responses of LLMs in the Contradictions testbed. The results are as shown in Figure 8.

STRICT PROMPT

You HAVE TO answer ONLY based on the context. Do not introduce any new information. If the context does not contain the information requested, state 'I don't know. Don't make up an answer.

STANDARD PROMPT

Use the following pieces of context to answer the question. If you don't know the answer, just say that you don't know. Don't try to make up an answer.

WEAK PROMPT

Consider the following context when answering the question. Don't try to make up an answer.

Figure 7. Strict, standard, and weak prompts used in the experiment.

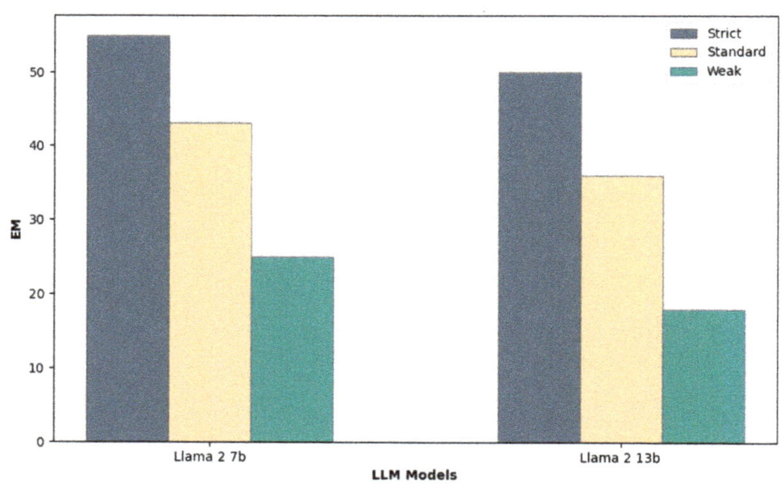

Figure 8. LLM responses to contradictions: prompt style impact.

From the results, we observe that while the type of prompt significantly influences answer alignment (with stricter prompts aligning more closely with external knowledge), the prompt alone is insufficient to fully adjust the system's behavior. Even when the retriever accurately provides necessary information, reliable answers are not assured as the generator may prefer the knowledge embedded in its training data.

The lack of clear guidelines on how models combine knowledge in answer evidence documents with prior knowledge can lead to problems. With LLMs set to be widely used in various fields, users and developers must be aware of potential unintended consequences, especially if they assume RAG-enabled systems are always truthful.

There are two main limitations in our study: (1) QA_RAG was only tested on factoid questions without involving complex reasoning; (2) we did not evaluate the system on GPT-3.5 and GPT-4 due to cost constraints, which prevented us from conducting comprehensive evaluations on other state-of-the-art models.

5. Conclusions

In this study, we rigorously evaluated QA systems using the TriviaQA dataset, comparing closed-book and open-book approaches. Based on the comprehensive evaluation, several key insights and findings emerged. Firstly, all Llama 2 models perform better in the open-book setting compared to the closed-book setting. This highlights the advantage of enabling models to access external information sources during answer generation. Our proposed $\text{QA-RAG}_{\text{llama2-13b}}$ approach excelled with the highest score of 83.3%. Secondly, the ablation study highlighted the efficacy of a dense retriever, achieving a context recall of 95%, crucial for enhancing system performance through precise context retrieval. Additionally, the investigation of knowledge gap detection ability revealed that Llama 2 13b correctly identified unanswerable questions, achieving 78% accuracy compared to 66% for Llama 2 7b. The results underscore the critical importance of developing retrievers capable of extracting relevant context with minimal noise. However, despite effective retrieval, the reliability of answers remains somewhat unpredictable. Finally, our exploration integration of information that contradicts general truth facts into the knowledge base emphasized the complex underlying tension between a model's prior knowledge and the information presented in reference documents, highlighting room for future research and improvements.

Author Contributions: Conceptualization, A.N.; data curation, A.M. (Aiganym Mansurova); formal analysis, A.M. (Aigerim Mansurova); funding acquisition, A.N.; investigation, A.M. (Aigerim Mansurova) and A.M. (Aiganym Mansurova); methodology, A.M. (Aigerim Mansurova); project administration, A.N.; resources, A.M. (Aigerim Mansurova); software, A.M. (Aigerim Mansurova); supervision, A.N.; validation, A.M. (Aigerim Mansurova); visualization, A.M. (Aiganym Mansurova); writing—original draft, A.M. (Aigerim Mansurova). All authors have read and agreed to the published version of the manuscript.

Funding: This research was funded by the Ministry of Science and Higher Education of the Republic of Kazakhstan, grant number AP19677756.

Data Availability Statement: The code and datasets used in this study are available in the GitHub repository https://github.com/Tbinma/Exploring-LLM-Reliance-on-External-Knowledge (accessed on 1 August 2024).

Acknowledgments: We express our sincere gratitude to Aliya Kalykulova for her invaluable assistance in collecting the data used in this study.

Conflicts of Interest: The authors declare no conflict of interest.

References

1. OpenAI. *ChatGPT* (Mar 14 Version) [Large Language Model]. 2023. Available online: https://chat.openai.com/chat (accessed on 17 June 2024).
2. Chase, H. *LangChain*; GitHub: San Francisco, CA, USA, 2022. Available online: https://github.com/langchain-ai/langchain (accessed on 17 October 2022).
3. Bang, Y.; Cahyawijaya, S.; Lee, N.; Dai, W.; Su, D.; Wilie, B.; Lovenia, H.; Ji, Z.; Yu, T.; Chung, W.; et al. A multitask, multilingual, multimodal evaluation of chatgpt on reasoning, hallucination, and interactivity. *arXiv* **2023**, arXiv:2302.04023.
4. Guo, C.; Lu, Y.; Dou, Y.; Wang, F.Y. Can ChatGPT boost artistic creation: The need of imaginative intelligence for parallel art. *IEEE/CAA J. Autom. Sin.* **2023**, *10*, 835–838. [CrossRef]

5. Ji, Z.; Lee, N.; Frieske, R.; Yu, T.; Su, D.; Xu, Y.; Ishii, E.; Bang, Y.J.; Madotto, A.; Fung, P. Survey of hallucination in natural language generation. *ACM Comput. Surv.* **2023**, *55*, 1–38. [CrossRef]
6. He, H.; Zhang, H.; Roth, D. Rethinking with retrieval: Faithful large language model inference. *arXiv* **2022**, arXiv:2301.00303.
7. Shen, X.; Chen, Z.; Backes, M.; Zhang, Y. In ChatGPT we trust? measuring and characterizing the reliability of ChatGPT. *arXiv* **2023**, arXiv:2304.08979.
8. Lewis, P.; Perez, E.; Piktus, A.; Petroni, F.; Karpukhin, V.; Goyal, N.; Küttler, H.; Lewis, M.; Yih, W.; Kiela, D.; et al. Retrieval-augmented generation for knowledge-intensive nlp tasks. *Adv. Neural Inf. Process. Syst.* **2020**, *33*, 9459–9474.
9. Gao, Y.; Xiong, Y.; Gao, X.; Jia, K.; Pan, J.; Bi, Y.; Dai, Y.; Sun, J.; Wang, M.; Wang, H.; et al. Retrieval-augmented generation for large language models: A survey. *arXiv* **2023**, arXiv:2312.10997.
10. Borgeaud, S.; Mensch, A.; Hoffmann, J.; Cai, T.; Rutherford, E.; Millican, K.; Van Den Driessche, G.B.; Lespiau, J.-B.; Damoc, B.; Sifre, L.; et al. Improving language models by retrieving from trillions of tokens. In Proceedings of the International Conference on Machine Learning, Baltimore, MD, USA, 17–23 July 2022; PMLR. pp. 2206–2240.
11. Roberts, A.; Raffel, C.; Shazeer, N. How much knowledge can you pack into the parameters of a language model? *arXiv* **2020**, arXiv:2002.08910.
12. Elaraby, M.; Lu, M.; Dunn, J.; Zhang, X.; Wang, Y.; Liu, S. Halo: Estimation and reduction of hallucinations in open-source weak large language models. *arXiv* **2023**, arXiv:2308.11764.
13. Stechly, K.; Marquez, M.; Kambhampati, S. GPT-4 Doesn't Know It's Wrong: An Analysis of Iterative Prompting for Reasoning Problems. *arXiv* **2023**, arXiv:2310.12397.
14. Huang, R.; Li, M.; Yang, D.; Shi, J.; Chang, X.; Ye, Z.; Wu, Y.; Hong, Z.; Huang, J.; Watanabe, S.; et al. Audiogpt: Understanding and generating speech, music, sound, and talking head. In Proceedings of the AAAI Conference on Artificial Intelligence, Vancouver, BC, Canada, 20–27 February 2024; Volume 38, pp. 23802–23804.
15. Izacard, G.; Lewis, P.; Lomeli, M.; Hosseini, L.; Petroni, F.; Schick, T.; Dwivedi-Yu, J.; Joulin, A.; Riedel, S.; Grave, E.; et al. Atlas: Few-shot learning with retrieval augmented language models. *J. Mach. Learn. Res.* **2023**, *24*, 1–43.
16. Guu, K.; Lee, K.; Tung, Z.; Pasupat, P.; Chang, M. Retrieval augmented language model pre-training. In Proceedings of the International Conference on Machine Learning, Vienna, Austria, 13–18 July 2020; PMLR; pp. 3929–3938.
17. Trivedi, H.; Balasubramanian, N.; Khot, T.; Sabharwal, A. Interleaving retrieval with chain-of-thought reasoning for knowledge-intensive multi-step questions. *arXiv* **2022**, arXiv:2212.10509.
18. Chen, J.; Lin, H.; Han, X.; Sun, L. Benchmarking large language models in retrieval-augmented generation. In Proceedings of the AAAI Conference on Artificial Intelligence, Vancouver, BC, Canada, 20–27 February 2024; Volume 38, pp. 17754–17762.
19. Wang, H.; Huang, W.; Deng, Y.; Wang, R.; Wang, Z.; Wang, Y.; Mi, F.; Pan, J.Z.; Wong, K.F. UniMS-RAG: A Unified Multi-source Retrieval-Augmented Generation for Personalized Dialogue Systems. *arXiv* **2024**, arXiv:2401.13256.
20. Mansurova, A.; Nugumanova, A.; Makhambetova, Z. Development of a question answering chatbot for blockchain domain. *Sci. J. Astana IT Univ.* **2023**, *15*, 27–40. [CrossRef]
21. Jacob, T.P.; Bizotto BL, S.; Sathiyanarayanan, M. Constructing the ChatGPT for PDF Files with Langchain–AI. In Proceedings of the 2024 International Conference on Inventive Computation Technologies (ICICT), Bangkok, Thailand, 16–17 April 2024; IEEE: Piscataway, NJ, USA, 2024; pp. 835–839.
22. Topsakal, O.; Akinci, T.C. Creating large language model applications utilizing langchain: A primer on developing llm apps fast. In Proceedings of the International Conference on Applied Engineering and Natural Sciences, Konya, Turkey, 10–12 July 2023; Volume 1, pp. 1050–1056.
23. Pandya, K.; Holia, M. Automating Customer Service using LangChain: Building custom open-source GPT Chatbot for organizations. *arXiv* **2023**, arXiv:2310.05421.
24. Singh, A.; Ehtesham, A.; Mahmud, S.; Kim, J.H. Revolutionizing Mental Health Care through LangChain: A Journey with a Large Language Model. In Proceedings of the 2024 IEEE 14th Annual Computing and Communication Workshop and Conference (CCWC), Las Vegas, NV, USA, 8–10 January 2024; IEEE: Piscataway, NJ, USA, 2024; pp. 73–78.
25. Devlin, J.; Chang, M.W.; Lee, K.; Toutanova, K. Bert: Pre-training of deep bidirectional transformers for language understanding. *arXiv* **2018**, arXiv:1810.04805.
26. Lyu, Y.; Li, Z.; Niu, S.; Xiong, F.; Tang, B.; Wang, W.; Wu, H.; Liu, H.; Xu, T.; Chen, E. CRUD-RAG: A comprehensive chinese benchmark for retrieval-augmented generation of large language models. *arXiv* **2024**, arXiv:2401.17043.
27. Cormack, G.V.; Clarke, C.L.; Buettcher, S. Reciprocal rank fusion outperforms condorcet and individual rank learning methods. In Proceedings of the 32nd International ACM SIGIR Conference on Research and Development in Information Retrieval, Boston, MA, USA, 19–23 July 2009; pp. 758–759.
28. Ni, J.; Qu, C.; Lu, J.; Dai, Z.; Abrego, G.H.; Ma, J.; Zhao, V.; Luan, Y.; Hall, K.; Chang, M.-W.; et al. Large dual encoders are generalizable retrievers. *arXiv* **2021**, arXiv:2112.07899.
29. Touvron, H.; Martin, L.; Stone, K.; Albert, P.; Almahairi, A.; Babaei, Y.; Bashlykov, N.; Batra, S.; Bhargava, P.; Scialom, T.; et al. Llama 2: Open foundation and fine-tuned chat models. *arXiv* **2023**, arXiv:2307.09288.
30. Joshi, M.; Choi, E.; Weld, D.S.; Zettlemoyer, L. Triviaqa: A large scale distantly supervised challenge dataset for reading comprehension. *arXiv* **2017**, arXiv:1705.03551.
31. Rajpurkar, P.; Zhang, J.; Lopyrev, K.; Liang, P. Squad: 100,000+ questions for machine comprehension of text. *arXiv* **2016**, arXiv:1606.05250.

32. Zhang, Z.; Reddy, R.G.; Small, K.; Zhang, T.; Ji, H. Towards Better Generalization in Open-Domain Question Answering by Mitigating Context Memorization. *arXiv* **2024**, arXiv:2404.01652.
33. Liu, Y.; Huang, L.; Li, S.; Chen, S.; Zhou, H.; Meng, F.; Zhou, J.; Sun, X. Recall: A benchmark for llms robustness against external counterfactual knowledge. *arXiv* **2023**, arXiv:2311.08147.
34. Nakano, R.; Hilton, J.; Balaji, S.; Wu, J.; Ouyang, L.; Kim, C.; Hesse, C.; Jain, S.; Kosaraju, V.; Schulman, J.; et al. Webgpt: Browser-assisted question-answering with human feedback. *arXiv* **2021**, arXiv:2112.09332.
35. Reiter, E. A structured review of the validity of BLEU. *Comput. Linguist.* **2018**, *44*, 393–401. [CrossRef]
36. Chiang, C.H.; Lee, H.Y. Can large language models be an alternative to human evaluations? *arXiv* **2023**, arXiv:2305.01937.
37. Liu, Y.; Iter, D.; Xu, Y.; Wang, S.; Xu, R.; Zhu, C. Gpteval: Nlg evaluation using gpt-4 with better human alignment. *arXiv* **2023**, arXiv:2303.16634.
38. Svikhnushina, E.; Pu, P. Approximating online human evaluation of social chatbots with prompting. In Proceedings of the 24th Annual Meeting of the Special Interest Group on Discourse and Dialogue, Prague, Czechia, 11–15 September 2023; pp. 268–281.
39. Es, S.; James, J.; Espinosa-Anke, L.; Schockaert, S. Ragas: Automated evaluation of retrieval augmented generation. *arXiv* **2023**, arXiv:2309.15217.

big data and cognitive computing

MDPI

Article

LLMs and NLP Models in Cryptocurrency Sentiment Analysis: A Comparative Classification Study

Konstantinos I. Roumeliotis [1,*], Nikolaos D. Tselikas [1] and Dimitrios K. Nasiopoulos [2]

[1] Department of Informatics and Telecommunications, University of Peloponnese, Akadimaikou G. K. Vlachou Street, 22131 Tripoli, Greece; ntsel@uop.gr

[2] Department of Agribusiness and Supply Chain Management, School of Applied Economics and Social Sciences, Agricultural University of Athens, 11855 Athens, Greece; dimnas@aua.gr

* Correspondence: k.roumeliotis@uop.gr; Tel.: +30-271-037-2216

Abstract: Cryptocurrencies are becoming increasingly prominent in financial investments, with more investors diversifying their portfolios and individuals drawn to their ease of use and decentralized financial opportunities. However, this accessibility also brings significant risks and rewards, often influenced by news and the sentiments of crypto investors, known as crypto signals. This paper explores the capabilities of large language models (LLMs) and natural language processing (NLP) models in analyzing sentiment from cryptocurrency-related news articles. We fine-tune state-of-the-art models such as GPT-4, BERT, and FinBERT for this specific task, evaluating their performance and comparing their effectiveness in sentiment classification. By leveraging these advanced techniques, we aim to enhance the understanding of sentiment dynamics in the cryptocurrency market, providing insights that can inform investment decisions and risk management strategies. The outcomes of this comparative study contribute to the broader discourse on applying advanced NLP models to cryptocurrency sentiment analysis, with implications for both academic research and practical applications in financial markets.

Keywords: cryptocurrency sentiment analysis; cryptocurrency classification; news sentiment analysis; llms cryptocurrency; nlp cryptocurrency; crypto signals; trading signals; cryptocurrency news; news classification

1. Introduction

In recent years, cryptocurrencies have emerged as a significant asset class in the global financial landscape, attracting substantial interest from investors seeking diversification and alternative investment opportunities. The decentralized nature and technological innovations underpinning cryptocurrencies, such as Bitcoin and Ethereum, have reshaped traditional financial paradigms, introducing new dynamics driven by market sentiment and information dissemination.

The volatility of cryptocurrency markets is often influenced by a myriad of factors, including news articles, social media discussions, crypto signals, and investor sentiment [1–3]. Understanding and accurately gauging sentiment in this rapidly evolving environment is essential for making informed investment decisions and managing risks effectively. As a result, sentiment analysis techniques using advanced natural language processing (NLP) models have gained traction as valuable tools for extracting sentiment from textual data related to cryptocurrencies.

By understanding public sentiment for a specific cryptocurrency in advance and monitoring market tension, we can predict price movements. Negative sentiment in the crypto market often leads to price drops, while positive sentiment tends to drive price increases. For instance, the recent fear of potential conflict between Israel and Iran caused a marginal 10% decrease in the value of all cryptocurrencies.

In this context, our study focuses on the comparative analysis of large language models (LLMs) and NLP techniques in the domain of cryptocurrency sentiment analysis. Specifically, we investigate the efficacy of fine-tuned models such as GPT-4, BERT, and FinBERT for discerning sentiment from cryptocurrency news articles. By leveraging the capabilities of these sophisticated language models, we aim to explore how effectively they can capture nuanced sentiment patterns, thus contributing to a deeper understanding of sentiment dynamics within the cryptocurrency market.

The primary objectives of this study are twofold: firstly, to evaluate the performance of LLMs and NLP models in cryptocurrency sentiment analysis through a comparative classification study, providing insights that can inform investment strategies and risk management practices within cryptocurrency markets; and secondly, to address specific research inquiries that previous studies have not adequately covered.

- Q1: Among the fine-tuned models of GPT-4, BERT, and FinBERT, which one demonstrates superior predictive capabilities in cryptocurrency news sentiment analysis and classification?
- Q2: What is the impact of fine-tuning LLMs and NLP models for specific tasks?

To fulfill the goals of our study, we undertake an extensive review of the existing literature on sentiment analysis and classification pertaining to cryptocurrencies in Section 2. Section 3 details the materials and methodology utilized in this study, while Section 4 provides the prediction outcomes for all three models and their variations before and after fine-tuning. In Section 5, we delve into a detailed discussion of the results, extracting valuable insights derived from our research findings.

2. Literature Review

Cryptocurrency sentiment analysis involves employing sophisticated NLP models to analyze textual data sources like news articles, social media posts, forums, and blogs related to cryptocurrencies. The primary objective is to extract and quantify sentiment—whether positive, negative, or neutral—expressed in these texts to comprehend the prevailing market sentiment towards specific cryptocurrencies or the broader market as a whole.

The significance of cryptocurrency sentiment analysis in financial markets is underscored by several compelling reasons:

- Market sentiment understanding: Cryptocurrency markets are highly sensitive to sentiment influenced by news events, social media trends, regulatory developments, and investor perceptions [4]. Sentiment analysis aids in assessing the prevailing sentiment and mood of market participants, offering insights into potential market movements.
- Insights into investor behavior: By analyzing sentiment, researchers and investors gain valuable insights into investor behavior and sentiment dynamics [5,6]. Understanding investor sentiment facilitates predicting market trends, identifying sentiment shifts, and assessing associated risks.
- Decision-making support: Sentiment analysis plays a pivotal role in guiding investment decisions. Traders and investors leverage sentiment-driven insights to make informed decisions; positive sentiment may signal buying opportunities, while negative sentiment could prompt caution or sell signals [7,8].
- Risk management: Assessing sentiment contributes to managing risks linked with cryptocurrency investments [9]. Sudden shifts in sentiment towards specific cryptocurrencies could indicate potential price volatility or market downturns.

In the cryptocurrency ecosystem, sentiment analysis offers unique advantages owing to the decentralized and rapidly evolving nature of cryptocurrencies. The wealth of online data sources, including social media platforms and cryptocurrency news websites, renders sentiment analysis particularly relevant and valuable for comprehending market behavior and investor sentiment in this domain.

By harnessing sentiment analysis techniques, researchers and market participants attain deeper insights into the factors driving cryptocurrency markets, empowering them to make more informed decisions based on sentiment-driven intelligence. This underscores the pivotal role of sentiment analysis in enriching market intelligence and facilitating effective decision-making within the dynamic and volatile cryptocurrency landscape.

2.1. NLP in Sentiment Analysis

NLP is integral to the field of sentiment analysis, offering tailored techniques to effectively extract sentiment from textual data. In sentiment analysis, NLP methods are essential for discerning the emotions and opinions conveyed through language. Some of the most widely used techniques and applications within financial contexts include:

- Sentiment lexicons: Sentiment lexicons are curated dictionaries featuring words or phrases annotated with sentiment scores (e.g., positive, negative, neutral) [7], aiding sentiment analysis by quantifying sentiment from specific word usage. Widely used lexicons like SentiWordNet and Vader are foundational resources. In financial sentiment analysis, specialized lexicons capturing financial terminology enhance accuracy by accounting for domain-specific expressions and market conditions.
- Deep learning approaches: Deep learning architectures, such as convolutional neural networks (CNNs), recurrent neural networks (RNNs), and bidirectional encoder representations from transformers (BERT) are extensively applied in sentiment analysis [10]. CNNs are effective for feature extraction, while RNNs excel in sequence modeling [11], and BERT specializes in capturing contextual information from language. Their application demonstrates remarkable accuracy in deciphering intricate patterns within text. These models undergo fine-tuning with financial datasets to better understand the nuances of financial language, thereby improving sentiment analysis in financial markets. Furthermore, integrating domain-specific features through NLP techniques enhances their effectiveness, enabling the extraction of meaningful signals from financial text data [12].

2.2. Previous Studies on Sentiment Analysis in Cryptocurrencies

Our literature review presents a comprehensive overview of 49 papers on the evolving role of sentiment analysis in understanding and predicting cryptocurrency market dynamics. The studies showcase a diverse array of methodologies, ranging from traditional sentiment analysis to cutting-edge deep learning models, that highlight the significant impact of sentiment-driven factors on cryptocurrency price movements and investor behavior. By leveraging data sources such as social media platforms, news articles, and market indicators, researchers demonstrate the potential of sentiment analysis to provide valuable insights for navigating the volatile cryptocurrency landscape and making informed investment decisions. Despite the progress made, challenges such as bias mitigation in sentiment data and the nuanced interplay between sentiment and fundamental market factors underscore the ongoing need for further exploration and refinement in this burgeoning field of research. Through innovative approaches and practical applications, the reviewed studies collectively contribute to advancing sentiment analysis as a powerful tool for cryptocurrency market analysis and decision-making.

2.2.1. Traditional Supervised Learning

Seven papers have explored cryptocurrencies using traditional supervised learning techniques. Notably, Rouhani et al. [7] identified a prevailing positive sentiment towards cryptocurrencies on Twitter, indicating the potential for accurate sentiment prediction through supervised methods like SVM. Colianni et al. [13] achieved notably high prediction accuracies in algorithmic trading strategies based on Twitter sentiment analysis, highlighting the feasibility of utilizing sentiment data for effective trading strategies. Loginova et al. [14] made significant advancements in directional cryptocurrency price prediction by integrating fine-grained sentiment analysis into online textual data, showcasing the effectiveness of innovative sentiment analysis techniques. Sureshbhai et al. [9] introduced KaRuNa, a blockchain-based sentiment analysis framework addressing risks in cryptocurrency schemes, achieving remarkable accuracy in risk assessment. Köse Ozan [15] automated the classification of crypto assets and sentiment analysis of news, providing valuable tools for informed decision-making based on the sentiment analysis of news sources. Ghazanfar et al. [16] successfully integrated social media sentiment analysis into cryptocurrency price prediction models, emphasizing its importance for financial forecasting. Seroyizhko et al. [17] introduced a sentiment and emotion annotated dataset for Bitcoin price forecasting based on Reddit posts, advocating for sophisticated social media integration techniques in crypto market analysis.

2.2.2. Deep Learning

Thirteen of the papers have utilized deep learning to enhance cryptocurrency price prediction. Huang et al. [1] pioneered the integration of sentiment from Chinese social media platform Sina-Weibo into LSTM models, demonstrating superior performance over traditional methods in predicting cryptocurrency prices. Building upon this approach, Parekh et al. [18] introduced DL-GuesS, a framework combining deep learning and sentiment analysis to forecast Dash and Bitcoin Cash prices based on historical data and Twitter sentiment. Raju et al. [19] further emphasized the significance of public sentiment by correlating Twitter and Reddit data with Bitcoin prices, achieving enhanced accuracy through supervised learning algorithms. Pant et al. [10] extended this sentiment analysis to predict Bitcoin price volatility using RNNs, offering insights into market sentiment dynamics. Pang et al. [20] highlighted the superiority of sentiment data models over conventional approaches in capturing market dynamics and predicting price fluctuations through machine learning techniques. Farimani et al. [21] contributed a methodology leveraging latent economic concepts and sentiments in financial news for market prediction, offering superior performance compared to baselines. Gadi et al. [22] investigated annotator selection's impact on sentiment corpus creation, while Farimani et al. [23] integrated sentiment analysis with technical indicators for real-time market prediction tools. Zamani et al. [2] developed an XLNet-GRU sentiment regression model for cryptocurrency news, showcasing effectiveness across languages. Nasekin et al. [24] constructed sentiment indices from StockTwits data, informing cryptocurrency market returns and volatility prediction. Wołk et al. [25] analyzed social media sentiment's impact on cryptocurrency prices, emphasizing psychological and behavioral attitudes. Vo [26] focused on the sentiment analysis of news for Ethereum price prediction, providing actionable insights for investors. Aslam et al. [27] emphasized understanding public sentiment towards cryptocurrency, achieving high accuracy through ensemble deep learning models.

2.2.3. Lexicon-Based Sentiment Analysis

Six of the examined papers utilized lexicon-based sentiment analysis for cryptocurrency price forecasting. Chen et al. [4] utilized sentiment data from StockTwits to investigate sentiment-induced bubbles, employing a smooth transition autoregression model to identify speculative bubbles and linking sentiment dynamics with market volatility. Their findings suggested that sentiment-driven exuberance can lead to locally explosive price dynamics, characteristic of speculative bubbles. Erdogan et al. [8] focused on the sentiment analysis of social media data, specifically Twitter, to discern user perceptions of cryptocurrencies. Through big data tools, they analyzed Twitter data to extract insights and classify user attitudes, providing valuable insights into public sentiment towards crypto assets, which can inform market strategies. Dwivedi et al. [28] contributed to understanding sentiment evolution pre- and post-COVID-19 using topic modeling techniques on Twitter data, extracting key themes in public sentiment towards Bitcoin and cryptocurrency. Şaşmaz et al. [29] delved into tweet sentiment analysis for cryptocurrencies like NEO, exploring correlations between sentiment and daily prices through an RF classifier trained on labeled tweet data. They demonstrated the feasibility of using automated sentiment analysis for cryptocurrency trading decisions based on Twitter data. Kraaijeveld et al. [30] explored the predictive capacity of Twitter sentiment across multiple cryptocurrencies, finding predictive power for returns in specific cryptocurrencies such as Bitcoin, Bitcoin Cash, and Litecoin. Additionally, they detected cryptocurrency-related Twitter bot accounts, highlighting the complexity of sentiment analysis in this domain. Gurrib et al. [31] introduced a machine learning approach, combining linear discriminant analysis and sentiment analysis to predict Bitcoin price movements, leveraging BTC price data and crypto-related news sentiment to forecast next-day price directions.

2.2.4. BERT and Transformer Models

Four studies have utilized BERT and other transformer-based models to delve into the understanding and prediction of cryptocurrency market behavior. Ider et al. [32] employed BERT classifiers and weak supervision techniques to improve the predictive power of text-based features for cryptocurrency return prediction. Their incorporation of weak labeling techniques addresses the challenge of unlabeled text data, showcasing the potential of NLP advancements in financial forecasting models. Similarly, Kulakowski et al. [33] developed sentiment classification solutions tailored to cryptocurrency-related social media posts, such as CryptoBERT and LUKE sentiment lexicon. Their study fine-tuned BERT models and integrated emoji sentiment analysis, offering investors tools for sentiment-based trading strategies. Nguyen Thanh et al. [34] explored ChatGPT for the sentiment analysis of Twitter data and its impact on Bitcoin returns, underscoring the influence of AI-generated sentiment indicators on market dynamics. Lastly, Raheman et al. [35] examined various NLP models for sentiment analysis in the cryptocurrency domain, emphasizing the importance of interpretable AI methods in practical financial prediction tasks. Their study highlighted correlations between sentiment metrics and Bitcoin price movements, shedding light on sentiment-driven market dynamics.

2.2.5. Time-Series Analysis

In their study, Georgoula et al. [36] utilized a combination of time-series analysis and sentiment analysis to probe the determinants of Bitcoin prices. Leveraging machine learning techniques such as SVMs, they scrutinized sentiment data sourced from Twitter feeds, alongside economic and technological factors. Their findings unveiled noteworthy correlations: a positive relationship between Twitter sentiment ratio, public interest gauged through Wikipedia searches, and Bitcoin prices. Conversely, they underscored the negative influences of exchange rates and stock market indices on Bitcoin's valuation. Meanwhile, Chalkiadakis et al. [37] introduced a novel framework aimed at evaluating multimodal statistical causality within cryptocurrency markets. By employing multiple-output Gaussian processes and delving into sentiment time-series data, their research delved into the intricate causal relationships between sentiment, price dynamics, and blockchain indicators. Through their investigation, they shed light on sentiment-driven market behaviors and the consequential impacts of investor sentiment on cryptocurrency market dynamics.

2.2.6. Computational Text Analysis

Anamika et al. [38] focused on assessing the influence of investor sentiment, particularly towards Bitcoin, on cryptocurrency returns. Using a direct survey-based measure from the sentix database, they found that optimistic sentiment among investors correlates with Bitcoin price appreciation. This sentiment measure also holds predictive power for Bitcoin prices even after accounting for other relevant factors. Moreover, they noted that Bitcoin sentiment can influence the prices of other cryptocurrencies, suggesting a broader impact on the market beyond Bitcoin itself. In a similar vein, Bouteska et al. [39] explored the predictive power of investor sentiment for Bitcoin returns during the COVID-19 pandemic. Using computational text analysis on social media messages, they constructed a sentiment index and analyzed its impact on cryptocurrency market returns through vector autoregressive analysis. Their findings suggest that investor sentiment significantly influences Bitcoin returns, especially in the short term, demonstrating practical implications for investors.

2.2.7. Hybrid Models

Seven papers adopt hybrid approaches to improve cryptocurrency price prediction. Critien et al. [40] investigated the relationship between Twitter sentiment and Bitcoin price changes, employing neural network models to enhance prediction accuracy. Similarly, Girsang et al. [41] proposed a hybrid LSTM and GRU model integrating social network sentiment analysis to forecast cryptocurrency prices, surpassing benchmark models in performance. Serafini et al. [11] explored the sentiment-driven price prediction of Bitcoin, comparing statistical and deep learning approaches, highlighting the significance of sentiment in predicting market stocks. Chalkiadakis et al. [42] developed a hybrid ARDL-MIDAS-Transformer model, emphasizing the interplay between sentiment, price dynamics, and technology factors in cryptocurrency markets. Li et al. [43] focused on the sentiment analysis of Twitter data to predict ZClassic price fluctuations, revealing a strong correlation between predicted and actual price movements. Valencia et al. [44] leveraged machine learning techniques to predict cryptocurrency price movements across multiple coins, showcasing the effectiveness of sentiment analysis in forecasting market behavior. Finally, Amirshahi et al. [45] proposed a hybrid neural network model utilizing sentiment extracted from tweets for cryptocurrency price prediction, shedding light on the role of social media sentiment in financial forecasting.

2.2.8. Other Techniques

Finally, eight papers employed a diverse set of technologies, including sentiment analysis, statistical methods, and text preprocessing techniques, to comprehend and forecast cryptocurrency market behavior. Lamon et al. [5] leveraged labeled news and social media data for cryptocurrency price prediction, utilizing sentiment analysis as a core technology to directly correlate sentiment with market behavior. Sattarov et al. [46] applied sentiment analysis specifically to Twitter data to forecast Bitcoin price movements, showcasing the predictive power of social media sentiment analysis. Oikonomopoulos et al. [47] utilized granger causality testing alongside the sentiment analysis of Twitter data to identify causal relationships between sentiment and cryptocurrency price fluctuations, demonstrating the integration of statistical techniques with sentiment analysis technologies. Pano et al. [48] delved into text preprocessing techniques as a technology to enhance sentiment analysis accuracy, emphasizing the importance of refining preprocessing methods for effective prediction models during market volatility. Kyriazis et al. [49] employed sentiment analysis measures from Twitter to analyze the influence of social media sentiment on cryptocurrency returns and volatility, highlighting the utilization of sentiment analysis tools for quantitative analysis in financial research. Gaies et al. [50] utilized sentiment analysis to examine the interactions between investor sentiment and Bitcoin prices, showcasing the application of sentiment analysis technologies to understand sentiment-driven dynamics in cryptocurrency markets. Naeem et al. [51] utilized sentiment analysis tools, including the FEARS index and Twitter happiness sentiment, to predict cryptocurrency returns, underscoring the utilization of sentiment analysis technologies for predictive modeling in financial markets. Rognone et al. [52] employed sentiment analysis to compare news sentiment between the cryptocurrency market and Forex, demonstrating the application of sentiment analysis technologies for comparative analysis across financial markets.

3. Materials and Methods

This study initially focuses on utilizing the innovative GPT-4 LLM, alongside a parallel comparison with BERT and FinBERT NLP models. All the models have demonstrated proficiency in comprehending human text. In this proposed approach, the models will undergo fine-tuning on a dataset using few-shot learning, and their sentiment analysis capabilities will be evaluated through direct comparisons before and after fine-tuning.

In the early stages of our research, we rigorously assess GPT-4's ability to accurately identify sentiments within a crypto news article. This involves conducting an exhaustive performance evaluation by comparing the base GPT-4 model with its fine-tuned counterpart. Subsequently, we proceed to fine-tune the BERT and FinBERT models for cryptocurrency sentiment analysis. We compare the fine-tuned LLM and NLP models, demonstrating how the fine-tuning process enhances their capability to effectively address the complex challenges of sentiment analysis with improved precision.

Our research findings confirm that both the LLMs and NLP models are highly accurate in their predictions, with the fine-tuned GPT demonstrating significantly higher performance compared to its base version and the BERT model. The complete codebase used in this study, including dataset cleaning classes, fine-tuning procedures, and datasets, is openly available in a GitHub repository under the MIT open-source license [53].

To meet this paper's goals, a tailored research methodology was crucial, chosen to facilitate data cleaning, feature engineering, model implementation, and fine-tuning. Subsequent subsections elaborate on this framework, offering a comprehensive strategy for the study.

3.1. Dataset Splitting, Cleaning, and Preprocessing

For our study, we utilized the Crypto News + dataset compiled by Oliviervha from various sources including cryptonews.com, cryptopotato.com, and cointelegraph.com [54]. Available on Kaggle under the Database Contents License (DbCL) v1.0, this dataset offers comprehensive data for cryptocurrency sentiment analysis. With a usability rating of 8.24, and containing 31,037 rows and six columns, it holds promise for uncovering insights into cryptocurrency sentiment analysis.

To ensure the quality and effectiveness of our predictive modeling and fine-tuning procedures, we meticulously prepared the dataset through a systematic approach comprising several essential steps designed to enhance its suitability for classification and sentiment analysis tasks.

Initially, we parsed the 'sentiment' column, extracting solely the class label from dictionaries like `{'class': 'negative', 'polarity': -0.01, 'subjectivity': 0.38}`. Following this, we focused on data preprocessing to enhance dataset quality, specifically removing special characters and unnecessary white spaces to maintain data integrity and coherence. This step was crucial to ensure compatibility for modeling purposes and prevent unwanted noise that could affect NLP model performance.

Additionally, text normalization played a crucial role in ensuring uniformity and standardization of text data. Operations included converting accented characters to their base forms, ensuring consistent treatment of words with accent variations. Furthermore, to achieve case-insensitivity, we systematically converted all text to lowercase.

For our few-shot learning study, we randomly selected 5000 rows from the dataset of 31,037, ensuring equal distribution of labels across the three sentiment categories.

In NLP tasks, dataset division is pivotal for effective model development, refinement, and evaluation. Our methodology involved splitting the dataset into training, validation, and test sets, facilitating model learning from input data during fine-tuning, tuning hyperparameters for enhanced generalization, and ultimately evaluating model performance through predictions on the test set.

Fine-tuning BERT or its variants (like FinBERT) typically requires label encoding due to the nature of the underlying frameworks (like PyTorch and TensorFlow). These frameworks expect numerical labels for classification tasks. Although higher-level libraries (such as Hugging Face's Transformers) allow working with string labels at a more abstract level, internally, these labels are converted to numerical values. For example, when using Hugging Face's Transformers library, you can specify labels as strings in the configuration or during dataset preparation, but the framework will encode these labels into integers for processing by the model. For our classification task, we selected transforming the string sentiment labels into integers using nominal encoding: positive as 1, negative as 0, and

neutral as 2, without implying any order. Additionally, we employed cross-entropy loss, the default loss function in `BertForSequenceClassification`, which is well suited for classification tasks with nominally encoded labels.

3.2. GPT Prompt Engineering

Our objective was to develop a prompt that seamlessly integrates with various LLMs, enhancing the accessibility of their results through our code. We focused not only on the prompt's content but also on its output formatting. To provide further clarity on the process of deriving the prompt design, we elaborate on several key aspects:

1. Initial research and understanding: The process began with a thorough examination of various language model architectures, including but not limited to GPT-3, GPT-4, LLaMA-2, and others. This involved understanding their capabilities, limitations, and unique features. This foundational research ensured that our prompt design would be compatible and effective across a diverse range of models.
2. Identification of challenges: We identified two primary challenges in crafting the prompt: (a) creating content that would be model-agnostic and (b) ensuring the accessibility of the output format [55]. The former required developing a prompt that could be understood and responded to by any LLM, regardless of its architecture. The latter involved designing an output format that would facilitate ease of use and integration into code, particularly emphasizing JSON formatting for versatility and compatibility.
3. Finalization and validation: After rigorous testing and refinement, we arrived at a finalized prompt that effectively elicited responses in the desired output format. Validation through Source Code 1 demonstrates the prompt's ability to generate meaningful responses comprehensible to all models, thus fulfilling our objectives of accessibility and compatibility.

```
conversation.append({'role': 'system', 'content': "You are a crypto expert."})
conversation.append({'role': 'user',
'content': 'Evaluate the sentiment of the news article. Return your response in JSON format
{"sentiment":
"negative"} or {"sentiment": "neutral"} or {"sentiment": "positive"}. Article:\n' +
input['text'] + ''})
```

- Source Code 1. Model-agnostic prompt.

3.3. Model Deployment, Fine-Tuning, and Predictive Evaluation

As discussed earlier in this study, we employ two distinct models to address sentiment analysis and classification tasks within the cryptocurrency sector. While previous research has explored cryptocurrency sentiment analysis using various algorithms and techniques, there is a significant gap in utilizing LLMs for this purpose. In this study, we have decided to extensively test the GPT-4, BERT, and FinBERT models both before and after fine-tuning. Below, we present an overview of how each model is deployed, showcasing our innovative approach to utilizing them for this specific task.

3.3.1. GPT Model Deployment and Fine-Tuning

In this stage, we utilized the GPT-4 Turbo base model, also referred to as `gpt-4-0125-preview`, for the sentiment analysis and classification of news articles. [56]. Leveraging the extensive pre-training of large language models (LLMs), our approach enabled the model to discern nuanced cues within the textual content of news articles. This section details the fine-tuning process to adapt the pre-trained model for our specific task.

Conceptual Background of LLM Fine-Tuning

Fine-tuning an LLM involves taking a pre-trained language model and training it further on a specific dataset to adapt it for a particular task. This process allows the model to learn task-specific patterns and nuances that may not be covered during its general pre-training phase.

The GPT-4 model, a closed-source LLM, is exclusively accessible through its API. Users can directly interact with the model or fine-tune it for specific tasks via the API or the user interface/website. They do not need to handle the fine-tuning process or import any libraries; instead, they simply provide the appropriate hyperparameters and ensure that the training and validation sets are in the appropriate format. According to Azure CTO Mark Russinovich [57], the model will be fine-tuned using default training techniques, including:

- Low-rank adaptation (LoRA): this technique reduces the number of trainable parameters by decomposing the weight matrices into lower-rank matrices, making the training process more efficient.
- Parameter-efficient fine-tuning (PEFT): PEFT methods focus on fine-tuning only a small subset of the model's parameters, reducing the computational load and memory usage.
- DeepSpeed: an optimization library that facilitates efficient large-scale model training by improving GPU utilization and memory management.

Fine-Tuning Phase

We fine-tuned the `gpt-4-0125-preview` base model using the official OpenAI API, incorporating the following steps:

1. Data preparation: We generated two JSONL files for training and validation, containing prompt–completion pairs (Source Code 2). As described in Section 3.1, these pairs were derived from our training and validation CSV files, which contain the textual content of news articles and their corresponding sentiment labels.
2. Training configuration: the fine-tuning was conducted with the following hyperparameters:
3. Job ID: `ft:gpt-4-turbo-0125:personal::9Aa7kYOh`.
4. Total tokens: 765,738.
5. Epochs: 3.
6. Batch size: 6.
7. Learning rate (LR) multiplier: 8.
8. Seed: 65426760.
9. Training process: The model underwent a multi-epoch training strategy, iteratively refining its understanding and capabilities. The initial training loss was 0.9778, which gradually decreased to nearly 0.1, indicating significant improvement in model performance over time.

Sentiment Analysis and Evaluation Phase

Following fine-tuning, the model was deployed to perform sentiment analysis on a test set of news articles. The process included the following steps:

1. Prediction generation: The fine-tuned model was tasked with predicting the sentiment of each article in the test set by making calls to the OpenAI API, specifying the ID of the fine-tuned model. Analyzing the textual content, the model examined the articles and generated sentiment labels based on the patterns learned during fine-tuning, presenting the results in a JSON format.
2. Comparison with original labels: The predicted sentiment labels were rigorously compared against the original labels in the dataset. This comparison facilitated a comprehensive analysis to assess the model's effectiveness in capturing article sentiments and its alignment with human judgments.
3. Integration of results: the outcomes of the sentiment analysis were integrated into the `test_set.csv` file, providing a consolidated view for subsequent comparative analyses.

4. Performance metrics: To evaluate the model's performance, standard metrics such as accuracy, precision, recall, and F1-score were computed. These metrics provided insights into the model's ability to generalize and perform accurately on unseen data.

The same prediction and evaluation procedure was applied to the GPT-4 base model using zero-shot training. This allowed for a direct comparison between the base model and the fine-tuned model, underscoring the necessity of fine-tuning for specific tasks.

```
{"messages": [
{"role": "system", "content": "You are a crypto expert."},
{"role": "user", "content": "Evaluate the sentiment of the news article."
"Return your response in JSON format {\"sentiment\": \"negative\"}"
"or {\"sentiment\": \"neutral\"} or {\"sentiment\": \"positive\"}."
"Article:\n ..."},
{"role": "assistant", "content": "{\"sentiment\":\"negative\"}"}
]}
```

- Source Code 2. Fine-tuning training and validation samples in JSONL format.

3.3.2. BERT and FinBERT Model Deployment and Fine-Tuning

In this phase, we utilized both the `bert-base-uncased` and FinBert models [58,59]. FinBert is specifically designed for financial sentiment classification, achieved by further training the BERT language model on a large financial corpus [60].

Training Phase

1. Data preparation: the dataset, as described in Section 3.1, was prepared for our task, resulting in the creation of three files: test, train, and validation CSV files.
2. Training configuration: both `bert-base-uncased` and FinBert models were trained with the following hyperparameters:
3. Optimizers: Adam and AdamW.
4. Epochs: 3.
5. Batch size: 6.
6. Learning rate: 6.
7. Maximum sequence length: 512.
8. Training process: The training procedure took place in the Google Colab environment. Each model underwent three epochs of training, with progress monitored using the `tqdm` library. The training involved backpropagation, optimization, and validation, leveraging an A100 GPU for accelerated computations. Post-training, the fine-tuned models and tokenizers were saved to a directory in Google Drive for future use

Sentiment Analysis and Evaluation Phase

Following training, both models were deployed to perform sentiment analysis on the same test set previously used by the GPT models for predictions. The resulting predictions were saved in two separate columns within the same test set. Subsequently, the evaluation process was conducted in a manner similar to that described in Section 3.3.1. The code, along with training and validation metrics, is available in an `ipynb` Jupyter file on GitHub [53].

4. Results

In Section 3, we explore the methodological approach used to assess the predictive abilities of the GPT-4 LLM, BERT, and FinBERT NLP models in crypto sentiment analysis and classification, seeking to understand their underlying complexities. This section reveals the results of the comparative analysis conducted between these three models at various stages of our research.

Before presenting our findings, it is crucial to emphasize the importance of model evaluation. In the fields of machine learning and NLP, evaluating models is crucial for understanding their performance. This is especially true in finance and cryptocurrencies, where informed decisions are paramount. Table 1 summarizes a comprehensive range of evaluations for each model, incorporating a variety of essential evaluation metrics. In this table, the "Pr" represents the precision metric, "Re" is the recall metric for each class, "F1" signifies the F1-score, and "T" indicates the time in seconds required to fine-tune a model. Notably, the 0 class denotes the negative, the 1 class signifies the positive, and the 2 class indicates neutrality.

Table 1. Model performance metrics comparison.

Model	Accuracy	Pr_0	Pr_1	Pr_2	Re_0	Re_1	Re_2	F1_0	F1_1	F1_2	T
base:gpt-4-0125-preview	0.829	0.832	0.855	0.803	0.85	0.796	0.841	0.841	0.824	0.822	-
ft:gpt-4	0.867	0.873	0.888	0.842	0.865	0.859	0.877	0.869	0.873	0.859	5518
ft:bert-adamw	0.801	0.713	0.817	0.917	0.88	0.793	0.731	0.788	0.805	0.813	107.38
ft:bert-adam	0.833	0.797	0.849	0.856	0.838	0.826	0.835	0.817	0.837	0.845	74.94
ft:finbert-adamw	0.836	0.817	0.867	0.828	0.856	0.784	0.868	0.836	0.823	0.848	132.29
ft:finbert-adam	0.843	0.863	0.804	0.865	0.829	0.85	0.85	0.846	0.826	0.858	91.76

4.1. GPT Base Model Evaluation Phase

In the initial phase of our study, we used the GPT-4 LLM base model, specifically `gpt-4-0125-preview`, to conduct sentiment analysis and classification on cryptocurrency news articles. We employed the test set consisting of 1000 articles with the goal of assessing the accuracy of the GPT base model in categorizing each article's sentiment (positive, neutral, or negative).

Upon thorough analysis of the model's outputs and comparison with the original user-provided labels, we made several notable observations. The `gpt-4-0125-preview` model exhibited a commendable level of accuracy, correctly predicting the sentiment class for 82.9% of the articles. This equates to successful predictions for 829 out of the 1000 articles in our test dataset. These results demonstrate that even the base model, without specific fine-tuning, shows a significant ability to infer sentiment from content based on contextual clues.

It is important to highlight that achieving an 82.9% accuracy rate in predictive modeling is quite high, indicating that the model can be confidently applied to sentiment analysis and classification tasks. Nonetheless, further improvements can be achieved by fine-tuning the models to better suit the specific task at hand. This refinement process can enhance their ability to capture and understand complex patterns and relationships within the data.

4.2. Fine-Tuned Models Evaluation Phase

In the subsequent phase of our research, we focused on fine-tuning the GPT-4, BERT, and FinBERT models using two different optimizers. This fine-tuning process was conducted using a training set of 3200 cryptocurrency articles, with the primary objective of enhancing the models' performance and their ability to analyze cryptocurrency sentiment.

From Table 1, we draw valuable insights showcasing the significant applicability of both LLMs and NLP models for the specific task, particularly after fine-tuning. The fine-tuned GPT-4 model emerges as the top performer, boasting an impressive accuracy rate of 86.7%, closely followed by FinBERT with 84.3%, and BERT with 83.3%. Notably, it is crucial to highlight that both the BERT and FinBERT models achieved higher accuracy when using the Adam optimizer instead of AdamW.

Precision values, indicating the models' ability to accurately classify instances within each class, vary across models and classes. Interestingly, the GPT base and fine-tuned models demonstrate relatively higher precision in predicting positive labels (class 1), while both the BERT and FinBERT models excel in predicting neutral labels (class 2), suggesting a higher tendency for false positives in the class 0 and 1.

The recall values reflect the models' proficiency in correctly capturing instances of each class. For instance, the `ft:finbert-adamw` model exhibits high recall for class 2, highlighting its effectiveness in identifying instances belonging to that class.

The F1-score, striking a balance between precision and recall for each class, showcases the `ft:gpt-4` model's superior performance with the highest F1-score for class 1, indicating its balanced precision and recall for that class.

In summary, while each model displays strengths in specific metrics, the fine-tuned GPT-4 model emerges as the standout performer with high accuracy, balanced precision and recall, and low mean absolute error, suggesting its superior performance across multiple evaluation criteria. Nevertheless, the choice of model may vary depending on specific use cases or priorities, where other models may offer advantages in certain aspects such as recall for specific classes or precision in particular scenarios.

4.3. Assessing Models' Performance and Proximity with Original Labels

To visualize our findings, we chose to use stacked bar charts generated by the `crosstab` function from the pandas library (Figures 1–3). This method will provide readers with more detailed insights into the distribution of predictions compared to the corresponding sentiment labels given by users.

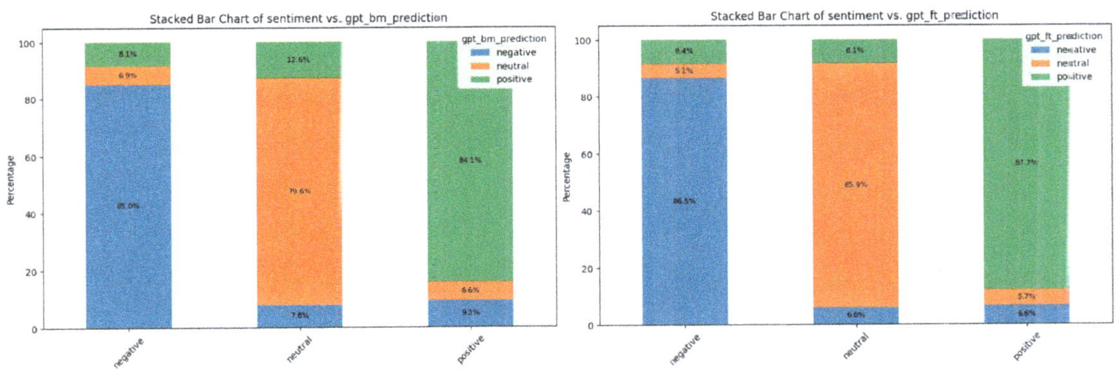

Figure 1. Stacked bar charts comparing the GPT-4 base model with its fine-tuned counterpart.

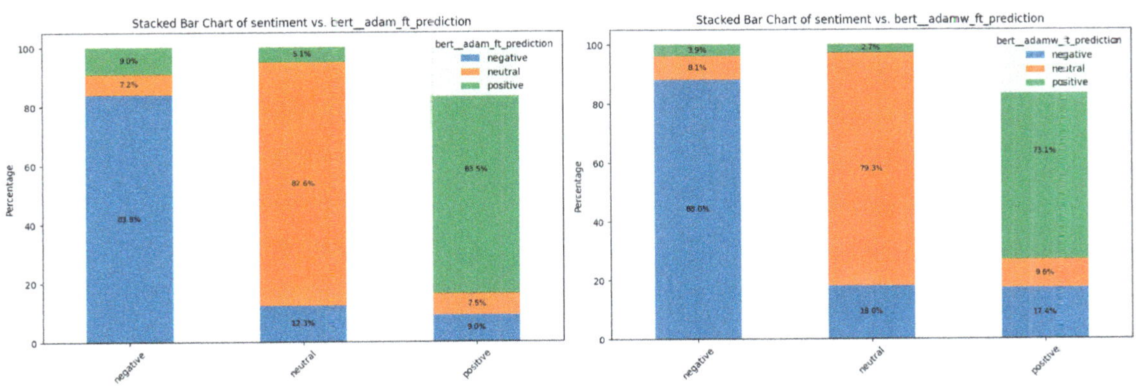

Figure 2. Stacked bar charts comparing the fine-tuned BERT models using different optimizers.

Analyzing the stacked bar charts offers valuable insights into model behavior after fine-tuning. In Figure 1, both the base and fine-tuned GPT-4 models demonstrate a balanced distribution of predictions for positive and negative labels. However, the base GPT-4 model exhibits significantly more errors in predicting neutral labels compared to its fine-tuned counterpart, highlighting the necessity of fine-tuning to improve accuracy in predicting neutral sentiment.

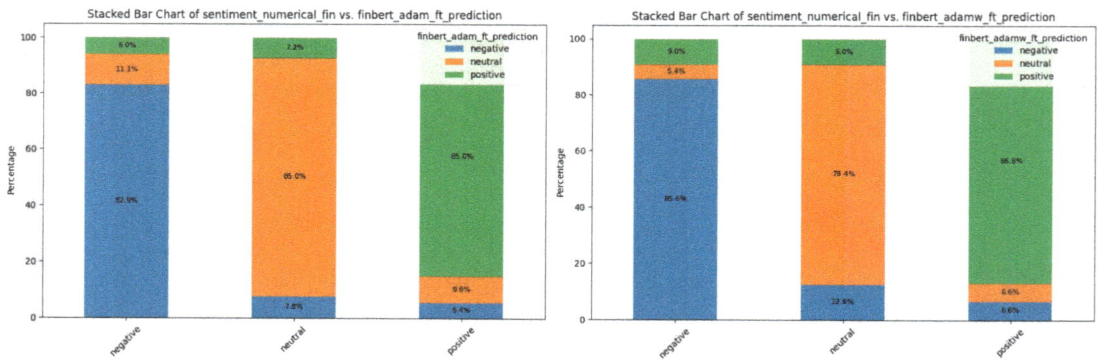

Figure 3. Stacked bar charts comparing the fine-tuned FinBERT models using different optimizers.

Continuing this analysis in Figure 2, focusing on the fine-tuned BERT models, we observe similar challenges with the ADAMW optimizer in accurately identifying positive labels, despite achieving 88% accuracy in predicting negative labels.

Armed with these insights, further optimizations can be pursued through adjustments to enhance overall model performance.

5. Discussion

In earlier sections, we delved into the methodology and outcomes related to the predictive performance of the GPT-4 LLM, BERT, and FinBERT NLP models before and after fine-tuning for cryptocurrency news sentiment analysis and classification. This section unveils the research discoveries and insights gained by the authors concerning the effectiveness of LLMs and NLP models as valuable tools for sentiment analysis in the cryptocurrency domain, addressing pertinent research inquiries.

5.1. Research Findings

In Section 4.2, we presented the outcomes of our study on the effectiveness of the fine-tuned GPT-4, BERT, and FinBERT models in analyzing crypto sentiment. We used a set of 1000 crypto news articles for this investigation. Remarkably, the models demonstrated almost flawless prediction accuracy post-fine-tuning with few-shot learning, achieving a maximum of 86.7%. Specifically, the fine-tuned GPT model achieved 86.7%, while BERT achieved 83.3% accuracy when using the ADAM optimizer. Interestingly, using the ADAMW optimizer led to a slight decrease in accuracy, around 3.2% lower compared to the ADAM optimizer. The FinBERT model presented slightly higher accuracy, with 83.6% when trained using the ADAMW optimizer and 84.3% when trained using the ADAM optimizer. These results imply that even subtle adjustments in fine-tuning parameters can yield diverse outcomes, underscoring the complexities of model optimization.

Moreover, both the BERT and FinBERT models with the ADAM optimizer nearly matched the predictive capability of a robust LLM, differing by only 3.4% and 2.4%, respectively. This small variation could be attributed to differences in their pre-training phases, where the GPT-4 model had the advantage of exposure to a wider and more varied set of public datasets. This extensive training likely facilitated more comprehensive and targeted fine-tuning, granting the GPT model a deeper comprehension of nuanced cryptocurrency themes. Consequently, the GPT model might be better positioned to produce precise and contextually relevant responses.

It is important to note that each model exhibits higher accuracy for specific labels. For instance, the fine-tuned GPT-4 model is more accurate in predicting positive labels, while BERT and FinBERT excel in predicting neutral labels. This highlights that each model has its own strengths and weaknesses, suggesting that a hybrid approach would be more effective in maximizing results in a production environment.

Additionally, there are more specialized variants of BERT models, such as `CryptoBERT`, which are trained on a broader range of data sources, including crypto news articles, Telegram, and social media [33,61].

Finally, it is imperative to highlight that even without fine-tuning, the GPT-4 base model achieved 82.9% accuracy. This demonstrates that LLMs, due to their extensive pre-training with billions of parameters, can perform tasks with high accuracy whether fine-tuned on a specific dataset or not. Such capabilities could lead to the development of zero-shot, simple yet accurate tools for non-specialized teams and organizations.

5.2. The Impact of Fine-Tuning

Customizing LLMs and NLP models via fine-tuning for specialized tasks within domains like finance and cryptocurrency is essential to optimize their effectiveness in practical applications. Models such as OpenAI's GPT-4 or BERT are initially trained on vast text datasets from diverse sources, which equips them to understand and generate human-like text across various domains. However, fine-tuning these models for specific tasks like sentiment analysis significantly boosts their performance and relevance in focused contexts. For instance, the FinBERT model, a variant of BERT, is fine-tuned on specialized financial label and unlabeled data. Moreover, even after fine-tuning, these models can undergo further fine-tuning for specific tasks.

Based on the results derived from this study, fine-tuning an LLM or an NLP model on large and representative datasets allows it to gain a deeper comprehension of the nuances and patterns unique to sentiment analysis, such as in the crypto domain, leading to more accurate predictions. This adaptation involves learning to recognize crypto-related terminology, grasp context, and extract relevant features from textual inputs. Through iterative adjustments in the fine-tuning process, using both training and validation data, the model becomes increasingly proficient at capturing these domain-specific intricacies, resulting in improved accuracy and other performance metrics.

5.3. Exploring the Cost and Usability of LLMs and NLP Models

Our research revealed that both the GPT and NLP models achieved high accuracy in the sentiment analysis of cryptocurrency news articles. While the fine-tuned GPT model showed slightly higher accuracy compared to BERT and FinBERT, it is important to note that BERT is an open-source model available for free use in a self-hosted environment. On the other hand, GPT-4 requires access through the official OpenAI API, which incurs a cost.

For stakeholders or investors seeking accurate and immediate predictions, the GPT API, despite its cost, offers a more convenient and sustainable solution due to its user-friendly interface. Conversely, for companies equipped with an AI team, deploying a self-hosted solution with BERT or similar NLP models may be a more cost-effective choice.

Specifically, within the cryptocurrency sector, where prices can fluctuate within minutes, software equipped with NLP technologies can detect market trends through news blogs, Telegram, or socials, providing crypto investors with information to adjust their strategies and potentially maximize profits. For instance, if a global event like a conflict between two countries is imminent, an investor could rely on the model to analyze user comments on platforms like Telegram and preemptively sell certain cryptocurrencies to avoid a significant drop in their value. Conversely, investors could also take advantage of low-cost cryptocurrencies that, based on crypto signals, might rapidly increase in value, leading to substantial gains.

Nevertheless, it is prudent to caution investors about spam comments or articles deliberately created to stimulate investment. For example, many articles are written daily speculating that Ethereum could reach $10,000 by 2025. Such articles serve two purposes:

generating clicks and enticing inexperienced investors to invest in the cryptocurrency with the expectation of substantial value multiplication.

6. Conclusions

In summary, the integration of LLMs and NLP models for cryptocurrency sentiment analysis represents a powerful toolset that enhances investment decision-making in the dynamic cryptocurrency market. This study showcases the efficacy of state-of-the-art models like GPT-4 and BERT in accurately interpreting and categorizing sentiments extracted from cryptocurrency news articles. The key strength of these models lies in their ability to capture subtle shifts and complexities in market sentiments, enabling investors to navigate the volatile cryptocurrency landscape with greater insight and confidence.

By leveraging advanced NLP capabilities, including few-shot fine-tuning processes, this study highlights the adaptability and robustness of LLMs and NLP models in analyzing sentiment data within the cryptocurrency domain. These findings underscore the transformative potential of advanced NLP techniques in empowering investors with actionable insights, enabling them to proactively manage risks, identify emerging trends, and optimize investment strategies to maximize returns.

Specifically, the application field of the research results extends to cryptocurrency investment and risk management. By providing a deeper understanding of sentiment dynamics in cryptocurrency markets, this study facilitates a more informed and data-driven approach to cryptocurrency investment, enabling investors to make well-informed decisions based on the real-time sentiment analysis of news articles and other relevant sources.

Author Contributions: Conceptualization, K.I.R. and N.D.T.; methodology, K.I.R., N.D.T. and D.K.N.; software, K.I.R.; validation, K.I.R. and N.D.T.; formal analysis, K.I.R., N.D.T. and D.K.N.; investigation, K.I.R., N.D.T. and D.K.N.; resources, K.I.R.; data curation, K.I.R.; writing—original draft preparation, K.I.R. and N.D.T.; writing—review and editing, K.I.R., N.D.T. and D.K.N.; visualization, K.I.R.; supervision, D.K.N. and N.D.T. All authors have read and agreed to the published version of the manuscript.

Funding: This research received no external funding.

Data Availability Statement: Data supporting the reported results can be found at ref. [53].

Conflicts of Interest: The authors declare no conflicts of interest.

References

1. Huang, X.; Zhang, W.; Tang, X.; Zhang, M.; Surbiryala, J.; Iosifidis, V.; Liu, Z.; Zhang, J. LSTM Based Sentiment Analysis for Cryptocurrency Prediction. In *Lecture Notes in Computer Science*; Springer: Berlin/Heidelberg, Germany, 2021; Volume 12683, pp. 617–621. [CrossRef]
2. Azmina, N.; Zamani, M.; Liew, J.; Yan, S.; Yusof, A.M. XLNET-GRU Sentiment Regression Model for Cryptocurrency News in English and Malay. *ACl Anthol.* **2022**, *24*, 36–42.
3. Sakas, D.P.; Giannakopoulos, N.T.; Margaritis, M.; Kanellos, N. Modeling Supply Chain Firms' Stock Prices in the Fertilizer Industry through Innovative Cryptocurrency Market Big Data. *Int. J. Financ. Stud.* **2023**, *11*, 88. [CrossRef]
4. Chen, C.Y.H.; Hafner, C.M. Sentiment-Induced Bubbles in the Cryptocurrency Market. *J. Risk Financ. Manag.* **2019**, *12*, 53. [CrossRef]
5. Lamon, C.; Nielsen, E.; Redondo, E. Cryptocurrency Price Prediction Using News and Social Media Sentiment. *SMU Data Sci. Rev.* **2017**, *1*, 1–22.
6. Sakas, D.P.; Giannakopoulos, N.T.; Kanellos, N.; Migkos, S.P. Innovative Cryptocurrency Trade Websites-Marketing Strategy Refinement, via Digital Behavior. *IEEE Access* **2022**, *10*, 63163–63176. [CrossRef]
7. Rouhani, S.; Abedin, E. Crypto-Currencies Narrated on Tweets: A Sentiment Analysis Approach. *Int. J. Ethics Syst.* **2020**, *36*, 58–72. [CrossRef]
8. Erdoğan, M.C.; Canayaz, M. Crypto-Currency Sentiment Analyse on Social Media. In Proceedings of the 2018 International Conference on Artificial Intelligence and Data Processing, IDAP 2018, Malatya, Turkey, 28–30 September 2018. [CrossRef]
9. Sureshbhai, P.N.; Bhattacharya, P.; Tanwar, S. KaRuNa: A Blockchain-Based Sentiment Analysis Framework for Fraud Cryptocurrency Schemes. In Proceedings of the 2020 IEEE International Conference on Communications Workshops, ICC Workshops 2020—Proceedings, Dublin, Ireland, 7–11 June 2020. [CrossRef]

MDPI AG
Grosspeteranlage 5
4052 Basel
Switzerland
Tel.: +41 61 683 77 34

Big Data and Cognitive Computing Editorial Office
E-mail: bdcc@mdpi.com
www.mdpi.com/journal/bdcc

10. Pant, D.R.; Neupane, P.; Poudel, A.; Pokhrel, A.K.; Lama, B.K. Recurrent Neural Network Based Bitcoin Price Prediction by Twitter Sentiment Analysis. In Proceedings of the 2018 IEEE 3rd International Conference on Computing, Communication and Security, ICCCS 2018, Kathmandu, Nepal, 25–27 October 2018; pp. 128–132. [CrossRef]
11. Serafini, G.; Yi, P.; Zhang, Q.; Brambilla, M.; Wang, J.; Hu, Y.; Li, B. Sentiment-Driven Price Prediction of the Bitcoin Based on Statistical and Deep Learning Approaches. In Proceedings of the International Joint Conference on Neural Networks 2020, Glasgow, UK, 19–24 July 2020. [CrossRef]
12. Jatoth, C.; Jain, R.; Fiore, U.; Chatharasupalli, S. Improved Classification of Blockchain Transactions Using Feature Engineering and Ensemble Learning. *Future Internet* **2022**, *14*, 16. [CrossRef]
13. Colianni, S.; Rosales, S.; Signorotti, M. Algorithmic Trading of Cryptocurrency Based on Twitter Sentiment Analysis. *CS229 Proj.* **2015**, *1*, 1–4.
14. Loginova, E.; Tsang, W.K.; van Heijningen, G.; Kerkhove, L.P.; Benoit, D.F. Forecasting Directional Bitcoin Price Returns Using Aspect-Based Sentiment Analysis on Online Text Data. *Mach. Learn.* **2021**, *113*, 4761–4784. [CrossRef]
15. Köse, O. Crypto Asset Taxonomy Classification and Crypto News Sentiment Analysis. Master's Thesis, Middle East Technical University, Ankara, Turkey, 2020.
16. Bhatt, S.; Ghazanfar, M.; Amirhosseini, M.H. Sentiment-Driven Cryptocurrency Price Prediction: A Machine Learning Approach Utilizing Historical Data and Social Media Sentiment Analysis. *Mach. Learn. Appl. Int. J.* **2023**, *10*, 1–15. [CrossRef]
17. Seroyizhko, P.; Zhexenova, Z.; Shafiq, M.Z.; Merizzi, F.; Galassi, A.; Ruggeri, F. A Sentiment and Emotion Annotated Dataset for Bitcoin Price Forecasting Based on Reddit Posts. In Proceedings of the FinNLP 2022—4th Workshop on Financial Technology and Natural Language Processing, Proceedings of the Workshop 2022, Abu Dhabi, United Arab Emirates, 8 December 2022; pp. 203–210. [CrossRef]
18. Parekh, R.; Patel, N.P.; Thakkar, N.; Gupta, R.; Tanwar, S.; Sharma, G.; Davidson, I.E.; Sharma, R. DL-GuesS: Deep Learning and Sentiment Analysis-Based Cryptocurrency Price Prediction. *IEEE Access* **2022**, *10*, 35398–35409. [CrossRef]
19. Raju, S.M.; Tarif, A.M. Real-Time Prediction of BITCOIN Price Using Machine Learning Techniques and Public Sentiment Analysis. *arXiv* **2020**, arXiv:2006.14473.
20. Pang, Y.; Sundararaj, G.; Ren, J. Cryptocurrency Price Prediction Using Time Series and Social Sentiment Data. In Proceedings of the BDCAT 2019—6th IEEE/ACM International Conference on Big Data Computing, Applications and Technologies 2019, New York, NY, USA, 2 December 2019; pp. 35–42. [CrossRef]
21. Farimani, S.A.; Jahan, M.V.; Fard, A.M.; Haffari, G. Leveraging Latent Economic Concepts and Sentiments in the News for Market Prediction. In Proceedings of the 2021 IEEE 8th International Conference on Data Science and Advanced Analytics, DSAA 2021, Porto, Portugal, 6–9 October 2021. [CrossRef]
22. Gadi, M.F.A.; Sicilia, M.A. Annotators' Selection Impact on the Creation of a Sentiment Corpus for the Cryptocurrency Financial Domain. *IEEE Access* **2023**, *11*, 131081–131088. [CrossRef]
23. Anbaee Farimani, S.; Vafaei Jahan, M.; Milani Fard, A.; Tabbakh, S.R.K. Investigating the Informativeness of Technical Indicators and News Sentiment in Financial Market Price Prediction. *Knowl. Based Syst.* **2022**, *247*, 108742. [CrossRef]
24. Nasekin, S.; Chen, C.Y.-H. Deep Learning-Based Cryptocurrency Sentiment Construction. *Digit. Financ.* **2020**, *2*, 39–67. [CrossRef]
25. Wołk, K. Advanced Social Media Sentiment Analysis for Short-Term Cryptocurrency Price Prediction. *Expert Syst.* **2020**, *37*, e12493. [CrossRef]
26. Vo, A.-D. Sentiment Analysis of News for Effective Cryptocurrency Price Prediction. *Int. J. Knowl. Eng.* **2019**, *5*, 47–52. [CrossRef]
27. Aslam, N.; Rustam, F.; Lee, E.; Washington, P.B.; Ashraf, I. Sentiment Analysis and Emotion Detection on Cryptocurrency Related Tweets Using Ensemble LSTM-GRU Model. *IEEE Access* **2022**, *10*, 39313–39324. [CrossRef]
28. Dwivedi, D.N.; Vemareddy, A. Sentiment Analytics for Crypto Pre and Post COVID: Topic Modeling. In *Lecture Notes in Computer Science*; Springer: Berlin/Heidelberg, Germany, 2023; Volume 13776, pp. 303–315. [CrossRef]
29. Şaşmaz, E.; Tek, F.B. Tweet Sentiment Analysis for Cryptocurrencies. In Proceedings of the 6th International Conference on Computer Science and Engineering, UBMK 2021, Ankara, Turkey, 15–17 September 2021; pp. 613–618. [CrossRef]
30. Kraaijeveld, O.; De Smedt, J. The Predictive Power of Public Twitter Sentiment for Forecasting Cryptocurrency Prices. *J. Int. Financ. Mark. Inst. Money* **2020**, *65*, 101188. [CrossRef]
31. Gurrib, I.; Kamalov, F. Predicting Bitcoin Price Movements Using Sentiment Analysis: A Machine Learning Approach. *Stud. Econ. Financ.* **2022**, *39*, 347–364. [CrossRef]
32. Ider, D.; Lessmann, S. Forecasting Cryptocurrency Returns from Sentiment Signals: An Analysis of BERT Classifiers and Weak Supervision. *arXiv* **2022**, arXiv:2204.05781.
33. Kulakowski, M.; Frasincar, F.; Cambria, E. Sentiment Classification of Cryptocurrency-Related Social Media Posts. *IEEE Intell. Syst.* **2023**, *38*, 5–9. [CrossRef]
34. Nguyen Thanh, B.; Nguyen, A.T.; Chu, T.T.; Ha, S. Chatgpt, Twitter Sentiment and Bitcoin Return. *SSRN* **2023**. [CrossRef]
35. Raheman, A.; Kolonin, A.; Fridkins, I.; Ansari, I.; Vishwas, M. Social Media Sentiment Analysis for Cryptocurrency Market Prediction. *arXiv* **2022**, arXiv:2204.10185.
36. Georgoula, I.; Pournarakis, D.; Bilanakos, C.; Sotiropoulos, D.N.; Giaglis, G.M. Using Time-Series and Sentiment Analysis to Detect the Determinants of Bitcoin Prices. *SSRN Electron. J.* **2015**. [CrossRef]
37. Chalkiadakis, I.; Zaremba, A.; Peters, G.W.; Chantler, M.J. On-Chain Analytics for Sentiment-Driven Statistical Causality in Cryptocurrencies. *Blockchain Res. Appl.* **2022**, *3*, 100063. [CrossRef]

38. Anamika; Chakraborty, M.; Subramaniam, S. Does Sentiment Impact Cryptocurrency? *J. Behav. Financ.* **2023**, *24*, 202–218. [CrossRef]
39. Bouteska, A.; Mefteh-Wali, S.; Dang, T. Predictive Power of Investor Sentiment for Bitcoin Returns: Evidence from COVID-19 Pandemic. *Technol. Forecast. Soc. Change* **2022**, *184*, 121999. [CrossRef]
40. Critien, J.V.; Gatt, A.; Ellul, J. Bitcoin Price Change and Trend Prediction through Twitter Sentiment and Data Volume. *Financ. Innov.* **2022**, *8*, 45. [CrossRef]
41. Girsang, A.S.; Stanley. Hybrid LSTM and GRU for Cryptocurrency Price Forecasting Based on Social Network Sentiment Analysis Using FinBERT. *IEEE Access* **2023**, *11*, 120530–120540. [CrossRef]
42. Chalkiadakis, I.; Peters, G.W.; Ames, M. Hybrid ARDL-MIDAS-Transformer Time-Series Regressions for Multi-Topic Crypto Market Sentiment Driven by Price and Technology Factors. *Digit. Financ.* **2023**, *5*, 295–365. [CrossRef]
43. Li, T.R.; Chamrajnagar, A.S.; Fong, X.R.; Rizik, N.R.; Fu, F. Sentiment-Based Prediction of Alternative Cryptocurrency Price Fluctuations Using Gradient Boosting Tree Model. *Front. Phys.* **2018**, *7*, 98. [CrossRef]
44. Valencia, F.; Gómez-Espinosa, A.; Valdés-Aguirre, B. Price Movement Prediction of Cryptocurrencies Using Sentiment Analysis and Machine Learning. *Entropy* **2019**, *21*, 589. [CrossRef] [PubMed]
45. Amirshahi, B.; Lahmiri, S. Investigating the Effectiveness of Twitter Sentiment in Cryptocurrency Close Price Prediction by Using Deep Learning. *Expert Syst.* **2023**, e13428. [CrossRef]
46. Sattarov, O.; Jeon, H.S.; Oh, R.; Lee, J.D. Forecasting Bitcoin Price Fluctuation by Twitter Sentiment Analysis. In Proceedings of the 2020 International Conference on Information Science and Communications Technologies, ICISCT 2020, Tashkent, Uzbekistan, 4–6 November 2020. [CrossRef]
47. Oikonomopoulos, S.; Tzafilkou, K.; Karapiperis, D.; Verykios, V. Cryptocurrency Price Prediction Using Social Media Sentiment Analysis. In Proceedings of the 13th International Conference on Information, Intelligence, Systems and Applications, IISA 2022, Corfu, Greece, 18–20 July 2022. [CrossRef]
48. Pano, T.; Kashef, R. A Complete VADER-Based Sentiment Analysis of Bitcoin (BTC) Tweets during the Era of COVID-19. *Big Data Cogn. Comput.* **2020**, *4*, 33. [CrossRef]
49. Kyriazis, N.; Papadamou, S.; Tzeremes, P.; Corbet, S. The Differential Influence of Social Media Sentiment on Cryptocurrency Returns and Volatility during COVID-19. *Q. Rev. Econ. Financ.* **2023**, *89*, 307–317. [CrossRef]
50. Gaies, B.; Nakhli, M.S.; Sahut, J.M.; Schweizer, D. Interactions between Investors' Fear and Greed Sentiment and Bitcoin Prices. *North Am. J. Econ. Financ.* **2023**, *67*, 101924. [CrossRef]
51. Naeem, M.A.; Mbarki, I.; Shahzad, S.J.H. Predictive Role of Online Investor Sentiment for Cryptocurrency Market: Evidence from Happiness and Fears. *Int. Rev. Econ. Financ.* **2021**, *73*, 496–514. [CrossRef]
52. Rognone, L.; Hyde, S.; Zhang, S.S. News Sentiment in the Cryptocurrency Market: An Empirical Comparison with Forex. *Int. Rev. Financ. Anal.* **2020**, *69*, 101462. [CrossRef]
53. GitHub—Kroumeliotis/LLM-and-NLP-Models-in-Cryptocurrency-Sentiment-Analysis: Crypto. Available online: https://github.com/kroumeliotis/LLM-and-NLP-models-in-Cryptocurrency-Sentiment-Analysis (accessed on 12 April 2024).
54. Crypto News +. Available online: https://www.kaggle.com/datasets/oliviervha/crypto-news (accessed on 12 April 2024).
55. Zhang, K.; Zhou, F.; Wu, L.; Xie, N.; He, Z. Semantic Understanding and Prompt Engineering for Large-Scale Traffic Data Imputation. *Inf. Fusion* **2024**, *102*, 102038. [CrossRef]
56. Models—OpenAI API. Available online: https://platform.openai.com/docs/models/gpt-4-and-gpt-4-turbo (accessed on 1 April 2024).
57. What Runs ChatGPT? *Inside Microsoft's AI Supercomputer | Featuring Mark Russinovich—YouTube.* Available online: https://www.youtube.com/watch?v=Rk3nTUfRZmo (accessed on 17 December 2023).
58. BERT—Transformers 3.0.2 Documentation. Available online: https://huggingface.co/transformers/v3.0.2/model_doc/bert.html#berttokenizer (accessed on 17 December 2023).
59. ProsusAI/Finbert · Hugging Face. Available online: https://huggingface.co/ProsusAI/finbert (accessed on 18 May 2024).
60. Araci, D.T. FinBERT: Financial Sentiment Analysis with Pre-Trained Language Models. *arXiv* **2019**, arXiv:1908.10063.
61. ElKulako/Cryptobert · Hugging Face. Available online: https://huggingface.co/ElKulako/cryptobert (accessed on 15 April 2024).